American Jewry

Understanding the history of Jews in America requires a synthesis of over 350 years of documents, social data, literature and journalism, architecture, oratory, and debate, and each time that history is observed, new questions are raised and new perspectives found. This book presents a readable account of that history, with an emphasis on migration patterns, social and religious life, and political and economic affairs. It explains the long-range development of American Jewry as the product of "many new beginnings" more than a direct evolution leading from early colonial experiments to latter-day social patterns.

This book also shows that not all of American Jewish history has occurred on American soil, arguing that Jews, more than most other Americans, persist in assigning crucial importance to international issues. This approach provides a fresh perspective that can open up the practice of minority-history writing, so that the very concepts of minority and majority should not be taken for granted.

ELI LEDERHENDLER is Stephen S. Wise Professor of American Jewish History and Institutions at the Hebrew University of Jerusalem.

American Jewry

A New History

ELI LEDERHENDLER
Hebrew University of Jerusalem, Israel

CAMBRIDGE
UNIVERSITY PRESS

University Printing House, Cambridge CB2 8BS, United Kingdom

Cambridge University Press is part of the University of Cambridge.

It furthers the University's mission by disseminating knowledge in the pursuit of education, learning and research at the highest international levels of excellence.

www.cambridge.org
Information on this title: www.cambridge.org/9780521196086

First published 2017

Printed in the United States of America by Sheridan Books, Inc.

A catalogue record for this publication is available from the British Library

Library of Congress Cataloguing in Publication data
Names: Lederhendler, Eli, author.
Title: American Jewry : a new history / Eli Lederhendler.
Description: New York : Cambridge University Press, [2016]
Identifiers: LCCN 2016025954 | ISBN 9780521196086 (hardback)
Subjects: LCSH: Jews – United States – History.
Classification: LCC E184.J5 L567 2016 | DDC 973/.04924–dc23
LC record available at https://lccn.loc.gov/2016025954

ISBN 978-0-521-19608-6 Hardback
ISBN 978-1-316-63262-8 Paperback

To Henry L. Feingold, esteemed teacher and friend

Contents

List of Figures   *page* viii

List of Tables   ix

Preface   xi

Acknowledgments   xxii

1   First Encounters, New Beginnings: From Colonial Times
    to the Civil War   1

2   Changing Places: Migration and Americanization,
    1860s–1920s   56

3   Finding Space in America, 1920s–1950s   132

4   The European Nexus: Spain, Germany, and Russia   190

5   Recapitulations and More Beginnings, 1950s to the
    Twenty-first Century   248

Epilogue   306

Index   313

Figures

2.1 US residents in urban and metropolitan areas, 1910: native-born, foreign-born, and Jewish   *page* 58

2.2 Dohany Synagogue, Budapest, 1859   73

2.3 Central Synagogue (Ahavath Chesed), New York City, 1872   74

2.4 Immigrants lined up for entry to the United States at Ellis Island   93

2.5 Hanukah greeting card, JWB, 1918   124

3.1 US union membership (millions), 1904–29   137

3.2 Estimated US emigration, 1915–39 (citizens and non-citizens)   159

4.1 AJDC expenditures in Germany and Poland, 1933–7 (US dollars)   225

5.1 Postwar growth in higher education and veteran enrollment   250

Tables

1.1 Earliest Jewish presence in selected American cities
 founded 1730s–1790s   *page* 9
1.2 Jewish households in selected cities in 1820   22
2.1 Jews and foreign-born residents as percent of city
 population   59
2.2 Rates of marriage across group boundaries, New York
 City, 1908–12, per hundred marriages   87
3.1 Jewish refugee immigrants to Britain, Palestine,
 and the United States   173
4.1 Central European rabbis in America   213

Preface

Histories of particular ethnic groups frequently highlight their strengths and accomplishments. Often, such histories have a reassuring "Whiggish" tone, in the sense that the past always seems to confirm the present. This book aims to be a little different in that it seeks primarily to describe, to annotate, and to understand, but it is less invested in confirmation. It is ethnocentric, to be sure: my interest lies in describing social, cultural, economic, political, and religious life in America from one group's point of view. As a Jewish historian, I find this of intrinsic interest; but while the narrative strives to orient the reader to one group's history, it does not set out to *justify* that history. I have sought to write a fair book that is content to offer partial answers to large questions.

It is, however, a book that does not lack a point of view. I regard the Jews in America as part of America's past (and present), but I also see America as part of the Jews' historical experience – within a longer, larger, non-American canvas. That implies, in essence, that there is a "gap" between the two histories that has never been bridged and that Jews, *qua* Jews, present challenges to the historian in the context of American society.

Perhaps for that reason, Jews continue to be rather marginal in the writings of most American historians. This makes sense, in numerical terms, since Jews represent a very small segment of the American population. What is interesting, however, is that the Jews' relative obscurity in standard academic histories contrasts with the prominence of Jewish individuals who enjoy cachet or notoriety in American public life and popular culture. That asymmetry between academic and popular perceptions has something to do with my underlying agenda. The issue is not how to give the Jews "due credit," in some compensatory fashion. The question is, rather, why notability is readily granted while an entire sectoral history finds only intermittent, shadowy reflection. Beyond the mere fact that celebrity is easily earned in a culture based on mass communication, I wanted to discover what might explain the Jews' paradoxical position in America.

I found that Jews have straddled the boundary between minority history and majority history, between the exotic and the pedestrian. On the one hand, their small numbers have made it unessential for general historians to consider them when tracing the course of the national American experience. It is really only since the multicultural turn of American scholarship in the final quarter of the twentieth century that so-called minor voices have merited a closer inspection, or that the purported "mainstream" has been turned inside-out in order to discover just how it came to be thus construed.

On the other hand, because many Jewish people were able to overcome the stigmas and burdens of marginality – those born in America were likeliest to do so – the same multicultural turn that eagerly sought to take the measure of minor voices found fewer compelling reasons to do so with regard to Jews. The more successful that Jews appeared to be in pursuing social, economic, cultural, and political integration, the more nondescript they seemed to the multicultural investigator.[1]

Either way, by holding up a mirror to the Jewish paradox, I have sought to drive a theoretical wedge between majority and minority histories. This undefined conceptual space may prove to be useful beyond the Jewish case, bearing in mind the growing number of Americans who consider themselves multi-racial. In the not-too-distant future, sociologists and historians may be hard pressed to draw strict boundaries, such as we have known until recently, between majority and minority perspectives. This is not at all to imply that minorities (as such) will no longer exist. It is also not simply that each minority's history is inevitably embedded and reflected in the history of the "majority" – as a multiculturalist scholar might say – and vice versa. Rather, it is that we may not be able to reduce all such social differences to a simple majority–minority paradigm.

The bi- or multi-racial population is just one instance waiting to be addressed. Similar questions could be raised about other groups with

<hr/>

[1] Ira Katznelson, "Two Exceptionalisms: Points of Departure for Studies of Capitalism and Jews in the United States," in *Chosen Capital: The Jewish Encounter with American Capitalism*, ed. Rebecca Kobrin (New Brunswick, NJ and London: Rutgers University Press, 2012), p. 19.

an in-between status. Spanish-speaking Americans, for instance, are so large a "minority" in the United States today (or, rather, a grouped set of minorities) that they appear to challenge classic definitions. As an aggregate, they transcend older "racial" distinctions, they mix elements of indigenous and migrant histories, and their culture(s) pose(s) a unique challenge to the narrative of Anglo-American hemispheric dominance. The Jewish case, I suggest, is no less apt to illuminate the conceptual issues that are at stake when we think beyond majority–minority models.

Comparability with other groups is important but it is still the background, not the foreground, in this portrayal of American Jewish history. However, as noted, there is another sense in which I have made an effort to look "outward" from the subject at hand. Not all that is pertinent to American Jewish history has occurred within American geographical space. A focus on the Jewish historical experience *in* the United States does not mean limiting the discussion *to* the United States. This approach is one that I learned long ago from my teacher, Henry L. Feingold, who used to remark that American Jewish historians must be aware of several histories: American history in general, the annals of the Jews in the United States, and European Jewish history. His history of American Jewry, *Zion in America*, was the first professional historian's study of the subject that I read as an undergraduate.[2]

I have tried to remain true to his critical spirit. In my turn, I have set out to add new perspectives based upon my own work and a mass of research by other Jewish historians, written over the forty-odd years that have elapsed since *Zion in America* first appeared in print. I have sought to bridge some gaps: just as I try to strike a new balance between the domestic and foreign dimensions of American Jewish history, I also seek to grapple with the economic side of Jewish history, to reintegrate religious history with social and political history, and to suggest a revised chronology of events.

In each chapter, I try to break some new ground. In the first chapter, I ask whether a pattern of urban Jewish settlement in the British colonies and in early America can be discerned. I believe that it can, and that it is linked to the grid of urban development itself. The earliest Jewish inhabitants chose mostly to live in established towns that exhibited substantial potential as market centers. Moreover, they rarely stayed in one place for very long. This leads me to raise, in turn, the issue of "founding myths" (local Jewish communities' claims of historical antiquity) and

---

[2] Henry L. Feingold, *Zion in America* (New York: Twayne Publishers, 1974).

their relationship to the actual, more gradual processes by which communities eventually took shape. When transiency is factored in, nearly all
communities appear dependent on new arrivals, as much as on the older
resident veterans. Thus, "founders" are not the exclusive claimants to the
"origins" of the community. Each new arrival is also a new beginning;
history is re-made (and not just re-told) by successive generations.

   Further on, I attempt to arrive at a more satisfactory explanation of
Jewish economic integration, trying to settle some lingering questions
about what helped immigrant Jews to promote their economic welfare,
despite discrimination and despite their heavy concentration in particular
occupations. I argue that no single factor (including the oft-cited educational advantage) can explain Jewish occupational achievement levels,
but that an unusual array of circumstances, including demographic and
social conditions, interacted to produce distinctive patterns.

   I have sought to re-integrate into this narrative certain themes such
as labor history and radical history that have fallen out of the limelight
in recent years. I have also endeavored to give an adequate account of
Orthodox Jewry as a religious culture with its own history and value
system. Another distinctive feature of this book is the attention that it
pays to the manner in which Jews, mainly an urban people, nevertheless
developed a rural or "pastoral" imagination as part of their foray into
American life.

   For the purposes of chronology – the "phrasing" that lends composition to the narrative – I have collapsed the Colonial, Early National, and
Antebellum periods of American history into one, long, opening phrase
(1650s to 1860), and divided the rest into three periods: the 1860s to
1920; the 1920s to the 1950s; and the 1950s to the turn of the twenty-
first century. The underlying logic here is to link the major transitions of
American Jewish history to America's national history. Thus, the entire
first period represents an intermittent but formative history that parallels
in some respects the piecemeal expansion of the American republic. The
second period (1860–1920) links the Jewish narrative to industrializa-
tion, urbanization, America's first major overseas wars, and the political
ferment of the Progressive Era. The third segment (the shortest, chrono-
logically) covers the virtual cessation of large-scale Jewish immigration,
the Great Depression, and the immediate aftermath of World War II.

   After these three chronological chapters and before the final, fifth
chapter, I have inserted an "intermezzo" that is thematic in nature, in
order to introduce the foreign dimension of American Jewish history as a
distinguishing feature with a coherence of its own.

The last and most contemporary chapter is the most tentative, in that its very definition as a historical phase remains open-ended. In it, I follow the course of domestic developments from the redistribution of the metropolitan population and the crisis of the inner cities to the renewal of large-scale immigration to America. I also engage international issues linked to the Cold War, the establishment of the state of Israel, and the final years of the Soviet Union.

I lay no claim to comprehensiveness. This book is only a selective version of the recorded past. At the same time, the scope of the narrative is wide enough so that anyone familiar with it will be equipped to wade without confusion into the more specialized scholarship available in this field. In any case, the selection of subject matter is by no means random: four cornerstones or thematic schemes seem to me to be essential – the setting, the human variable, culture, and worldwide connections.

The Setting

The characteristic geo-historical feature of America is its large land area and the relatively low ratio of population to territory, by world standards. The inhabitants live in sections of the whole, rather than spread evenly throughout its expanse. All of that applies in even more pronounced ways to American Jewish history. For instance, although Jews have historically lived in various sections of the country, they were (and still are) far less evenly distributed than the American population at large. A select handful of places have been the sites of the most concentrated groups of Jewish inhabitants, while in other places the Jewish presence has been peripheral, at best. In the eighteenth and early nineteenth centuries, the major sites of Jewish settlement included Philadelphia, New York, and Charleston. In later periods, Chicago, San Francisco, Los Angeles, and Miami joined New York and Philadelphia near the top of the list. Other regional centers like Pittsburgh, St. Louis, New Orleans, Atlanta, and Boston have similarly served as centers of Jewish communal life, far afield from the historical Middle Atlantic communities.

Cities are transit points where a constant turnover of population takes place, where intermittent inflows of domestic and foreign immigration alter the social landscape, and where continual residential expansion spreads across county lines. These protean features also pervade the urban history of the Jews. Usually, two generations of any given family are the most that remain in any one city for all or most of a lifetime. Concrete expression of this transience may be seen in the persistent migration of synagogues from one site to another within cities, and – at a later stage – from city neighborhoods to suburban communities. This institutional movement mirrors the drift of Jewish residents across social boundaries and across district lines. Landmark synagogues that have persisted at one permanent site since their foundation are rare in the extreme, in contrast to some of the nation's well-known historical churches. Even the landmark synagogues, indeed, have not served a constantly renewed community of worshippers, but have tended rather to become museums.

The Human Variable

The second commonplace or unifying theme consists of the Jews themselves – both the Jews *in* society and the Jews *as* a society. The key proposition concerning the Jews in American society is their religious distinctiveness and this, in essence, lends them their minority status. Distinctiveness can stimulate self-awareness and motivate adaptive strategies. It may also be a cultural disadvantage, which people may feel that they must finesse. Typically, four ways of doing so may be observed historically among American Jews:

Turning disadvantage to advantage: by cultivating an ethno-religious niche of their own, insiders belonging to a small group may resolve certain problems of status (by keeping outsider perspectives at bay), and can reinforce a sense of co-responsibility. In some periods this pattern has a "racializing" effect (that is, Jews are mostly related to one another by "blood") and group identity markers are sufficiently strong as to appear virtually "ineradicable," at least over the short term.

Turning difference into a compromise: live-and-let-live tolerance – by forging alliances (including marital alliances) across the religious divide. This may have a "de-racializing" effect: that is, a blurring of separate group markers.

Turning difference into a "contribution" via civic "boosterism," including the sponsorship of enterprise, politics, and philanthropy. A small, nearly marginal group like the Jews might thereby seek to magnify its visibility and, in turn, trade its marginality for "influence."

Addressing the religious issue at its source by de-exoticizing Judaism, by bringing its practices closer into line with those of mainline Protestant ideas. A great deal of energy has been invested over generations to domesticate American Judaism. One goal of this book's discussion of Jewish religion is to unpack the cumulative layers of that ideological project.

Religious distinctiveness vis-à-vis the majority of other Americans is, however, only one aspect of the Jews' social world. As noted, American Jewish history also involves examining the Jews *as a society*, characterized by internal diversification, conflict, and debate – indeed, just the sort of divisions one encounters in American society at large, or indeed in any social system.

Among the salient aspects of the Jewish social system that we will discuss are the following:

Sub-ethnicities: the formation of sub-communities based on such factors as countries of origin, variations in religious rites, and linguistic heritage. In turn, these subdivisions have reinforced the proliferation of individual synagogues, social clubs, newspapers, political movements, and welfare networks.

Sub-classes: occupational and class diversity has always been a feature of Jewish social life, even in those eras when it might seem, stereotypically, that Jews are economically homogeneous. Divisions between status groups produce class tensions, which in turn challenge notions of the Jews' mutual solidarity. By the same token, these divisions prompt some Jews to initiate civic, political, or social work across racial and ethnic boundaries by reaching out to non-Jews.

Migration: essential to any understanding of American Jewish history is an analysis of Jewish migration. In this book, migration is treated as an ongoing series of "new beginnings" – multiple, contiguous singularities – rather than as a conflated, collective genealogy. Indeed, the importance of migration history for American Jewry (as for the United States in general) establishes a way of talking about "natives" and "strangers" within the overall Jewish population. Finally, I also discuss Jewish re-emigration *from* America – re-emigration being a standard feature of virtually all instances of migration, in every land, and of some relevance (albeit minor) to the American Jewish case.

Spatial dimensions: in comparison with other populations, in Jewish history the movement from rural to urban spaces appears to be less significant. That is due to the mainly urban background of Jewish social life. This does not absolve the historian from grappling with the urban–rural distinction, however. As we will see, agriculture and rural life in general exercised a certain fascination for and among Jews. Moreover, it was through this rural (or as I refer to it, "pastoral") dimension that Jews in America first began to come to terms with "native" American sub-cultures.

Culture

A historical panorama of this sort would be incomplete without an aesthetic and intellectual component. In discussing Jews as creators and consumers of ideas and culture, more is at stake than the popularly rehearsed catalogue of individual Jews' "contributions" to the arts, sports, science, the media, or academia. What I have in mind is, rather, an analysis of Jewish self-representation. Evidence for this is as likely to emerge in their religious discourse as it is in forms like poetry, novels, songs, and drama.

The quest to discover a cultural dimension of Jewish experience often leads to a debate between *essentialist* and *constructionist* approaches. When (if at all) is a popular American song, written by an artist of Jewish birth, worth considering in the context of "Jewish" history, and why? The essentialist point of view places a great deal of weight on what may be construed as a thread of inner consistency or "authenticity," however thinly drawn the thread might be. The constructionist approach insists, rather, on the plastic, dynamic quality of all cultural products.

The essentialist mode of representing Jews and Jewish culture generally reduces Jewish civilization to a single, overriding principle, transcending time and space. Such essentialism crops up, for example, in claims (promoted mainly by Jewish liberals, which is not surprising) that liberalism represents an "essence" of Judaic principles – indeed, that Judaism is fundamentally identical with liberalism, if not its primordial source.

Actually, that quest for a definitive, intrinsic, Jewish–liberal nexus is most common in the United States and is latent or nearly absent in other Jewish communities around the world. That marks the idea as an artifact of the Jewish experience in America, rather than as a "Jewish" characteristic, per se. It is, to be precise, a cultural construction, and that leads us to consider the constructionist point of view.

Constructionists see all things that any Jews might do as equally "Jewish," without reference to core values or claims of authenticity. Such approaches are useful in certain discussions, such as some American Jews' engagements with hybrid affinities: nineteenth-century Jews who engaged with German culture, early twentieth-century Jews who engaged with Russian radicalism, and so forth. None of these affinities may be said to transcend the context in which they were bred; they are not "timeless" or efficient proxies for "Judaism" writ large.

A peculiarly American Jewish version of the constructionist approach involves an adaptation of the notion of American "exceptionalism." This approach posits that (for the Jews) America *is different*: it is the antithesis of all previous eras and contexts in the Jewish historical experience. By extension, all Jewish behaviors in America (and their cultural representations) are always partly or wholly re-invented and must be seen as self-sufficient, rather than dependent upon historical precedent. The hypothetical "otherness" of American Jewish history, namely the notion that it constitutes a separate, unique, open-ended journey of self-discovery and self-invention invites critical scrutiny. The foreign dimension of US Jewish life, which complicates the claims for domestic self-sufficiency, presents one opportunity to test such notions. Jews' experiences in America may have a qualitatively different aspect, in the world Jewish context, but how, when, or why they are different points toward comparability, not isolation.

Worldwide Connections

Ethnic subgroups have their source in migrations and they often retain an engagement with their countries of origin. That is clearly relevant to the American Jews, as well; but the Jewish case presents aspects that one encounters less often, if at all, in other ethnic groups. Jews in America have extended their overseas involvements and concerns to countries other than their particular countries of origin. Further, their overseas engagements surpass co-ethnic family networks of the type we see among other dispersed populations (as in the case of South Asians, for example), insofar as Jewish involvements are formalized, institutionalized, and persist even in the absence of common language or extended family connections.

For all these reasons we will have occasion to discuss the domestic reception of foreign events, including wars and revolutions; American foreign policy; "mission"-like projects undertaken abroad by Jewish agencies based in the United States; and even the intervention of American Jewish volunteers in armed conflicts not involving the United States.

Beyond Diversity and Adversity

Two alliterative signposts – "diversity" and "adversity" – have, between them, marked out some of the most popularly accepted approaches to the study of American Jewish history. In an earlier generation, Columbia University's foremost historian of European Jewry, Salo Wittmayer Baron (1895–1989), entitled his collection of lectures and essays about American Jewry *Steeled by Adversity*. The theme of adversity is, indeed, an important keynote throughout the realm of Jewish letters: namely, that the Jewish historical experience might be read as a long-running series of crisis, affliction, and anxieties about survival. However, one of Baron's important critical interventions was his insistence that during the long periods that interrupt the various episodes of adversity, Jews' lives have been far more "normal" than one might think – and that this was interesting and worth researching.[3] In the present volume, "adversity"

---

[3] Salo W. Baron, *Steeled by Adversity: Essays and Addresses on American Jewish Life* (Philadelphia, PA: Jewish Publication Society of America, 1971), p. 33; Jonathan

remains relevant, but is not the structuring pillar of my discussion. I do not see adversity as a metaphorical anvil upon which a sense of positive purpose has been forged. I have tried, rather, to integrate the better and the worse within the larger context.

The second motif, "diversity," has frequently been deployed as a pathway for inserting Jewish topics into discussions about multiculturalism. Diversity, as construed in today's environment, is not a bothersome "itch" on the skin of social discourse. It is, rather, considered a positive quality, rendering America more universal, more tolerant, and more democratic: in a word, more "American." In the political economy of contemporary America, diversity seems to have only benefits, no costs. Scholars in the field of American Jewish history have paid homage to the opening-up of American culture to diverse and distinctive voices. (Others, however, have taken the opposite tack, and have pointed rather to the involvement of Jews in the entrenchment of majoritarian cultural norms, particularly racialized norms, as practiced by white Americans.)[4]

Here, once again, I believe that some new approach needs to be suggested. Sacvan Bercovitch, one of the foremost interpreters of American political culture, has done much to clarify the mechanisms by which all supposedly diverse and dissident strands somehow end up by confirming "American" ideology.[5] I, too, explore the field of diversity in order to re-examine its ingrown ideological premises. So often, the discourse about diversity turns out mostly to be about self-esteem. One might wonder, however, how far-removed are Americans' habits of positive self-regard from Judaism's teachings of self-criticism? In turn, we might ask how Jews deal with such dissonances.

Woocher, *Sacred Survival: The Civic Religion of American Jews* (Bloomington and Indianapolis: Indiana University Press, 1986), p. 137.

[4] Many works promote the idea that Jews in America fostered cultural diversity. See, e.g. Susanne Klingenstein, *Jews in the American Academy, 1900–1940: The Dynamics of Intellectual Assimilation* (New Haven, CT: Yale University Press, 1991) and David A. Hollinger, *Science, Jews, and Secular Culture: Studies in Mid-Twentieth Century American Intellectual History* (Princeton, NJ: Princeton University Press, 1996). Works that reflect the contrasting view, that Jews in America mainly fell into line with white America's cultural hegemony, include Michael P. Rogin, *Blackface, White Noise: Jewish Immigrants in the Hollywood Melting Pot* (Berkeley: University of California Press, 1996), and Karen Brodkin, *How Jews Became White Folks and What that Says about Race in America* (New Brunswick, NJ: Rutgers University Press, 1998).

[5] Sacvan Bercovitch, *The Rites of Assent: Transformations in the Symbolic Construction of America* (New York and London: Routledge, 1993).

In short, this version of American Jewish history responds to a need, as I see it, for a history that absorbs and exhibits the ironies, the paradoxes, and the anxieties of life in America and is less fixated upon the successes and achievements of notable Jews. I ask that we observe American Jewry not just as providing evidence for the nation's diversity, but also as a product of a ramified, world-embracing history of Jewish existence.

Acknowledgments

I have incurred numerous debts along the way and it is now my pleasure to acknowledge them.

During the years spent writing this book I had the good fortune to be involved with several research groups at my home institution, the Hebrew University of Jerusalem. One was a two-year cycle of workshops in the field of migration studies, along with an able and amiable team of scholars based in Europe, Israel, and the United States. The group focused on the twentieth-century experiences of Jewish migrants from Russia and Eastern Europe.[1] Gleanings from these conversations are evident throughout this book. I would like to thank the Leonid Nevzlin Research Center for Russian and East European Jewry, and its head, Jonathan Dekel-Chen, for initiating and supporting this worthwhile endeavor, and to express my thanks to my fellow group-members: Anna Lipphardt, Kenneth Moss, Rafi Tsirkin-Sadan, Jeffrey Veidlinger, and Frank Wolff.

I also collaborated for three consecutive years in a research seminar on "Jews and Cities" at "Scholion," the Interdisciplinary Research Center for Humanities and Jewish Studies at the Hebrew University. Again, the experience was very rewarding and this book reflects some of what I gleaned. I am grateful for the generous grant afforded by the Jack, Joseph, and Morton Mandel Foundation, the sponsor of "Scholion," which enabled me to reduce my teaching load and to pursue my work with the greatest efficiency. I also take this opportunity to express my gratitude to my

---

[1] See a few of the published papers, which appeared in *East European Jewish Affairs* 44(2–3) (2014).

colleagues, among whom I was able to test out various ideas and theories: Sidra Dekoven Ezrahi, Aziza Khazzoom, Michael L. Miller, Dimitry Shumsky, Michael Silber, and Scott Ury. I thank, with special affection, my Scholion "kids," the doctoral students who were an integral part of our research group: Gali Drucker Bar-Am, Yakir Englander, Na'amah Meishar, Dvir Tzur, and Sara Yanovsky. Gali, in particular, delighted me on several occasions with treasures from the world of Yiddish letters that were particularly pertinent to my work. All of them have since earned their degrees. יישר כחכם – נעמתם לי מאוד!

In the early stages of my research, I was fortunate to have the assistance of Daniel Gross, one of my doctoral students, whom I thank warmly for his efforts. During that time, I was also able to rethink my understanding of ethnicity theory when I edited a volume of essays on the subject of Jewish ethnicity for the annual journal, *Studies in Contemporary Jewry*. I have been associated with *Studies* for most of my professional career, and this is but one of many occasions on which I have been grateful for this constantly refreshing encounter with thought-provoking new research. I thank my friends at the editorial staff, Laurie Fialkoff and Hannah Levinsky Koevary, and my co-editors, Uzi Rebhun, Anat Helman, and Richard Cohen.

I should also like to convey special thanks to friends who took the trouble to read preliminary versions of this book or draft chapters: Jack Wertheimer, Steven Zipperstein, Jonathan Dekel-Chen, and the anonymous reader for Cambridge University Press who offered valuable and constructive suggestions. Of course, I take full responsibility for any errors or other remaining drawbacks in the text.

I have the pleasure, as well, of acknowledging here (as well as in the footnotes) my indebtedness to graduate and doctoral students whose research I supervised over the years, who augmented my knowledge and afforded me much satisfaction from our collaborations, and whose work figures in this book in several places. Thank you, Nir Barkin, Hagit Cohen, Ze'ev Deutsch, Moshe Fox, Carmel Frenkel, Ari Katorza, Linda Maizels, Amos Morris-Reich, Yael Ohad-Karny, and Matthew Silver.

As noted at the outset, the person most responsible for shaping my thinking about American Jewish history is Henry Feingold, with whom I studied years ago at the Jewish Theological Seminary in New York. At the time, my chief interest lay in Eastern Europe, but studying with Henry opened my intellectual horizons and, as things turned out, became a lasting influence in my life. Our friendship has only deepened since then. Henry, this book is dedicated to you, in admiration and gratitude.

As always, the ones who share the author's intimate life are the ones who have to live with the gestation of the book and make room for it in their lives. I recall such occasions as when Lisa, my wife, handed me a flashlight from her bedside table, so that I would not need to keep on hopping out of bed to jot down suddenly inspired notes under the bathroom light. Thanks, Lisa, for shining light into my life in unexpected and marvelous ways.

My grown and still growing children – Adina, Aryeh, Sivan, and Yoav – have been the mainstay of the domestic part of my life. A previous book of mine that dealt with New York in the 1960s was dedicated to them, as it contained much that was relevant to our long family trek from Poland to America (via stopovers in Japan and China), and from America to Israel. With this book, I am happy to bequeath to them a much more comprehensive account. The completion of the manuscript coincided with Aryeh's return from a two-year period of graduate studies in the States, accompanied by his wife, Michal, who is herself the daughter of American ex-pats. Their "return to the scene" for yet another "new beginning" makes this book all the more timely. תודה יקירי על כל האהבה והפרגון.

First Encounters, New Beginnings

From Colonial Times to the Civil War

"Although religion-based explanations for economic achievement have been largely discredited by recent scholarship, most historians agree that a shared religion, especially in a diaspora group, helps to provide a basis for the formation of values, coherence, [and] social organization [...] among the members of the community."[1]

Introduction: The European Background, Sixteenth to Eighteenth Century

Most Jews in America today are native-born, and most can claim American-born forebears going back two, three, or more generations. The majority, however, can also point to a prior cultural and family heritage that is distinctly European, and others have roots in the Mediterranean region and the Middle East. Regardless of these genealogies, however, the context in which Jewish life developed on the American continent over several centuries was undoubtedly that of the Euro-American social world. Hence, we must begin our survey with a glance at the European dimension and, as we progress, we must continue to bear it in mind.

Through conquest and settlement, Spain, Portugal, France, Holland, and England established extensive Atlantic and Caribbean possessions in the Americas during the sixteenth and seventeenth centuries. These gave rise to plantation, smallholder, and merchant colonies consisting of transplanted Europeans, African slaves, and (in some cases) forced native

---

[1] Jessica Vance Roitman, *The Same but Different? Inter-Cultural Trade and the Sephardim, 1595–1640* (Leiden and Boston, MA: Brill, 2011), pp. 68–9.

labor. Distant as those colonies were from their European sponsors, they were nevertheless vital strategic and economic assets over which the leading European economies of the day competed and fought. Colonies were therefore a matter of high policy whose governance was entrusted to high-ranking figures or to chartered corporations; they, in turn, nurtured these prime assets of empire and looked for ways to maximize their profitability. The colonial experience at its height eventually combined shipping (oceans, rivers, canals) and financial ventures on an unheard of scale, and the transfer of large populations.

The new economic thinking that underwrote colonialist ventures was crucial for the development of the modern European state system – and for the emergence of modern Jewish communities. The same ideology that promoted colonial and commercial expansion embraced the concept that human endeavor was fundamentally expansive: it was not meant to be fixed or limited except by the variety of "native" capacities to be found at random in nature and human society. In the most forward-looking states, the push for recruitment of human resources for economic development began to take priority and it tended to push aside the once crucial matter of religious convictions and national origins. To a greater or lesser degree, tolerance for certain religious differences found its way into statecraft, with the result that foreigners, minorities, and Jews in various parts of the world found easier access to employment and business ventures. Thus, the link between these aspects of modern political economy and Jewish history is not fortuitous.

All this took at least a century to evolve, however, and the pace of social and economic integration varied widely from place to place. The terms of Jewish integration in any given country were framed by certain abiding legal and social inhibitions, and these shifted ground with the changing of rulers and governors. To track the Jews' encounter with the Atlantic world, therefore, we need to orient ourselves to the peculiar geopolitics of Jewish life at the onset of the classical era of European colonial expansion.

At that time, about half of the world's Jewish population lived in Europe (approximately half a million souls), but they were not evenly distributed: in most of Western Europe, they were scarcely present at all. The bulk of Europe's Jews were concentrated in the Habsburg-ruled lands of Central Europe and in the Polish-Lithuanian Commonwealth (1569–1795). A second major body of Jewish population, comprising another half-million people, lived under the scepter of Islam, mostly under the Ottoman Empire, which was the seat of major trading networks.

The relative scarcity of Jewish population across large swaths of Western Europe prior to the mid-seventeenth century was a legacy of the medieval era. Jewish communities of long standing (some with antecedents dating as far back as Roman times) had been expelled from England, France, most of Italy, and many German principalities from the late 1200s to the fifteenth century. Those expulsions would be partially reversed only in the mid-1600s, in the wake of the Thirty Years' War. Restoring population size, urban commerce, and international trade were prioritized after the Peace of Westphalia of 1648, which constituted a window of opportunity for Jewish resettlement. Gradually, Jews from Habsburg and Polish lands migrated west and established communities in northwestern Europe, where they were joined by Jews of Spanish-Portuguese background who were migrating north.

Spain had been the last country to join the cycle of medieval Jewish expulsions. The "Catholic monarchs" Ferdinand II and Isabella I of Aragon and Castile "cleansed" their realm of infidels in the summer of 1492, after subduing the Moslem emirate in Granada. Considerable numbers of Spanish Jews who wanted to avoid religious persecution during the century preceding the expulsion had sought recourse to conversion, and their ranks were newly augmented after the expulsion decree. In neighboring Portugal, to which some of the refugees initially fled, all Jews were forcibly converted by royal edict in 1497. In 1536 Portugal (like Spain before it) granted wide powers to the Holy Office of the Inquisition, the arm of the Church that enforced Catholic theological purity and purged alleged heresies. Part of its task was to discover and to punish secret practitioners of Jewish rites among the *conversos* ("converts") or New Christians, as former Jews and their descendants were known.

A number of such conversos resettled in New Spain (Mexico) during the reign of Philip II (1556–98). As many as 300 New Christians were living there by the first half of the seventeenth century, but the Inquisition, transplanted to the New World, gradually put an end to their existence. Capture by the Inquisition and prosecution for secret Judaizing led to punishment ranging in severity from imprisonment, flogging, and expropriation of property, to eternal banishment from New Spain, and in some cases capital punishment. By 1640, New Christians were nearly eradicated from Mexico but instances of alleged crypto-Jews burned at the stake at the Inquisition's behest in Spanish America continued to the end of the century.[2]

---

[2] Martin A. Cohen, "The Religion of Luis Rodriguez Carvajal: Glimpses into the Passion of a Mexican Judaizer," in *Critical Studies in American Jewish History*, ed. Jacob Rader

In the wake of the Iberian persecutions, large colonies of former Iberian Jews were established in North Africa, in Ottoman Turkish realms in the Balkans and the eastern Mediterranean, in southern France (Provence and Bordeaux), in northern Italy (chiefly the trading superpowers, Livorno and Venice), in northern Germany (chiefly around Hamburg), and the Netherlands. In the mid-seventeenth century, a handful of Jewish *conversos* lived in London, their Jewish identities being a discreet matter that was not openly acknowledged. Once their status as residents and merchants was regularized in the 1650s, others joined them and the community grew to several hundred. At about the same time (1645), as many as a thousand Jews settled in Dutch colonial settlements in northeastern Brazil, among an estimated 3,400 other colonists, and it was there that Jews were first able to engage freely in public religious worship in the New World.

Jews' encounters with the Atlantic world of trade and European expansion began slowly, therefore, and (apart from the ill-fated episode of New Spain) were closely associated with England and the Low Countries. By 1795, the fast-growing Dutch Jewish population reached about 40,000, making it an especially important center of Jewish cultural and economic

Marcus (New York and Cincinnati, OH: Ktav/American Jewish Archives, 1971), vol. II, pp. 1–26; and *The Martyr: The Story of a Secret Jew and the Mexican Inquisition in the Sixteenth Century* (Philadephia, PA: Jewish Publication Society of America, 1973); Pinhas Bibelnik, "Bein iberiyut leyahadut: 'al zehutam shel 'notzrim hadashim' bisefarad hahadashah bameah ha-17" (Between Iberian and Jewish Identities: On the Jewish Identity of New Christians in New Spain in the 17th Century), in *Be'ikvot kolumbus: amerikah 1492–1992 (In the Wake of Columbus, 1492–1992)*, ed. Miriam Eliav-Feldon (Jerusalem: Mercaz Zalman Shazar, 1996), p. 465; Jonathan Israel, "Jews and Crypto-Jews in the Atlantic World Systems, 1500–1800," in *Atlantic Diasporas: Jews Conversos, and Crypto-Jews in the Age of Mercantilism, 1500–1800*, ed. Richard L. Kagan and Philip Morgan (Baltimore, MD: Johns Hopkins University Press, 2009), p. 17; Eva Echmany, "The Participation of New Christians and Crypto-Jews in the Conquest, Colonization, and Trade of Spanish America, 1521–1660," in *Jews and the Expansion of Europe to the West, 1450–1800*, ed. Paolo Bernadini and Norman Fiering (New York and Oxford: Berghahn Books, 2001), pp. 186–202; Robert Rowland, "New Christian, Marrano, Jew," in Bernadini and Fiering, *Jews and the Expansion of Europe*, pp. 125–48; Nathan Wachtel, "Marrano Religiosity in Hispanic America in the Sixteenth Century," in *ibid.*, pp. 149–71; Solange Alberro, "Crypto-Jews and the Mexican Holy Office in the Seventeenth Century," in *ibid.*, pp. 172–85; Yosef Kaplan, *Minotsrim hadashim leyehudim hadashim (From New Christians to New Jews)* (Jerusalem: Mercaz Zalman Shazar, 2003); Renée Levine Melammed, *A Question of Identity: Iberian Conversos in Historical Perspective* (New York: Oxford University Press, 2004); Alicia Gojman de Backal, "Crypto-Judaism in Mexico: Past and Present," in *Identities in an Era of Globalization and Multiculturalism: Latin America in the Jewish World*, ed. Judit Bokser Liwerant et al. (Leiden and Boston, MA: Brill, 2008), pp. 223–30.

life. The organized life of the community was dominated by well-to-do Iberian (in Hebrew, Sephardi) families. Fanning out wherever commerce was developing, members of such families established trading networks that spanned international borders and sea-going trade routes. From the 1630s to early 1650s, representatives of these mercantile families had settled in Dutch colonies along the northeastern coast of South America and in French, British, and Dutch possessions in the Caribbean and the coastal waters of North America. Settling individually or in small family clusters, they formed a natural extension of a wider network of Atlantic traders. Merchants like Mordekay Enriques, David Robbles, and Joseph Bueno were active in commerce linking New Netherland, Curaçao, and Surinam. They were but a small part of the colonial population, but the paper trails they left in the archives exemplify the functions of coastal Atlantic cities as commercial outposts of the European mercantile world.[3]

Civic Development and Jewish Settlement in North America

Jewish settlers generally appeared several decades after a mercantile European town was already established. Dutch New Amsterdam, for instance, had been in existence for nearly thirty years when about two dozen Jews arrived in 1654. The majority of these were en route northward from the Caribbean, after having abandoned former Dutch settlements in Brazil, which had recently fallen to Portuguese control. After British rule replaced that of the Dutch in New Amsterdam (1664), the small town that was re-designated New York more than tripled its population (from 1,000 in 1650 to 3,200 in 1680). In this enhanced

---

[3] Jonathan Israel, *Diasporas Within a Diaspora: Jews, Crypto-Jews, and the World Maritime Empires (1540–1740)* (Leiden: Brill, 2002); Roitman, *The Same but Different*; Francesca Trivellato, *The Familiarity of Strangers: The Sephardic Diaspora, Livorno, and Cross-Cultural Trade in the Early Modern Period* (New Haven, CT and London: Yale University Press, 2009); Malcolm H. Stern, "Portuguese Sephardim in the Americas," in *Sephardim in the Americas: Studies in Culture and History*, ed. Martin A. Cohen and Abraham J. Peck (Tuscaloosa and London: University of Alabama Press, in cooperation with the American Jewish Archives, 1993), pp. 141–78. See also Wim Klooster, "Networks of Colonial Entrepreneurs," in Kagan and Morgan, *Atlantic Diasporas*, p. 33; Zvi Loker, *Jews in the Caribbean: Evidence on the History of the Jews in the Caribbean Zone in Colonial Times* (Jerusalem: Misgav Yerushalayim, 1991), pp. 90–7, 186–8; Max J. Kohler, "Phases of Jewish Life in New York Before 1800," *Publication of the American Jewish Historical Society (PAJHS)* 2 (1894): 77; Richard D. Brown, *Modernization: The Transformation of American Life, 1600–1865* (New York: Hill and Wang, 1976).

urban setting, a Jewish congregation in New York was functioning by around 1682.[4]

Likewise, Jews also settled in Charles Town (Charleston) in the British colony of Carolina some thirty years after the colony's establishment in 1670. From 1697 to 1750, but mainly after 1720, the number of Jews in Charleston increased along with the growth of the town itself. Philadelphia, to take another example, was founded in 1683, home to English, Welsh, and German settlers. Starting about twenty years later, occasional Jewish sojourners and eventually some permanent Jewish residents appear in local documentation. The seminal period of the Jewish community's formation occurred in subsequent years, however, when Philadelphia, which boasted over 10,000 inhabitants by 1740, established itself as the second-largest city in British America (after Boston). Although bolstered numerically during the years of the American Revolution, when Jews who fled British-held New York relocated temporarily to Philadelphia, leaders of the veteran Sephardi "Mikveh Israel" congregation complained in the early 1790s of drastically dwindling members, insufficient funds to pay for basic religious services, and the shouldering of congregational responsibilities by barely "9 or 10 individuals."[5]

In Newport, Rhode Island (founded 1638), the intermittent presence of several Jewish settlers is documented for the 1650s and 1660s and for the years from 1693 to 1700. After another hiatus, an established Jewish community reappeared later in the 1740s, by which time Newport was a substantial town with over 6,000 inhabitants. New Haven, Connecticut, which likewise was founded in 1638, did not attract Jewish settlers for 120 years, until two brothers – Jacob and Solomon Pinto – arrived in

---

[4] Holly Snyder, "English Markets, Jewish Merchants, and Atlantic Endeavors," in Kagan and Morgan, *Atlantic Diasporas*, pp. 57–62; Simon Rosendale, "An Early Ownership of Real Estate in Albany, New York, by a Jewish Trader," *PAJHS* 3 (1895): 61; Leon Hühner, "Asser Levy, a Noted Jewish Burgher of New Amsterdam," *PAJHS* 8 (1900): 9; Albion Morris Dyer, "Points in the First Chapter of New York Jewish History," *PAJHS* 3 (1895): 41; Howard B. Rock, *Haven of Liberty: New York Jews in the New World, 1654–1865* (New York and London: New York University Press, 2012), pp. 10–23.

[5] Thomas L. Purvis, *Colonial America to 1763. Almanacs of American Life* (New York: Facts on File, Inc., 2009), pp. 224–6; Edwin Wolf 2nd and Maxwell Whiteman, *The History of the Jews of Philadelphia from Colonial Times to the Age of Jackson* (Philadelphia, PA: Jewish Publication Society of America, 1956, 1975), pp. 9–35; "Benjamin Nones to Congregation Beth Elohim, 1792," in *The Jews of the United States, 1790–1840, A Documentary History*, ed. Joseph L. Blau and Salo W. Baron (New York and Philadelphia: Columbia University Press and the Jewish Publication Society of America, 1963), vol. II, p. 584.

1758. The Reverend Ezra Stiles noted the arrival in 1772 of a Venetian Jewish family who conducted a private Sabbath rite.[6]

A partial exception to this pattern might be Savannah, where the earliest Jewish colonists arrived directly from Britain in 1733, virtually together with the initial group of British settlers. Two groups of Jews were involved: some relatively well-off Portuguese Jews, including one Dr. Nuñez, a native of Lisbon, and a number of Ashkenazic Jews – that is, Jews hailing from Europe north of the Alps and east of the Rhine – in this case apparently from Bavaria, who were dependent on the good graces of the London Jewish community. (The practice of transporting poor Jews from Britain to North America or to West Indian colonies continued in some cases into the early nineteenth century.) True to the pattern in other colonies, however, the original group of Jewish settlers in Savannah was soon depleted, leaving behind only a few individuals. A stable community was established only toward the end of the 1760s and a synagogue was founded still later, after the American Revolution (1791).[7]

The French colony at New Orleans was laid out in 1718 and several thousand colonists soon populated the settlement, including French, Germans, and Swiss, as well as African slaves. By the early 1730s, some thirty years prior to the earliest sojourns there by Jews, the city was an important economic and administrative hub for a very large district. The strictly Catholic French and Spanish administrations in the Louisiana territory were decidedly inhospitable to a Jewish presence, and it was only after the Louisiana Purchase (1803) by the US government that several Jews arrived to take up permanent residence. In any event, it actually took much longer for Jews to create a stable community in New Orleans. The handful of Dutch Jewish merchants who lived in the city mostly married

[6] William Pencak, *Jews and Gentiles in Early America, 1654–1800* (Ann Arbor: University of Michigan Press, 2005), pp. 87–8; Morris Gutstein, *The Story of the Jews of Newport* (New York: Bloch Publishing Co., 1936), pp. 46, 53; Holly Snyder, "Rethinking the Definition of 'Community' for a Migratory Age," in *Imagining the American Jewish Community*, ed. Jack Wertheimer (Hanover, NH and London: Brandeis University Press/ University Press of New England, in association with the Jewish Theological Seminary of America, 2007), pp. 7–8; Purvis, *Colonial America to 1763*, pp. 180, 227.

[7] Eli Faber, *A Time for Planting: The First Migration, 1654–1820. The Jewish People in America*, vol. I (Baltimore, MD and London: Johns Hopkins University Press, 1992), p. 41; Charles C. Jones, Jr., "The Settlement of the Jews in Georgia," *PAJHS* 1 (1892): 5–12; Leon Hühner, "The Jews of Georgia in Colonial Times," *PAJHS* 10 (1902): 65; Saul S. Friedman, *Jews and the American Slave Trade* (New Brunswick, NJ: Transaction, 1998), p. 168. See the case of Levy Joseph, sent by the London Talmud Torah committee in 1807 to Charleston: cited in Todd Endelman, *The Jews of Georgian England, 1714–1830* (Philadelphia, PA: Jewish Publication Society of America, 1979), p. 231.

French Catholic women, whose children were raised in the Church. Thus, although a Jewish cemetery was started in 1828, a functioning community took shape only in the 1830s, thanks to the activities of German Jewish immigrants. The latter were able to erect a synagogue by 1850.[8]

The predominant pattern of Jews' settling in relatively small numbers in established towns of several decades' standing, forming themselves into communities by a drawn-out series of fits and starts, can be explained in large part by the fluctuations of economic opportunity. Jews, who were neither planter-gentry nor landless farmers, were attracted nearly always to towns where they were likeliest to find mercantile opportunities in trade or craftwork. A town had to have reached a certain level of social coherence and economic viability before it might be attractive to a mercantile element (see Table 1.1).

Furthermore, we should bear in mind that Jews were not recruited as colonists by the founding owners or the development corporations. New England and Virginia, between them, were home to 90,000 European colonists and hundreds of African slaves by the 1660s.[9] By contrast, the settlement of Jews was neither sought nor organized, neither encouraged nor planned. Rather, Jews were part of an unorganized, sporadic migration, settling down along known routes, seldom if ever venturing beyond an already existing line of major European-settled towns or cities.

Jews in the colonies (like many other settlers) were frequently transient, continuing to move between London, the Caribbean, and the North American colonies. Benjamin Bueno de Mesquita left Dutch Brazil for the Italian port of Livorno, journeyed back to the Caribbean (Jamaica) by 1660, and later moved on to New York. The prominent Gomez family of British New York thrived on spatial mobility: its members had marital connections with other Jewish families in Newport (Rhode Island), Jamaica, Barbados, and Curaçao. Creating multiple home-base sites suited their economic needs admirably. Their commercial connections, about half of which directly involved other Jews, fanned out to New

---

[8] Blau and Baron, *The Jews of the United States*, vol. III, pp. 853–54; see also letter of Rebecca Gratz to Joseph Gratz, November 1, 1807, in Bertram W. Korn, *The Early Jews of New Orleans* (Waltham, MA: American Jewish Historical Society, 1969), p. 210: "There are many who call themselves Jews, or at least whose parentage being known are obliged to acknowledge themselves such, but who neglect those duties which would make that title honorable and [...] respected." Robert P. Swierenga, *The Forerunners: Dutch Jewry in the North American Diaspora* (Detroit, MI: Wayne State University Press, 1994), pp. 211–13, 219.

[9] Michael G. Kammen, *Colonial New York: A History* (New York: C. Scribner's Sons, 1975; Oxford University Press, 1996), p. 38.

TABLE 1.1. *Earliest Jewish presence in selected American cities founded 1730s–1790s**

	Founding date	First recorded Jew(s)	Town size (overall population)
Richmond, VA	1737–42	Joseph Myers, 1787; burial plot and first entry of congregational records, 1791	State capital (1780); Richmond county population in 1790: *c.* 7,000
Pittsburgh, PA	1764	Michael Gratz and others intermittently resided in the 1780s; first permanent resident of Jewish ancestry: Samuel Pettigrew (1814)	*c.* 8,000 (1815)
St. Louis, MO	1764	Bloch family, 1816; prayer quorum (*minyan*) in 1837	6,000 (1830)
Louisville, KY	1776	Israelite Benevolent Society, est. 1832	Over 10,000 (1830)
Cincinnati, OH	1780s	Joseph Jonas, from Plymouth, England, 1817; 16 Jews listed in 1820	6,000 (1815), with 7 churches; 9,642 (1820)
Lexington, KY	1782	Benjamin Gratz, 1818	C. 1800 already a large town, known as "the Philadelphia of Kentucky"
Utica, NY	1786–98	Abraham Cohen, from Poland, 1847; *minyan* formed 1848	17,656 (1850)

*Lewis N. Dembitz, "Jewish Beginnings in Kentucky," *PAJHS* 1 (1893): 99–101; Jacob Ezekiel, "The Jews of Richmond," *PAJHS* 4 (1896): 21–7; Nancy Klein, "Cincinnati," in *Encyclopedia Judaica*, 2nd ed., vol. IV (New York: Macmillan Reference USA, 2006), pp. 727–30; David Philipson, "The Jewish Pioneers of the Ohio Valley," *PAJHS* 8 (1900): 43–57; and, "The Cincinnati Community in 1825," *PAJHS* 10 (1902): 97–9; S. Joshua Kohn, *The Jewish Community of Utica, New York, 1847–1948* (New York: American Jewish Historical Society, 1959); Richard C. Wade, "Urban Life in Western America, 1790–1830," in *The Old Northwest. Studies in Regional History, 1787–1910*, ed. Harry N. Scheiber (Lincoln: University of Nebraska Press, 1969), pp. 229–48.

Haven, Newport, Raritan (New Jersey), Charleston, and Philadelphia as well as Barbados, Curaçao, Nevis, Amsterdam, London, Dublin, Liverpool, Venice, Madeira, and Brazil.[10]

Transiency was also, at times, the effect of larger historical shifts. The earliest arrivals by Jews on the North American mainland had coincided (rather inauspiciously for them) with the end of the Anglo-Dutch war of 1652–4 and the defeat of Dutch imperial and trading interests. The Amsterdam connection, which was the lynchpin in the Atlantic trading networks of the Sephardi merchants and a key to Dutch–Spanish–Portuguese trade, was an initial source of strength that won Jews a precarious foothold in colonial ports, but that strength did not last very long. In terms of North American trade in particular (as compared with Caribbean or Mediterranean commerce), the crucial fact of that era was British commercial and naval ascendancy. Although there was some transfer of Dutch Sephardi traders to London (especially after 1688, when William of Orange gained the English throne), their share in Britain's overseas trade was peripheral: perhaps only 1 or 2 percent.[11]

It is noteworthy in this regard that the Torah scroll that the first Jews in Manhattan used for communal prayer until 1663 was borrowed from Amsterdam, and it was then returned to its original home when these early Jewish colonists dispersed. As noted, a small Jewish population conducted regular religious and communal life in New York from the early 1680s, but it still constituted only a tiny fragment of the growing colony. They included Asser Levy, butcher and trader, originally from the Lithuanian part of the Polish kingdom, probably the only Jew in British New York who had maintained his residence there since the Dutch colonial period. In the first two decades of the 1700s, there were perhaps seventeen to twenty Jewish households in New York City. These accounted for about 1 percent of the city's inhabitants at the time.[12]

---

[10] Adam Sutcliffe, "Jewish History in an Age of Atlanticism," in Kagan and Morgan, *Atlantic Diasporas*, p. 26; Klooster, "Networks of Colonial Entrepreneurs," p. 37; Francesca Trivellato, "Sephardic Merchants in the Early Modern Atlantic and Beyond," in Kagan and Morgan, *Atlantic Diasporas*, pp. 99–120; Bruno Feitler, "Jews and New Christians in Dutch Brazil, 1630–1654," in Kagan and Morgan, *Atlantic Diasporas*, pp. 123–51; Max J. Kohler, "Jewish Activity in American Colonial Commerce," *PAJHS* 10 (1902); Stephen A. Fortune, *Merchants and Jews: The Struggle for British West Indian Commerce, 1650–1750* (Gainesville: University of Florida Press, 1984), pp. 133–5; see also Faber, *Time for Planting*, pp. 35, 47–8, 86; Roitman, *The Same but Different*, pp. 113–14.

[11] Trivellato, *Familiarity of Strangers*, p. 212.

[12] Jonathan D. Sarna, *American Judaism: A History* (New Haven, CT: Yale University Press, 2004), p. 10; Snyder, "English Markets, Jewish Merchants," p. 58; Leo Hershkowitz,

While the general population of New York increased (it reached 18,000 in 1760), the Jewish population straggled along in a fairly static fashion. One synagogue served them all: the need for a larger building did not become a practical issue for a hundred years. By comparison, there were sixteen churches in the city in 1774, twenty-two in 1794, and fifty-five by 1811, including three that served the African American population.

Looking beyond New York to Britain's North American colonies as a whole, it is indicative that between 1660 and 1750 the number of synagogues in North America went from one to a total of five, while the number of churches increased nearly ten-fold, from 156 to 1,461.[13]

We may sum up, then, that a modest number of Jews were involved in the settlement and the commercial economy of British America, and that they tended to take stronger root as occupational opportunities became more developed. That was true especially after 1700, notably in such key centers as Philadelphia, Charleston, and New York. The gradual growth of the Jewish population in the colonies was associated with the considerable influx of Jews into Britain from 1710 to 1735, many of whom (some 1,500) were fleeing a renewed spate of Inquisitorial persecution against New Christians and their descendants in Spain and Portugal. Still other Jews arriving in Britain in that period were Ashkenazic Jews from Holland, Germany, and Poland. The colonies in America apparently absorbed some of the overflow of these inter-European migrations.[14]

The larger significance of the tentative, small-scale settlement by Jews in North America's European colonies is two-fold. First, as we will discuss in the next section, the loosely structured colonial context proved relatively accommodating of Jewish religious difference. The handful of

---

"Some Aspects of the New York Jewish Merchant in Colonial Trade," *Migration and Resettlement: Proceedings of the Anglo-American Jewish Historical Conference* (London: Jewish Historical Society, 1971), p. 102. Moses Franks, son of Jacob and Abigaill Franks, a key family in the New York Jewish community of the day, moved between New York, London, and Philadelphia in the 1730s before returning permanently to England. See Faber, *A Time for Planting*, pp. 44–5.

[13] Kammen, *Colonial New York*, pp. 161, 181, 279; Hershkowitz, "Some Aspects"; Ira Rosenwaike, *Population History of New York City* (Syracuse, NY: Syracuse University Press, 1972), pp. 10, 24, 27, 28. Rosenwaike (p. 10) gives the breakdown into "families" belonging to various churches in 1695 in a contemporary minister's report: Chapel in the fort (Anglican): 90 families; Dutch Calvinists, 450; Dutch Lutheran, 30; French, 200; Jews Synagogue, 20; Haarlem (Dutch Calvinist], 25; English (Anglican), 40; Dissenters (no number stated).On the physical expansion of the Mill St. Synagogue, see Rachel Wischnitzer, *Synagogue Architecture in the United States* (Philadelphia, PA: Jewish Publication Society of America, 1955), p. 25.

[14] Endelman, *Jews of Georgian England*, p. 168.

Jewish residents encountered few difficulties in carrying out normal social and economic functions. In some respects, similarities existed between the status occupied by Jews in the colonies and their fellow Jewish traders in the port cities of southern France, Holland, Italy, and Britain. Ultimately, however, the American colonies went well beyond the bounds of European ideas of civic propriety in terms of Jewish integration.[15]

Second, Jews in America – despite their dependence on and constant communication with their confreres abroad – were apt to pursue their lives in the colonies in ways that separated them from the main currents of Jewish life, not just in civil terms, but also in religious terms. The fragmentary and transient nature of their communities, combined with geographical distance, put them more than just an ocean apart from European and Mediterranean Jewries. Here, a few general background remarks are in order.

The seventeenth and early eighteenth centuries constituted a pivotal phase in the modern remaking of Jewish social and religious history. In the 1650s and 1660s, Jews across most of Europe, North Africa, and the eastern Mediterranean were plunged into a period of intense religious and geographic turmoil. This was due partly to the insurrections and invasions of Poland and Ukraine (beginning in 1648–9), whose course was marked by the massacre of many thousands of Jews (and many thousands more lost their homes and livelihoods). In addition, the era was marked by the heretical millennialism of Sabbetai Zevi, the Jewish messianic pretender of Smyrna (Izmir, Turkey), that peaked around 1666 and continued to generate aftershocks of theological controversy for nearly a century.[16]

Buffered by distance, Jews in colonial America were only minimally exposed to much of this. Though some individuals, scattered around the Atlantic and Caribbean European colonies, evidently harbored spiritualistic leanings, there was no pietistic revival resembling those of the Old World. At once linked to world Jewry but also adrift in a frontier zone, their ritualized confirmations of Judaic belief in the afterlife and in an

[15] David Sorkin, "Is American Jewry Exceptional? Comparing Jewish Emancipation in Europe and America," *American Jewish History* 96(3) (2010): 175–200.

[16] On Sabbateanism and Frankism, see Gershom Scholem, *Sabbetai Sevi, The Mystical Messiah, 1626–1676*, trans. R. J. Zwi Werblowsky, *The Bollingen Series XCIII* (Princeton, NJ: Princeton University Press, 1973); Stephen Sharot, *Messianism, Mysticism, and Magic. A Sociological Analysis of Jewish Religious Movements* (Chapel Hill: University of North Carolina Press, 1982), pp. 86–138; Pawel Maciejko, *The Mixed Multitude: Jacob Frank and the Frankist Movement, 1755–1816* (Philadelphia: University of Pennsylvania Press, 2011). Frank and his retinue converted to Catholicism.

End of Time that would usher in an era of eternal redemption, it has been shown, tended to be "more [like] a quotidian messianism than an intense revitalization movement."[17] Intense eschatological interest and speculation linked to events in the Jewish world of the 1660s was far more characteristic of millenarian New England Puritans than of colonial Jews.[18]

The Civil and Political Status of Colonial Jews

The experience of the Atlantic Sephardi trading diaspora captures in microcosm the pathos and contradictions that characterized that era. As former converts to Christianity or their descendants, living in cultural, political, and religious border zones, and operating in the interstices of international trade, the conduct of their lives was made possible solely through the competitiveness of the maritime powers whose prime interest lay in promoting new ventures.

Yet at the same time, their very predicament – expatriate members of a decimated and scattered population that had thrived materially and spiritually for centuries in Spain only to end up in humiliation, trauma, and expulsion – could only be imagined in a world where religious difference was considered an affront, heresy or blasphemy a punishable crime, and faithlessness an obscenity. It would be difficult to draw the line between the pragmatism of the commercial revolution, which broadened the terms of personal existence for any number of people, and the jealousy with which resources and opportunities were guarded and controlled. Zealous vigilance was needed to thwart the designs of the foreigner, the stranger, the non-believer, and the sectarian. In practice as well as in principle, Jews were tolerated only under circumscribed conditions defining their occupational pursuits, controlling and limiting their overall numbers, requiring them to police other Jewish travelers and transients, and imposing particular fees and taxes. Urban Jewries of seventeenth- and eighteenth-century Europe were caught in a tug-of-war between the central government, which sought tighter control over commerce and manufacturing, and the municipal councils, which wanted to assert their prerogatives of local self-administration. The banning or limitation of Jewish tradesmen and the geographical and juridical sequestering of Jews were common

---

[17] Laura Arnold Leibman, *Messianism, Secrecy, Mysticism: A New Interpretation of Early American Jewish Life* (London and Portland, OR: Valentine Books, 2012, 2013), quotation from p. 13.

[18] Sacvan Bercovitch, *The American Jeremiad* (Madison: University of Wisconsin Press, 1978), pp. 74–5, 86–8.

weapons in the arsenal of city elders, which they wielded in defense of their ancestral rights.[19]

In contrast, a number of the colonial regimes in North America often permitted Jews and members of other minority religions to avoid most sorts of religious controls. The chances of bending or neutralizing the rules, of maximizing one's chances, were greater on the far periphery of European civilization, particularly where no single established church predominated (and in particular, where the Catholic Church was not in the ascendant). Although the colonies continued to uphold the legal and religious traditions of the mother countries in many respects, in other ways colonists circumvented or subverted the system. As a result, both lenient loopholes and the sporadic attempts to eliminate them existed. Jews represented an element that was traditionally outside the regulated or semi-regulated Christian social order; accommodating them tended to be part of the overall disturbance of status and propriety that characterized the colonies.

The Dutch colonial authorities, in founding New Netherland, originally sought to restrict public religion in the colony to the Dutch Reformed (Calvinist) Church; yet, they found it necessary, for the economic welfare and general peace of the colony, to make certain exceptions – making an accommodation with the presence of English settlers (Presbyterians and Puritans) as well as Lutherans on lands along the Delaware River. Upon seizing the Dutch colonies in 1664, the English authorities extended freedom of religious conscience as previously upheld by the Dutch. Restrictions against public worship by Jews, Quakers, and Catholics were enacted or reinforced in the early 1680s, only to be struck down again in 1686. Five years later, Jews and Catholics again lost their civic and public religious rights. By 1695, however, the Jews in New York opened a small synagogue on Mill Street (today South William Street).

In Maryland, legislation of an "Act concerning Religion" in 1649 provided that no person professing a belief in Jesus Christ should be molested, but that anyone blaspheming or denying "Jesus Christ to be the Son of God" might be punished with death. Curiously known as the "Toleration Act," it was the basis for the arrest in 1658 of a Jewish physician, one Jacob Lumbrozo, who was, however, released from custody. Subsequently, Jews resided in Maryland with no recognized civil status

---

[19] Hillel Kieval, "Antisemitism and the City: A Beginner's Guide," in *People of the City: Jews and the Urban Challenge. Studies in Contemporary Jewry*, vol. XV, ed. Ezra Mendelsohn (New York: Oxford University Press, 1999), pp. 3–18.

in law, but nevertheless in "undisturbed domicile" in practice, and were "gradually allowed the exercise of certain undefined rights." The anti-blasphemy clauses of 1649 were reiterated in a new act of 1723: "If any person shall hereafter [...] deny our Saviour Jesus Christ to be the Son of God, or shall deny the Holy Trinity, he should for the first offense be fined and have his tongue bored; for the second, fined, and have his head burned; for the third, be put to death."[20] This was evidently directed against Christian offenders, in the main, but it is noteworthy that no synagogue was organized in Maryland until 1830.

English policy regarding the status of alien residents in the colonies underwent a certain evolution. The Navigation Acts of the 1650s and 1660s sought to inhibit the trading status of "Jews, French, and other foreigners." In order to trade without penalty, it was necessary to petition the colonial governor or the king for certification ("letters patent") as an English subject or "denizen." With such special license in hand, a denizen could engage in wholesale and overseas trade, but had no rights of inheritance and property, and bore no civic responsibility. Those could only be obtained by applying for full-fledged naturalization. After 1740, when Parliament anchored this policy in a new Naturalization Act, conditional upon seven years' residence, Jews in the colonies increasingly applied for naturalized status.[21]

Those who were naturalized or endenizened could also apply to become freemen, which entitled one to engage in retail trade, to vote, and to serve in public office; but apparently the status of freeman was easily obtained, thus ameliorating the restrictive intention of the law. Freemanship both in New York City and Albany, for instance, was a fairly non-restricted privilege, and fees for "merchant-trader" or "shop-keeper" status were reduced to nominal rates. In 1702, New York City made it possible for those who "are poor and not able to purchase Their Freedoms [to] be made Freemen of this Citty [*sic*] Gratis." Moreover, it proved increasingly difficult to restrict trading privileges in the colony to bearers of the franchise. As one scholar put it, "The pressing need for population in the colonies overcame official reluctance [...] to [grant] citizenship."[22]

[20] J. H. Hollander, "The Civil Status of the Jews in Maryland, 1634–1776," *PAJHS* 2 (1894): 33–58.

[21] Simon Rosendale, "An Act Allowing Naturalization of Jews in the Colonies," *PAJHS* 1 (1893): 93–8; Sorkin, "Comparing Jewish Emancipation in Europe and America," p. 187.

[22] Kammen, *Colonial New York*, 86–7, 132; Milton M. Klein, *The Politics of Diversity: Essays in the History of Colonial New York* (Port Washington, NY and London: Kennikat Press, 1974), p. 21; Hershkowitz, "Some Aspects," pp. 105–6.

Jews were among the many who were occupied in trades and crafts and who sought Freemanship in New York: from 1688 to 1770 some sixty Jews, engaged in various pursuits (distillers, bakers, chandlers, gold- and silversmiths, barbers, and watchmakers), were recorded as freemen.[23] No special taxes were levied on Jews in the North American colonies, in contrast to standard practices throughout most of Europe and even in certain British colonial settings, like Jamaica and Barbados. Acts passed by the New York Assembly barred Jews from the polls in 1701 and again in 1737, but by the 1760s quite a few Jewish family names appeared on New York's voters lists. It is important, moreover, to take into consideration that between half and two-thirds of those eligible to vote in New York regularly failed to exercise their franchise, which raises the possibility that voting rights were not necessarily highly valued.[24]

Fluctuations between law and reality were common. Rhode Island permitted both Jews and Catholics to vote and to hold office as early as 1665, though this precedent was disregarded or annulled some fifty years later. Jewish merchants in eighteenth-century Rhode Island obtained naturalization, but not freeman rights. The same applied in South Carolina; nevertheless, one English Jew, Francis Salvador, was elected to the South Carolina Assembly and served in his state's first and second Revolutionary Provincial Congresses.[25] Some observers – not at all unsympathetic – believed that the social integration of Jews in the colonies was bound to remain controversial and to arouse opposition. Ezra Stiles, the Congregational minister and future president of Yale College, wrote in 1762: "Jews will never become incorporated with the people of America any more than in Europe, Asia, and Africa."[26]

A number of the American colonies maintained sectarian restrictions on the franchise until close to the Revolution, or beyond. The 1776 Pennsylvania constitution upheld a Christian religious test clause for

---

[23] See appendix in Hershkowitz, "Some Aspects," pp. 116–17.
[24] Snyder, "English Markets, Jewish Merchants," p. 74; Faber, *A Time for Planting*, p. 17; Klein, *Politics of Diversity*, p. 24; Kammen, *Colonial New York*, p. 209.
[25] Pencak, *Jews and Gentiles*, pp. 100–3, 123; Richard B. Morris, "The Role of the Jews in the American Revolution in Historical Perspective", in *Jewish Life in America: Historical Perspectives*, ed. Gladys Rosen (New York: Ktav, 1978), p. 12; Hühner, "Jews of Georgia in Colonial Times," p. 91.
[26] Quoted by Stanley F. Chyet, *Lopez of Newport* (Detroit, MI: Wayne State University Press, 1970), pp. 37–8; Ezra Stiles, *Extracts from the Itineraries and Other Miscellanies of Ezra Stiles*, ed. Franklin B. Dexter (New Haven, CT: Yale University Press, 1916), pp. 52–3.

holding political office, which was dropped in 1790. South Carolina also amended its previous restrictions in that year; Delaware two years after that; and Vermont in 1793. In Virginia, the Act for Religious Freedom that Thomas Jefferson authored (1785) removed civic and political restrictions based on any sort of religious bar or condition. Just to the north, in Maryland, Jews could not exercise political rights until as late as 1826. In North Carolina, Jacob Henry, a Jew elected to the state House of Commons in 1808, could not by law take his rightful seat (the prescribed oath of office required swearing by both the Old and New Testaments). The House nevertheless voted to seat him, regardless of the statute. The North Carolina state constitution was not actually amended until after the Civil War.[27]

In the main, however, the process of civic integration for Jews was rather unremarkable. This reflects the fact that Jews formed under 0.05 percent of the colonial population (less than five Jews for every ten thousand inhabitants). Moreover, their numbers failed to keep pace with the growth of the rest of the populace, in a society that continued to absorb new immigrants and had an especially high rate of natural population growth.[28]

For the majority of Jews in America, by the end of the colonial period they were either citizens or eligible for citizenship, and most of the males among them enjoyed or were soon eligible to obtain political rights. At the Federal constitutional convention in 1787 in Philadelphia, the prohibition against any religious test or oath as qualification for federal office was adopted with little dissent (Article 6, section 3). The process of reformulating the state constitutions in the ensuing decades was residual in nature and took explicit form in later years as state constitutional standards were subordinated to those of the United States Constitution.

[27] Morris, "Jews in the American Revolution," pp. 12, 21–2; Stanley F. Chyet, "The Political Rights of the Jews in the United States: 1776–1840," in *Critical Studies in American Jewish History*, ed. Jacob Rader Marcus (Cincinnati, OH: American Jewish Archives, 1971), vol. II, pp. 28–30; Morton Borden, *Jews, Turks, and Infidels* (Chapel Hill and London: University of North Carolina Press, 1984), pp. 11–15.

[28] Peter D. McClelland and Richard J. Zeckhauser, *Demographic Dimensions of the New Republic: American Interregional Migration, Vital Statistics, and Manumissions, 1800–1860* (Cambridge: Cambridge University Press, 1982), pp. 13, 54; Pencak, *Jews and Gentiles in Early America*, pp. 1, 37–8. See also Richard Cohen, "The Demography of the Jews in Early America," in *Modern Jewish Fertility*, ed. Paul Ritterband (Leiden: Brill, 1981), pp. 144–59; and "The Life Cycle of the Jewish Family in Eighteenth Century America," in *Papers in Jewish Demography 1977*, ed. U. O. Schmelz et al. (Jerusalem: Institute of Contemporary Jewry, Hebrew University, 1980), pp. 19–31.

This state of affairs contrasted to civic arrangements in most of Europe, even though it resembled certain cases in Western European port cities. It bears noting, for instance, that despite their overall civic equality, Jewish traders were blocked from establishing retail businesses in the City of London until 1831. The key distinction between Europe's civil codes and those adopted in early America lay in the realm of economic and civic custom, but even more so in the realm of political rights. Even in relatively benign England, non-Anglican Protestant and Catholic men were politically emancipated in England only in 1828 and 1829, respectively, and Jews were fully enfranchised there only in 1858. In Lower Canada, Jews obtained the right to be elected to the Assembly only in 1834. In Revolutionary France, full civil and political equality was granted to Sephardi Jews in 1790 and a year later to their far more numerous (though much less acculturated) Ashkenazi brethren; but Napoleon Bonaparte rolled back their civil equality in 1808 for what he intended to be a probationary period of ten years. Outside France, under the Restoration regimes after 1815, most of continental European Jewry was left in the status of second-class citizens, to await political emancipation in the 1860s and 1870s – or, in the case of Russia, 1917.[29]

The ambiguities and relative laxity of social relations in American colonial society formed the context for the inclusion of Jewish colonists as individuals in the economic and civic life of their communities. If Western Christian societies produced programmatic ideas related to gendered, racial, and class differences, and drew particular attention to religious difference, the colonial American experience attenuated rather than accentuated the Jewish factor. While even Thomas Jefferson (to take one significant instance) casually accepted conventional, culturally embedded notions (the Jews' "sharp dealings and strange rituals"), it is remarkable that these notions left no trace in what he and other leading figures wrote in the core documents of American governance. Jewishness was, perhaps, a liability, but not an egregious one.[30]

Perhaps above all, these circumstances were also linked to the fact that Jews lived in America as individuals, without any collective authorization or communal umbrella to sanction their arrival. They lacked any statutory or corporate standing as a group, and this corresponded with the

[29] David Sorkin, "Comparing Jewish Emancipation in Europe and America," in *Paths of Emancipation: Jews, States, and Citizenship*, ed. Pierre Birnbaum and Ira Katznelson (Princeton, NJ: Princeton University Press, 1995).
[30] Borden, *Jews, Turks, and Infidels*, p. 6.

way in which Jewish difference was accommodated by the civil order.[31] In every other land where Jews eventually attained citizenship rights, their collective religious and civil corporate "personhood" – their registered status under the law as a *group* of Jews, subject to Jewish judicial, religious, and taxation authority – had first to be dismantled, as a prerequisite for granting civil liberties to Jews as individuals.

The American case emerges, in that context, as a contrasting alternative. It was a by-product of frontier conditions, in which no apparatus of Jewish self-governance existed such as might require disestablishment prior to the Jews' naturalization. The American historian, Michael Kammen, has used the term "an invertebrate society" to describe colonial America – highlighting the disjointed nature of relations among the thirteen colonies. If we may borrow his phrase, Jews in the American colonies were "an invertebrate community."[32] Though they formed synagogues and established other institutions in local communities whenever their numbers grew sufficiently large, the world they inhabited for most everyday purposes was that of the wider civic society around them. The synagogue did not constitute the focal point of their lives and, because Jews were not restricted to certain occupations (as was still so often the case in Europe), their livelihoods and other household affairs were not bound up with their sectarian identity.

Ironically, the rudimentary state of their internal group life may have spared them (at least for a while) the doctrinal fissures – but also the enthusiasms – that characterized their Protestant and Catholic neighbors, who staked so much on their religion and their churches. Indeed, Christian (especially Protestant) values and terminology continued to pervade America's civil and political code – ranging from state constitutions and oaths of office to Sabbath-observance ordinances, public prayers and benedictions, courthouse oaths, and anti-blasphemy clauses. Judaism, in contrast, was never regulated or particularly referred to in public American documents. It was, in consequence, not intertwined with the civic sphere to begin with. As Jews maintained a low institutional profile, their impact as a religious group within the civic realm was minimal. American society's capacity to absorb Jewish difference with relative ease was not always replicated for Christian religious difference – as illustrated by the strongly politicized and at times violent opposition

[31] Faber, *Time for Planting*, p. 82.
[32] Kammen, *People of Paradox*, chapter 3.

to Catholics, Quakers, and Mormons. Perhaps that was because Jewish difference staked no claim that countered Christian ascendancy or Protestantism as such.

Urban Economy and Jewish Geography

In many parts of early modern Europe, Jews were stereotypically and at times legally required to be identified with certain trades, such as street-peddling, tavernkeeping, and pawnbroking. Jews in the American colonies, in contrast, did not introduce or predominate in any particular trade. In one sense, their presence nearly exclusively in towns and in mercantile trades and crafts placed them in a minority, given that most of the other Euro-American inhabitants were farmers. But mercantile and urban occupational specializations never created an ethno-cultural demarcation between Jews and non-Jews. Commerce was very much the essence of the whole colonial enterprise, and towns, which soon became cities, initiated the trading economy that made further inland colonization possible. Jewish commerce, crafts, and trade were more a matter of indifference than a kind of difference.[33]

That is not to say that small groups of traders did not have their own specific identities. Diasporized minorities active in trade – including Scots, Quakers, and Huguenots, as well as Jews – may have enjoyed some advantages due to their networks of mutual trust and closely knit kinship ties. Still, the generic forms of town commerce commonly cut across religious or ethnic lines. In what one scholar has dubbed "the twilight of the trading diasporas," the relatively small Caribbean and North American outposts served what remained of what had formerly been a far-flung commercial network, but this was, for them, the end of an era.[34]

Jews in the American colonies and increasingly in the early Republic were a polyglot population. They followed closely in the wake of mercantile and urban development. They were involved in a variety of businesses, all of which came into being once a consumer market emerged for

[33] James E. Vance, Jr., *The Merchant's World: The Geography of Wholesaling* (Englewood Cliffs, NJ: Prentice Hall, 1970), pp. 10–11, 68.
[34] Sutcliffe, "Jewish History in an Age of Atlanticism," pp. 24, 29; Israel, "Jews and Crypto-Jews," pp. 16–17; and "The Jews of Dutch America," in Bernardini and Fiering, *The Jews and the Expansion of Europe*, p. 346; Charles Maier, "Consigning the Twentieth Century to History," *American Historical Review* 105(3) (2000): 817 (quotation on "networks of shipping right"); see also Philip Curtin, *Cross-Cultural Trade in World History* (Cambridge: Cambridge University Press, 1984), pp. 230–54.

wares like "Scotch snuff, spermaceti candles, tea, and fine wines."[35] The diversity of Jews' occupations, enterprises, and social stations is noteworthy, in that they implied a range of close interactions with fellow-inhabitants on a daily basis. In the mercantile life of the colonies it was often possible for members of heterogeneous groups to achieve, if not a melting pot, then a commonality of sorts.[36]

By 1820, seven states contained Jewish "seed" communities in which at least ten households were recorded, concentrated mainly in six urban centers (see Table 1.2). The figures cited below probably represent an undercount, and some households (especially in Philadelphia and New York) probably contained more than just immediate family members – there were sometimes extended or combined households (see the data in Table 1.2).

An additional 500–600 Jews lived elsewhere in the United States. Overall, the total Jewish population of America in 1820, estimated at between 2,650 and 2,750, corresponds to under 0.04 percent of the US population of 7.23 million.

The seventy-four Jewish households listed for New York City in 1820 were roughly equivalent to the number of family units that had been claimed by the community over two decades earlier. Their very limited growth was partly accounted for by the assimilation of some Jewish inhabitants within the Christian populace, primarily through intermarriage, which most often withdrew the next generation, at the very least, from the sphere of Jewish activity. In America as a whole, according to contemporary records, of nearly 700 marriages involving Jews between

---

[35] Snyder, "English Markets, Jewish Merchants," pp. 64–5.

[36] D. W. Meinig, *The Shaping of America: A Geographical Perspective on 500 Years of History* (New Haven, CT and London, 1998), vol. I, p. 140. In contrast, when Austria annexed the southwestern portions of the Polish-Lithuanian Commonwealth, the Austrian authorities accepted the petition by the royal city of Craców and upheld the late fifteenth-century decree denying Jews the right to engage in any merchandising or commerce, apart from pawnbroking. In Venice in 1777 the city authorities carried out an enforcement order against Jews living outside the ghetto (first established in 1516). In Germany, Jews had participated for generations in the trade fair at Leipzig – a major international entrepôt – but it was not until 1713 that a single Jew was allowed to establish residence there with his family, and another forty years until this privilege was extended to include a second family. Majer Bałaban, *Toledot hayehudim bekrakuv uvekazhimizh (A History of the Jews in Craców and Kazimierz, 1304–1868)* (Jerusalem: Hebrew University Magnes Press, 2002), vol. I, pp. 52–5; Jacob Katz, *Out of the Ghetto: The Social Background of Jewish Emancipation, 1770–1870* (Cambridge, MA: Harvard University Press, 1973), pp. 16–17, 20; Benjamin Ravid, "All Ghettos were Jewish Quarters but Not All Jewish Quarters were Ghettos," *Jewish Culture and History* 10(2–3) (2008): 5–24.

TABLE 1.2. *Jewish households in selected cities in 1820**

City	Charleston	New York City	Philadelphia	Richmond	Baltimore	Savannah	Total
Data							
No. of Jewish households	109	74	58	32	21	21	315
No. of white individuals	674	528	402	191	120	94	2,009
Average no. of white persons per household	6.2	7.1	6.9	6.0	5.7	4.5	6.4
No. of persons engaged in:							
Commerce	93	27	36	31	6	12	205
Manufacture	12	10	17	5	11	–	55

* Ira Rosenwaike, "The Jewish Population of the United States as Estimated from the Census of 1920," *American Jewish Historical Quarterly* 53 (September 1963–June 1964), pp. 131ff, Table 2.

1790 and 1840, some 200 Jews married Christians (28.5 percent). Conditions in colonial and early-national America were not conducive to religious or ethno-cultural exclusivity (or resilience), and America was only just attractive enough to bring in sufficient new Jewish immigrants to offset the attrition.[37]

In addition, Jews remained quite mobile, frequently changing their place of residence or returning to Europe. We have the remarkable example of one Joseph Cohen (1745–1822) who migrated from Westphalia, Germany to England (1764); resettled in Philadelphia (1768); returned to Germany briefly and thence moved again to England. Having failed in business in London, he took ship once more to Pennsylvania (this time taking up residence in Lancaster). He then served the Shearith Israel ("Remnant of Israel") Jewish congregation in New York City as a *shohet* (kosher slaughterer/butcher), before moving on to Charleston, and finally re-migrating to live out the remainder of his days in London.[38]

However, in the transition to the nineteenth century a noticeable change took place, including a larger volume of immigration, which gave rise to a more stable pattern of numerical growth. Between the American Revolution and the 1830s, a stream of migrating Dutch Jews – many of them of Ashkenazic background and many of them quite poor – arrived either directly from Holland or as trans-migrants via England. In 1790, they comprised 10–11 percent of all Jews in Charleston and in New York City; 42 percent of the Jews in New York State outside New York City; and 27 percent in Baltimore. In 1795 they helped establish a new synagogue in Philadelphia and their entry was increasingly felt in other cities, including New Orleans and Richmond.[39]

In the years following the Napoleonic Wars and the establishment of Restoration regimes in Europe, these Ashkenazim were increasingly joined by a swelling stream of migrant Jews from Central Europe – a small but disproportionate current within the larger Atlantic migration of that period. Jews in America had formed twelve synagogue congregations

[37] Letter by Alexander Hirsch and Solomon Joseph Simson, 1795, in I. J. Benjamin, *Three Years in America* (Philadelphia, PA: Jewish Publication Society of America, 1956), vol. I, p. 63; Ira Rosenwaike, *On the Edge of Greatness: A Portrait of American Jewry in the Early National Period* (Cincinnati, OH: American Jewish Archives, 1985), p. 3; Frederic Cople Jaher, "American Jews in the Revolutionary and Early National Periods," in *Encyclopedia of American Jewish History*, ed. Stephen H. Norwood and Eunice G. Pollack (Santa Barbara, CA: ABC-CLIO, 2008), vol. I, p. 18.

[38] Jacob Rader Marcus, *Memoirs of American Jews, 1775–1865* (Philadelphia, PA: Jewish Publication Society of America, 1955–1956), vol. I, pp. 27–30.

[39] Swierenga, *The Forerunners*, pp. 12–15, 25–6, 41, 42–3; Rosenwaike, *Edge of Greatness*.

by 1830; ten more would be founded in the following decade; and from 1841 to 1851, fifty more sprouted across the country.

The America to which these new arrivals came was an independent society, established on a democratic, constitutional foundation. Mercantile and urban development was moving into high gear, even as the nation still remained largely agrarian. American cities founded west of the Alleghenies were often laid out before the surrounding countryside was populated by farmers: they were meant to be the first and critical stage of what would eventually become a wider, rural periphery. The ascendancy of the mercantile and manufacturing branches of the economy gave the new wave of Jewish migrants a vital niche in America's civic life as petty merchants, peddlers, and skilled craftsmen and women. It was precisely because Jews rarely if ever came to an American "wilderness," but rather settled in urban settings already developed by others, that they interacted primarily with town- and cityfolk very much like themselves and adapted to their ways. In that environment they did not stand out as exceptions to an agrarian social milieu, but rather found themselves part of a mercantile and manufacturing America.

Because urban centers developed differently depending on their region and location, the density of population, as well as on natural, economic, and political circumstances, there were some typical patterns of growth and types of occupation, but there were also some interesting variations.

Thus, for example, the heads of Baltimore Jewish households enumerated in the 1830 census were occupationally diverse, though they concentrated in small businesses and direct sales (nearly half), followed by individuals plying various occupations (musician, doctor, lottery and exchange office, and "priest of the Jews"), manufacturers of light consumer goods, and one housepainter. In contrast, in Philadelphia, merchandisers were somewhat more common (60 merchants out of 105 economically occupied Jews). Likewise, there were no civil servants or holders of government office among the Jews of Baltimore, but these categories were quite well represented among Jews in both New York City and Charleston. Baltimore Jews' early involvement in light manufacturing paralleled that of Jews in New York (14–15 percent), compared to less than 10 percent in Philadelphia and less than 6 percent in Charleston.[40]

---

[40] Compiled from Rosenwaike, *Edge of Greatness*, pp. 95–101, Tables 23–7. In Baltimore, Dutch Jews were noted for their concentration in dry goods retailing (as was the case, as well, in New Orleans), but in New York a greater diversity occurred (such as fancy goods dealers, clothiers, pawnbrokers, watchmakers, gilders, spectacle makers, quill pen makers, tailors, and carders): Swierenga, *Forerunners*, p. 61.

To some extent, these early nineteenth-century patterns recapitulated some important features of the colonial experience: the largest cities absorbed the greatest share of Jewish newcomers and, in general, Jews were apt to arrive once a viable economic base was already in place. It is significant that in 1820 the American urban population grew at an even pace along with the national population at large; but from 1820 to 1830, and especially from 1840 to 1860 (when Jewish immigration increased), towns and cities were growing at a much faster rate than the US population as a whole. Apart from New York and Philadelphia – the two largest cities in the nation – there were four other cities with over 30,000 inhabitants in 1830: Baltimore, Boston, Charleston, and New Orleans. Five additional cities had grown to over 15,000 inhabitants: Cincinnati, Albany, Providence, Richmond, and Washington, DC.[41] Of these, all except Providence had Jewish households. Albany and Washington had some Jewish inhabitants, but did not yet have any organized Jewish community. The biggest cities had a head start in the development of Jewish populations and it was there that an infrastructure of Jewish civic life first arose. In Baltimore, New Orleans, and Cincinnati, Jewish communities were established on an organized footing during the course of the 1820s and 1830s. The first lodges of the new Jewish fraternal order, B'nai B'rith, were founded in the 1840s in New York, Philadelphia, Baltimore, and Cincinnati, to be followed during the 1850s by an array of branches in cities in the Midwest (Louisville, Cleveland, St. Louis, Chicago, Detroit, and Milwaukee), the South (Memphis, New Orleans), and the West Coast (San Francisco).[42]

A typology of Jewish urban settlement from the 1820s to the 1850s would show a range from larger cities to small-to-medium towns or frontier hubs, with the addition of the western boom town as another case.

Large Mercantile Cities: Cincinnati

Cincinnati grew from a modest city of 6,000 in 1815 to become the sixth-largest in the nation by 1850. In the mid-1830s, the city was nicknamed "Porkopolis" because of the importance of its hog-meat packing industry: a doubtful "welcome mat" for Jews, perhaps, but one that did not seem to deter them unduly. The growth of a new Jewish community was

---

[41] Brian J. L. Berry, "Urbanization and Counterurbanization in the United States," *Annals of the American Academy of Political and Social Science* 451 (1980): 13–16.

[42] Rosenwaike, *Edge of Greatness*, pp. 30, 34; Tobias Brinkmann, *Von Gemeinde zur "Community": Jüdische Einwanderer in Chicago 1840–1900* (Osnabrück: Universitätsverlag Rausch, 2002), p. 108.

intimately related to the occupational opportunity and material security offered by the local economy.

Ten immigrants who hailed respectively from England, Germany, and Barbados established the first Jewish congregation, Bene Israel ("Children of Israel"), in 1824. At that time, the city housed over 10,000 inhabitants. By 1830 a number of other new Jewish households had been established: alongside five merchants and an equal number of clothiers there were also a dry-goods dealer, a boarding-house manager, and a jeweler. The total number of Jews at the time was somewhat over 100; it increased to an estimated 400 persons by the end of the decade, and then tripled within the next few years.[43] Alongside Congregation Bene Israel, which was able to build its own house of prayer by 1836, the community also established a school (subsequently a Sunday school), a benevolent society (dedicated to providing burial services in the communal cemetery), and two women's charity groups "instituted for the purpose of assisting distressed widows and orphans."[44]

We might compare the patterns of Jewish life in Cincinnati to the quite different situation in Boston, for example, where Jewish communal activity took shape with a time-lag of nearly two decades behind the Queen City. There was a very small growth of Jewish immigrant life in Boston at that time, with Jews from southern, northern, and eastern Germany predominating (along with a handful from Poland) during the 1840s and 1850s. Two out of five Jews who settled in Boston were single. The great majority of those Jews involved in mercantile trades were peddlers, and the number of manual or semi-skilled laborers and artisans nearly matched the number of peddlers, clerks, and merchants. Cincinnati Jews, by contrast, were most likely to be classified as merchants, with a secondary tier employed as clerks; peddling came in at a distant third place. The establishment and management of clothing manufacturing enterprises grew to assume a central role in the local Jewish occupational structure.[45]

---

[43] Rosenwaike, *Edge of Greatness*, pp. 31, 102; Jacob Rader Marcus, *To Count a People: American Jewish Population Data, 1585–1984* (Lanham, MD: University Press of America, 1990), p. 172.

[44] Jacob Rader Marcus, *Memoirs of American Jews*, pp. 206–7, 212–13; Jonathan D. Sarna and Nancy H. Klein, *The Jews of Cincinnati* (Cincinnati: Hebrew Union College – Jewish Institute of Religion, 1989), p. 181.

[45] Stephen Mostov, "A Sociological Portrait of German Jewish Immigrants in Boston: 1845–1861," *AJS Review* (1978): 121–52; and "A Jerusalem on the Ohio: The Social and Economic History of Cincinnati's Jewish Community, 1840–1875" (PhD dissertation, Brandeis University, 1981), p. 107; Avraham Barkai, *Branching Out: German-Jewish Immigration to the United States, 1820–1914* (New York and London: Holmes and

Cincinnati drew a chain migration of Jews from Bavaria, and by 1850, a majority (51.4 percent) of the city's 2,800 Jews were German-born (compared to 35 percent in Philadelphia and just 13 percent in Charleston). Cincinnati was a major center for migration from Germany, of which the great majority, of course, were non-Jewish. By the 1850s, Cincinnati's German-born residents accounted for about a third of the population. The conspicuous presence of German migrants in Cincinnati was especially evident in the neighborhood popularly nicknamed "Over-the-Rhine," and it was reflected in the dual-language German–English track offered in the city's public schools. By the late 1860s, this "German department" would enroll over half (53 percent) of all elementary school children in the city's public schools. Private Jewish and Catholic schools similarly provided German-language programs.[46]

What were the implications of this German cultural embeddedness? We will address some of these issues in a later chapter, but a brief treatment here of the American encounter between Jews and Germans is in order. The comfort level that a common language and common frames of reference provided for migrants coming from the same country, and now living again at close quarters, is conveyed by various Jewish documents of the day. Cincinnati's German-language Jewish newspaper for women, *Die Deborah*, for instance, approvingly declared in 1858 that in the Queen City "the blithe [*munter*] German spirit has here more than elsewhere subdued Puritanical rigor and austerity [and] our Israelites have a large share in this victory of the joy of life." Part of that "joy" was no doubt imparted in the more than 2,000 saloons and beer gardens in Cincinnati (as of 1860), a decidedly non-Puritan form of recreation.[47]

Meier, 1994), p. 85, Table 3.3; Rudolph Glanz, "The German Jewish Mass Migration, 1820–1880," *American Jewish Archives* 22 (1970): 63.

[46] "English-only" monolingual education, demanded in a backlash against German in American schools in the Midwest, began only toward the late 1880s. Roger Daniels, *Coming to America: A History of Immigration and Ethnicity in American Life* (New Delhi: Affiliated East-West Press, 1990), pp. 145–64. See also Barkai, *Branching Out*, p. 79, Table 3.2, citing Roseman, "The Jewish Population of America, 1850–1860" (PhD dissertation, Hebrew Union College, 1971); Stephan F. Brumberg, "The Cincinnati Bible War (1869–1873) and its Impact on the Education of the City's Protestants, Catholics, and Jews," *American Jewish Archives Journal* 54(2) (2002): 13.

[47] Gerhard Grytz, "Triple Identity: The Evolution of a German Jewish Arizonan Ethnic Identity in Arizona Territory," *Journal of American Ethnic History* 26(1) (2006): 21; *Die Deborah*, 1858–9, p. 126, cited by Morris A. Goldstein, *A Priceless Heritage: The Epic Growth of Nineteenth Century Chicago Jewry* (New York: Bloch Publishing Co., 1953), pp. 28–9; Daniels, *Coming to America*, p. 151.

Social boundaries undeniably existed between ex-German nationals of different faiths – Jews, Lutherans, Catholics, and others – and there were cultural, linguistic, and ethnic distinctions between people who hailed from different parts of the greater German orbit (including the sundry German states that joined up to create the post-1869 unified German empire, as well as Austrian-ruled Bohemia, Moravia, Galicia, and Hungary). But those boundaries also had some degree of permeability. Middle-class households, for instance, typically included female domestic help, and the general trend among middle-class Jewish families was to hire non-Jewish, German-speaking women. Aspects of these Jews' cultural orientation – previously focused on specific localities of origin – were generalized to all things "German" and, indeed, reinforced over time. Even as they acquired English and began to live "American" lives, immigrants discovered that their links with Germany and its culture possessed cachet and did not inhibit their aspirations for higher status. They looked to Germany for models of artistic, literary, philosophical, and scientific achievement. Jews living in communities with a large German immigrant presence were most likely to emphasize their German identities, while at the same time committing themselves to a sectarian Jewish identity. Quite a lot of people are evidently capable of maintaining a serial set of voluntary, not necessarily overlapping relationships with others. With their Jewish associations secured, as one recent study has shown, involvement by Jews in ethnic German social groups "likely was complementary, causing little interference with their Jewish commitments." The outcome was a Germanocentric Jewish milieu that was both part of, and separate from, the wider German-speaking milieu.[48]

---

[48] Anton Hieke, *Jewish Identity in the Reconstruction South: Ambivalence and Adaptation* (Berlin and Boston, MA: De Gruyter, 2013), pp. 202–03; Maria T. Baader, "From 'the Priestess of the Home' to 'the Rabbi's Brilliant Daughter': Concepts of Jewish Womanhood and Progressive Germanness in *Die Deborah* and the *American Israelite*, 1854–1900," *Leo Baeck Institute Year Book* 43 (1998): 48; Tobias Brinkmann, "'German Jews?' Reassessing the History of Nineteenth-Century Jewish Immigrants in the United States," in *Transnational Traditions: New Perspectives on American Jewish History*, ed. Ava F. Kahn and Adam D. Mendelsohn (Detroit, MI: Wayne State University Press, 2014), pp. 144–64; "Exceptionalism and Normality: 'German Jews' in the United States 1840–1880," in *Towards Normality? Acculturation and Modern German Jewry*, ed. Rainer Liedtke and David Rechter (Tübingen: Mohr Siebeck, 2003), p. 314; "Jews, Germans, or Americans? German-Jewish Immigrants in the Nineteenth-Century United States," in *The Heimat Abroad: The Boundaries of Germanness*, ed. Krista O'Donnell et al. (Ann Arbor: University of Michigan Press, 2005), pp. 132–4; and *Von Gemeinde zur "Community"*, p. 212, note to Table 5; Stanley Nadel, *Little Germany: Ethnicity, Religion, and Class in New York City, 1845–1880* (Urbana: University of Illinois Press, 1990); and "Jewish Race and German Soul in Nineteenth-Century America," *American Jewish History* 77(1) (1987): 6–26.

Within the realm of sectarian institutions per se, the organizing principle was the separate bond that Jews established with their fellow Jews, and here subgroups came into play. In 1840, a second synagogue was established in Cincinnati (Bene Yeshurun), and under its aegis, a Jewish day school was organized (1849–51). A third synagogue, formed by Polish and Lithuanian Jews, was organized in the 1840s (later known as Adath Israel), to be followed during the following decade by yet another traditionalist congregation, Shearith Israel, which similarly relied on Eastern European migrants. Two lodges of the B'nai B'rith fraternal order were opened in Cincinnati in 1849 and 1850, respectively. In 1850, the Jewish community added a hospital to its philanthropic undertakings.[49]

The level of self-organization, through which Jews took part in the construction of a civic realm in the city, was particularly accelerated: Cincinnati Jews had by the 1850s matched in the space of two or three decades what it had taken sixty or as many as a hundred years to construct in older venues like New York, Philadelphia, and Charleston. As for their numerical visibility, the size of the Jewish community in 1860 can be estimated at between 7,500 and 10,000 – or roughly twice the number of Jews who had been living in the entire United States as recently as three decades earlier. They constituted about 5 percent of the entire population of Cincinnati.[50]

Medium-range Inland Cities and Towns, 1820–1850: The Case For and Against Local Founding Myths

As we have seen, already established towns and cities offered Jewish immigrants the most opportune venues for resettlement. In some instances, however, recorded local histories suggest a different pattern. A "first settler" paradigm – where a Jew was named among the earliest residents of a new town – is claimed for such places as Green Bay, Wisconsin; Easton, Pennsylvania; Des Moines, Iowa; Detroit, Michigan; and Montgomery, Alabama. Yet, a critical reading of the evidence shows that only a small portion of such cases support any direct, sustained connection between "first settlers" and the crystallization of a viable Jewish social milieu.

Des Moines, Iowa (originally a log-cabin encampment known as Racoon Forks) counted one Jewish couple, William Kraus and his wife Minnie Lauer Kraus, formerly of Cincinnati, among the first two-dozen civilian white inhabitants. After living and selling clothing and general

---

[49] Sarna and Klein, *Jews of Cincinnati*, pp. 40–4, 61.
[50] *Ibid.*, pp. 3, 4, 6, 181.

merchandise in the town for eight years – during which time William Kraus supported his neighbors when they built their Methodist, Baptist, and Catholic churches, respectively – the couple returned in 1853 to Cincinnati. Subsequently, several Jewish immigrants from Germany arrived in Des Moines. The 1860s, therefore, were the actual context for a sustainable Jewish community life. The city's first directory, printed in 1866, reported a population of 7,500 residents, among whom eleven single Jewish men and three Jewish couples can be identified.[51]

The colorful saga of the supposed Jewish "founder" of Montgomery, Alabama was even more idiosyncratic. One Abram Mordecai from Pennsylvania was a Revolutionary War veteran who traded with the local Indians. Despite an enterprising career as a local trader and cotton gin operator, he lived as a virtual hermit, sharing a small cabin with a half-Indian, half-black woman. According to Albert James Pickett's *History of Alabama*:

Abram Mordecai was a queer fellow. He traded extensively with the Indians, exchanging his goods for pink root, hickory-nut oil and peltries of all kinds. These he carried to New Orleans and Mobile in boats, and to Pensacola and Augusta on pack-horses [...]. Mordecai bought cotton of the Indians in small quantities [and] ginned it [...]. He was a darkeyed Jew, and amorous in his disposition. Tourculla, (Captain Isaacs), the Chief of the Coosawdas, hearing of his intrigues with a married squaw, approached his house with twelve warriors, knocked him down, thrashed him with poles until he lay insensible, cut off his ear, and left him to the care of his wife. They also broke up his boat, and burned down his gin-house.[52]

Abram Mordecai's misadventures appear quite unrelated to the founding of a congregation by some thirty Jews quite a while afterward, in 1846.[53]

Dubuque, Iowa (once part of Michigan and later the Wisconsin Territory) was established in 1833. In that year a solitary Jewish settler named Alexander Levi arrived. The area became important as a center for lead mining. According to a local historian, Levi "engaged in the grocery and provision business ... [and in] dry goods and clothing. [Subsequently] he engaged in mining on a large and extensive scale ... [He] became the state's first naturalized citizen in 1837."[54]

[51] Frank Rosenthal, *The Jews of Des Moines: The First Century* (Des Moines, IA: Jewish Welfare Federation, 1957), pp. 3–8, 16–17.

[52] Concerning this incident as well as other circumstances in the life of Abram (Abraham) Mordecai, see also Joseph L. Blau and Salo W. Baron, *The Jews of the United States, 1790–1840* (New York and Philadelphia, PA: Columbia University Press and Jewish Publication Society of America, 1963), vol. III, p. 852.

[53] Rader, *To Count a People*, p. 13; Barkai, *Branching Out*, p. 75.

[54] William D. Houlette, "Introduction: The Land between the Rivers," in Rosenthal, *The Jews of Des Moines*, pp. xi–xii; see also Karin Pritikin, "Family and Community

Levi remained in the community and therefore has some historical claim as a Jewish "first settler"; but the notion of a "Jewish presence" would be more credible if we could base it on something other than quasi-racial criteria. That is to say, an individual's Jewish descent in and of itself may not attest to the fact that anything "Jewish" was going on in a given locality. A mere nose-count of the children of Abraham amounts to no more than ethnic score-keeping. We ought therefore to ask: when did Jews begin to actively promote activities related to each other and to their Jewish identity? In the case of Dubuque, it was only after Alexander Levi had been a resident for over twenty years that a second Jewish household was established in town. Moses Cahana of St. Louis, who had business dealings with Levi, moved to Dubuque in 1855 with his wife Eva, where they opened a jewelry and millinery shop. The town then had a population of 13,000. Eight years later, after a number of other Jewish newcomers took up residence in town, Cahana became a trustee of the Jewish cemetery, and in the same year a synagogue congregation was formed.[55]

St. Louis, founded originally in 1763, was a frontier trading hub under the French and then the Spanish colonial regimes. A trio of Jewish brothers, the Philipsons, had migrated to Philadelphia from Prussian Poland around the turn of the century, and in 1807 they went to settle in St. Louis. They opened a general store as well as a brewery. Nearly a decade later, they were followed by yet another "first Jewish family," the Blochs (or Blocks). Because the Philipsons seem not to have conducted themselves Jewishly or associated with anything Jewish, local historians give the Blochs credit for having been the nucleus for later communal growth. A prayer quorum (*minyan*) was established in the late 1830s, over twenty years after the Blochs' arrival. Other organized Jewish institutions came into being in the 1840s, a decade in which St. Louis's population topped 70,000 and it became the eighth-largest American city.[56]

Typically, it was from the 1840s on that Jewish migrants became a not unknown, if still unusual feature of the social landscape. Memphis, Tennessee, for example, was founded in 1819 and soon attracted German and Irish settlers. Several Jews settled in Memphis sometime in the 1840s.

History – A Serendipitous Quest," adapted from a lecture presented August 23, 2008 at Temple Beth El, Dubuque, IA. Available at www.levicelebration.com (accessed November 10, 2010). Citation drawn from *The History of Dubuque County, Iowa* (1880).

55 Pritikin, "Family and Community History."
56 Walter Ehrlich, *Zion in the Valley: The Jewish Community of St. Louis* (Columbia and London: University of Missouri Press, 1997, 2002), vol. I, pp. 1–2, 14, 18–26, 29–33.

Jewish residents accounted for some of the thirty-one dry-goods merchants and the forty grocery and commission merchants in the city
at the end of the 1840s. In 1847 they bought a burial plot. Gathering
momentum, they founded a Benevolent Society (to care for the cemetery) in 1850, a synagogue congregation in 1854, and a Ladies' Hebrew
Benevolent Society in 1855.[57]

The major basis of Memphis's economy was cotton. In 1857 it was
linked by rail to Charleston, and like Charleston it was a major slave
market. Twenty-eight percent of the inhabitants were either slaves or (less
frequently) free Blacks. Jews living there formed perhaps up to 3 percent
of the white population. While they were not cotton planters, it was likely
that they, like many of their fellow merchants, hired the services of Black
slaves for help in their places of business. Hiring slaves from planters
was fairly common in the South's urban mercantile class – indeed, city
councils in the 1840s and 1850s were pressed by slave-owning interests
to ensure the continued urban employment of hired slaves, even when
German and Irish immigrants sought to ban the practice.[58]

One characteristic of the rural hub environment was the large
number of itinerant Jews plying the peddling trade in the surrounding
countryside. Directory listings indicate that at various times during the
1850s, sixty-five Jewish peddlers were based in Utica, New York, which
then boasted a population of some 17,000. The nucleus of the resident Jewish community, however, seems to have been much smaller, and
there was a wide discrepancy between the settled residents and the itin-
erants. During the 1850s there were about thirty resident Jewish breadwinners, including five dry-goods and fancy-goods store owners, four
cap makers, three grocers, three tailors, three "pastors," two clothing
store owners, two cigar makers, and one each of the following: baker,
boarding-house operator, coppersmith, laborer, mason, and painter.[59]

[57] Lawrence Charles Meyers, "Evolution of the Jewish Social Service Agency in Memphis,
Tennessee, 1847 to 1963" (MA thesis, Memphis State University, 1965, in author's pos-
session), pp. 7–8.
[58] Beverly G. Bond and Janann Sherman, *Memphis in Black and White* (Charleston, SC,
Chicago, IL, Portsmouth, NH and San Francisco, CA: Arcadia Publishing/Tempus,
2003), pp. 30, 36; Will of Isaac Judah, 1827, in Blau and Baron, *The Jews of the United
States*, vol. I, pp. 206–7; Randall M. Miller, "The Enemy Within: Some Effects of Foreign
Immigrants on Antebellum Southern Cities," in *The Making of Urban America*, ed.
Raymond A. Mohl (Wilmington, DE: Scholarly Resources, 2nd ed., 1997), pp. 58–9.
[59] Kohn, *Jewish Community of Utica*, pp. 161–7, Table XI. See Hasia Diner, *Roads Taken:
The Great Jewish Migrations to the New World and the Peddlers Who Forged the Way*
(New Haven, CT: Yale University Press, 2015).

Boom Towns and the West Coast: Regional Economies and Racialized Environments

Jewish peddlers, merchants, and a few members of the professions like the law, medicine, and the clergy began to settle in southwestern, Western Plains, Rocky Mountain, and Pacific Coast communities starting in the 1840s, gaining numerically after the Mexican–American War and the Gold Rush. By 1855, there were an estimated 6,000 Jews in California (half of them in San Francisco), and by 1859 there may have been as many as 10,000 Jews living in California, Washington, and Oregon together. There were also nearly a thousand, respectively, in both Kansas and Texas, and scattered handfuls in Utah. When Julius and Fanny Bruck (Brooks), born in the German city of Breslau (today: Wrocław, Poland), headed west in the mid-1850s, they encountered a former Jew, also a former Breslauer, living in Salt Lake City as a Mormon.[60]

Mining, especially for gold, provided the initial impetus for the almost overnight appearance of some towns. San Francisco is famous as an "instant" city that grew suddenly from 850 settlers in 1848 to 35,000 only four years later, boasting more inhabitants than either Chicago or Richmond.[61] The mining boom, in turn, generated an entire ancillary economy: the mercantile needs of these brand new, bustling communities provided livelihoods for dealers in tools, food, shoes and clothing, housing, watches and jewelry (including repair and pawnshops), as well as for those involved in the legal profession, shipping and overland transportation services, railroad development, brokerages and management, provision of leisure activities, entertainment, health care, religious services, newspaper publication, translation services, painting, and photography. By 1859, the most well-represented occupations practiced in San Francisco were (in this order): liquor sellers (388), merchants and salesmen (363), grocers (348), lawyers (296), hotel, boarding-house, and lodging-house operators (269), doctors (173), wholesale and retail clothing dealers (149), tailors (136), carpenters and builders (134), and shoe- and boot-makers and repairers (128). There was also one astrologer.[62]

The *Nevada Journal* reported in 1852 on the shipment of nearly $3 million in gold dust out of San Francisco, including shipments by firms

---

[60] Marcus, *To Count a People*, pp. 20, 74, 181, 211, 218; *Jewish Voices of the California Gold Rush: A Documentary History, 1849–1880*, ed. Ava F. Kahn (Detroit, MI: Wayne State University Press, 2002), p. 117.

[61] "Continuation of the Annals of San Francisco," *California Historical Society Quarterly* 15(3) (1936): 266–82.

[62] Benjamin, *Three Years in America*, vol. I, pp. 182–5.

like Jacobs and Levi, J. Seligman & Co., and S. F. Meyer & Co. In May
1855, US Land Commissioners confirmed the claim of Joel S. Polack to
the Island of Yerba Buena (in San Francisco Bay). The *Mountain Echo*
and the *Weekly Sierra Citizen* of Downieville, northeast of Sacramento,
and the Sonora *Union Democrat* advertised some of the following Jewish
enterprises: E. W. Haskell & Bro., "Just Received – Ladies' White Kid
and Silk Gloves"; H. Levi & Co., "Importers and Jobbers in Groceries,
Provisions, Liquors, etc." Readers of the western press in 1856 could have
followed breathless reports on the arrest and trial of Arthur A. Cohen,
manager of a San Francisco banking house, for the alleged embezzlement
of $120,000. (Cohen was subsequently acquitted.) The *Weekly Ledger* in
Jackson, east of Sacramento, extravagantly estimated the Jewish population of the United States to be a quarter of a million in 1857 – perhaps
extrapolating from the recent increase of the local Jewish presence.[63]

The Volcano *Weekly Ledger* reported in December 1856, "There
are nine Jewish synagogues in California, as follows: San Francisco,
3; Sacramento, 2; Shasta, 1; Stockton, 1; Grassvalley, 1; Sonora, 1."
Occasionally these synagogues were "a sometime thing" rather than
a regularly attended house of prayer. Thirty-five Jews in Jackson,
California, for example, put up a synagogue in 1857 but had no Torah
scroll (required for the thrice-weekly public reading of the Law in the
company of a prayer quorum). Once a year, for the High Holidays, a
scroll was borrowed from San Francisco, but otherwise the synagogue
was "closed and deserted the rest of the year."[64]

In San Francisco itself, the community's needs were served by a
Benevolent Society that was founded in 1849 by English and Polish Jews
(who struck a Jewish visitor from abroad as being "not ... particularly
liberal to strangers and travelers"). A second such society (the Eureka
Benevolent Association) was founded in 1850, after a major outbreak of
cholera. Organized by both men and women, such groups proliferated
over the decade to come, in the Jewish community as in all the other
ethnic and religious groups in town.[65]

The civic life of the "instant city" emerged fitfully and uneasily from
a threatening and at times dangerous shantytown metropolis, where the
sale of liquor, we recall, outweighed any other trade. The initial reign by

[63] Card index of California newspaper items, in possession of the author; Benjamin, *Three Years in America*, vol. I, p. 167; "Continuation of the Annals of San Francisco," p. 280.
[64] Benjamin, *Three Years in America*, vol. II, p. 96.
[65] Benjamin, *Three Years in America*, vol. I, pp. 210–27; Kahn, *Jewish Voices of the California Gold Rush*, pp. 199–211.

"vigilance committees" that summarily administered the lynch justice of kangaroo courts attested to the impatience with (or the absence of) due process, as well as the fear and greed that were so close to the surface. Defining some freedoms as liberating seemed to demand that other kinds of lax behavior be defined as vicious and corrupt. Casual violence, sexual license, and alcoholism – all of which were widely in evidence – could most conveniently be displaced onto those who were perceived as primitive, perverse, and "disorderly," and thus could have no legitimate claim upon the liberal commonality.

"There is a great deal of freedom in America," wrote one European Jewish visitor in describing California. "The thieves, gamblers, and vagabonds know it well." But though "freedom flourishes," he wrote, "anything for which a native is readily forgiven is a crime if a Chinaman does it. [T]hey certainly deserve the deepest sympathy." Blithely repeating every nasty epithet and gross opinion that his local informants must have confided to him, he also averred:

John Chinaman's person has no agreeable odor; the color of his face and its features are odd; his poverty is too great; his lies, knavish tricks and innate cowardice have become proverbial. [...] They are as a rule quiet and industrious members of human society, generous toward their fellow-countrymen, temperate men who do not indulge in drink [... though] a large part of the Chinese population gives itself up to gambling [and] the women carry on the still worse trade of prostitution.[66]

The heterogeneous boom-town environment was, therefore, far from a level playing field. Jews, Catholics, and other foreign-born Europeans or native-born whites enhanced their freedoms and their prosperity, but this took place within a racial hierarchy in which they occupied an advantageous position. Jews, so we are informed by several regional historians, were "placed among the 'best [class of] citizens,' separating them from the despised Asians, Indians, Mexicans, and blacks ... [and were] recognized for their business skills, their Euro-American appearance and habits, and their commitment to religion, family, and community life."[67]

Boom-town Jews went about their normal business of creating associations, congregations, benevolent funds, and so on – all the familiar voluntary activities that everywhere gave form and weight to self-discipline and self-help and, therefore, worked to the common good; but, as the

[66] Benjamin, *Three Years in America*, vol. I, pp. 278, 280.
[67] Meinig, *The Shaping of America*, vol. III, pp. 52–3; Ellen Eisenberg, Ava F. Kahn, and William Toll, *Jews of the Pacific Coast: Reinventing Community on America's Edge* (Seattle: University of Washington Press, 2009), pp. 19, 41–2, 46.

San Francisco case seems to indicate, these projects in civic improvement were sometimes more than casually related to an un-civil undertow.

Urban and Rural Spaces in America

There were thus marked similarities but also distinct local differences in experiences Jews had across a variety of urban settings. The kind of place it was – big commercial city, developing inland urban hub, or boom town; slave-state or free; the cultural identity or preponderance of certain migrant groups and the definitions and rules used to distinguish between the different parts of the local population – shaped the timing and the manner in which Jewish residents took part in civic and economic life. Almost everywhere, there was a tipping point at which a critical mass of Jewish inhabitants was established and the balance shifted from anonymity or individual happenstance toward an established, institutionalized presence.

Urban geography matters a great deal in the history of Jews in America, as it does for American society as a whole. Jewish residential clustering near workplaces, synagogues, specialty shops, and other amenities are a basic feature of Jewish life in America. Our consideration of how Jews found their place in American society, however, requires us to consider the topographical dimension of this history in relation to its wider implications. American economic, political, and social history has an intrinsic fascination with the spatial realm. Along with Russia, Australia, Indonesia, Canada, and Brazil, the United States is one of the few countries not contained within a single time zone. America's capacious, continental landscape has been its paramount defining quality and its quintessential natural resource throughout much of its history. That was true during the long eras prior to European settlement and conquest, and it remained fundamentally true during the centuries that followed.

Much was derived from that fact. It may be hackneyed to refer to Turner's hoary "frontier hypothesis," in which the basic elements of the American experience are traceable to the historical availability of surplus land, but it bears restating that geography matters a great deal in US history. One could point, for example, to the diversity of social forms and cultures, arrayed in a series of local climates and eco-systems, local economies, local accents and dialects, and to the ability of the land to sustain them – albeit not without conflict. Localism and sectionalism, in turn, were clearly related to the political constitution of the American nation, which sought to balance fiscal centralization, local self-government, republican federalism, a common legal order, and an integrated market system.

In light of this, it is noteworthy that the standard pattern of Jewish organizational activity was a decentralized one – "invertebrate," as we have described it earlier. Later in our discussion, we will see how religious, educational, social, and philanthropic institutions continued to develop in a pattern that confirmed their autonomy from one another. The logic behind this derived in some measure from the physical distances that separated Jewish congregations.

Another spatial aspect of Jewish life derives from traditional burial practices. Religious custom requires Jews to locate their burial plots at some distance from homes and synagogues ("churchyard" cemeteries are thus not part of the synagogue tradition). Nascent Jewish communities often took their first steps toward incorporation by acquiring burial grounds – an immediate need, unfortunately, that took precedence over constructing or purchasing a house of prayer, since Jewish prayer can be conducted at home or virtually anywhere. The historic Jewish cemetery in Newport, Rhode Island, for instance, is about a quarter of a mile distant from the colonial Touro Synagogue. In larger cities, Jewish burial grounds were often located even further afield, and they came to be outlying "satellites" of Jewish neighborhoods. Chicago's Jewish Burial Ground Society, founded in 1845, acquired an acre of land near Lake Michigan, at a spot beyond city limits in those days. Later, the community augmented its cemetery grounds with another plot two miles north of the city. With the purchase of burial grounds, a spatial grid could be described linking the residential cluster, the house of worship, and at least one other point on the local map.[68]

The question of non-urban space is more perplexing, however, for one of the abiding characteristics of the Jewish population has been the very low proportion (generally below 3 percent) engaged in agricultural pursuits. Yet it is precisely non-urban space – the "land" or "the country" – that figures so compellingly, and on such an epic scale, in the American national narrative. The pastoral imagination afforded many people a crucial sense of what it meant to be American, to see oneself in relation to one's environment, to claim it as one's own turf. Was the slippage between the agrarian image of the historic American countryside and the urban setting of most American Jews a significant cultural factor? Did it

---

[68] Morris A. Gutstein, *A Priceless Heritage: The Epic Growth of Nineteenth Century Chicago Jewry* (New York: Bloch Publishing Co., 1953), pp. 25, 28.

prompt certain Jews to pay special homage to the homespun, rural ethic? Given the prevalent tendency to adapt to American cultural and political norms, in what ways did Jews relate to the "wilderness," to the vastness of the land, to the collective rural legend of their country, and to those people who seemed most representative of the pastoral hinterland?

The history of Jews in early nineteenth-century America offers several initial examples of this kind of pastoral impulse, though these were all fleeting episodes. In the 1820s, the prominent New York journalist and civic figure, Mordecai Noah, proposed what he called his "Ararat" project at Grand Island in the Niagara River (near the site of Buffalo, New York) as a blueprint for a Jewish pioneering settlement and as a refuge for European Jews in distress. Likewise, there was a Jewish colonization project in Florida, floated by Moses Levy, which was designed to support a landed population of Jewish colonists. Noah's "folly" never materialized, and Levy's troop of about seventy Jewish settler-families quickly dispersed. Another attempt to found a Jewish farming community, called Sholem ("Peace"), was made in New York's Catskill region in 1837 – again, with no long-term results. Further west, Jews set up a short-lived farm settlement near Chicago in the early 1840s.[69]

These stand as more or less isolated instances, and given the limited numbers of Jews in America at the time, that is not so surprising. However, the question of rural life, farming, and the relationships between Jews and other Americans who were seen as native to the countryside did not simply disappear. Somewhat counterintuitively, these issues loomed larger as new immigration accelerated and urban commercial and manufacturing economies became ever more dominant. Jewish farmers never represented a significant sector; yet the phenomenon of Jewish agriculture merits the historian's attention, if only as the flip-side of Jewish urbanism. The countryside was a powerful vector of identity: it represented an alternative life-style which was idealized as the theater of American nativity. As we will see in later chapters, this cluster of questions found greatest traction in Jewish life in America from the 1880s to the 1950s.

[69] Abraham D. Lavender and Clarence B. Steinberg, *Jewish Farmers of the Catskills: A Century of Survival* (Gainesville: University Press of Florida, 1995), pp. 9–12; Tobias Brinkmann, "Between Vision and Reality: Reassessing Jewish Agricultural Colony Projects in Nineteenth Century America," *Jewish History* 21 (2007): 305–24; Leonard G. Robinson, "Agricultural Activities of Jews in America," *American Jewish Year Book* 5673 (1912–13), pp. 56–7; Leon A. Jick, *The Americanization of the Synagogue 1820–1870* (Hanover, NH and Waltham, MA: University Press of New England for Brandeis University Press, 1976), p. 32.

Beliefs and Practices: Folk Religion in
American Judaism

Within a majority culture informed mainly by the heritage of Christian churches and denominations, Judaism's religious aspects could hardly have escaped notice, even if the Jews in America were statistically a small minority and only some of them observed their faith with any diligence. They were known to read a different Scripture; address a different Lord (whose name – "The Name," as devout Jews reverently referred to God – was never pronounced); keep a separate Sabbath; mark their own fasts and festivals; and subscribe to a different (contrary) prophecy of salvation. Jews calculated their months and holy days according to an antique lunar calendar and reckoned their years since Creation, not since the birth of Christ. They retained ancestral, "oriental" practices: a liturgy written right-to-left and recited in ancient Semitic languages (Hebrew and Aramaic); male infant circumcision as a rite of religious initiation; abstention from pork, amid an array of other culinary taboos; and a physical partition between men and women in the house of prayer. Jews were apt to be viewed (for better or for worse) as something of an exotic feature on the American religious landscape.

They were not averse, for the most part, to seeing themselves as representatives of a small, heritage-based, sacred community – as was also true of other Jewish populations around the world. However, like other modern Jewries, they also sought through various forms of display and reforms of ritual practice to place their beliefs on a par with the dominant faiths of their country. Absorbing Western norms, they rendered some of their liturgical music into forms more aesthetically pleasing to Western ears. They felt squeamish or embarrassed by the customary, private practices of hearth and home observed by earlier generations. Perhaps more consistently (and more successfully) than their contemporaries elsewhere, Jews in America went to great lengths to de-exoticize their religious rites and customs. Jews in America affirmed that, like the churches of their neighbors, Judaism's effect on its believers' comportment was wholesome, that it met the test of promoting the public peace, and that it was consistent with civic patriotism.

One circumstance that made it possible for Jews in British America and, later, the United States to tailor their religion to local norms was their hemispheric distance from the Old World. Distance resulted, among other things, in the fact that no ordained rabbis took up residence in early America. Jews in America were among the few Jewries anywhere in the world to have presumed the validity of their religious behavior and practices, rather than have them supervised and authorized by an ordained clergy. They did so over a period that lasted, cumulatively, over a century and a half. One would have to go very far afield (to the isolated Bene Israel Jews of India, for example) to encounter similar examples of a sustained "folk Judaism" – that is, a "common person's" religion – over so long a time.

Those who ministered to American Jews' religious needs in the era before the first ordained rabbis began to immigrate in the 1840s were, to a man, autodidacts. Often, they were employed on a part-time basis or received fees for performing ritual tasks or ceremonies: reading from the Torah scrolls in the synagogue and chanting the liturgy; preaching sermons; performing circumcisions; solemnizing weddings and divorces; slaughtering and preparing meat and fowl for consumption in accordance with kosher standards; administering religious instruction to children; preparing Passover *matzas*. In the earlier stages of community formation, such men also tended to pursue mercantile livelihoods as a "day job." Others were honorary lay officers, elected periodically, who oversaw the administration of the community, such as the purchase or lease of congregational property and the execution of corporate by-laws (as state law required), supervising charity and dues collections, maintaining a semblance of order during prayer assemblies, and performing or assigning the duties attendant on the burial of deceased co-religionists.[70]

Finally – and this was fully in keeping with global Jewish practice at the time – the domestic realm of religious observance was informally but effectively supervised nearly entirely by wives and mothers – a point to which we will return presently.[71]

Ritual, Community, and Society

Insofar as organized religion is the most publicly recognized aspect of American Jewish life, it has also been the most documented and the most commented upon; but not a great deal has been written of the Jewish

---

[70] Jick, *Americanization of the Synagogue*, pp. 4–5, 8–11.
[71] Holly Snyder, "Queens of the Household. The Jewish Women of British America, 1700–1800," in *Women and American Judaism, Historical Perspectives*, ed. Pamela S. Nadell and Jonathan D. Sarna (Hanover, NH and London: Brandeis University Press/ University Press of New England, 2001), pp. 16, 19, 21, 24; Leibman, *Messianism, Secrecy and Mysticism*, pp. 30–7, 40–50.

religion itself as a subjective experience.[72] What did America's Jews mean when they thought or spoke about "Judaism"?

To begin with, no spiritual Great Awakening beckoned to America's Jews. As we briefly noted earlier, Jews in other parts of the world from the mid-seventeenth to early nineteenth century were variously radicalized or scandalized by prophetic, charismatic, and esoteric religious movements. Little of this appears to have affected Jews on the North American continent. Leaning instead toward an unvarnished Judaic ritual – shorn of prophetic, mystical, and ascetic embellishments – they charted a course of their own toward a somewhat staid, temperate religious life. The main thrust of these developments was, as noted, a de-exoticizing effort that worked toward a reduction of what an anthropologist might call "religious shame" and the heightening of "religious pride."

"Religious shame" in this context refers to a complex of subliminal meanings and explicit practices rooted in classical forms of Judaism. (These fall, roughly, into three categories: *cultic shame*, *national guilt*, and *moral conscience*, which we will outline briefly below.) What emerged eventually in American Judaism was a virtually sinless, optimistic, this-worldly faith, fully accessible to American sensibilities and seemingly impervious to mystical or messianic notions that an earlier generation might have entertained.[73] As such, it was also fairly immune to the blandishments of American Protestant evangelical missionizing – a not insignificant "survival gene" for Jews living in the American environment, especially during the revivalist wave known as the Second Great Awakening (1790s to 1830s).

Cultic shame involved the almost visceral need to avoid taboos associated with sex, blood, and death. Death and the dead are associated with a state of ritual taint, which, in biblical times, was expiated by special sacrificial rites at the Temple in Jerusalem. In post-biblical Judaism, the ritual marking-off of mortality took other forms. For example, Jews whose genealogy linked them to the *kohen* (priestly, Aaronide) clan could not enter into close contact with the dead, such as approaching a gravesite. The same priestly condition, intended to demarcate an idealized form of ritual purity, dictated a sexual reticence not applied to Jews at large: alone of all Jewish males, men of the *kohen* line, when marrying, could not choose divorced women for their mates.[74]

---

[72] One recent exception to this is Leibman, *Messianism, Secrecy, Mysticism.*

[73] Leibman, *Messianism, Secrecy, Mysticism.*

[74] Often written in English as Cohen, Kahan, or Cohn, priests-by-lineage are not to be confused with rabbis. Nevertheless, although they have almost no clerical role, they are granted certain honorary functions in synagogue practice.

Both sexual and blood taboos were incorporated into Judaic practice through various ritual behaviors. Most well known, perhaps, is that of infant male circumcision: the token shedding of blood and flesh in early infancy establishes the link between body and soul, and "monitors" the conditions under which the grown male, in later years, will participate in the community and increase it through procreation. Under the same general heading of blood- and sex-related practices, sexual intercourse is licensed only during a woman's non-menstrual days. Similarly, the emission of semen (voluntary or involuntary), when not occurring during licensed sexual intercourse, is forbidden. Transgression of these rules incurs cultic shame, or sin.

A parallel concern with avoiding blood contact is channeled through food taboos: meat slaughtered for consumption must be drained of its blood; eggs containing "blood spots" are forbidden for kosher use; and it is forbidden to eat the flesh of carnivores and scavengers of any species – fish, fowl, or mammal – or to eat crustaceans, most insects, and reptiles. Meat and fowl must be eaten cooked, not raw, and they must be kept apart from dairy products, must be prepared using separate utensils, and must be consumed at separate meals. Other rules apply to the selection of dairy products and wines certified for Jewish consumption and to the requirements for hand-washing before eating a meal.[75]

These rules were not devised to "make sense" or "inspire"; rather, via schemes of classification between pure and impure, sacred and profane, life and anti-life, they addressed points of stress in human relations with the natural world. In retrospect, of course, they also had more instrumental effects: the menstrual taboos, for example, were apt to encourage procreation since they defined sexuality in terms of fertility; ritual hand-washing promotes hygiene; raw or nearly raw bloody meat may be less healthy, under certain conditions, than cooked meat; and so forth. Because they were ritualized, they acquired the aura of the sacred; and because many of these practices set them apart from their neighbors and reinforced other aspects of Jewish difference, the practices themselves

---

[75] Israel Knohl, "Sin, Pollution, Purity: Israel," in *Religions of the Ancient World: A Guide*, ed. Sarah Iles Johnston (Cambridge, MA: Belknap – Harvard University Press, 2004), pp. 502–4; Mary Douglas, *Purity and Danger: An Analysis of the Concepts of Pollution and Taboo* (London: Routledge and Kegan Paul, 1966), pp. 41–57, 120, 159; Jean Soler, "The Semiotics of Food in the Bible," in *Food and Drink in History: Selections from the Annales* (Baltimore, MD and London: The Johns Hopkins University Press, 1979), vol. V, 126–38; Charlotte Fonrobert, *Menstrual Purity: Rabbinic and Christian Reconstructions of Biblical Gender* (Stanford, CA: Stanford University Press, 2000).

became a Jewish trademark. The flesh–blood/life–death mysteries that they represent might be functionally compared in some ways to the mysteries of the Christian Eucharist.

In contrast to Christian practice, however, nearly all Jewish rites of this sort take place mainly in the home and (with a few exceptions) are mainly executed and maintained by women. A Jewish woman of the traditional sort was, to use a modern phrase, a "priestess of the home," performing sacred acts that transformed the home (bed, board, utensils, and all) into a site for numinous meaning.[76] Consequently, any move to "rationalize" or abolish these mythic aspects of Judaism and to focus, instead, on the synagogue and its liturgy, was, in equal measure, a move toward a de-feminized Judaism.

The second dimension of religious shame in classical Judaism is *national*. It is primarily associated in Jewish liturgy with the guilt or sinfulness that led to the Jewish people's fate in exile: "For our sins, we have been expelled from our land." These sins are collective, not individual violations. Salvation in Judaism, symbolically imagined as an ultimate reversal of Jewish exile through the enthronement of a messiah-king, is also a collective concept, not intrinsically linked to the spiritual state of the individual soul.

Conscience is the area in which individual morality is at stake, and care for the state of one's soul is related to notions of individual reward and punishment (in this life or in the hereafter).[77] However, in the classical tradition, the community bears co-responsibility for the transgressors in its midst. "We are guilty, we have betrayed, we have robbed" – thus begins a confessional litany recited by traditional Jews on weekdays. The entire catalogue of such sins is declared aloud by the congregation on Yom Kippur (Day of Atonement), the climax of the annual season of penitence. Characteristically, the confession is worded in the first-person plural, though nearly all the named transgressions are acts committed by and against individuals: "[Forgive] the sins we have committed against You by slandering [...], by gossiping [...], by sexual licentiousness [...], by contempt for our parents and teachers."

These three creedal elements – an intimate choreography of domestic practice, a recognition of the fallen spiritual and political state of the House of Israel, and a sense of individual and collective self-blame – formed a symbolic and emotional tripod on which much of classical

[76] Baader, "From 'the Priestess of the Home'."
[77] Leibman, *Messianism, Secrecy, Mysticism*, pp. 123–80, offers a fascinating portrait of such beliefs as they were expressed in the culture of seventeenth- and eighteenth-century Atlantic Jews.

Judaism rested. None of these elements might be executed by clergy or any intermediary; rather, they were incumbent on all adult persons, male or female. Therefore, even in early America, where no rabbi was on hand to provide guidance or authority, there was no inherent impediment to the transference of these basic beliefs and practices to new soil.

The primal need to guard against or expiate religious shame was certainly recognized among Jews who made their homes in the colonies of the New World.[78] This soon became contested ground, however, as not every item of the religious code elicited the same degree of loyalty. Death rituals, for instance, tended to retain an aura of strict sanctity. The acquisition and maintenance of burial grounds remained, throughout American Jewish history, almost a universally respected tradition.

In keeping with other domestic religious requirements, colonial era Jews were known to avail themselves of kosher slaughtering services for their tables. Congregations took it upon themselves to regulate meat provisioning, but the skills required were not limited to one or two individuals. As one historian reminds us, "The number of members conversant with the rules pertaining to *shehitah* [slaughter] was sufficient that *shohet* [slaughterer] and *bodek* [inspector] were competitive posts."[79] The laws of food consumption failed to retain universal acceptance, but in many households they were maintained for several generations, supervised personally by the woman of the household, even where (non-Jewish) kitchen help was available.[80]

Abigaill (Bilhah) Levy Franks of New York (1688–1746), whose letters to her eldest son, Naphtali, between 1733 and 1748 have been preserved, is a case in point. Naphtali Franks, at age seventeen, returned to England to be apprenticed in trade with his uncles. In her letters to her son, Abigaill admonished him:

I Desire you will Never Eat Anything with [my brother Asher] Unless it bread and butter nor noe where Else where there is the Least doubt of things not done after our Strict Judaicall method for whatever my thoughts may be Concerning Some Fables this and Some other foundementalls I Look Opon the Observence Conscientiously and therefore with my blessing I Strictly injoyn it to your care.[81]

[78] Leibman, *Messianism, Secrecy, Mysticism*, pp. 30–7, 40–50.
[79] Snyder, "Rethinking the Definition of 'Community'," p. 9.
[80] Aviva Ben-Ur, "The Exceptional and the Mundane. A Biographical Portrait of Rebecca (Machado) Phillips (1746–1831)," in Nadell and Sarna, *Women and American Judaism*, p. 55; Snyder, "Queens of the Household," pp. 24–5.
[81] *Lee Max Friedman Collection of American Jewish Colonial Correspondence: Letters of the Franks Family (1733–1748)*, ed. Leo Hershkowitz and Isidore S. Meyer (Waltham, MA: American Jewish Historical Society, 1968), p. 8.

Abigaill reverted in a subsequent letter to the theme of her religious skepticism, but implied that she had no thought to implement any ritual changes on her own. Having conveyed her thanks for the gift of a book which she found "agreeable to my Sentiments in regard to our Religeon," she wittily remarked that "Whoever wrote it I am Sure was noe Jew for he thought too reasonable." Apparently stimulated by the author's rational discussion, she added:

I Must Own I cant help Condemning the Many Supersti[ti]ons wee are Clog'd with & heartly wish a Calvin or Luther would rise amongst Us. I Answer for my Self, I would be the first of there followers for I don't think religion Consist in Idle Cerimonies & works of Suppererogations Wich if they Send people to heaven wee & the papist have the Greatest title too.[82]

Nevertheless, in due course she was emotionally devastated by the elopement and secret marriage of her daughter, Phila, with Oliver de Lancey, of one of New York's prominent (non-Jewish) families (1742), followed by her son David's marriage with Margaret Evans, a Philadelphia Episcopalian (1743). Abigaill, deeply shamed, barred her errant offspring from her life. It was one thing for her to discreetly entertain heterodox thoughts, but quite another for her children to set up households where they would no longer be within the safe and sanctified bounds of their ancestral faith. The key role of home and hearth in the maintenance of spiritual propriety comes through here very clearly.[83]

Jewish–Gentile marriages were, as noted, not uncommon. In later years, leading up to the 1840s, they constituted perhaps as many as 30 percent of marriages involving Jews. "The Jews [...] are dressed like all other citizens, shave regularly, and also eat pork [...] moreover do not hesitate to intermarry," reported one German officer who served during the American Revolution. More often than not, however, marriage to a non-Jew augured an estrangement among kin. As for Christian Americans, clearly there were some for whom the Judaism of a prospective spouse did not constitute a formidable barrier, socially or religiously. There were even some cases of conversion to Judaism, normally by a non-Jewish wife. This was quite unusual in that era, given the dearth of such cases in the Old World. There, where the weight of ecclesiastical pressure

[82] *Letters of the Franks Family*, p. 66.
[83] *Letters of the Franks Family*, pp. 63, 114, 116–19; see also *The Letters of Abigaill Franks 1733–1748*, ed. and intro. Edith B. Gelles (New Haven, CT and London: Yale University Press, 2004), Introduction, pp. xxxvi–xxxix; Anne C. Rose, *Beloved Strangers: Interfaith Families in Nineteenth Century America* (Cambridge, MA: Harvard University Press, 2001), p. 15.

and influence was greater, European Jews were thought rash, indeed, if they provoked Christian sensibilities.[84]

Within these patterns of extensive and, sometimes, intimate fraternization across religious lines, the reframing of Judaism as an appropriate religious rite within the symbolic system of American life gradually began to take shape. This entailed a reapportionment between practiced cult and verbalized assertions of faith – the reduction of the former and the elevation of the latter – as well as a more pronounced centering of Jewish religious life around the synagogue, as the formal (male-dominated) institution representing the congregation.

Several of these elements may be seen in tandem in a speech delivered by Mordecai M. Noah, on the occasion of a synagogue dedication in New York in 1818. Noah praised the "liberality and toleration" that characterized religious life in the United States, by which the nation's morals and philosophy were guided. He then placed Judaism squarely within this enlightened category of rational, "natural" religion: "The religion of the Jews requires no defence; it [...] is the religion of nature – the religion of reason and philosophy." The Jews' religion, Noah asserted, was an eminently reasonable philosophy of life, fully in keeping with Anglo-American deistic ideas – and not an exotic implant.[85]

Committed to subsuming Judaism within the civic ideology of their country, Jews and their spokesmen were not averse to trading one kind of exoticism for another, as may be seen in the following program for a Masonic cornerstone-laying ceremony for a synagogue in Savannah in 1820:

Form of Procession. The Tyler with his Sword, Two deacons with Wands, Three order Bible Square and Compasses, Stone on a cushion borne by Committee of

---

[84] Rose, *Beloved Strangers*, pp. 14–16, 20–24, 27–30, 36; Snyder, "Queens of the Household," pp. 25–6; Malcolm Stern, "Jewish Marriage and Intermarriage in the Federal Period (1776–1840)," *American Jewish Archives* 19(2) (1967): 142–3; Jacob R. Marcus, *The American Jewish Woman: A Documentary History* (New York: Ktav/Cincinnati, OH: American Jewish Archives, 1981), p. 51; Snyder, "Queens of the Household," p. 26; Sarna, *American Judaism*, p. 74; Dana Evan Kaplan, "Conversion to Judaism in America 1760–1897," (PhD dissertation, Tel-Aviv University, 1994), pp. 23, 27, 31–42, 60, 72–9, 102–4. Johann Conrad Doehla's diary is cited by Rudolph Glanz, *Studies in Judaica Americana* (New York: Ktav, 1970), p. 220, and by Jick, *Americanization of the Synagogue*, p. 7; originally published in German: "Amerikanische Feldzüge, 1777–1783, Tagebuch von Johann Conrad Doehlia," *Deutschamerikanische Geschichtsblätter* 17 (1917): 51.

[85] *Jews of the United States*, ed. Blau and Baron, vol. I, pp. 82–3, 85; Sarna, *Jacksonian Jew: The Two Worlds of Mordecai Noah* (New York: Holmes and Meier Publishers, 1981), pp. 54–5.

the building [...]. The Hebrew Members [of the Masonic lodge] in pairs will close the procession. On coming to the inclosure the bretheren [...] will arrange themselves round the Spot forming the hollow Square or circle as the Space may allow. [...] A charge or address will then be given after which a Masonic Sign, With three times three will be given [...].[86]

Masonic rites were increasingly apt to crop up at Jewish funerals. This neo-pagan intrusion caused great chagrin to Rabbi Abraham (Reiss) Rice (*c.* 1800–62), one of the first ordained European rabbis to migrate to America. In the 1840s, he served as the minister of the Nidche Israel ("The Dispersed of Israel") synagogue in Baltimore. Rabbi Rice was forced to retreat in the face of popular will on this and on other matters, as the laymen of the congregation exerted control over congregational policies. Rice resigned after less than a decade as the community's rabbi. Embittered over the lack of regard for his status and his beliefs, he opened a general store instead.[87]

In Charleston, a group of younger members of the Jewish congregation confronted their elders with a plan to rectify what they saw as undesirable features of synagogue proceedings. In 1824, they proposed an English repetition of a portion of the Hebrew liturgy and they urged stricter attention to "decency and decorum" (the usual hubbub in the synagogue was considered unseemly). Likewise, they proposed the elimination of "everything superfluous" other than the "principal parts" of the liturgy to shorten the length of prayer services, and the addition of a "discourse" to explain the meanings of prayers and Torah readings. Their spokesman, Isaac Harby (1788–1828), insisted:

To throw away rabbinical interpolations; to avoid useless repetitions; to read or chaunt with solemnity [...], is this sapping the foundations of our venerable faith? No, my friends, this is stripping it of foreign and unseemly ceremonies; divesting it of rubbish, and beautifying that simple Doric column [...]. [We ask] not to insult us with bad Spanish and Portuguese [the Sephardi congregation's inherited vernaculars, used as semi-sacred tongues]; to admit an English discourse; [...]; and to select the sublimer portions of such [...] prayers as taste and piety can approve, to be said or sung in the English language. We wish to [...] take away whatever is offensive to the enlightened mind; but to leave in its original grandeur whatever is worthy to be uttered by man, and to be listened to by the Deity.[88]

---

[86] *Jews of the United States*, ed. Blau and Baron, vol. III, p. 688; see also Edmund R. Sadowski, "A Jewish Masonic Prayer," *PAJHS* 48(2) (1958): 134–5.

[87] Jick, *Americanization of the Synagogue*, pp. 71, 73.

[88] *Jews of the United States*, ed. Blau and Baron, vol. II, pp. 554–65; see also Jeffrey S. Gurock, *Orthodox Jews in America* (Bloomington and Indianapolis: Indiana University Press, 2009), pp. 44–6.

The quest for a streamlined, easy-to-grasp, Bible-centered Judaic creed was felt, as well, in the realm of religious instruction for children. In 1839 Rebecca Gratz (1781–1869) introduced a catechism at her Hebrew Sunday School in Philadelphia, produced for this purpose by Isaac Leeser (1806–68), lay minister of Philadelphia's Mikveh Israel ("Hope of Israel") congregation. Leeser cribbed the text from a textbook written in Hamburg in 1814, adding his own elaborations and purging the original's heterodox, "reformist" tendencies.[89]

Intended for rote memorization and recitation, such texts were based on Christian models but with "Jewish answers" inserted, along with appropriate biblical quotations. One was written by Rachel Peixotto Pyke (b. 1814), another of Rebecca Gratz's collaborators. Similar pedagogical devices were introduced in New York a few years later, at the B'nai Jeshurun congregational school, and at a Jewish private school opened in that city by Rabbi Max Lilienthal (1814–82).

These schools taught "Religion" as a separate subject, which reflected the German philosophical trend of that era and reinforced the theological content of the religious heritage. Jews were familiar with declarative statements of their faith, as featured in the Book of Psalms and in the standard liturgy of the synagogue; but the educators we are discussing felt that Judaism lacked a highly articulated rationale in modern language. Customs practiced in the home (or not practiced, as the case may be) were insufficient in that regard. The definition of religious indoctrination as a matter of individual belief or conscience signaled a Westernized, Americanized religious sensibility.[90]

Civic consciousness, American middle-class cultural norms, and an amorphous boundary between Jewish and Christian didactic texts permeated Rebecca Gratz's Hebrew Sunday School in Philadelphia. A former pupil recalled that Gratz, as headmistress, "was extremely particular to instill neatness and cleanliness," and called her charges to order before

[89] *Jewish Education in the United States: A Documentary History*, ed. Lloyd P. Gartner (New York: Teachers College and Columbia University Press, 1969), p. 51; Gurock, *Orthodox Jews in America*, p. 80. The original work was written by Edward Kley, entitled *Catechismus der Mosaischen Religion*. See Michael A. Meyer, *Response to Modernity: A History of the Reform Movement in Judaism* (New York and Oxford: Oxford University Press, 1988), pp. 49, 54–5.

[90] Dianne Ashton, *Rebecca Gratz. Women and Judaism in Antebellum America* (Detroit, MI: Wayne State University Press, 1997), pp. 152–3, 159–60, 161; Bruce L. Ruben, *Max Lilienthal, The Making of the American Rabbinate* (Detroit, MI: Wayne State University Press, 2011), pp. 96–7; Lance J. Sussman, *Isaac Leeser and the Making of American Judaism* (Detroit, MI: Wayne State University Press, 1995), pp. 95–101, 133–5.

a table upon which rested "a much worn Bible containing both the Old and the New Testaments [...], Watts's Hymns, and penny contribution box 'for the poor of Jerusalem.' [...] Scripture lessons were taught from a little illustrated work published by the Christian Sunday School Union." The school day always ended with "a Hebrew hymn and a simple verse from Watts."

In catechism class, youngsters repeated formulas in response to questions such as: "Who formed you child, and made you live?" The question and the rhyming answer, "God did my life and spirit give," are close paraphrases of Christian models. On the occasion of the Philadelphia Hebrew Sunday School's first anniversary, in March 1839, a public examination of the pupils was held at the Masonic Hall. Isaac Leeser intoned a lengthy opening benediction and, as befitted such a civic event, concluded his remarks with a patriotic prayer for the peace and prosperity of his city and his country.[91]

In communities where a critical mass of German-speaking immigrant families had concentrated, catechisms that were already in use in Germany were simply imported. That was the case, for instance, in Cleveland in the mid-1840s, where a comprehensive Jewish day school was operated under the aegis of the city's Anshe Chesed congregation, and run by a veteran educator from Germany. Pupils were taught to decipher Hebrew texts by translating passages from the Book of Genesis and from the daily prayer book into German. The culmination of the school year was a public examination, a kind of commencement exercise, in which children "exhibited their skill." The annual exercises were a civic event attended by the mayor and members of the city council.[92]

The Jewish population was in constant flux, so each new cohort of migrants tended to recapitulate these adjustments in practice and rhetorical emphasis. Apparently oblivious to the implied dissonance, they insisted on strict provisions for kosher meat and the recitation in Hebrew of the entire, unabridged liturgy, while at the same time, they accorded little status or prestige to those they put in charge of their sacred rituals.

---

[91] Rosa Mordecai, a great-niece of Gratz's, wrote the memoir, quoted here from Gartner, *Jewish Education in the United States*, pp. 54–60; Isaac Leeser, *Discourses on the Jewish Religion*, vol. III (Philadelphia: Sherman & Co., 1867), pp. 365–8. The reference might be to either the Methodist *Hymns and Psalms* or the Presbyterian *Trinity Hymnal*, both of which featured hymns by the English theologian and hymn-writer, Isaac Watts (1674–1748).

[92] Lloyd P. Gartner, *History of the Jews of Cleveland* (Cleveland, OH: Western Reserve Historical Society and the Jewish Community Federation of Cleveland, 1978), pp. 52–3.

They also apparently accommodated themselves without too much difficulty to consuming non-kosher food when travelling around the countryside (as many of them did, as peddlers). Though initially apt to bar
membership in the synagogue to men known to keep their businesses
open on the Sabbath, in time they tended to turn a blind eye. Abraham
Rice, in his brief rabbinical career in Baltimore, sought at least to reserve
public honors in the synagogue for those whose enterprises were closed
for the day, but could not prevail. Nevertheless, with little if any sign
of consistency, his congregants refused his suggestion that the services
be shortened by eliminating some optional hymns. The congregation's
stalwarts required strict formalism in their liturgy but were lax in other
matters.

Charleston's Beth Elohim was the first synagogue to install an organ –
in direct emulation of their Gentile neighbors and in flagrant violation of
orthodox rabbinical precedent. But the governing board at Beth Elohim
flatly rejected the suggestion of its *hazan* (reader-minister), Gustav
Poznanski (1804–79), that the observance of the major festivals of the
Jewish calendar be shortened: that is, that they should be celebrated as
prescribed in the Bible for just seven, rather than the (post-rabbinic) customary eight days. Poznanski was reprimanded for his impertinence. This
and other cases led one historian to refer to the inconsistent "primitive
piety and opportunistic pragmatism" that seemed to guide Jewish lay
leaders in antebellum America.[93]

Individuals varied, of course, in their levels of observance, and
some were more particular than others about their religious duties. In
Cleveland, Ohio, some Jewish merchants counted themselves fortunate
in obtaining a favorable court ruling (in 1853) that permitted them to
open their clothing stores for business on Sunday, in consideration of the
fact that they kept Saturday as their Sabbath. But, they complained, there
were "several others in the same business [who] keep open on Sunday
[...] but they do [also] sell on Saturday and every other day."[94]

It is, therefore, not entirely out of character to read in one young woman's diary, recorded in New Orleans during 1861–2, that her customary
attendance at Sabbath services was sometimes canceled in order to store
up energy for the day's shopping expedition later that day (a flagrant
bit of sacrilege); that the Yom Kippur fast day was observed, but that

---

[93] Jick, *Americanization of the Synagogue*, pp. 49–53, 56–7, 71–2, 76, 85–95; Gurock,
    Orthodox Jews in America, p. 79.
[94] Gartner, *Jews of Cleveland*, p. 69.

the main topic of conversation was the seating arrangement in the synagogue's women's gallery; or, on another occasion, that a neighbor was delegated "to see about the [Passover] 'Motsas' [...]," but that obtaining them was "a mere farce surrounded as they [the matzas] are by bread and biscuits. But for form sake we must have them."[95]

This somewhat haphazard state of religious conduct and adherence – moving between diehard formalism, lax or indifferent practice, ethical chicanery, and devotion to tradition – might be imputed to the uneven adjustments being made by a great variety of different people. What appears inconsistent, quirky, or improvisational, however, might paradoxically mask an underlying consistency. It was apparently difficult for many people to scrap the system of "religious shame" forthwith, however haphazardly they might have understood it or "believed" in it. Codes of ritual conduct were apt to exert a resilient psychological pull. It was estimated, for example, that some thirty-five communities across the country employed at least one "professional *shohet*" in the 1850s, and that this figure had doubled by the end of the 1860s. Interposing a different religious idiom – or, indeed, attempting to give religious behavior a more explicit rationale – required real ideological work, of which people like Mordecai Noah, Isaac Harby, Rebecca Gratz, Gustav Poznanski, Isaac Leeser, and Max Lilienthal were fully capable. By the 1850s, at least sixty religious leaders (few of them ordained rabbis) were active in America, many of whom used the pulpit for English-language preaching. "If the masses are not yet sufficiently prepared for the changes unavoidably in store for us," opined Lilienthal, "it is the holy duty of the Jewish ministry and press to [...] assist them in overcoming the travails of the present state of transition."[96]

Though they occupied different positions along the spectrum between traditionalism and innovation (the traditionalist, East Coast-based Leeser and Gratz, both of them lay leaders, facing off against two Cincinnati Reform rabbis, Lilienthal and Isaac Mayer Wise [1819–1900]), these

---

95 *The Civil War Diary of Clara Solomon. Growing Up in New Orleans, 1861–1862*, ed. and intro. Elliott Ashkenazi (Baton Rouge and London: Louisiana State University Press, 1995), pp. 112–13, 318, 326.

96 Gurock, *Orthodox Jews in America*, p. 61; Max Lilienthal, "Rabbinical Codices, or the *Shulchan Aruch*," *Letters on Reform Addressed to the Rev. I. Leeser*, no. 5, December 26, 1856, reprinted in *Jewish Belief and Practice in Nineteenth Century America: Seminal Essays by Outstanding Pulpit Rabbis of the Era*, ed. Elliot B. Gertel (Jefferson, NC and London: McFarland and Co., 2006), p. 49; Robert V. Friedenberg, *"Hear O Israel": The History of American Jewish Preaching, 1654–1970* (Tuscaloosa and London: University of Alabama Press, 1989), p. 41.

mid-century communal figures all sought a new balance between performance-etiquette and inner conviction. They preferred to overcome the uneven pattern of individual whim and the force of unreflective habit with a definable religious sensibility. Backed by powerful propaganda media such as an emergent Jewish press and the introduction of regular preaching in the synagogue (Leeser and Wise were among the most active publishers and preachers), traditionalists and reformers alike worked to formalize Judaism as a synagogue-centered, clergy-led, "church-like" body. Folk Judaism on the American continent was about to enter upon a long eclipse.[97]

Women

The role of women in that process was, in retrospect, an irony. As we noted, as long as Judaism was orchestrated mainly in the home – the synagogue being reserved for more formal occasions – women's practical and ritual influence was considerable, even dominant, and their piety was recognized as the primary guarantor of a family's virtue. Upsetting that home-based ideal (as through intermarriage) could, for some, be a devastating prospect, as we saw in the case of Abigaill Franks and her daughter.

By the time of Leeser and Gratz, a Jew of their generation, born or raised in America, was apt to believe that a refined, genuine, individual, religious *feeling* was crucial; that routine household practices were derivative, at best a mnemonic device invented by rabbis in times gone by; at worst – "superstition"; and that an inter-generational family matrix of gendered life-tasks was a fine thing but not absolutely essential (neither Leeser nor Gratz ever married). Jewish fellowship was more likely to be enacted outside the home and outside the synagogue, in gender-separated fraternal lodges (B'nai B'rith) and female associations (like the wives of B'nai B'rith who organized the Treue Schwestern, or local charities like Rebecca Gratz's Female Hebrew Benevolent Society in Philadelphia).[98]

---

[97] Alan Silverstein, *Alternatives to Assimilation: The Response of Reform Judaism to American Culture* (Hanover, NH and London: Brandeis University Press/University Press of New England, 1994), pp. 23–4, 95–102.

[98] Ashton, *Rebecca Gratz*, pp. 93–119; Wolf 2nd and Whiteman, *The History of the Jews of Philadelphia*, pp. 276–7; Sussman, *Isaac Leeser*, pp. 96–7; Hasia R. Diner, *A Time for Gathering: The Second Migration, 1820–1880. The Jewish People in America*, vol. II (Baltimore, MD: The Johns Hopkins University Press, 1992), pp. 86–113; Deborah Dash Moore, *B'nai B'rith and the Challenge of Ethnic Leadership* (Albany, NY: SUNY Press, 1981), pp. 1–34; Cornelia Wilhelm, *Deutsche Juden in Amerika* (Stuttgart: Franz Steiner Verlag, 2007).

Synagogue membership was organized and paid for by heads of households – that is, by men – with only occasional membership provisions made for widows. As was true of American churches of that era, however, synagogues of the mid-nineteenth century were frequented, increasingly, by women more than by men. At times, indeed, smaller congregations could not even muster a traditional quorum of ten men, which led one pioneering young rabbi, Bernard Felsenthal (1822–1908), to propose counting women in the quorum. The board at his Adas Israel Congregation in Madison, Indiana in 1856 was aghast at this and his other proposed reforms. Felsenthal left that synagogue two years later.[99]

As home-based practice of a practical ritual code diminished, women's religious energies were inevitably drawn out of the home. At the synagogue they were met by a male-dominated establishment, but one to which they readily adapted, eliciting a good deal of ideological support from rabbis who encouraged women's "natural" feminine bias toward religious sentiment. Their religious demeanor was seen as an adjunct to their "natural" maternal and spousal callings. In the age of Darwin, these "naturalistic" ideas achieved a scientific standing that had been absent from the feminine mystique of earlier eras.

In Isaac Mayer Wise's German-language women's journal, *Die Deborah*, the prescription for ideal Jewish motherhood was a dual imperative: "God commands [women]: Be just, virtuous, pure, and faithful! God commands: Be rational and free!" What that meant in practice, as Wise saw it, was that a Jewish mother should "encourage her children to be charitable, grateful, truthful, gentle, orderly, and punctual." She should "accustom her children to attending the synagogue and should read to them from the Bible or from religious tracts."[100]

New synagogue buildings from that era featured family pews, putting an end to the separate seating reserved for women in traditional synagogues, highlighting the role of the house of prayer as a lynchpin of family-based decorum, and giving more visible expression to women's presence. Yet, any notion of a "feminized" synagogue must be considered a rhetorical exaggeration. As observers have noted, nineteenth-century Jewish women's role in the house of prayer was limited, compared to

[99] Gurock, *Orthodox Jews in America*, pp. 74–5; see also Barry A. Kosmin and Seymour P. Lachman, *One Nation Under God: Religion in Contemporary American Society* (New York: Harmony Books, 1993), pp. 211–12.

[100] *Deborah*, vol. I, December 28, 1855, p. 145; Baader, "Priestess of the Home," pp. 49, 55, 61, 64–8. (Published as *Deborah* during its first decade, the journal was called *Die Deborah* after 1865.)

that of contemporary women in American churches. Detached from
the sources of religious shame and therefore, the means of expressing
piety of previous generations, and educated to believe in the scientific
basis of human relations, the new Jewish woman of the mid-nineteenth
century bore only two major responsibilities: the raising of children
and the organizing of altruistic good works in the community. In that
sense, women's presence in the American synagogue fostered a kind
of "bridge" between the domestic and the communal realm, but that
bridge was a very narrow one. Sitting together with men did nothing
to widen it.[101]

Jewish Chaplaincy in the Civil War

The naturalization of Judaism as an American denomination, symbolized by its church, represented by its clergy, honored by civic leaders, and
designed to win the respect of neighbors, passed one significant milestone
in the heat of the Civil War. The question of Judaism's place in the civic
sphere arose when the estimated seven thousand Jewish men fighting for
the Union (and three thousand, perhaps, serving in the Confederate forces)
faced a lack of Jewish army chaplains. Military chaplains had served the
various Protestant denominations since 1781 and Roman Catholic clergy
served as volunteer chaplains (i.e., without military commissions) during
the Mexican–American War. Catholic priests were inducted as military
personnel for the first time in the Civil War. The Jewish case paralleled
that of the Catholics in some respects.

Initial attempts by units with considerable numbers of Jewish personnel to appoint volunteer prayer-leaders and religious advisors met
with official resistance, mainly from Federal authorities. (In the Rebel
army, unlike in the Union forces, no single regiment had sufficient Jewish
soldiers to warrant their own chaplain.) Nevertheless, at least one Jewish
soldier – a layman, as was the normal Jewish practice for so many

---

[101] Snyder, "Queens of the Household," p. 19; Ashton, *Rebecca Gratz*, pp. 19, 22, 116–17,
147, 221, 255; Karla Goldman, *Beyond the Synagogue Gallery: Finding a Place for
Women in American Judaism* (Cambridge, MA: Harvard University Press, 2001), pp.
1–3, 10–11, 93–9; and "Women in Reform Judaism: Between Rhetoric and Reality,"
in *Women Remaking American Judaism*, ed. Riv-Ellen Prell (Detroit, MI: Wayne State
University Press, 2007), pp. 109–13; Silverstein, *Alternatives to Assimilation*, p. 19;
Jonathan D. Sarna, "The Debate over Mixed Seating in the American Synagogue," in
The American Synagogue, A Sanctuary Transformed, ed. Jack Wertheimer (Cambridge
and New York: Cambridge University Press, 1987), pp. 363–94; Sarna, *American
Judaism*, pp. 127–8, 142; see also Ann Douglas, *The Feminization of American Culture*
(New York: Knopf, 1978), esp. pp. 97–101.

years – was serving in the capacity of regimental chaplain, not only for the Jewish ranks, but also for the men of other faiths, for whom he conducted a non-denominational service on Sundays. When brought to the attention of government authorities, this anomaly led to a legal test. By 1862, the existing law was amended so as to permit non-ordained representatives designated by an "ecclesiastical body" (defined as a board of five clergymen) to serve.[102]

The nineteenth century may, in retrospect, be viewed as having been a formative era in the history of Jews in America. By the time of the American Civil War, a steady migration of European Jews to the United States was underway and the people involved found their way without many obstacles into the heterogeneous urban sector of American society. Over the next half-century, however, many more Jews made many more "new beginnings" in America than ever before.

[102] Bertram W. Korn, *American Jewry and the Civil War* (Philadelphia, PA: Jewish Publication Society, 1951 and Marietta, GA: R. Bemis Publishing, 1995), pp. 56–97; Sarna, *American Judaism*, pp. 119–20; Albert Isaac Slomovitz, *The Fighting Rabbis. Jewish Military Chaplains and American History* (New York and London: New York University Press, 1999), pp. 10–22.

2

Changing Places

Migration and Americanization, 1860s–1920s

Closed are the portals of their Synagogue,
No Psalms of David now the silence break,
No Rabbi reads the ancient Decalogue
In the grand dialect the Prophets spake [...]
The groaning earth in travail and pain
Brings forth its races, but does not restore,
And the dead nations never rise again.
> – Henry Wadsworth Longfellow, "The Jewish
> Cemetery at Newport" (1859)

No signs of life are here: the very prayers
Inscribed around are in a language dead [...]
Nathless the sacred shrine is holy yet,
With its lone floors where reverent feet once trod.
Take off your shoes as by the burning bush,
Before the mystery of death and God.
> – Emma Lazarus, "In the Jewish Synagogue
> at Newport" (1867)

As we noted before, small numbers of Jews had lived in Newport, Rhode Island intermittently during the 1650s, the 1690s, and again, in the 1740s. After that, the community flickered into a sustained existence until about 1822. Neither of our two poets, Longfellow and Lazarus, quoted in the epigraphs above, found any Jews living in Newport when they visited just before and just after the Civil War, respectively.

The Jewish population of the United States in the mid-nineteenth century was alive and well elsewhere, however. In Lazarus's native New York City alone there were 35,000 Jews in 1860, supporting twenty-three synagogues and forty-four charitable societies. Of this she was well aware. Her maternal grandparents, Sarah Seixas and Isaac Mendes

Seixas Nathan, were members of the close-knit community clustered around Shearith Israel, the venerable Spanish-Portuguese synagogue in Manhattan. Her paternal grandfather, Eleazar Lazarus, another member and twice-elected president of Shearith Israel, had helped prepare the first bilingual Hebrew–English daily prayer book published in America (1826).[1] Two decades after Emma's musings over the extinguished lamp in Newport's historic (and empty) synagogue, close to three hundred Jewish congregations were active throughout the United States. Nearly forty were established in the 1860s, and over thirty more were founded in the 1870s. By 1880, the Jewish population neared an estimated 250,000 in the country as a whole. Why, then, was Newport a Jewish ghost town?

Jews lived mostly in cities where commerce and industry supported a broad occupational spectrum. Those cities typically had a substantial number of commercial travelers, hucksters, and peddlers; a sizeable concentration of industrial workers; and a sufficient network of banks and other financial institutions.[2] Newport did not even make it into the top hundred American cities, ranked by size of population, and the fact that it was overlooked by Jews moving to new homes need not surprise us too much. Newport did attract some part-time Jewish residents, however: Moses Lazarus, Emma's father, built a summer cottage there in 1870. Along with other socially prominent summer visitors, the Lazaruses joined the exclusive Town and Country Club.[3]

Jews were more metropolitan than most other Americans. By 1900, half of the Jews in the nation would be located in New York, Chicago, and Philadelphia. Though their urbanism may have been disproportional, Jews were certainly part of a general trend: by 1910, town and city dwellers outnumbered the rural population in New England, the Middle Atlantic states, and the Midwest east of the Mississippi. Across the rest of the Midwest and along the Pacific coast, urbanites were close to achieving parity with their rural neighbors. Native-born Americans were less apt to be living in major cities, but the foreign-stock population (immigrants and their children) was substantially more urban (see Fig. 2.1).

[1] Selma Berrol, *The Empire City, New York and its People 1624–1996* (Westport, CT and London: Praeger, 1997, 2000), p. 47; *The People and the Book: The Background of Three Hundred Years of Jewish Life in America: A Tricentennial Exhibition at the New York Public Library*, compiled by Joshua Bloch (New York: New York Public Library: 1954), p. 106; Esther Schor, *Emma Lazarus* (New York: Nextbook/Schocken, 2006), pp. 3–8.

[2] Meinig, *The Shaping of America*, vol. III, pp. 241, 298, 299; Vance, Jr., *The Merchant's World*, p. 36 (fig. 5).

[3] Bette Roth Young, *Emma Lazarus in Her World* (Philadelphia, PA: Jewish Publication Society of America, 1995), pp. 6–7, 44; Schor, *Emma Lazarus*, pp. 36–9.

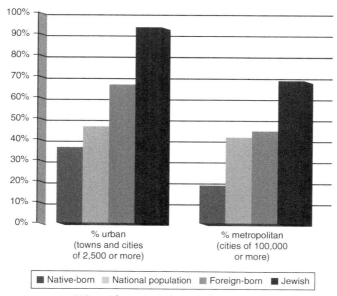

FIGURE 2.1. US residents in urban and metropolitan areas, 1910: native-born, foreign-born, and Jewish.

As early as 1870, a quarter of the foreign-born lived in major cities (of 100,000 population and up), and 44 percent did so by 1910 – higher than the national average. Jewish patterns, thus, tended to resemble the average for immigrant groups in general.[4]

Cities that had higher-than-average foreign-stock populations (between 29 and 40 percent) included Boston, Cleveland, Detroit, Milwaukee, Minneapolis, Newark, and San Francisco. In 1900, an overwhelming 84 percent of New York City's white heads of households were of foreign birth or had foreign-born parents. In contrast, in the nation at large, 57.5 percent of white heads of households were native-born of native parentage.[5] Jewish residential concentration in particular cities fell into step with these patterns: wherever immigrants were a significant part of the population, so were Jews (see Table 2.1). Altogether, some two-thirds of America's Jews were concentrated in large urban centers that were ethnically, culturally, racially, and religiously heterogeneous. Jews

[4] Alan Nevins, *The Emergence of Modern America 1865–1878* (New York: Macmillan, 1928), p. 75; Herbert S. Klein, *A Population History of the United States* (Cambridge: Cambridge University Press, 2004), p. 142.

[5] Rosenwaike, *Population History of New York City*, pp. 90–1.

TABLE 2.1. *Jews and foreign-born residents as percent of city population**

City	Foreign-born as percent of total population (1910)	Jews as percent of total population (1917)
New York City	41	26
Boston	36	10
Chicago	36	9
Cleveland	35	13
Detroit	34	6
Newark	32	14
Pittsburgh	27	10
Philadelphia	25	11

* Klein, *Population History of the United States*; Rosenwaike, *Population History of New York City*; and Marcus, *To Count a People*.

were embedded in that heterogeneity. Despite their small numbers, they augmented and changed the social fabric around them as they founded voluntary associations for social and religious purposes, alongside those of their neighbors.

The poems by Longfellow and Lazarus, quoted above, are thus not to be mistaken for reliable guides to the state of American Jewry after 1850. However, the historian would do well to register the sense of transience in these poets' elegiac, brooding verses. The span of family continuity in most Jewish communities can usefully be thought of in terms of several generations, rather than as a single, seamless line, stretching across centuries. The considerable expansion and variety of the country's Jewish population from about the mid-nineteenth-century was largely due to a constant influx of newcomers – all of them, by definition, building their lives anew, rather than carrying forward a continuous flow of lifestyles and experience. The summer sojourns of the Lazarus family in Newport, for instance, were hardly preconditioned by the sporadic Jewish presence in the town during the colonial era – long since faded into memory – despite the ironic coincidence that Bellevue Avenue, where the Lazaruses built their home, had once been a small lane, known as "Jew Street."[6]

Indeed, the family of Moses and Esther Nathan Lazarus illustrates the limits of intergenerational continuity. Emma and two of her sisters (Sarah and Josephine) never married. Three other siblings (Eleazar Frank, Mary, and Anna) married out of the Jewish faith. Anna became an Anglican and Mary moved to Germany upon her marriage to a Protestant son of

[6] Schor, *Emma Lazarus*, p. 36.

an ex-Jewish convert. Another sister, Agnes, married art critic Montague Marks, son of David Marks, rabbi at the West London (Reform) Synagogue. But one of their daughters, Adah Esther, remained a spinster and their son, Philip, who had a non-Jewish wife, was killed in action in France in 1915. Another son, Julian David, married a Hollingsworth from Philadelphia. Agnes and Montague's other daughter, Margaret, was buried in 1959 beside the grave of her husband in the Old Saint David Church yard near Philadelphia. Having lasted four generations in America and England, the fifth generation saw the Jewish Lazarus-Nathans passing into history.

Transitions of all sorts will be a guiding theme of this chapter. Jews, along with other Americans, were mobile not just in moving from place to place, but also in moving from one occupational status to another and exchanging older ways of life for new ones. In doing so, they found themselves occupying the same social zones as Americans from different backgrounds.

The dialogue between our two opening poems is emblematic of this as well. Emma Lazarus was literally imagining herself in Longfellow's place by adapting his poem and subtly altering the message.[7] Lazarus located her fanciful encounter with the ghosts of a once extant Jewish community in the synagogue – not the cemetery – and described it as a place where "Children's gladness and men's gratitude/ Took voice and mingled in the chant of praise." And while Lazarus found it sad that life and youth proved so transient ("And green grass lieth gently over all"), she avoided the final verdict in Longfellow's requiem.

No less significant than her literary impersonation of Longfellow, by which she audaciously claimed a place in the heartland of American poetry, Lazarus performed a second appropriation in this poem. She made historic Newport and its Jews her own in a self-reflexive way that Longfellow could not have considered, by inscribing herself as part of the scene through such phrases as "we gaze" and "we see." Where Longfellow invoked "History" as an eternal, magisterial arbiter, marking the passing of the Jewish "race," Lazarus inserted her own active consciousness and sketched a personal frame of reference – *a history* rather than History – by giving us the image of her shoes walking literally in the footsteps of her (figurative) forebears.

---

[7] My analysis of the dialogue between Lazarus and Longfellow's is essentially similar to Esther Schor's, and although I arrived at my reading of it well before having read Schor's masterly work, I am happy to acknowledge that she went down that road before me.

Ironically, just as Emma Lazarus claimed a proprietary interest in the Newport synagogue, whose members were long dead and gone, Emma herself attained a posthumous place in American Jewish consciousness because Jews of later generations took a proprietary interest in *her*. That was not because of her "Newport" poem but because of her most famous sonnet, "The New Colossus," which she penned in 1883 as her contribution to the campaign to erect a pedestal for Frederic Bartholdi's statue, "Liberty Enlightening the World," in New York harbor. Overlooked at the time by contemporaries (Emma herself never mentioned the poem again in her brief lifetime), the poem was rescued from oblivion in 1901 by a friend, Georgina Schuyler, and in 1903 it was inscribed on a plaque inside the statue's pedestal. Thus was Liberty Enlightening the World – celebrating the shared political values of the French and American republics – transformed into Lazarus's "mother of exiles," possessing a specific resonance among the masses of immigrants who passed it while entering the United States. Thus, too, Emma Lazarus, whose passing was little remarked beyond her immediate circle of friends, earned her posthumous career as a "patron saint for American Jews."[8]

Migration

The bulk of Jewish migration to the United States took place after 1850, although its beginning phases, as we have seen, had occurred over the three previous decades, following the end of the Napoleonic Wars. Statistics for pre-1900 Jewish immigration are not always precise, but the available information has yielded some fair approximations. Germany, Austria-Hungary, and Romania predominated as sources for transatlantic Jewish migration up through the 1870s. About two-thirds of the Jews living in the United States for at least five years prior to 1890 had mothers born in Germany. Another 16 percent were from Russian- or Polish-Jewish heritage; about 10 percent had American-born parents; and 8 percent had roots elsewhere.[9] From 1870 to 1914, about 75–100,000 Jews immigrated to America from Germany. This ongoing German-Jewish influx was reflected in 1908 public school attendance figures: according to the

[8] Young, *Emma Lazarus in Her World*, p. 4; Schor, *Emma Lazarus*, pp. 185–98, 254–5; John Higham, "The Transformation of the Statue of Liberty," in *Send These to Me: Jews and Other Immigrants in Urban America* (New York: Atheneum, 1975), pp. 78–87.

[9] John S. Billings, *Vital Statistics of Jews in the United States. Census Bulletin No. 19* (Washington, DC, 1890), as cited by Barry R. Chiswick, "The Occupational Attainment and Earnings of American Jewry, 1890–1990," *Contemporary Jewry* 20(1) (1999): 68–98.

data, almost 40,000 foreign-born "Hebrew" children from Germany were registered in public schools in thirty-seven cities, especially in Baltimore, Chicago, Newark, New York, and Philadelphia.[10] ("Hebrews" was the polite term often applied to Jews, in deference to the political correctness of the age.)

The large, multinational Habsburg Empire, or Austria-Hungary, straddled much of Central, East-Central, and Southeastern Europe, and was home to a Jewish population of two million (second in size only to Imperial Russia's at that time). From 1880 to 1914 the dual monarchy was the source of about 350,000 Jewish migrants to the United States. Many were from Galicia – the ethnically mixed Polish-Ukrainian-Jewish region then under Habsburg rule – and many of these were, culturally speaking, more East European than Austro-German.[11] Another 75–80,000 migrant Jews came from Romania, and a smaller but significant contingent arrived from Greece, Turkey (predominantly its pre-1918 Balkan and Mediterranean possessions), and several Moslem countries, totaling perhaps 8,000 up to 1912, but in time growing to a community of about 50,000.[12]

Several thousand Jews from Eastern Europe had migrated to America prior to the 1880s. Indeed, some of the earliest Russian and Polish Jewish synagogues and mutual benefit societies dated back to the 1850s and 1860s, such as New York's Beth Hamedrosh Hagodol congregation,

---

[10] The Immigration Commission, *Abstract of the Report on the Children of Immigrants in Schools* (Washington, DC: Government Printing Office, 1911), pp. 12–17 (Table 1).

[11] One way of judging the proportion of Eastern European Jews among immigrants from Austria-Hungary or imperial Germany is to look at US census data on mother tongue. In 1910, foreign-born immigrants who reported Yiddish (or Hebrew) as their mother tongue, though preponderantly from Russia (838,193), also included 124,588 from Austria; 19,896 from Hungary; and 7,910 from Germany. See Daniels, *Coming to America*, pp. 217–18.

[12] Simon Kuznets, "Immigration of Russian Jews to the United States," *Perspectives in American History* 9 (1975): 39, Table 1; Walter Nugent, *Crossings: The Great Trans-Atlantic Migrations, 1870–1914* (Bloomington and Indianapolis: Indiana University Press, 1992), p. 94; Andrew Godley, *Jewish Immigrant Entrepreneurship in New York and London, 1880–1914: Enterprise and Culture* (Basingstoke: Palgrave, 2001), p. 78; Devin E. Naar, "From the 'Jerusalem of the Balkans' to the Goldene Medina: Jewish Immigration from Salonika to the United States," *American Jewish History* 93(4) (2007): 435–73; Daniel Florentin, "Hagirat yehudim sefaradim miturkiyah umin habalkan lenyu york bein hashanim 1899–1924" (Sephardi Immigrants from Turkey and the Balkans to New York 1899–1924) (PhD dissertation, Tel-Aviv University, 2008); Aviva Ben-Ur, *Sephardic Jews in America: A Diasporic History* (New York: New York University Press, 2009), pp. 33–5; Joseph M. Papo, "Sephardim in North America in the Twentieth Century," in Cohen and Peck, *Sephardim in the Americas*, pp. 267–308.

founded in 1852. In the late 1870s, of the twelve synagogues in Chicago, four were founded by and for East Europeans.[13]

Immigration to America (by all immigrant groups) accelerated in the 1880s, after the American economy recovered from the economic panic of 1873. In tandem with the overall trend, the tempo of Jewish migration also picked up. Over time, the epicenter of Jewish emigration from Europe shifted eastward. Russo-Polish Jews came to comprise nearly 80 percent of all new Jewish arrivals. Out of a population of 5 million Russian Jews, 1.5 million migrated to the US from the 1870s to 1914.

What we might call the "migration regime" of the period was favorable in many respects. Rail transport in Europe and the advent of regular transatlantic steamship traffic in the 1870s – in particular the availability of low-price steerage passage in steamers' holds – brought transatlantic migration within the means of millions of people. There were, in addition, few formal or legal barriers to surmount. Even autocratic Russia had no explicit emigration policy, though documentation of various sorts was required. Those who feared the bureaucratic whims of local officials, those unable to obtain travel permits (such as young men of military age), or others in similar straits, had recourse to illegal border crossing. Such migrants exposed themselves to various risks, including exploitation at the hands of "agents" who specialized in human traffic.[14]

Over time, as the volume of rail and shipping traffic expanded, transmigrants traveling from Eastern Europe through Germany were subjected to stricter controls, especially health checks, administered at border crossings and ports of embarkation. These were performed at the behest of the American authorities, which sought to forestall undesirable migration. Yet, although formalized procedures and controls came to prevail, the outflow of European migrants to the United States continued to grow

---

[13] Brinkmann, *Von Gemeinde zur "Community"*, pp. 283, 299–300; Judah David Eisenstein, "The History of the Russian-American Jewish Congregation – The Beth Hamedrosh Hagodol," *PAJHS* 9 (1901): 63–74. In 1869, East European Jews from Prussian-ruled Posen (today's Poznań, Poland), established their own synagogue, separate from that of the socially upscale "Bavarians," in Portland, Oregon: see Ava F. Kahn, "Western Reality: Jewish Diversity during the 'German' Period," *American Jewish History* 92(4) (2004): 455–79.

[14] Gur Alroey, *Hamahapekhah hashketah: hahagirah hayehudit meha'imperiah harusit 1875–1924 (The Quiet Revolution: Jewish Emigration from the Russian Empire, 1875–1924)* (Jerusalem: Merkaz Zalman Shazar, 2008), pp. 107–15; and "Bureaucracy, Agents, and Swindlers: The Hardships of Jewish Emigration from the Pale of Settlement in the Early 20th Century," in *Jews and the State: Dangerous Alliances and the Perils of Privilege. Studies in Contemporary Jewry*, vol. XIX, ed. Ezra Mendelsohn (New York: Oxford University Press, 2003), pp. 214–31.

and the percentage that was turned away at various points along their route remained relatively small.[15]

The favorable conditions for international migration also encouraged short-term or temporary migrants. Between 15 and 30 percent of all US immigrants made repeated round-trips and homeland visits. As much as 30 percent of some immigrant groups (and in a few cases, over 60 percent) returned permanently to their native countries. Jews, however, were notably different in that regard: only about 7 percent of Jewish immigrants, on average (12 percent among those from Habsburg lands, 6 percent for those from Russia, and 4.5 percent of those from Romania) took the homeward journey between 1908 and 1914.[16]

As long as America maintained a virtual open-door policy toward European migrants, mass Jewish immigration continued unabated, except in wartime (1914–18), and spiked again in 1919–21. In the peak years of migration, from 1899 to 1914, Jews comprised an estimated 11 percent of all new arrivals on American shores – 14 percent if we count only those immigrants who remained permanently (net migration). The enactment of national origins immigration quotas (1921 and 1924) reduced the flow of immigration, especially from Eastern and Southern Europe, to a small fraction of its former volume.

From the 1840s to the 1920s, the cumulative proportion of Jews who left Central and Eastern Europe was about one out of every three, based on the total Jewish population in those regions – a large outflow by historical standards. By comparison, the emigration rate among Italians – numerically the largest single contingent of Europeans entering America in that era – was about one in ten. Several different factors precipitated the particularly heavy flow of Jewish migration, apart from the general "pull" factors that attracted millions to America's shores:

[15] Barbara Lüthi, "Germs of Anarchy, Crime, Disease, and Degeneracy? Jewish Migration and the Medicalization of European Borders around 1900" and Nicole Kvale, "Emigrant Trains: Jewish Migration through Prussia, 1880–1914," in *Points of Passage: Jewish Transmigrants from Eastern Europe in Scandinavia, Germany, and Britain, 1880–1914,* ed. Tobias Brinkmann (New York: Berghahn Books, 2013).

[16] Kuznets, "Russian Jews," p. 40, Table 1; see also Jonathan D. Sarna, "The Myth of No Return: Jewish Return Migration to Eastern Europe, 1881–1914," *American Jewish History* 71(2) (1981): 256–68; Neil Larry Shumsky, "Let No Man Stop to Plunder! American Hostility to Return Migration, 1890–1924," *Journal of American Ethnic History* 11(2) (Winter 1992): 56–75; Ewa Morawska, "Immigrants, Transnationalism, and Ethnicization: A Comparison of this Great Wave and the Last," in *E Pluribus Unum? Contemporary and Historical Perspectives on Immigrant Political Incorporation,* ed. Gary Gerstle and John Mollenkopf (New York: Russell Sage Foundation, 2001), chapter 5.

(a) Jewish population growth: in Eastern and East-Central Europe, natural increase among Jews outpaced that of their Christian neighbors, due mainly to lower infant and child mortality rates rather than to higher fertility as such. High population growth was of particular consequence for Jews living in the Russian Empire because their areas of residence were restricted by government decrees, with the result that population density continually rose, with scant opportunity for internal migration.

(b) Scarcity of sufficient livelihoods: poverty became endemic among East European Jews by the last decades of the nineteenth century, engendered by government restraints – some of them discriminating against Jews in particular, such as restricted access to schools and professions, residential restrictions, and special taxes; as well as by the mechanization of consumer goods production, which tended to impoverish previously independent craft workers, who formed a significant occupational sector among Jews.

(c) Negative factors that encouraged Jews to emigrate also included outbreaks of mob violence against Jews in Russia, especially its southern provinces, initially in 1881, but reaching intolerable levels from 1903 to 1906.

(d) Migration was vigorously promoted by shipping firms and their agents. Some migrants, already in transit, were persuaded to move on to America by government authorities (Germany in particular actively dissuaded migrant Jews from remaining and becoming naturalized in Germany) or by Jewish charitable associations (French-, German-, and Anglo-Jewish philanthropic groups encouraged trans-migrants to continue to destinations further west). Lastly, prior migrants made it possible for an increasing number of their family members and acquaintances to follow them, thus setting in motion a chain migration process. Between 60 and 90 percent of America's Jewish immigrants (depending on the years in question) had their passage paid by relatives already settled in the United States.[17]

All told, over 2.5 million Jews immigrated to the United States before World War I, transforming American Jewry into one of the world's largest Jewish concentrations. By the late 1920s, there were approximately 4 million Jews living in the United States. They constituted about

[17] Godley, *Jewish Immigrant Entrepreneurship*, p. 71; Kuznets, "Russian Jews," Table XIII.

3 percent of the national population of 120 million and, as we have seen, they were substantially over-represented in cities and especially in major metropolitan centers, New York City in particular.

Internal Migration

The geographical world of American Jewry was also shaped by internal migration. Americans in general were frequently on the move, particularly known for their westward thrust and the steady circulation of people moving between small towns and large cities. The rapid expansion of rail connections facilitated domestic migration and resettlement. By 1860, America's 30,000 miles of track represented half the world's total. By 1890, there were 140,000 miles of railway across the country, and 200,000 miles a decade later.[18]

Railroads served as vectors for new or growing urban centers. Even smaller towns became accessible and attractive because of rail transit. Three-quarters of the towns that had Jewish communities of at least a hundred souls by the 1870s had a direct rail connection. Jews first settled in Duluth, Minnesota in 1871, a year after the arrival of the railroad, when the population numbered 3,000. The railroad arrived in Davenport, Iowa and nearby Moline and Rock Island, Illinois in 1854. Seven years later, Temple Emanuel, the first Jewish congregation in the area, was founded. In Muncie, Indiana (later to become famous as "Middletown" in the classic social study by Helen and Robert Lynd), two Jewish brothers owned a dry-goods and clothing store in 1850, in a town of 600 people. But the town's Jews increased in number mainly after 1852, when rail connections facilitated new arrivals from Chicago, Cincinnati, Cleveland, and New Orleans. Sometimes, towns located at the terminus of a rail line became, for a time, burgeoning Jewish communities, until new track was laid to points further along and trade declined at the previous termini.[19]

America's cities served as transit points, and the volume of two-way traffic into and out of cities was sometimes greater than the net increase of

[18] Albert Fishlow, "Internal Transportation in the Nineteenth and Early Twentieth Centuries," in *The Cambridge Economic History of the United States. Vol. II: The Long Nineteenth Century*, ed. Stanley L. Engerman and Robert E. Gallman (Cambridge: Cambridge University Press, 2000), pp. 562–83.

[19] Lee Shai Weissbach, *Jewish Life in Small-Town America: A History* (New Haven, CT and London: Yale University Press, 2005), pp. 39, 62–3; Daniel J. Elazar, *Cities of the Prairie: The Metropolitan Frontier and American Politics* (New York: Basic Books, 1970), p. 68; *Middletown Jews: The Tenuous Survival of an American Jewish Community*, ed. Dan Rottenberg with an Introduction by Dwight W. Hoover (Bloomington and Indianapolis: Indiana University Press, 1997), p. x.

population experienced by a given city. Native New Yorkers who moved away from the city, for example, outweighed the number of native-born Americans moving to New York City in the post-Civil War decades. One-quarter to one-third of all Bostonians in 1890 were recent arrivals of ten years' standing or less, but they barely outweighed the number of those who left. "The typical urban migrant," it has been observed, "went not to one city but to three or four (or perhaps a dozen) in the course of his wanderings."[20]

Though they often remained local residents for one or two generations, Jews, too, were an unstable population, which meant that their communities and institutions were constantly changing in character and composition. Jews often moved between different parts of the United States. Many small- to medium-sized Jewish communities burgeoned into major ones in the latter decades of the nineteenth century, but others shrank or even disappeared entirely by the turn of the century. Itinerant Jewish peddlers moved around considerably before settling down in regional urban centers. A study of Chicago's Jewish residents in 1850–70 showed that most of them had previously lived in New York, Pennsylvania, Ohio, Indiana, Virginia, California, Iowa, or Wisconsin. After the Great Fire of 1871 destroyed a third of the city, many Chicagoans moved away, including Jews (whose property losses, concentrated in and around the inner business district, were considerable). Those Jews who remained or returned totaled no more than 5,000, but they were joined by as many as 10,000 newcomers over the decade that followed.[21]

Jews in Cleveland, Ohio hailed mainly from overseas, but also included domestic migrants who had come (as either children or adults) from the East Coast or from the South. At the same time, some Jewish Clevelanders moved away to such destinations as Pennsylvania, New York, California, Nebraska, and Washington, DC. Similarly, nearly half the Jews living in Reconstruction-era Atlanta had left by 1880, and 74 percent had done

---

[20] Rosenwaike, *Population History*, p. 63; Stephan Thernstrom and Peter R. Knights, "Men in Motion: Some Data and Speculations about Urban Population Mobility in Nineteenth-Century America," *Journal of Interdisciplinary History* 1(1) (1970): 22.

[21] Amy Hill Shevitz, *Jewish Communities on the Ohio River* (Lexington: University Press of Kentucky, 2007), p. 48; Weissbach, *Small-Town America*, pp. 29, 47–9, 352–5; Weissbach, "Decline in an Age of Expansion: Disappearing Jewish Communities in the Era of Mass Migration," *American Jewish Archives* 49(1–2) (1997): 39–61; Brinkmann, *Von Gemeinde zur "Community"*, pp. 77, 261, 282; Hieke, *Jewish Identity in the Reconstruction South*, pp. 194–8. On the subject in general of Jews and peddling, see Hasia R. Diner, *Roads Taken: The Great Jewish Migrations to the New World and the Peddlers Who Forged the Way* (New Haven, CT: Yale University Press, 2015).

so by 1896. Perhaps most indicative of all, 67 percent of Russian Jewish families in New York City surveyed in 1880 could not be located again in 1890.[22]

An egregious instance of this "restlessness" was an immigrant named Julius Basinski. German-born Basinski arrived in New York in 1865, moved to San Francisco four years later, and then peddled in a circuit of Montana mining towns. After various business ventures, he shifted his interests into raising sheep, but then sold up and moved yet again: this time, to Tacoma, Washington, the northern terminus of the Northern Pacific Railroad. Late in life, he and his family moved to Portland, Oregon.[23]

Benjamin Bloomingdale, born in Bavaria, resettled in North Carolina and in Kansas before moving to New York City. There, on the Lower East Side of Manhattan, his sons, Joseph and Lyman, opened a Ladies' Notions Shop, forerunner to the uptown emporium they would one day establish under their family name. Similarly, Hungarian-born Samuel Fox immigrated to New York in 1881, and four years later moved to San Francisco. Within two years, he had relocated twice: first to Los Angeles, then to San Diego. There, he helped establish the first local synagogue and, along with several other Jewish merchants, helped obtain federal subsidies that enabled their town to be linked by rail to the transcontinental system.[24]

Jews in America were as mobile as their neighbors. That having been said, the paths of Jewish internal migration may present a distinctive pattern. Jews settled mainly in such states as New York, Pennsylvania, Ohio, and Illinois – states that experienced net losses of population in the 1870s due to the westward flow of inland migrants. Concomitantly, of the states that saw the greatest gains in population from 1900 to 1910, such as the Rocky Mountain states, Arizona, and California, only the last saw a substantial increase in Jewish population.[25]

[22] Gartner, *History of the Jews of Cleveland*, pp. 14, 16, 22; Stephen Hertzberg, *Strangers Within the Gate City: The Jews of Atlanta, 1845–1915* (Philadelphia, PA: Jewish Publication Society of America, 1978), p. 143; Weissbach, *Small-Town America*, p. 92; Thomas Kessner, *The Golden Door. Italian and Jewish Immigrant Mobility in New York City 1880–1915* (New York: Oxford University Press, 1977), p. 142.

[23] Robert E. Levinson, "Julius Basinski: Pioneer Montana Merchant," *YIVO Annual of Jewish Social Science* 14 (1969): 219–33; Elliott R. Barkan, *From All Points: America's Immigrant West, 1870s–1952* (Bloomington and Indianapolis: Indiana University Press, 2007), pp. 49–50.

[24] Eisenberg, Kahn, and Toll, *Jews of the Pacific Coast*, pp. 61, 81–2. On the decline of boom-era mining towns in the 1870s, see Nevins, *Emergence of Modern America*, pp. 138–9; see also Weissbach, *Small-Town America*, pp. 78–80.

[25] Klein, *Population History of the United States*, pp. 137–8.

Spontaneous, individual movements, driven by personal decisions and market forces (transport, commerce, manufacturing, and mining), represented just one form of Jewish population change. Significant, as well, were the efforts aimed at planned population redistribution undertaken by Jewish philanthropists and organizations. With a view toward promoting Jewish civic integration and relieving the congested tenement neighborhoods on the East Coast, an association called the Industrial Removal Office (IRO), active between 1901 and 1922, relocated nearly 80,000 Jewish immigrants further inland, dispersing them among more than 1,600 locations across the country.[26]

A similar project channeled Jewish immigrants from Eastern Europe via the port city of Bremen, Germany directly to Galveston, Texas, avoiding the East Coast ports altogether. Texas already had a large population of European immigrants (especially Germans, who were a third of the inhabitants of San Antonio and almost two-thirds of the population of Dallas). Between 1907 and 1914, between eight and ten thousand Jews, mainly from Ukraine, were admitted at Galveston and dispersed to locations throughout the West and Midwest by the Jewish Immigrants' Information Bureau (JIIB). Kansas City, Missouri, for instance, received a large number of such immigrants. Other cities that figured in this program included Sioux City, Denver, Omaha, and Los Angeles. Sometimes, however, immigrants were dissatisfied with the arrangements made for their employment or housing, and they left outlying towns for more central locations. They were also likely to move on in order to establish families, since women were only 23 percent of the total among the Galveston immigrants (compared to 45 percent among Jewish arrivals at Ellis Island in New York harbor). In one instance, a client of the JIIB, following a tip received in a letter, left Texas and made his way to Wilkes-Barre, Pennsylvania to marry the daughter of a *landsman* (fellow home-townsman).[27]

[26] Jack Glazier, *Dispersing the Ghetto: The Relocation of Jewish Immigrants across America* (Ithaca, NY and London: Cornell University Press, 1998); John Livingston, "The Industrial Removal Office, the Galveston Project, and the Denver Jewish Community," *American Jewish History* 68(4) (1979): 434–58; Gary Dean Best, "Jacob H. Schiff's Galveston Movement: An Experiment in Immigration Deflection," *American Jewish Archives* 30(1) (1978): 43–79; Marc Lee Raphael, "The Industrial Removal Office in Columbus: A Local Case Study," *Ohio History* (Spring 1976): 100–8; Weissbach, *Small-Town America*, pp. 65–9, 74–7; Gur Alroey, *Bread to Eat and Clothes to Wear: Letters from Jewish Migrants in the Early Twentieth Century* (Detroit, MI: Wayne State University Press, 2011), pp. 5, 22–3, 71, 93–9, 110–24; Alroey, *Hamahapekhah*, pp. 221–36.

[27] Bernard Marinbach, *Galveston: Ellis Island of the West* (Albany, NY: SUNY Press, 1983); Alroey, *Hamahapekhah*, pp. 221–36; Barkan, *From All Points*, pp. 76–7; Livingston, "The Industrial Removal Office."

Efforts by well-to-do veterans to divert lower-class immigrants away from central cities were not unique to the stewards of Jewish charities. In Chicago, the Irish Catholic Colonization Society (founded in 1879), worked to relocate poor Irish migrants from the Windy City to Midwestern farms. Similarly, in the 1890s, Italian-American chambers of commerce, the Italian government, and several American states made concerted efforts to disperse recent Italian immigrants to agricultural colonies across a tier of southern states from Alabama to Texas, though with relatively little success.[28]

Migrants or Refugees?

The migratory impulse in the history of American Jewry from the mid-nineteenth century to the mid-1920s differed in its ramifications from the patterns we observed for the colonial era and the early years of the Republic. The travels, marital alliances, and economic endeavors of early American Jews were thinly spun out along the Atlantic coast, throughout the Caribbean basin, and overseas to the Netherlands, Britain, or Italy. Their communities were small way-stations within a larger Atlantic network; their sojourns in those communities (as in Newport) were sometimes episodic. Although they formed nuclei for an embryonic communal life, they did not attract a great deal of attention either from other Americans or from their fellow Jews abroad.

In contrast, the scale of the population transfer that took place between Europe and America in the years after 1840, and even more so after 1870, cast American Jewish communities in an entirely different light. Attracting a steady stream of Jewish migrants from Europe as well as the eastern Mediterranean, America was no longer merely an outpost on the far western rim of European civilization. Within just a few decades, it became a focal point of Jewish interest and activity in its own right. By the eve of World War I, there were more Jews living in New York City (1.5 million) than in most other *countries*, apart from Russia and Austria-Hungary.

Moreover, Jewish migrations before the 1800s had not been channeled toward a single, predominant destination: Germany, Hungary, Italy, the Netherlands, and the Turkish Empire all figured as important areas for Jewish resettlement before the nineteenth century. In contrast, from the

---

[28] Lawrence J. McCaffrey, Ellen Skerrett, Michael F. Funchion, and Charles Fanning, *The Irish in Chicago* (Urbana and Chicago: University of Illinois Press, 1987), p. 37; Humbert S. Nelli, *The Italians in Chicago, 1880–1930: A Study in Mobility* (New York: Oxford University Press, 1970), pp. 15–17.

1840s through the early 1920s, one country – the United States – was the destination of three-quarters of all international Jewish migrants. It was the ultimate destination, too, for trans-migrants who stopped en route, chiefly in Britain, before heading to America. Jewish migrants were still apt to be found anywhere from Buenos Aires to Bombay, but America became a singularly important and dynamic venue for the transplanted Jews of the Old World. From then on, whatever happened in the United States, especially with regard to its immigration and foreign policies, would be of consequence to Jews everywhere.

It should be noted that Jews arriving from Germany, Austria-Hungary, and even from the Polish Kingdom (constituted in 1815 and ruled by the Russian tsar) and the Ottoman Empire, were not refugees. They came from countries where governments had either already adopted, or were poised to initiate, fundamental civic reforms, including guarantees of religious freedom and the gradual civil and political emancipation of Jews and other religious minorities. America was no longer, in that sense, in a class by itself, and one can conceive of a certain graded continuum between those countries and the United States, insofar as the Jews' civil status is concerned.

Therefore, the issues of social and cultural integration confronting European Jews in the mid-nineteenth century were not fundamentally dissimilar to those facing Jews in America. As early as the 1820s one could read such sentiments in the fledgling Jewish press in Central Europe as the following, published by a Jewish writer from Habsburg Bohemia: "Fellow Jews! We will live our lives in our fair country, we will serve our God, and we will obey the word of our king [...]. We will have a common covenant with the people in whose midst we dwell." Somewhat later, one of his compatriots urged upon Jewish public opinion the wisdom of just that sort of national integration, averring that "Jews have to join themselves to some other nation, for they cannot sustain themselves as a nation apart, nor do they wish to do so."[29]

Because of that agenda, Jewish public discourse was apt to be particularly self-conscious. For those Jews who came of age from the 1830s to the 1850s, it became a matter of near universal consensus – both in America

[29] Jehuda Yeiteles, in *Bikurei ha'itim* 1827, p. 40, and David Kuh in *Allgemeine Zeitung des Judenthums*, 1844, both quoted by Shmuel Hugo Bergmann, "Prague," *Kenesset* 8 (1943): 113, 114. Yeiteles's comment was made in response to the proposal by Mordecai M. Noah, the American Jewish journalist and civic figure, to found a "city of refuge" for the Jews of the world on Grand Island in the Niagara River, near Buffalo, NY. I thank Dimitry Shumsky for drawing my attention to these texts.

and in Western and Central Europe – that they and their families, along with the Jewish religion they observed and its showcase, the synagogue, ought to project an image of civic probity and patriotic virtue. They therefore employed preachers who could address them in the national language of the country; they encouraged their congregations to exhibit proper decorum during prayers; and they hired teachers to school their children in subjects of general knowledge as well as religious instruction.

In the same spirit, they constructed large synagogues in conspicuous locations that would convey the image of a dignified citizenry with an honorable stake in the public arena. Frequently, their preference was for the so-called "Moorish" (that is, vaguely Islamic or "Semitic") style of synagogue architecture that swept through the Jewish world from the 1830s to the early 1900s (see Figs. 2.2 and 2.3). In adopting such aesthetic, religious, and cultural innovations, American Jews in the nineteenth century were acting very much like other Western Jewries and were responding to the same agenda. The "Moorish" style paid homage to Judaism's pre-Christian origins while also invoking the legacy of Iberian Jewry, construed as a high point in Jewish civilization, combining worldly aesthetics with nobility of religious spirit.[30]

The heightened link between American and European Judaism was also reflected in the fact that rabbis, who until the 1840s were entirely absent from Jewish life in America, increasingly made the journey to the New World in the ensuing decades, following in the wake of multitudes of their fellow Jews. Rabbis did not necessarily displace the lay religious functionaries and lay leaders who had previously served the congregational needs of the scattered Jewish flock in North America; but they did bring a European intellectual and professional consciousness to bear on the lives of their congregations. Those European scholars, in turn, founded rabbinical academies in America that resembled their Western or Central European counterparts. American and European Jewries were thus brought into greater synchronization.

Imperial Russia was altogether different in that regard: it did not seem to be part of the Jewish cultural continuum bridging both sides of the Atlantic. In the 1860s, Russia, the country with the world's largest concentration of Jewish population, was in the process of emancipating its peasants from

---

[30] Ivan Davidson Kalmar, "Moorish Style: Orientalism, the Jews, and Synagogue Architecture," *Jewish Social Studies* 7(3) (2001): 68–100; Olga Bush, "The Architecture of Jewish Identity: The Neo-Islamic Central Synagogue of New York," *The Journal of the Society of Architectural Historians* 63(2) (2004): 180–201.

FIGURE 2.2. Dohany Synagogue, Budapest, 1859. Photo: Dr. Theodore Cohen. Beit Hatfutsot Photo Archive, Tel Aviv, courtesy of Dr. Theodore Cohen, NY.

serfdom, but it still adhered to a strict political and social regime. Jews, along with other Russian subjects, had certain legal entitlements and suffered under certain legal disabilities. In the course of the long nineteenth century (up to World War I), some of those entitlements were expanded, others retracted, while disabilities were similarly either relaxed or reinforced, as the regime's Jewry policies remained deeply ambivalent. Basic concepts of citizenship and political rights would have to wait until 1905 to be considered and partially recognized; full political emancipation – until 1917.[31]

[31] John Doyle Klier, *Russia Gathers Her Jews: The Origins of the "Jewish Question" in Russia, 1772–1825* (Dekalb: Northern Illinois University Press, 1986); Michael Stanislawski, *Tsar Nicholas I and the Jews: The Transformation of Jewish Society in Russia 1825–1855* (Philadelphia, PA: Jewish Publication Society, 1983); Benjamin Nathans, *Beyond the Pale: The Jewish Encounter with Late Imperial Russia* (Berkeley: University of California Press, 2002).

FIGURE 2.3. Central Synagogue (Ahavath Chesed), New York City, 1872. Photo: Gabor Hegyi. Beit Hatfutsot Photo Archive, Tel Aviv, courtesy of Gabor Hegyi, Hungary.

Deep and lasting damage to the social fabric of Jewish life in the Russian Empire was the result of impoverishment more than physical or religious persecution. The signs of this were evident already by the 1870s, when emigrants began slowly to ply the routes to a better life in the West. Still, there was a noticeable worsening of the Jews' physical security and civil status under the last two Romanovs, Alexander III (1881–94) and Nicholas II (1894–1917). Political incitement against the Jews flared up and mob violence occurred in 1881–2 and especially from 1903 to 1906. Those were also peak years for Russian Jewish emigration: the volume of such migrants to the US increased by nearly 20 percent, while the corresponding increase of emigrants to Palestine skyrocketed upwards by 180 percent.[32]

The depredations against Jews in Russia became a *cause célèbre* in the West and the economic privations that had preceded and accompanied them were not perceived as an independent factor. Mentally attuned as they were to the more benevolent regimes of the West, Jewish communal leaders in receiver-countries like the United States were prone to cast Jews arriving from the "despotic East" in a different light from the thousands of migrants arriving from Central Europe. The incipient signs of a mass migration of Jews from Eastern Europe were viewed (with some alarm) as a refugee emergency rather than a mere continuation or expansion of earlier migrant outflows.

It was this perspective that also fostered the idea that there were two distinct Jewish populations in America – one "German" in origin (and in fact already mostly Americanized) and the other "Polish" or "Russian." The "refugee-ism" that took root as the main Jewish approach to social welfare policy fostered a dualistic hierarchy between natives and immigrants and, in due course, laid the established Jewish communal leadership open to charges of patronizing its immigrant clientele, at best, or regarding them, at worst, as a burden or potential threat to their own status.

In October 1882, a food riot took place among Jewish inmates of a refugee shelter at New York's Ward's Island (on the East River), which the financier and philanthropist Jacob H. Schiff (1847–1920) had established. Representatives of a hastily organized relief association, the Hebrew Emigrant Aid Society (HEAS), visited the site to investigate. A few months prior to that visit, HEAS and other Jewish aid committees had met in New York and resolved to adopt a policy of supporting

---

[32] Gur Alroey, "Jewish Immigration to Palestine and the United States 1905–1925," in *Research in Jewish Demography and Identity*, ed. Eli Lederhendler and Uzi Rebhun (Boston, MA: Academic Press, 2014), pp. 28–9.

only selectively recruited, able-bodied immigrants who could be accommodated in economically rational resettlement projects – rather than be caught in the quagmire of feeding an endlessly self-perpetuating stream of charity recipients.

One of the visitors to Ward's Island in the fall of 1882 was Emma Lazarus, who several months later would so gracefully portray New York as a "golden door" open for all the "huddled masses" of the world. There is some irony in the contrast between that soaring rhetoric of welcome and her response to her visit to Ward's Island. Striking a Social Darwinist pose, Lazarus argued that an "excess of sympathy" militated against natural processes, "artificially" propping up the weak at the expense of the strong. She also recommended that the immigrant hostel dwellers perform some essential tasks (such as laundry) and thus aid in their own upkeep; that English classes be instituted for both adults and children; and that a written contract be introduced that would spell out the mutual obligations of both clientele and staff.[33]

Convinced by her recent encounters that long-term prospects for Jewish resettlement in America were relatively limited, Lazarus published a serialized, fifteen-part manifesto, entitled "An Epistle to the Hebrews," in the New York paper, *The American Hebrew*. She advocated applying the lion's share of Jewish energy and funding toward reconstituting a Jewish homeland in Palestine, which she saw as the only reasonable solution for the masses of Jews in Russia:

As long as refugees arrive here by hundreds, or even by the thousands, *up to a certain point*, a helping hand may be extended to them [...]. But the question before us is one of *millions*, and when the limit [of space available in America] is reached, [...] where shall they turn? [...] It is our duty to anticipate this calamity [...] and the only method by which it can be anticipated is by the united action of American and free European Jews, in deliberating upon the ways and means of securing the proper asylum, and contributing the sum necessary for its purchase and establishment.[34]

---

[33] *Proceedings of the Conference of Hebrew Emigrant Aid Societies and Auxiliary Committees, Representing the Various Cities of the United States and Canada, at New York, 4th June 1882. American Hebrew* XII(10) (October 20, 1882), pp. 114–15, 119–20; see also George M. Price, "The Memoir of Doctor George M. Price," *PAJHS* 47(2) (1957): 101–10 and "The Russian Jews in America," *PAJHS* 48(2) (1958): 78–133. See also Yaakov Kellner, "Mered hamityashvim berishon letsiyon be-1887 umered hamehagrim hayehudim benyu-york be-1882" (The Settlers' Rebellion at Rishon Leziyon in 1887 and the Immigrants' Revolt in New York in 1882), *Kathedra* 5 (1978): 3–29.

[34] Emma Lazarus, *An Epistle to the Hebrews*, ed. Morris U. Schappes (New York: Jewish Historical Society, 1987), pp. 44–5.

By the time that Lazarus wrote her "Epistle," the notion of a Jewish "restoration" to Palestine was by no means far-fetched. Jews had been augmenting their presence in the Ottoman-ruled province over the second half of the nineteenth century. Recent arrivals from Romania, Yemen, the Bukhara (Uzbek) region of Russian-ruled Central Asia, as well as European Russia had swelled the ranks of the polyglot, long-established Jewish population of Palestine. A Jewish agricultural school was established in 1870 at a site close to today's Holon, a southern suburb of Tel Aviv-Jaffa. In 1884, a league of "Lovers of Zion" (in Hebrew: *Hovevei tsiyon*) was organized in Russia with the purpose of supporting land purchases in Palestine and encouraging Jewish resettlement there. By the end of the century, when Theodor Herzl convened the first Zionist Congress at Basle, Switzerland (1897), Jews living in Jerusalem already represented a solid majority (62 percent) of the city's inhabitants.[35]

Yet there seemed something almost risible about Lazarus's suggestion that the continental expanse of the United States was insufficient for accommodating the number of Jews who sought to leave Eastern Europe, yet a country the size of New Jersey might absorb those millions with ease. The argument was not very prescient: two million Jews arrived in America over the subsequent decades, and they constituted only a fraction of all US immigrants from around the world. (Today, the average population density of the United States is still among the lowest in the world, ranked 179th out of 240. Israel, incidentally, is ranked thirty-second.) Lazarus's perception that there might be a *political* upper limit for Jewish immigration, however, proved correct, even though that insight jarred awkwardly with her magnanimous invitation to the world's "tired and poor." She was not a consistent political thinker and she was, evidently, caught up by the poetry of the Jews' restoration to their ancient land. But she was also convinced that refugee Jews from Europe would neither be welcomed nor would prove sufficiently adaptable to justify their wholesale reception on American shores.

In contrast to her proto-Zionist ideas, which most American Jews declined to support at the time, the bifurcation that Lazarus assumed between American strength and freedom, on the one hand, and Jewish hardship elsewhere in the world, on the other, was well within the prevailing consensus. What was at stake during the 1880s and for the subsequent

---

[35] Evyatar Friesel, *Atlas of Modern Jewish History* (New York: Oxford University Press, 1990), p. 128; Yehoshua Ben-Arieh, *Jerusalem in the Nineteenth Century*, 2 vols. (Jerusalem: Yad Izhak Ben-Zvi, 1984–6), vol. II, pp. 152–274, 466–7.

decades of large-scale Jewish migration to the United States was whether East European Jews, emerging from conditions of un-freedom and poverty, would lend strength to American Jewry or would burden the community through its association with a stigmatized, lower-class, "ghetto" population. Jewish immigrants were typically saddled with a negative popular image. Rarely were they thought of as particularly literate, let alone gifted. Many still adhered to religious practices sometimes denigrated as Old World "superstition"; conversely, others amongst them were decidedly estranged from their parents' religion and were dangerously tainted by nihilism, anarchism, or Marxism.

Mobility

The particular American Jewish dilemma captured by Emma Lazarus's misgivings reflected a broader national malaise that persisted in late nineteenth-century America. The underlying issues of governance, civil rights, and republicanism that had been part of the national debate prior to, during, and after the Civil War were not really resolved. Westward expansion and accelerated economic development had brought into the open an array of intractable divisions over the "civilizing" and "democratic" values of American institutions. The 1870s, with the economic downturn and political turmoil in America's domestic affairs of that decade, left in their wake a heightened consciousness of class differences. During the ensuing decades, there was considerable anxiety over the urban poor, social pathologies (vice, crime, alcoholism) associated with tenement districts, and the threat of political violence – starkly symbolized by Chicago's Haymarket Riot of May 1886 and the subsequent hanging of accused anarchists.

The social profile of America's Jews – which in recent memory had been so solidly mercantile – altered considerably during this period. As America industrialized, foreign Jews arriving in the country now included a large working-class element. Jews now ranged across a wider spectrum from poor to affluent: from manual laborers and barely subsisting street vendors to menial white-collar wage earners; from small business proprietors, middle-ranking managers, professionals, and real estate owners (or "speculators"), to high-powered executives and financial tycoons. Moreover, in earlier decades, when most Jewish households were based on mercantile activity, many married Jewish women had routinely been involved in family businesses or had run enterprises of their own. Now, among immigrant Jewish women – especially if they were young and single – large numbers were wage earners in factories, shops, and, eventually, as office clerical staff. Immigrant youngsters of both sexes in their early to mid-teens were most likely to find employment in factories.

Although there were grounds for solidarity and common endeavor among Jews of different social classes, as there obviously were among American Christians across different denominations and classes, there were also antagonisms that divided them. Class-based divisions among Jews encouraged the forging of cross-ethnic and non-sectarian ties with fellow workers in the form of labor unions.

Finally, beneath and alongside the legal economy there was also a seedier element, including pimps and prostitutes, protection racketeers, gamblers, and other shady operators on the fringes of the business community. There were bona fide bankers specializing in the immigrant community whose unconcern with legal and fiscal niceties eventually cost thousands of simple working people their life savings. And there were sweatshop and factory owners who engaged in unsavory practices that, at the time, were well within the letter of the law – such as operating plants that offered little or no ventilation, ignored basic fire safety precautions, and offered no sick leave or compensation for work accidents. Their egregious disregard for their employees' health and safety caused much hardship and a few severe tragedies – eventually spawning a battery of Progressive-era industrial reform legislation.[36]

Class distinctions were often represented in stereotypical, ethnic or racial terms, with entire subgroups perceived as inadequately endowed with innate ability or discipline and dangerously prone to vice, violence, and criminality. If it was common to speak of "lace-curtain" Irish and "shanty Irish" or "black Irish," the Jews divided themselves without much difficulty into "uptown" Jews and "ghetto" Jews, snobbish German Jewish "Yahudim" and uncouth "Russians."

(As late as the 1950s, some leading American sociologists still conflated ethnic labels with social and quasi-racial categories. They classified

---

[36] Jenna Weissman Joselit, *Our Gang: Jewish Crime and the New York Jewish Community, 1900–1940* (Bloomington and Indianapolis: Indiana University Press, 1983); Eugene Bristow, *Prostitution and Prejudice: The Jewish Fight against White Slavery 1880–1939* (Oxford: Oxford University/Clarendon Press, 1982); Arthur A. Goren, *New York Jews and the Quest for Community: The Kehillah Experiment 1908–1922* (New York: Columbia University Press, 1970); Harold Gastwirt, *Fraud, Corruption, and Holiness: The Controversy over the Supervision of Jewish Dietary Practice in New York City, 1881–1940* (Port Washington, NY: Kennikat Press, 1974); Rebecca Kobrin, "Destructive Creators: Sender Jarmulowsky's Bank, Financial Failure, and the Writing of American Jewish Economic History," *American Jewish History* 97(2) (2011).

Jews who acquired the habits required for successful assimilation as belonging to the so-called "Light Caucasoid" population; whereas others – those Jews whose assimilation was delayed, whose ethnic networks were thicker, and whose status was lower – were described as being relatively swarthy "Dark Caucasoids.")[37]

Yet, the complex social and class relations within the Jewish populace make it difficult to accept a starkly drawn, simply bifurcated social map of the Jewish population based on just two large ethno-linguistic subgroups (Americanized German-born or native-born English speakers on the one hand, and un-acculturated Yiddish-speakers from Eastern Europe, on the other). In the world of small manufacture and petty trade, some working-class immigrants made it into the ranks of sub-contractors, employers, and shop owners. The limitations that quasi-racial branding placed on the life chances of many Jews were, in practice, not crippling. As many studies agree, Jewish immigrants and, even more so, their children, exhibited unusually high degrees of social and occupational mobility. The typical East European Jewish immigrant at the turn of the twentieth century was able to achieve parity in income and occupational status with the average native-born American worker after about fourteen years.[38]

In their attempts to account for the success of Jewish mobility strategies, previous observers have cited two factors: widespread self-employment in the immigrant generation and the boosting of second-generation attainments via secondary and higher education. In explaining the roots of these strategies, it is tempting to enlist broad generalizations regarding Jewish "traits" and affinities, such as an "inbred" Jewish respect for learning, ostensibly absorbed via traditional religious norms. Similarly, as some have claimed, mercantile and crafts employment prior to immigration was seen as a facilitator, priming the Jews' transition into the urban American economy and promoting their long-term success.[39]

---

[37] W. Lloyd Warner and Leo Srole, *The Social Systems of American Ethnic Groups* (New Haven, CT: Yale University Press, 1945), pp. 283–96. The pertinent section of this study was republished in sociology textbooks, such as Charles F. Marden, *Minorities in American Society* (New York: American Book Company, 1952), pp. 452–3; and *American Minorities: A Textbook of Readings in Intergroup Relations*, ed. Milton L. Barron (New York: Alfred A. Knopf, 1957), pp. 434–45. Marden taught sociology at Rutgers University and Barron taught at the City College of New York.

[38] Barry Chiswick, "Jewish Immigrant Skill and Occupational Attainment at the Turn of the Century," *Explorations in Economic History* 28(1) (1991): 75.

[39] Eli Lederhendler, *Jewish Immigrants and American Capitalism, 1880–1920: From Caste to Class* (New York: Cambridge University Press, 2009), pp. 40–57.

In reviewing the relevant data, I have found that the most popular theories of Jewish upward mobility based on "culture" or other human capital advantages are plagued with preconceptions, exaggeration, and imprecision. A more careful approach would have to take into account some structural features that helped to determine Jewish economic activity in turn-of-the-century industrial America.

Heightened Workforce Participation

In America, Jewish workforce participation rates were double what they had been in Russia, partly because the working-age population predominated in the migration stream, and partly because work opportunities were more readily available in the United States. Jewish workforce participation also compared favorably with US national averages: between 1899 and 1914, the share of the Jewish immigrant population that was earning a livelihood reached 56.7 percent, at a time when the national rate stood at about 51 percent. The Jewish immigrant population, which had a younger median age (33) than was the case among other European immigrants (39), was also better able to compete over the long term in the labor market, well into the post-World War I period.[40]

The occupational profile of Jewish immigrants at the beginning of the twentieth century was unremarkable in the context of other European migrant populations. Manual and mechanical work (crafts workers, machine operators, and laborers) made up the largest sector of employment for both Jewish and non-Jewish immigrants: 58–59 percent in both cases. Relatively fewer Jews than other foreign-born Americans were employed in clerical work, agriculture, and service jobs. Jews were somewhat more involved than non-Jews in sales and in running some form of business. (The scale of these differences was modest.) According to turn-of-the-century census data, for both Jewish and non-Jewish European migrants, previous work experience had a negligible effect on either earnings or occupational

---

[40] Chiswick, "Occupational Attainment and Earnings," pp. 69 (Table 2), 75; and "Jewish Immigrant Skill," pp. 64–86; Arcadius Kahan, "Economic Opportunities and Some Pilgrims' Progress," in *Kahan, Essays in Jewish Social and Economic History*, ed. Jonathan Frankel (Chicago, IL: University of Chicago Press, 1986), p. 113; *The Immigration Commission* (1911), vol. I, pp. 352, 367, 439, 474; Robert Higgs, *The Transformation of the American Economy 1865–1914* (New York: John Wiley, 1971), pp. 116–18; Lederhendler, *Jewish Immigrants and American Capitalism*, pp. 87–8.

attainment. Income levels of American immigrants tended to follow closely the number of years they had resided in the United States.[41]

The most significant fact about Jewish immigrant participation in the labor force was not their human capital – that is, their prior work experience and their allegedly special talents or particular pursuits – but rather their transition from a pre-industrial, relatively marginalized and virtually closed ethnic labor market in Eastern Europe to a radically different American environment. As immigrants, they found work in expanding industrial branches engaged in the manufacture of mass-produced consumer goods, a core American urban sector. Those occupational niches included garment manufacture (including furriers and shoemakers), food and tobacco products, building trades (glaziers, painters, carpenters, plumbers), and printing. In these and similar economic pursuits, immigrant Jews for the first time in their lives entered into positions on a par with vast ranks of non-Jews.

Neither previously acquired skills nor entry-level opportunities at higher wages appear to have been disproportionally present in the Jewish immigrant sector. With some caution, we may propose, therefore, that the resources and strategies necessary to enhance American Jewish immigrants' social and occupational profile had other roots.

Public Education

Public education played a crucial role in promoting occupational mobility for children of immigrants. That was true for Jews, too, but this should not be overgeneralized. For the earlier decades of the mass migration period, the separate impact of schooling on employment was not particularly great, since high school education was rarely available. The picture is more complex than we might imagine, given prevailing stereotypes.

The United States Immigration Commission (1908–9) found that of the schoolchildren in nearly forty American cities surveyed, 15.7 percent of early primary grade pupils had fathers belonging to various "Hebrew" categories (German, Polish, Romanian, Russian, and other). For older grades, however, that percentage began to drop. Jewish children were 14.2 percent of the total in grammar (middle) school grades and 9.15 percent in high school. Concomitantly, the proportion of native-born American pupils *increased* from grammar school (42.76 percent)

---

[41] Chiswick, "Occupational Attainment and Earnings," p. 89, Table 2; and "Jewish Immigrant Skill," 76–7, 79; *Report of the U.S. Immigration Commission* (Washington, DC: Government Printing Office, 1991), vol. I, pp. 352, 367, 439, 474.

to high school (58 percent). The data indicate, therefore, that foreign-born children – including those from immigrant Jewish families – did not remain in the school system's higher grades in equal proportion to their younger siblings in the compulsory lower grades.

The pattern of declining numbers in the upper grades is even more pronounced when looking at the "Russian Hebrews" alone (that is, subtracting the other Jewish pupils, from German families, for instance): Russian Jewish children were 11.84 percent among primary grade pupils, 9.59 percent in the grammar school grades, and only 5.53 percent of the student body in high schools.[42]

In Chicago, for example, of the eight public schools where a significant percentage of pupils were Jewish (ranging from 20 to 93 percent), three of the schools had no seventh- or eighth-grade classes. In the schools where upper grades existed, there was a significant fall-off in registration. Dropout rates began to be significant in the fifth and sixth grades. Only 10 percent of the students reached seventh grade, and only 5 percent reached eighth grade. Work permits for youths aged 14–16 were issued to considerable numbers of "Russians" (that is, mostly Jews, since Poles and Finns from the Russian Empire were counted separately and non-Jewish ethnic Russians were few), alongside somewhat larger numbers of children from German, English, Bohemian, and Irish families. Those work permits enabled younger teens to leave school and contribute to family incomes.[43]

Thus, in foreign-born families in general (including Jewish ones), older children were apt to leave school with a sixth-grade or at best a junior high school education. However, it appears that immigrant Jewish families were more likely than families from other ethnic groups to invest in a high school education for their children: foreign-born Jews in high school were 21.75 percent of all foreign-born pupils. For the "Russians" alone, that share was 13.15 percent – just slightly above their parents' share in the immigration stream. Localized studies, such as a cross-ethnic comparison of public school students in Providence, Rhode Island, confirmed that Russian Jewish boys constituted nearly 20 percent of high school graduates, even though they were only 7 percent of that particular age cohort. Nonetheless, the same data also show that their scholastic

[42] The Immigration Commission, *Abstract of the Report*, p. 26 (Table 6).
[43] Edmund J. James et al., *The Immigrant Jew in America* (New York: B. F. Buck & Co. for The Liberal Immigration League, 1906), pp. 211–12; Nelli, *Italians in Chicago*, pp. 69–70.

performance (based on average grades) was not noticeably different from that of pupils from other ethnic backgrounds.[44]

The role of public education was no doubt considerable, but within limits. Its contribution to second-generation mobility would grow in later years.

Family and Household Structure

The foreign-born population of the United States was disproportionally male. Only 30 percent of the migrants arriving between 1889 and 1914, for example, were female. Among immigrants who remained permanently (net migration), foreign-born men still outnumbered women (61 percent to 39 percent). Among Italian immigrants, males outnumbered females three to one from the 1880s to the 1920s. The gender imbalance could sometimes go the other way: young Irish migrants (age 15–24) had been fairly evenly divided between males and females up to about 1870; but from the 1880s to the 1920s, women took an ever greater share, and by 1921 they outnumbered their male counterparts two to one.[45]

The Jewish influx exhibited a much more balanced sex ratio: about 56 percent males, 44 percent females. That gap was further reduced – 53 percent males to 47 percent females – among those who remained permanently in the United States. The importance of this factor as an enhancer of economic performance has been underestimated. A balanced sex ratio, combined with the presence of a higher than average proportion of children under fourteen, helped enormously to stabilize the Jewish immigrant household, boosted male immigrants' motivation to remain permanently in the United States, and heightened Jewish immigrant families' capacity to enter the workforce at several different skill and wage levels simultaneously. Successful economic adaptation depended, in the first instance, on remaining long enough in America to ride out short-term employment difficulties and to exercise informed judgment as to the best available residential and job options. The exceptionally high retention rate among the Jewish immigrant population was related to demographic structure and was, therefore, a significant factor in later mobility patterns.

---

[44] Joel Perlmann, *Ethnic Differences: Schooling and Social Structure among the Irish, Italians, Jews, and Blacks in an American City, 1880–1935* (Cambridge and New York: Cambridge University Press, 1988), pp. 151–3.

[45] Klein, *Population History*, pp. 132–3; Kuznets, "Russian Jews," p. 96 (Table X); Daniels, *Coming to America*, pp. 142, 194.

The demographics of the Jewish immigrant sector enabled many house-holds to enjoy more than one income. When married women moved out of factory work, they continued to earn income "on the side" in home-based activities. Their teenaged sons and daughters augmented family earnings with their factory and shop wages. Moreover, the presence of women in large numbers helped to promote quality of life in terms of food consumption, household hygiene, and disease control – all of which also tended to promote job stability. Jews in tenement districts exhibited favorable rates of recovery from serious illness. Tuberculosis, one of the great killers of that period, claimed far more lives in America as a whole (112.8 per 100,000) than among East European Jewish immigrants (71.8 per 100,000). Such patterns, in turn, had a favorable impact in lowering rates of infant and child mortality, which again had a ripple effect on later economic performance.[46]

The social and economic benefits of a stabilized sex ratio and family structure were never limited to the Jewish immigrant population alone. Increasingly, after 1900, the flow of Italian immigrants began to shed its overwhelmingly male preponderance. This lent the immigrant Italian immigration a more permanent character, helped to liberate Italian work-ing men from exploitative practices of ethnic labor recruiters (*padroni*), and facilitated processes of occupational mobility.[47] Such collateral ben-efits demonstrate that, no matter what the ethnic group, the demographic profile of the community was a significant contributor to economic welfare.

Northeastern Residential Concentration

The Jewish map, which in the antebellum era had been fairly evenly di-vided between North and South, was reshaped after the Civil War and accorded with national trends. By 1906, nearly three-fourths of American

---

[46] Susan A. Glenn, *Daughters of the Shtetl: Life and Labor in the Immigrant Generation* (Ithaca, NY and London: Cornell University Press, 1990); Deborah Dwork, "Health Conditions of the Jews on the Lower East Side of New York 1880–1914," *Medical History* 25 (1981): 1–33; Jacob Jay Lindenthal, "*Abi Gezunt*: Health and the Eastern European Jewish Immigrant," *American Jewish History* 70(4) (1981): 420–41; Michael M. Davis, Jr., *Immigrant Health and the Community* (New York: Harper and Brothers, 1921), pp. 42–69. Figures for the United States in the years from 1885 to 1915 show that infant mortality rates among Jews were about 50 percent lower than in the gen-eral population: Gretchen A. Condran and Ellen A. Kramarow, "Child Mortality among Jewish Immigrants to the United States," *Journal of Interdisciplinary History* 22(2) (1991): 223–54; see also Davis, *Immigrant Health*, p. 61.

[47] Nelli, *Italians in Chicago, 1880–1930*, pp. 65–6.

Jewry resided in New York, New Jersey, Massachusetts, Pennsylvania, and Illinois. Only 3 percent of Jewish male immigrants (and 5 percent of all European male immigrants) lived in the South, compared with 28 percent of native-born white males. The South was religiously and ethnically more homogeneous, it was far more rural, and its population was poorer. Per capita income (PCI) in the southern states in 1900 ranged from a low of $71 (North Carolina) to a high of $125 (Louisiana); whereas the states that absorbed most Jewish immigrants at the turn of the century had PCIs ranging between $254 and $257 (Pennsylvania and Illinois) and $307 and $308 (New York and Massachusetts).[48]

Clearly, statewide averages are not direct indicators of individual experience. Economic achievement and wealth were possible in the South and poverty was dire in the cities of the North. Nor do inter-regional gaps help us to account for statistical differences in mobility and achievement rates between Jewish and non-Jewish European immigrants, since both populations were substantially northern or midwestern. Nevertheless, the regional factor may help to account for the relative rapidity by which Jewish immigrants achieved occupational and income parity with native-born white males.

Along with other factors, the selective regional residential pattern may have been relevant for health care services and for the education and the job options available to members of the second-generation cohort, who were favorably positioned to maximize their opportunities.

Endogamy, Extended Support Networks, and Group Economic Behavior

Often overlooked as an economic factor, high levels of Jewish endogamy may be considered as another contributor to Jewish economic performance, insofar as close family bonds could be parlayed into support networks and employment boosters.

At the turn of the century, marriages between Jews and non-Jews were extremely rare, especially among Jews who hailed from Eastern and East-Central Europe and who inhabited densely populated urban centers. The proportion of ethno-religious mixed marriages in New York City from 1908 to 1912, for instance, was only 0.36 per hundred marriages among first-generation Russian Jewish immigrants and 3.4 per hundred among

---

[48] Meinig, *The Shaping of America*, vol. III, p. 227; Chiswick, "Jewish Immigrant Skill," pp. 70, 78; Stanford Spatial History Group, www.stanford.edu/group/spatialhistory.

TABLE 2.2. *Rates of marriage across group boundaries, New York City, 1908–12, per hundred marriages**

Ethnic group	1st generation women	1st generation men	1st generation men and women	2nd generation men and women
Jews from Russia	0.47	0.26	0.36	3.40
Jews from Germany	2.62	4.83	3.74	6.02
Jews from Austria	0.50	0.55	0.52	5.68
Northern Italians	19.68	11.89	15.73	30.57
Southern Italians	2.15	9.13	5.95	3.51
North Germans	45.61	57.08	52.04	70.58
South Germans	49.54	59.60	55.16	71.87
Poles from Russia	10.71	27.00	19.70	65.21
Irish	18.66	9.61	14.54	39.99

* Drachsler, *Democracy.*

their native-born offspring. The rates were similar among Jews from Austria and Germany (see Table 2.2). This, too, it should be recalled, is related to the nearly balanced sex ratio among Jewish immigrants. Marriages involving Jews and non-Jews were not just low in absolute terms, but also low in relation to other immigrant groups. In 1910, for America as a whole, some 10 percent of immigrant men and women wed spouses from national-origin groups other than their own, and another 10 percent married native-born Americans. In the second generation, levels of marriage outside the ethnic group reached 60 percent for men and 55 percent for women. In contrast, Jews – a religious minority as well as an ethnic group – were far more endogamous.[49]

Extensive (and nearly exclusive) marital ties within a group multiply and "thicken" close kinship networks (in-laws, uncles, cousins, etc.). Among first-generation immigrants, family or marital kinship was often the basis for business partnerships. Close family ties could also account for a degree of resilience in times of sickness, unemployment, strikes, or business failure. Given the low involvement of government agencies in social welfare at the time, the underdeveloped state of meritocratic standards in hiring, and the need to overcome obstacles such

[49] Robert McCaa, Albert Esteve, and Clara Cortina, "Marriage Patterns in Historical Perspective: Gender and Ethnicity," in *A Companion to American Immigration*, ed. Robert Ueda (Malden, MA and Oxford: Blackwell Publishing, 2006), p. 360; Julius Drachsler, *Democracy and Assimilation: The Blending of Immigrant Heritages in America* (New York: Macmillan, 1920).

as job discrimination in certain professions, family-based ethnic cohesion could – and evidently did – constitute a qualitative market asset. In turn, this often translated into work opportunities for young people. Ties bred of family networks, especially in families that ventured into small businesses, would partially explain the increase of clerical and sales jobs among second-generation Jews with East European immigrant parents.[50]

This feature of Jewish life reinforced the tendency of critics and ill-wishers to invoke the infamous "C"-word ("clannish") to describe Jewish cohesiveness. As a counterweight, apologists for the Jews sought to extract the negative freight of that epithet by presenting the matter in a more positive light. The following laudatory comments, for example, appeared in the *New York Evening Post* in 1905 to mark the 250-year anniversary celebrations of New York Jewry:

> Let it be said [...] that no section of our variegated population has ever set up a higher ideal of what the home ought to be than the Jews. [...] There is in all their relations of family life a mutual regard and respect, with a recognition of the claims of kinship, well worthy of imitation.[51]

Self-Employment

Minority status placed a premium on self-employment, since the self-employed did not risk falling prey to discrimination in hiring or promotion. Self-employment (including peddling) in the Jewish population was rather high, with estimates ranging between 18 and 25 percent in New York and other major cities in the 1880s and 1890s, and increasing to between 34 and 38 percent in 1910–20. The economic rewards of self-employment in petty trade or small-scale manufacturing were in most cases quite modest, as such income was only marginally better than income from industrial wages. East European Jewish entrepreneurs in Baltimore, for instance, were not considered properly middle-class: socially invisible, they ranked far below those establishments that merited a listing in that city's business directories.[52]

---

[50] Chiswick, "Occupational Attainment and Earnings," p. 89, Table 2.
[51] "Jewish Idealism," reprinted in *PAJHS* 14 (1906): 214–15.
[52] Kahan, "Economic Opportunities," pp. 109–10; Godley, *Jewish Immigrant Entrepreneurship*, p. 59; Nathan Glazer, "Social Characteristics of American Jews," in Finkelstein, *The Jews*, vol. II, pp. 1702, 1707; Chiswick, "Occupational Attainment and Earnings," p. 89, Table 2; Eleanor S. Bruchey, *The Business Elite in Baltimore: 1880–1914* (New York: Arno Press, 1976), cited by Aaron M. Glazer, "Entrepreneurship

Social considerations, however, as well as the entrepreneurial culture of American business life, may have tipped the balance in favor of aspirations for self-employment. Comparative analysis shows that there was more entrepreneurial activity among Russian Jewish immigrants in New York, despite falling profits from small business, than was true among their counterparts in London, where profits were rising. In America more immigrants were willing to risk self-employment (and business failure) for far less remuneration. Jews in America had absorbed a different commercial ethic from their new surroundings, where risk was socially acceptable and class mobility a bit more flexible.[53]

Low- or middle-level entrepreneurship associated with immigrant life could be observed in sectors other than business and manufacturing. Ownership of real estate, for example, became a noticeable track for upwardly mobile immigrants who bought up tenement buildings in the neighborhoods where they lived. A 1914 canvass of Philadelphia slum housing, for examples, found that Jews and Italians were the most widely represented groups among local tenement owners. Twenty-seven percent of the city's tenements were actually inhabited by their owners. Of the two groups, however, Jews were more apt than Italians to buy property outside their immediate ethnic environment.[54]

Entrepreneurship did not necessarily remain at the small business level. Simon Kuznets, the Nobel laureate in economics, once pointed out that minority group members sometimes reap structural advantages when they gravitate toward newly founded or newly expanding branches of the economy, in which other people are not already well entrenched. Subsequent development in those branches make it possible for a significant sub-group of immigrants to climb vertically within such sectors, or to move from one to the other while continuing to "network" within their own ethnic niche.[55]

Those who fit this description included Jews who worked in apparel manufacture and sales, dealt in scrap metal and other industrial waste

among Eastern European Jewish Immigrants in Baltimore, 1881–1914" (MA thesis, The Johns Hopkins University, [n.d.]), p. 27.

[53] Godley, *Jewish Immigrant Entrepreneurship*, pp. 14–15, 59, 107, 109–11.

[54] John F. Sutherland, "Housing the Poor in the City of Homes: Philadelphia at the Turn of the Century," in *The Peoples of Philadelphia: A History of Ethnic Groups and Lower-Class Life, 1790–1940*, ed. Allen F. Davis and Mark H. Haller (Philadelphia, PA: Temple University Press, 1973), pp. 175–201.

[55] Simon Kuznets, "Economic Structure and Life of the Jews," in *The Jews: Their History, Religion, and Culture*, ed. Louis Finkelstein (Philadelphia, PA: Jewish Publication Society of America, 1966), vol. II, pp. 1602–3.

materials, entered such new media as radio and the film industry, or specialized in new commodities. One notable case was that of Samuel Zemurray, an immigrant from Kishinev (then in the Bessarabian province of the Russian Empire, today in Moldova). Zemurray was working as a dock-worker in Mobile, Alabama when he took a bunch of ripening bananas languishing in the port, sold them to grocers, and went on eventually to found the United Fruit Co., a Central American-based plantation empire – the "largest privately owned agricultural domain in the world" (and the original model for the "banana republic" style of political exploitation and corruption).[56]

The "Russian" Factor

The two-sidedness of the Jewish immigrants' position in the American economy around the turn of the twentieth century thus begins to emerge. On the one hand, there were specific characteristics that set them apart not just from native-born Americans but also from some other immigrant groups. These characteristics included a more pronounced regional concentration; higher levels of endogamy; a moderately higher level of investment in public schooling for older children; a high level of self-employment; and a higher-than-average presence of women in the immigrant stream, which correlated with household stability, quality of life, and sustained residence in the United States. On the other hand, in America a sizeable industrial Jewish working class took shape, which at one point represented as much as 65 percent of first-generation Jewish immigrant households. There may be much to learn, therefore, by looking at the Jewish immigrant experience from the point of view of labor history.

Jews, as noted, were able to achieve job status and income parity with average American working people within a dozen years or so after immigration. In part, as we have seen, there were structural reasons that might account for that; but an additional factor that may have helped was the widespread recruitment of Jewish workers to labor unions. Unlike many native-born American skilled workers who organized themselves into craft-based professional unions in order to raise wages, and whose ranks were jealously controlled and kept exclusive, immigrant workers were swept up into large industrial unions that organized all employees on a plant-wide basis and fostered the mass organization of entire

---

[56] Howard M. Sachar, *A History of the Jews in America* (New York: Knopf, 1992), pp. 344–5.

industries. That meant that co-ethnic ties, so important at the family or neighborhood level, were both instrumental in labor recruitment but also – crucially – secondary to common economic struggles. Immigrants, once organized, were in a less dependent position, vis-à-vis employers, and over time were able to win more favorable contracts, better working conditions, a shorter work week, and an hourly wage in place of piece-work. The standards of economic independence and equity demanded by veteran American craft workers were thus adapted and absorbed within the framework of immigrant-dominated industrial unionism.

The typical Jewish immigrant did not arrive in America with a modern, working-class outlook. In Russia and Poland there were, of course, Jewish factory workers, but they were relatively few, compared with the far greater numbers of menial craftsmen in one-man shops, as well as the legions of petty tradesmen and those chronically out of work. In Eastern Europe, Jews' job profiles had set them apart from the vast majority of their neighbors, who were peasant villagers. Having made it to America, however, Jews readily took up positions in growing industries alongside millions of non-Jews working in the same manufacturing branches. Americanization in the economic sense meant integration into large-scale industries, occupational parity with non-Jews, and ways of earning a living that were fairly stable and offered some chance for advancement.[57]

These features provided the kind of economic and social leverage that was virtually unknown in the "old country." The "Russian" factor, then, may be a misnomer: migration to an urban, industrial center like America made it possible for the co-ethnic solidarity among Jewish workers to expand and to metamorphose into labor union loyalties, improved wages, and the adoption of democratic (small "d") social values.

The "German" Factor
East European Jewish immigrants around the turn of the twentieth century did, nevertheless, have one group-specific feature that must be taken into account: their link (however tenuous) to an established group of middle- and upper-middle-class Americans: namely, the native-born and "German"-Jewish business class and its communal leadership, headed by financier-philanthropists. German-American Jewish businesses were among the first to offer employment to Jewish immigrant men, women, and adolescents.

[57] Lederhendler, *Jewish Immigrants and American Capitalism*, pp. 6–7, 30–5, 66–79.

The posture of "German"-Jewish communal establishment figures vis-à-vis their poor cousins has already been referred to: the initial organizational work that was done to provide immediate relief; the subsequent misgivings that were voiced regarding the scale of the Jewish refugee influx; and the attempts to divert some of the migrants away from "ghetto" districts in cities along the eastern seaboard.

In fact, however, the infrastructure for a Jewish welfare establishment was much more far-reaching than that, and in very short order it also included a number of supporters and staff from among the more well-established of the East Europeans. The battery of Jewish social services included hospitals and health-care sanitariums under Jewish sponsorship; settlement houses, visiting-nurse services, and fresh milk distribution to mothers of young children; direct subsidies to the sick and the poverty stricken, as well as loan societies that circulated small sums to households and petty tradespeople for little or no interest; English language and American civics classes and popular lectures for working adults; playgrounds in tenement districts and fresh-air funds to provide brief summer respites in the country for urban ghetto children; vocational and technical training programs for boys and girls and boarding schools for orphans (which typically served indigent families generally). Guided as much by instincts of self-preservation as by progressive social thought (indeed, bearing some resemblance to church-based "social gospel" initiatives), this veritable "war on poverty" created a crucial welfare basket – a fair portion of which went toward non-sectarian social services – well ahead of the advent of the welfare state.[58]

Surprisingly, the well-heeled Jewish communal establishment even provided legal advice and representation to those immigrants most likely to become a burden: those who were detained at Ellis Island for suspected ill health or who, for other reasons, were candidates for deportation. By standing up on behalf of these weakest candidates for entry into the country, who were potential liabilities in both material and social terms, representatives of established Jewish groups offered critical support that appreciably reduced the actual number of Jewish deportees (Fig. 2.4).[59]

---

[58] Herman D. Stein, "Jewish Social Work in the United States, 1654–1954," *American Jewish Year Book* 57 (1956): 18–44; Shelly Tenenbaum, *A Credit to Their Community: Jewish Loan Societies in the United States 1880–1945* (Detroit, MI: Wayne State University Press, 1993); Jenna Weissman Joselit, *Lending Dignity: The First One Hundred Years of the Hebrew Free Loan Society of New York* (New York: Hebrew Free Loan Society, 1992).

[59] Zosa Szajkowski, "The Yahudi and the Immigrant: A Reappraisal," *American Jewish Historical Quarterly* 63(1) (1973): 13–44.

FIGURE 2.4. Immigrants lined up for entry to the United States at Ellis Island. Photo: Edwin Levick. New York Public Library Digital Collection: Photographs of Ellis Island 1902–1913. Image title: The Pens at Ellis Island, Main Hall.

"Ours is the era of social service," said Boris Bogen (1869–1929), a Russian Jewish immigrant and settlement worker who played a pivotal role in the professionalization of Jewish charity services in America. Writing in 1917, Bogen summed up his credo: "Society is beginning to realize its responsibility for the care of those who have been cast out of the human mill." Sectarian philanthropic impulses were thus translated into a broad, civic vision: "The waste of society is being reduced [by virtue of our intervention] to a minimum." Within that framework, sectarian Jewish social service agencies were neither separatist nor assimilationist, but rather focused upon maintaining "the positive characteristics" of the Jewish clients' human and ethno-religious individuality – "the guarantee of their good citizenship."[60]

It was all, of course, perfectly imperfect: hierarchical, sometimes bureaucratically rigid and insensitive, and slow to regard the clients of the system as endowed with positive cultural resources of their own. However, considering that comparatively little was spent on direct welfare payments

[60] Boris Bogen, *Jewish Philanthropy: An Exposition of Principles and Methods of Jewish Social Service in the United States* (New York: Macmillan, 1917), p. 1.

and that a great deal more went toward educational, health-care, and other professional services, it was a support system that subsidized the poor while seeking to avoid subsidizing dependency. Without the social services thus provided, we may well speculate that Jewish immigrant adjustment and upward mobility would have followed a longer, slower curve.

Secularization

One of the hidden intangibles that may have influenced the occupational mobility of some Jewish immigrants and, in particular, the educational and professional advancement of their children, was the religious disparity between Jews and those closest to them in social origins – fellow foreign-born or foreign-stock Southern and Eastern Europeans and Irish Americans – the vast majority of whom were Catholics.

Sometimes, Jews' employment and advancement was unfavorably affected by religious discrimination. Yet, at the same time, not being Christian – and in particular, not being Catholic – could also be a hidden advantage. The Church, after all, was a centralized, hierarchical institution with the ability to exert a certain degree of social control among its adherents. The Jews' communal life was extremely decentralized by comparison. By extension, their individual progress was left relatively unmonitored and uninhibited by religious institutions and religious mores. There was no Jewish equivalent of the bishop or diocesan office, and no strong network of parochial schools in the Jewish community, as did exist among Catholic communities. Habits of social conservatism, aligned with Church-inflected values and teachings, were noticeably weakened among the majority of Jews and less frequently articulated by public figures. Such residual conservatism as did permeate Jewish lives in the parental immigrant generation (particularly in the realm of sexual and marital mores) was relatively easily overturned by youthful rebellion. Indeed, it has been suggested that Jewish parents were tacit collaborators in their children's rebellion against the constraints of tradition, hierarchy, and Old World notions of decorum.[61] This may have

---

[61] On the proactive stance of Catholic bodies and Italian immigrants, vis-à-vis enhancing the structural and cultural integrity of immigrant church communities, see Silvano M. Tomasi, *Piety and Power: The Role of the Italian Parishes in the New York Metropolitan Area, 1880–1930* (New York: Center for Migration Studies, 1975), pp. 117–68, 178–83. Catholic pastors' estimates of attendance at Sunday Mass may be accurate or not, but as a general indicator, the percentages they cite of between 40 and 70 percent average attendance (pp. 137–8) appear to be roughly double the average Jewish attendance at Sabbath services on a weekly basis. On Vatican influence and the role of the Church in

put greater independence into the hands of individuals and families – a greater willingness to move on, even at the expense of leaving old neighborhoods.

Further, Jews exercised a more pronounced individualism in family decision-making, with virtually no input from clergy. That applied to such crucial matters as the planning of family size, the spacing of births, the choice of schools, and the abandonment of immigrant neighborhoods for greener pastures. Talented Jewish sons and daughters were not recruited into celibate religious avocations (as was the case among Catholics). These "soft" or psycho-social effects, which may collectively have reinforced a secularizing trend among rank-and-file Jews and their offspring, have not been thoroughly researched, but their economic ramifications – including risk-taking and enterprise as well as intensive investment in smaller numbers of children – may have had some long-term significance.

Rural America: Jews Imagining Nativity

Although Jews were one of the most urbanized elements in American society, some Jews, including those who were born and raised in small towns, were bound to reflect on the contrasts between rural and city life. Such encounters bore the deep impress of revered American traditions along with some less savory impressions about social discomfort and marginalization.

We encounter such a case in the writer Edna Ferber (1885–1968), author of *Show Boat*, *So Big*, and other popular works of her day. Ferber spent her early childhood years in Ottumwa, Iowa – a town of moderate size, located amidst farms and coal mines. Writing her memoirs in New York in the early 1940s, Ferber remembered Ottumwa as possessing "all the sordidness of a frontier town with none of its picturesqueness [...] unpaved, bigoted, anti-Semitic, undernourished, [where] there were seven murders one year, and no convictions." Yet, she also said, "Those Ottumwa years were more enriching, more valuable than all the fun and luxury of the New York years."[62]

debates over American and modern values at the turn of the century, see Jay P. Dolan, *The American Catholic Experience* (Garden City, NY: Doubleday, 1985), pp. 298–303, 315–20. On autonomy, liberalism, and the individual, see John T. McGreevy, *Catholicism and American Freedom: A History* (New York and London: W. W. Norton, 2003), pp. 49, 53, 127–57, 196.
[62] Edna Ferber, *A Peculiar Treasure* (New York: Doubleday, Doran and Co., 1944), pp. 2, 31, 37, 38, 42, 50, 393.

Such contrasting images – town and country, bitterness and nostalgia, open vistas and stunted perspectives, limits and freedom – were ripe for the poetic imagination. Here, for instance, are the words of poet Alter Brody (1895–1981), a young New York immigrant, writing around the time of World War I, describing the space outside his bedroom window:

> Walls and windows and clothes lines
> Wherever you look [...]
> Sometimes there is a moon
> And some stars,
> In that square piece of heaven
> That the walls cut out.
> It's a little piece to have
> But a good enough sample to see –
> People are spoiled
> Getting the whole sky to look at
> Every time they choose.[63]

A few years later, another immigrant poet, Israel Jacob Shvarts (1885–1971), limned the social and physical landscape of a different America in a Yiddish verse epic, entitled *Kentucky*. Shvarts's ballad of the modern South was replete with images of blacks and whites, Jews and non-Jews, Biblical allusions, traces of the land's aboriginal inhabitants, and snatches of gospel songs ("*Oy Miriam, veyn nit mer*" – "Oh, Mary don' ya weep").

In *Kentucky*, Shvarts portrayed a Jewish itinerant peddler, "Joe," who – following a shotgun wedding with a local farmer's daughter – has become a tiller of the soil. Joe experiences an American epiphany. Following a visit to the local town, he finds that he has lost any hankering for the bustle of town life. He dismisses the local Jewish shopkeepers' invitations to sit and drink with them:

> He knew they would snicker behind his back.
> They would pass judgment on his Christian wife and his household. [...]
> What did he care? [...]
> Without realizing it, he'd become part of the soil,
> As if he'd been rooting there [...].
> Only now did he begin to grasp the potency, the truth [...]
> And the tranquil greatness of
> "My old Kentucky home" and "Old Glory."[64]

[63] Alter Brody, "From the Third Story Window," in *A Family Album and Other Poems* (New York: B. W. Huebsch, 1918), pp. 39–50.
[64] I. J. Shvarts, *Kentucky*, trans. Gertrude W. Dubrovsky (Tuscaloosa: University of Alabama Press, 1990), pp. 216–17.

Shvarts lived in Lexington, Kentucky, a small city with 55,000 people when he moved there in 1918. During Shvarts's lifetime, Lexington nearly quadrupled in population. His poetic landscape of farms and bluegrass, of twilight sounds of neighing horses and wafting notes of banjo music and black voices was very much a town-dweller's pastoral idyll. To the rest of the Yiddish literary community in America, however, Shvarts's view from the hinterland looked like the "real McCoy." Shmuel (Charney) Niger (1883–1955), a leading Yiddish literary critic, opined that *Kentucky* represented something novel in Yiddish letters: "We have had such names in Yiddish books as 'East Broadway' or 'New York,' but East Broadway became Yiddish-country long ago and New York, after all, isn't exactly America ... Kentucky is America!" Here at last was a poem that "we can show our [American-born] children," because it was written in a major – not a minor – key: free of the mordant tones that marked so much of modern Yiddish literature.[65]

Shvarts, however, had more at stake than just the representation of a free people's relaxed mentality. He invested the landscape itself with a moral dimension. Thus, "Joe" not only experiences a release from the emotional bondage of the peddler's life and the mean-spirited pecking order of town life, but also achieves a veritable salvation, cleansed of every transgression (sexual and religious) by virtue of his labor on the soil.

To fully appreciate this facet of the American Jewish imagination, we need to briefly revisit its Old World background. A small fraction of European Jewry lived by growing crops or animal husbandry. More often, Jews were embedded in the rural economy as processors or refiners of agricultural or forest produce: they engaged in dairying, flour milling, timber and the lumber trade, distilling grain for alcoholic beverages, beetroot sugar refining, tanning leather, or bristle-making. The Russian government offered incentives in the early nineteenth century to encourage the establishment of Jewish farm colonies, with modest results. By the 1890s about 5 percent of the Jews in White Russia (Belarus), Lithuania, and Ukraine were engaged in agricultural work. The southern and southwestern provinces (Ukraine), where the bulk of Jewish farmers lived,

[65] Shmuel Niger, *Yidishe shrayber fun tsvantsikstn yorhundert (Yiddish Writers in the Twentieth Century)*(New York: Yidisher Kultur Kongres, 1973), vol. II, p. 141. The review of *Kentucky* was first published in 1925. Shmuel Niger was the brother of Baruch (Charney) Vladeck, the New York socialist political activist.

also supplied the greatest share of Jewish emigrants who resettled on American farms.[66]

The Jewish "back to the soil" movement enjoyed the support and organizational backing of major philanthropists on an international scale. Charitable foundations established in France, Britain, and Germany – such as the *Alliance Israélite Universelle* (AIU, founded in Paris, 1860), the Jewish Colonization Association (established in 1891 by Baron Maurice de Hirsch [1831–96], and known by its acronym ICA [pronounced "Eeka"]); Baron Edmond de Rothschild (1845–1934); and the *Hilfsverein der Deutschen Juden* (founded 1901, also known by its Hebrew name, "*Esra*") – all were involved in promoting agricultural and technical training, land-purchase, and organized farm settlement. Their activities fanned out across Russia, Argentina, Canada, the United States, and then Ottoman-ruled Palestine. The philanthropic establishment saw this as a way to deliver on its civic commitments, and in particular to promote Jewish social integration.[67]

Apart from the philanthropists, small bands of radical Jewish students in Russia and Ukraine also touted farming as a Jewish cause. They were influenced by Russian *narodnik* (populist) ideology which promoted an idealistic cult of peasant life. The fundamental crisis of modern life, they believed, was that "nature" and "culture" were pitted against each other. Only a grand, new synthesis could bring society back into harmony with nature. An agrarian life, based on communal sharing and equality (including sexual equality), appeared to offer that kind of secular salvation.

In the early 1880s, in the wake of the first wave of anti-Jewish pogroms that rocked southwestern Russia and Ukraine, student-idealists and the philanthropists formed an unlikely partnership. While some set their sights on Palestine, others organized themselves under the Hebrew name, *Am oylom* ("the universal/eternal nation"), and looked to America

---

[66] Mordecai Zalkin, "Hakla'ut vehakla'im bamerhav hatarbut hayehudit-halita'it" (Farming and Farmers in the Cultural Realm of Lithuanian Jewry), *Zion* 77(4) (2012): 531–43; Kuznets, "Immigration of Russian Jews," pp. 73–4; Israel Bartal, "Farming the Land on Three Continents: Bilu, Am Oylom, and Yefe Nahar," *Jewish History* 21 (2007): 249–50, 252; Ellen Eisenberg, *Jewish Agricultural Colonies in New Jersey 1882–1920* (Syracuse, NY: Syracuse University Press, 1995), pp. 117–22; Robinson, "Agricultural Activities of Jews in America," p. 38.

[67] Derek Penslar, *Shylock's Children: Economics and Jewish Identity in Modern Europe* (Berkeley and Los Angeles: University of California Press, 2001), pp. 107–22, 195–216; Ellen Eisenberg, "Cultivating Jewish Farmers in the United States and Argentina," in *Transnational Traditions*, ed. Kahn and Mendelsohn, pp. 212–29.

as the ideal site for fulfillment of their agrarian-collectivist ideals. With the help of sympathetic backers, these sincere but woefully inexperienced young people hired themselves out initially as farm hands in the country-side near New York City, while others went further afield, attempting to establish their own communes: Sicily Island, Louisiana; Bethlehem-Judea and Crémieux (named for Adolphe Crémieux [1796–1880], a French Minister of Justice and a leader of the AIU), both of which were in South Dakota; New Odessa, in Oregon; and several sites in Kansas (named Beersheba, Hebron, Montefiore, Touro, and Gilead), as well as a few in California, Texas, and Iowa.[68]

Most of these homesteads were wiped out by drought, floods, and disease-bearing mosquitoes. Others languished fitfully for several years until their members dispersed. In 1891, for example, twelve immigrants from Russia set up a colony called Palestine in Bad Axe, Michigan, where they held out against crop failure and indebtedness for nearly nine years before the colony disintegrated. One Jewish colony was established in Arpin, Wisconsin, northeast of Milwaukee, in 1904. The colony was reduced by setbacks in 1911, but held its own until the mid-1920s. "The children left for the cities – and the parents followed, one by one."[69]

Some particularly rugged individuals managed against all odds to scratch out an existence in the most unlikely places:

We arrived to North Dakota to a little town, Devils Lake and there my boy-friend's older brother waited for us to take us home. That means to the farm. [...] We broke out of the tall grass into a cleared space, and I beheld [our shack],

[68] George M. Price, "The Russian Jews in America," *Publications of the American Jewish Historical Society* 48(2) (1958): 78–100; Eisenberg, *Jewish Agricultural Colonies*, pp. 25–58, 61–89; Robinson, "Agricultural Activities of Jews in America," pp. 57–62; Lavender and Steinberg, *Jewish Farmers of the Catskills*, pp. 15–20; Joseph Brandes, *Immigrants to Freedom: Jewish Communities in Rural New Jersey since 1882* (Philadelphia, PA: Jewish Publication Society, 1971), pp. 18–19, 23–32, 43–50; Elias Tcherikower, "Revolutsyonere un natsyonale ideologyes fun der rusish-yidisher inteligents" (Revolutionary and National Ideologies among the Russian-Jewish Intelligentsia), and Abraham Menes, "Di 'am-oylom' bavegung" (The Am Oylom Movement), both in *Geshikhte fun der yidisher arbeter-bavegung in di fareynikte shtatn* (*History of the Jewish Labor Movement in the United States*), ed. Elias Tcherikower (New York: Yivo Institute, 1945), vol. II, pp. 138–202 and 203–38, respectively; Jonathan Frankel, *Prophecy and Politics: Socialism, Nationalism, and the Russian Jews, 1862–1917* (Cambridge: Cambridge University Press, 1981), pp. 90–97, 121–2. See also Harris Rubin, "Worker on the Land," *American Jewish Archives* 33(1) (1981): 18–28.

[69] Louis J. Swichkow, "The Jewish Agricultural Colony of Arpin, Wisconsin," *American Jewish Historical Quarterly* 54 (1964–5): 82–91; Holly Teasdle, "Jewish Farming in Michigan," *Michigan Jewish History* 42 (2002): 3–6.

twelve-by-fourteen [...], not only lacking a floor but roofless as well. [...] Dear God, I thought, whatever your reason, haven't I suffered enough in my nineteen years to pay for the rest of my life?[70]

The percentage of American Jewish immigrants whose declared occupation was agriculture rose from 1.6 to 3.9 percent between 1899 and 1914, and stabilized around 3 percent from 1920 to 1924.[71] The more successful ventures in Jewish farming were located in the east, close to large urban markets (chiefly Camden, Philadelphia, and New York City), where they catered to city dwellers' demand for fresh produce, eggs, and dairy products. Cultivation of cash crops such as strawberries and grapes – the latter often going for the kosher wine trade – was augmented with canneries and small manufacturing workshops. One report on Jewish farms in southern New Jersey, written in 1905, combined hyped rhetoric with an appreciation for the hardships of farming and a hard-headed appraisal of business practices:

With an enthusiasm that often amounted to a creed, men from different walks of life worked side by side, dreaming of the regeneration of a race too long excluded from the field and the forest. [Colonies called] Alliance, Carmel, Rosenhaym, and finally Woodbine grew [...].When the poor, wild soil did not yield what it could not yield, when willing hands failed to find work that would help fill the bread basket, and when the aid of charity had to be invoked; there was little sunshine to cheer the dismal gloom. [...] The survival of the four colonies is due to the establishment of factories.[72]

Dairying and poultry, boarding house, and guest house businesses were the mainstays of independent Jewish farmers located northwest of New York City in the Catskills, in Ulster and Sullivan Counties. These families formed associations, and by 1910, there were ten of these in the lower Catskills, with memberships ranging from a few dozen to over a hundred. These networks were based on dairy cooperatives, a fire insurance cooperative, health insurance, literary societies, and synagogues.

[70] Rachel Bella Calof, *Rachel Calof's Story: Jewish Homesteader on the Northern Plains*, trans. Jacob Calof, ed. J. Sanford Rikoon (Bloomington and Indianapolis: Indiana University Press, 1995), pp. 22, 26, 29. A recent scholar has noted the varnished and dramatized American version supplied by Jacob Calof's English rendition of the Yiddish original. I have included two lines from the original. See Kristine Peleg, "The Original Text of Rachel Calof's Memoir," *American Jewish History* 92(1) (2004): 108.
[71] Kuznets, "Immigration of Russian Jews," p. 102.
[72] *The Russian Jew in the United States*, ed. Charles S. Bernheimer (Philadelphia, PA: John C. Winston Co., 1905), pp. 376–9; see also Brandes, *Immigrants to Freedom*, pp. 50–72, 75–99, 145–69; Eisenberg, *Jewish Agricultural Colonies*, pp. 90–159.

Meetings were "occasions for picnics, festivals and other social gatherings for the wives and children of the Jewish farmers."[73]

A New York-based agency, the Jewish Agricultural Society – a mainstay
of this population – provided over 7,400 loans (totaling $4.73 million)
to Jewish farmers in thirty-nine states and Canada between 1900 and
1924. The Chicago-based Jewish Agriculturalists' Aid Society assisted in
settling over 400 Jewish farmers between 1900 and 1908 throughout the
Midwest, the Mountain states, and the Pacific Northwest. In 1910 it was
estimated that there were 3,000–5,000 Jewish farm families in America,
and by 1925 about 10,000 families, totaling some 50,000 individuals, or
somewhat over 1 percent of the American Jewish population.[74]

Entering the Public Arena

As befitted a large and diverse population subdivided by region, social
class, country of birth, and religious outlook, Jews in the United States
did not have a unified political position in the late nineteenth and early
twentieth centuries. Many of the foreign-born among them were not yet
naturalized and were therefore ineligible to vote. Women, of course, did
not yet have voting rights, although many were active in public affairs in
various other ways: grassroots social organizations, settlement houses,
spontaneous expressions of solidarity with those in need, trade union
membership, and in some prominent cases, major ventures in period-
ical publication and leadership of national, representative women's
organizations.[75]

---

[73] Lavender and Steinberg, *Jewish Farmers of the Catskills*, pp. 31–83; Herman J. Levine
and Benjamin Miller, *The American Jewish Farmer in Changing Times* (New York: The
Jewish Agricultural Society, Inc., 1966), p. 74.

[74] Gabriel Davidson, *Our Jewish Farmers and the Story of the Jewish Agricultural Society*
(New York: L. B. Fischer, 1943), p. 35; Levine and Miller, *The American Jewish Farmer*,
p. 21; Robinson, "Agricultural Activities of Jews in America," pp. 76–100; Bogen, *Jewish
Philanthropy*, pp. 128–9; *The Jewish Agricultural Society, Inc. Report for the Period
1900–1924* (New York: Jewish Agricultural Society, Inc., 1924), pp. 18–19; J. Sanford
Rikoon, "The Jewish Agriculturalists' Aid Society of America: Philanthropy, Ethnicity,
and Agriculture in the Heartland," *Agricultural History* 72(1) (1998): 8; Louis Rosenberg,
Canada's Jews: A Social and Economic Study of the Jews in Canada (Montreal: Bureau
of Social and Economic Research, Canadian Jewish Congress, 1939), p. 226.

[75] See Philip J. Ethington, *The Public City: The Political Construction of Urban Life in
San Francisco, 1850–1900* (Berkeley and Los Angeles: University of California Press,
2001 [orig., New York: Cambridge University Press, 1994]) on the role of women in
the emergence of an expanded urban political public domain in the late nineteenth century: pp. 209–10, 327–36, 355–400.

Yet, as variegated as they were in their political affinities, they were, like other Americans, influenced by the nation's political trends. At the end of World War I there were six Jews in the US House of Representatives. Four were Republicans; one – Chicago's Adolph Joachim Sabath – was a Democrat; and one, New York City's Henry M. Goldfogle (1856–1929), a Tammany man, was on this occasion backed by both major parties. On Goldfogle's home turf, the New York County (Manhattan) Republican Party had a Jewish chairman in the 1890s – Edward Lauterbach. Another Jewish Republican, Samuel Koenig, a Hungarian-born clothing salesman, was New York's Secretary of State in 1909–10 and Republican Party chairman in New York County (1911).[76]

What Republicanism represented at that time was in flux. Toward the end of the nineteenth century, Lincoln's party became the base of an emergent cadre of politicians from the professional middle class, with links to government reform platforms of various sorts. The "GOP" had at various times accommodated a range of progressive positions (such as anti-trust and anti-monopoly legislation and anti-child labor laws) alongside conservative economic and monetary (gold standard) policies. Its business and political elites backed "an ideology of merit and efficiency," and were allied with the Progressive movement.

The Republicans trumpeted their historical record as the party of Lincoln, urged equal justice for black Americans and an end to statutes that violated the letter and spirit of the Thirteenth, Fourteenth, and Fifteenth amendments to the Constitution. In a reference to discrimination against US Jewish citizens by foreign governments – Russia was the culprit, though it was not named – the GOP pledged itself "to insist upon the just and equal protection of all our citizens abroad." (The topic will be discussed further in Chapter 4.) The party's platform for 1912 spoke of freedom of emigration as a fundamental human right and upheld the role of America as a land of asylum. Yet it also pledged the party to "the enactment of appropriate laws to give relief from the constantly growing evil of induced or undesirable immigration, which is inimical to the progress and welfare of the people of the United States."[77]

---

[76] *American Jewish Year Book*, vol. XXI (1919), p. 599; Moses Rischin, *The Promised City: New York's Jews 1870–1914* (Cambridge, MA: Harvard University Press, 1962; New York: Harper and Row, 1970), pp. 221, 229.

[77] Ira Katznelson, *City Trenches: Urban Politics and the Patterning of Class in the United States* (Chicago, IL and London: University of Chicago Press, 1981), pp. 121–3; *National Party Platforms, Volume I: 1840–1956*, compiled by Donald Bruce Johnson (Urbana, Chicago, and London: University of Illinois Press, rev. edition, 1978), pp. 158–61, 186–7.

Republicans dominated the White House from the Grant administration (1869–77) through the Progressive era, with the exceptions of Grover Cleveland's terms of office (1885–9, 1893–7) and Woodrow Wilson's presidency (1913–21). The Senate had a Republican majority until the 46th Congress (1879–81) and then again from the 48th Congress (1883–5) to the 63rd (1913–15). In the House of Representatives, Republicans held a consistent majority between 1895 and 1911. This long Republican ascendancy in American politics must be taken into account when we consider how American Jewish political attitudes were shaped. Many if not most Jewish immigrants living in the United States by 1914 had arrived while Theodore Roosevelt, a Republican and later a Progressive ("Bull Moose") Party leader, had been New York State Governor (1898–1901) and then US President (1901–09). Roosevelt had been an anti-corruption crusader in New York, a "trust-buster," an advocate of free immigration and a strong proponent of rapid Americanization of the immigrant. It was also Roosevelt who, in 1906, appointed Oscar Straus (1850–1926) to his cabinet as Secretary of Commerce and Labor (thereby also making him head of the Bureau of Immigration).

Republican affinities were strong in parts of the Jewish immigrant community in New York City. Although the most heavily distributed Yiddish daily, *Der Forverts*, was pro-labor, two of the other leading Yiddish dailies (*Morgen zhurnal* [Jewish Morning Journal] and the *Yiddishes tageblatt* [Jewish Daily News]) took pro-Republican positions.[78] Republicans predominated in state politics in most Northern and Midwestern states throughout this period, which is where most American Jews lived. In gubernatorial elections in New York State between 1906 and 1910, Jewish wards in Rochester and Syracuse polled between 40 and 60 percent for Republican candidates – very close to the average Republican support in those cities among German and Italian voters.[79]

In Chicago there was a strong Republican tradition in the Jewish community in state and national elections until the 1930s. Republican sympathies in local political affairs also thrived in Jewish communities outside the North–Midwestern quadrant. In San Francisco, where local politics were Republican-dominated for fifty years, the Jews of the city, mainly

---

78 Arthur A. Goren, *The Politics and Public Culture of American Jews* (Bloomington and Indianapolis: Indiana University Press, 1999), pp. 100–09; Glenn, *Daughters of the Shtetl*, pp. 202–3.

79 Robert F. Wesser, *A Response to Progressivism: The Democratic Party and New York Politics, 1902–1918* (New York and London: New York University Press, 1986), pp. 230–1.

of German immigrant origin, were active in the GOP as both voters and holders of elective office.[80]

At the same time, major metropolitan cities – prominently those in New York, Boston, and Chicago – were dominated politically by Democratic Party machines. Machine politics were widely identified with political corruption and electoral manipulation. Perhaps that was one reason why some Jews chose to vote Republican, as in urban wards in Boston, where Republican support among Jews continued into the late 1920s. But, by the same token, the Democratic Party machine won the support of many shopkeepers and peddlers through its control of pay-offs, licensing, and health and fire hazard inspections. The machine "took care" of its own, settled neighborhood disputes, arranged employment for young people, and it got out the vote on Election Day.

Big Tim (Timothy) Sullivan was the most powerful political fixer for the Tammany machine in lower Manhattan, and one of his main tasks was to recruit new immigrants and turn them into Democratic voters. Apart from organizing country outings ("chowders") for thousands, Sullivan provided free shoes and woolen socks every February to the poor and appointed ethnic "captains" (lawyers, merchants, liquor dealers) to marshal the vote among the German, Jewish, and Italian immigrant communities. "The Sullivan machine," we are told, "occasionally employed rival gangs for strong-arm support at election time. [...] The largest and most notorious of these were the Jewish Monk Eastman gang and the Italian Paul Kelly Association." Closely associated with Sullivan was his Jewish lieutenant, Martin Engel, a bail bondsman and poultry wholesaler, whose brother Max owned one of the most notorious brothels on the Lower East Side.[81]

(Party machines and party "bosses" were not limited to the Democrats. In San Francisco a Jewish political boss, Abe Ruef, ran the Union Labor Party and the mayor's office in high-handed style until convicted for bribery and sent to San Quentin Penitentiary. In turn-of-the-century Cincinnati, Republican George Cox presided over a legendary, ironclad, patronage machine that made the city governable and "appeased" special

[80] David Dalin, "Jewish and Non-Partisan Republicanism in San Francisco, 1911–1963," *American Jewish History* 38(4) (1979): 492–516.
[81] Lawrence H. Fuchs, *The Political Behavior of American Jews* (Glencoe, IL: The Free Press, 1956), p. 72; Daniel Czitrom, "Underworlds and Underdogs: Big Tim Sullivan and Metropolitan Politics in New York, 1889–1913," in *The Making of Urban America*, ed. Raymond A. Mohl (Wilmington, DE: Scholarly Resources, 2nd ed., 1997), pp. 131–40.

interest groups in the city by constructing a broad coalition, including civic and middle-class reformers, African Americans, and Jews.[82])

Jews in New York City gave about half their votes to Democratic candidates for governor between 1906 and 1918 (somewhat lower in Brooklyn), and from 36 to 44 percent in Syracuse and Rochester. Jewish Democrats were rarely prominent in elective office; but there were several veteran congressional incumbents, such as the aforementioned Henry M. Goldfogle who represented the heavily Jewish Lower East Side (1901–15 and 1919–21).[83]

The Democrats, as well as minor or so-called third parties, sometimes garnered Jewish support for ideological reasons. Republicans' coziness with big business made it harder for some progressives to remain stalwart supporters of the GOP. The so-called "Mugwump" faction of reform-minded Republicans who crossed over to the Democratic Party in the mid-1880s, as well as fusion candidates, economic and civic reformers, Henry George's social-egalitarian campaign for a single tax, and Teddy Roosevelt's "Bull Moose" third-party candidacy all succeeded among sections of the Jewish electorate. Louis D. Brandeis (1856–1941), for instance, a Louisville lawyer transplanted to Boston who would later become the first Jewish Supreme Court Justice (1916), bolted the Republican Party with the Mugwumps; considered (but turned down) an offer to run for mayor of Boston on a Good Government ticket against the Democrats' John F. Fitzgerald; returned to the Republican fold when the liberal Robert M. LaFollette, Sr. ran for the Republican presidential nomination in 1912; and finally ended up in the Democratic camp as a Wilson supporter.[84]

Political participation in minor parties was particularly associated, in the case of the East European Jewish working-class sector, with the brief ascendancy of American socialism. The Socialist Party, at the peak of its voter appeal in 1912, enrolled about 150,000 members nationwide. Although no more than 10 percent of Jewish voters actually cast ballots for Socialist candidates, the Socialists had a wider following among Jewish immigrants than voting records alone would suggest. Jews (along

[82] Dalin, "Republicanism," p. 492; Zane L. Miller, "Boss Cox's Cincinnati: A Study in Urbanization and Politics, 1880–1914," *Journal of American History*, vol. 54 (1968): 823–38; Walton Bean, *Boss Ruef's San Francisco* (Berkeley: University of California Press, 1967).

[83] Wesser, *Response to Progressivism*, p. 232.

[84] Melvin Urofsky, *Louis D. Brandeis, A Life* (New York: Pantheon Books, 2009), pp. 84–5, 193.

with Germans and Finns) figured among the largest ethnic constituencies in the socialist camp. There were, in addition, Italian, Lithuanian, Norwegian, Polish, Hungarian, South Slavic, and Bohemian sections ("federations") in the Socialist Party.[85]

Some young Jewish men and women arrived from Russia imbued with radical ideologies, and they were destined to play an important role in the subculture of American radicalism, trade unionism, and socialist politics. But, crucial as they were to the shaping of a radical Jewish intelligentsia, it was more the tough reality of American economic and political life that prompted their followers to look to them for guidance.

Moreover, in America, Jewish socialist politics were metamorphosed to compete in the arena of public opinion and electoral affairs. The revolutionary fervor characteristic of Russian radical underground groups had been focused on the task of toppling the autocratic tsarist state. In America, this relatively simple formula for regime change had no ready application; for in the American case, the "enemy of the people" was not a personal ruler or coterie of aristocratic officialdom. Rather, the entire republic – constitution, ballots, and system of representative government – was permeated at every level by a social ideology and economic ethos based on private gain, and it was effectively entrenched. Partly for such reasons, partly because most immigrants focused on their immediate concerns to get ahead in America, radicalism lost its appeal among many who might otherwise have become its natural constituency.[86]

Affiliation with a third party was always burdened with the likelihood of electoral defeat in a system dominated by two major parties. But where three, four, or more parties divided the vote in municipal, state, and national elections, the campaigns of minor-party candidates were sometimes surprisingly viable. Under such conditions, it proved possible on rare occasions to defeat a major party machine. The Socialist Party's Meyer London was sent to Congress three times (1914, 1916, and 1920) as representative of the Lower East Side of Manhattan.[87]

[85] Ira Kipnis, *The American Socialist Movement, 1897–1912* (New York: Columbia University Press, 1952), pp. 274–6, 364.

[86] Marcus Lee Hansen, *The Immigrant in American History* (Cambridge, MA: Harvard University Press, 1948), p. 95; Sigmund Diamond, "The Recruitment and Integration of an Immigrant Labor Force," in *Hartsaot biknasei ha'iyun behistoriah: nedudei he'amim vehagirah betoledot yisrael uvetoledot he'amim (Historical Conference Lectures: Migration of Peoples and Jewish Migration in World History)* (Jerusalem: Israel Historical Society, 1973), pp. 127–9.

[87] Steven J. Rosenstone, Roy L. Behr, and Edward H. Lazarus, *Third Parties in America: Citizen Response to Major Party Failure* (Princeton, NJ: Princeton University

On the other hand, with less revolutionary action in the offing, the socialist Left was in a position to offer its devotees something more than "pure" politics. The milieu created by a leftist press, left-wing social and fraternal organizations, adult lecture forums, summer camps for children, and youth organizations was, in its way, similar to other all-encompassing movements that combined home, work, public affairs, and community – such as the Grange movement in rural America. The Workmen's Circle (*Arbeter ring*) Jewish fraternal order had nearly 40,000 members by 1910, mainly drawn from the labor sector.[88]

As a sectoral phenomenon, the Jewish involvement with the labor movement and the political Left reflected the location of large numbers of Jews in the nation's industrial cities. As a lifestyle, much of it conducted in Yiddish, it exemplified group pride and was a formative influence for an entire generation. As politics, it allowed recent immigrants to enter the fray alongside allies from other subgroups in the American population and to join the political nation of Americans.

Inventing Denominational Judaism

By the post-Civil War years, American Judaism was becoming a house divided by doctrinal and cultural issues. Once begun, the drift toward a civic, American, middle-class Judaism inspired numerous congregations to reformulate their religious heritage. That project, always fraught with tension over personal and doctrinal disagreements, grew ever more contested in the era of mass migration.

This was conveyed in the rhetoric that accompanied the campaign to purge Judaism of its "Asiatic," cultic elements that set it at a social and religious disadvantage, as the Reformers saw it. A Rochester, New York congregation honored their rabbi by declaring: "He led his congregation out of Orientalism." In Chicago in 1874, Rabbi Kaufmann Kohler (1843–1926) introduced Sunday prayer services at his congregation, Temple Sinai, thus turning the Christian Sabbath into a day on which

Press, 2nd ed., 1996), p. 6; Wesser, *Response to Progressivism*, pp. 214, 239; William Hesseltine, *Third-Party Movements in the United States* (Princeton, NJ: D. Van Nostrand Co., 1962), pp. 13–14, 46–74. On Jewish socialism, see Gerald Sorin, *The Prophetic Minority* (Bloomington: Indiana University Press, 1985), and Arthur Liebman, *Jews and the Left* (New York: John Wiley, 1979).
[88] Sorin, *Prophetic Minority*, p. 79; Tony Michels, *A Fire in Their Hearts: Yiddish Socialists in New York* (Cambridge, MA and London: Harvard University Press, 2005), p. 294 n. 63.

Jews, too, would pray together. This move was seconded by Rabbi Joseph Krauskopf (1858–1923) at Philadelphia's Keneseth Israel, in 1887.[89]

At the same time, significant numbers of Jewish households retained traditionalist practices, as was the case in this San Francisco home:

> The kitchen was the temple in which Mother was priest and Maggie Doyle [the Irish maid], Levite. When Maggie first came to us to do general housework, Mother explained to her the custom regarding diet and the use of kitchen utensils. [...] No butter must touch meat of any kind nor be served at table when meat was a course; no meat pot must know the contact of milk. The distinction held to the least knife and teaspoon.[90]

Nonetheless, many households were shifting away from such traditions. The cookbook sponsored by the Women's Auxiliary of Temple de Hirsch in Seattle included a recipe for baked oysters – an egregiously non-kosher commodity – alongside one for chicken soup with noodles. Indeed, with one minor exception, *none* of the Jewish cookbooks published in America before World War I prescribed kosher recipes.[91]

The doctrinal formulation of Reform Judaism's outlook, known as the Pittsburgh Platform, adopted in that city in 1885 at the behest of Kohler and his rabbinical colleagues, enunciated what was already implied by grassroots adaptations. The text of the Reform platform repeatedly used the term "modern" in association with reason and science and specifically rejected traditional ritual practices, especially those that "regulate diet, priestly purity and dress." It affirmed "only the moral laws and [...] only such ceremonies as elevate and sanctify our lives"; denied restorationist hopes linked to Palestine as the Holy Land and, in consequence, also abandoned the ritual symbols linked to descendants of the Levite and priestly (*kohen*) clan (these were symbolic reminders of the rites at the

---

[89] Jick, *Americanization of the Synagogue*, p. 191; Herbert Bronstein, "From Exclusivity to Inclusivity in Reform Judaism," in *Platforms and Prayer Books: Theological and Liturgical Perspectives on Reform Judaism*, ed. Dana Evan Kaplan (Lanham, MD and Oxford: Rowman and Littlefield, 2002), p. 29; Silverstein, *Alternatives to Assimilation*, p. 106. See also Jonathan Freedman, *Klezmer America: Jewishness, Ethnicity, Modernity* (New York: Columbia University Press, 2008), pp. 279–80.

[90] Harriet Lane Levy, *920 Farrell Street: A Jewish Girlhood in Old San Francisco* (Berkeley, CA: Heyday Books, 1996 [orig. 1937]), p. 136.

[91] Yaakov Ariel, "Miss Daisy's Planet: The Strange World of Reform Judaism in the United States, 1870–1930," in Kaplan, *Platforms and Prayer Books*, p. 58. Ariel cites the cookbook's recipes, as noted by Mary McCarthy, *Memoirs of a Catholic Girlhood* (Harmondsworth: Penguin, 1957), p. 175; see also Barbara Kirshenblatt-Gimblett, "Kitchen Judaism," in *Getting Comfortable in New York: The American Jewish Home, 1880–1950*, ed. Susan L. Braunstein and Jenna Weissman Joselit (New York: The Jewish Museum, 1990), p. 78.

ancient Temple in Jerusalem). A central postulate of the new credo was that religion – and Judaism in particular – was a doctrine by which society defined and sustained a system of ethics. By overturning older, ritual-centered practices and by explicitly legitimizing one form of Judaic belief and practice – while seeking to marginalize other forms – the Pittsburgh Platform was a watershed in the emergence of Jewish denominational religion on American shores.[92]

Translating these ideas into oratory and broadcasting them to the Jewish public at large was the task of congregational rabbis, who delivered the message in their sermons. The texts of these sermons reveal much about the nature of denominational religiosity in the heyday of the early Reform movement in America. That applies, particularly, to those sermons judged worthy to represent the Reform rabbinate in a collection published in the mid-1890s.

I. S. Moses (1847–1926), rabbi of the KAM (Kehilath Anshe Mayriv [People of the West]) Temple of Chicago, for example, contributed one of his Yom Kippur sermons to this homiletic digest. His homily on "Sin and Forgiveness" opened by expounding the Jewish view of sin, as he saw it, which was not based on the doctrine of innate human wickedness, but rather appealed to the innate goodness of people. The crucial issue of penitence was not about placating divine anger or about fear of punishment for specific sins of commission or omission. The crux was, rather, about character: how might a person attain true integrity through constant self-correction? "It is to ourselves that we must turn, pleading before the tribunal of our conscience, testifying before the majesty of our convictions, that we have been false to our truths, low in our desires, selfish and insatiable in our cravings, cruel and ungrateful in our dealings with others."[93]

Compare that text to a sermon preached on "Sin and Repentance" over half a century earlier by Isaac Leeser of Philadelphia, and we would see a marked difference in tone, mentality, and theology. Leeser – a man of an earlier generation and a religious conservative – asserted that there were things that God did, indeed, prescribe or proscribe. Leeser conceded, further, that human nature is dualistic, including both divine and base inclinations ("evil does exist"), but that the potential for good had

[92] Meyer, *Response to Modernity*, pp. 387–8; Silverstein, *Alternatives to Assimilation*, pp. 116–20; Sarna, *American Judaism*, pp. 148–50.

[93] *Sermons by American Rabbis*, edited and published under the auspices of the Central Conference of American Rabbis (Chicago, IL: Central Conference Publication Committee, 1896), pp. 55–65.

to be effected through obedience to "the revealed word of God, for this is the guide which will lead us in the path we should go." The self was not sovereign and the state of one's soul did not depend solely on self-motivation: "True, the exercise of religious duties may interfere with our convenience; true, the precepts of revelation may not be all alike clear and intelligible to us; but then [...] to doubts springing from a not sufficiently explained reason of any particular precept, we can oppose a firm confidence in the Supreme Wisdom."[94]

The later sermon, by I. S. Moses, divested sin of its capacity to be *ritually* corrected (by proper execution of the religious code). That ritual option, a point of contention in Judaism ever since the biblical prophets had critiqued pure formalism (see Isaiah 58), was here peremptorily discarded. It bears noting that this gentler, humanistic, and less authoritarian model of atonement was remarkably similar in tone and substance to shifts in American Protestant theology around the mid-nineteenth century, with regard to Jesus as the great symbol of atonement. In the wake of that shift, it was accepted among liberal pastors that "God is no longer expressing hatred of sin in his sacrifice of his son but love of man; he ceases to govern by the direct imposition of his will and begins to sway by the influence of example."[95]

The Chicago rabbi's discourse was remarkable at yet another level. He counseled his parishioners to cultivate humility as a means of coping with life's sorrows and unpredictable turns of fortune. Knowing his audience as he did, he capped this argument with a plea to their self-esteem and their pocketbook. Moses's parishioners were genteel, well-to-do people. The KAM congregation had just recently built a new synagogue, its construction and extremely opulent interior having cost $110,000 (in today's terms, about $2.75 million). It had 190 pews in the "auditorium" and 90 additional pews in the galleries, offering seating for 1,500 persons, and was described as being "more imposing and majestic than any other building of a similar kind in this great city of architectural achievements, if not the entire West."[96] Humility was, perhaps, not their strongest suit. However, Moses turned his congregants' affluence into an opportunity for practicing charity: "Humility," he told them, "is not exclusively the virtue of poverty and misfortune; it is no less the crowning glory of

[94] Isaac Leeser, *Discourses on the Jewish Religion*, vol. I (Philadelphia, PA: Sherman and Co., 1836), p. 101; see also Friedenberg, *"Hear O Israel"*, pp. 26–38.
[95] Douglas, *Feminization of American Culture*, p. 124.
[96] Gutstein, *A Priceless Heritage*, pp. 78–80.

wealth and happiness." It thus behooved the members of the congregation to apply the homily in practice and to double their previous year's donations to Chicago's Jewish charity fund, the United Hebrew Relief Association. "By thy own strength, thou art reconciled unto thyself, thy fellow-men and thy God. Amen."[97]

Were nostrums about humility and charity just what the Jews in Moses's congregation wanted to hear? Was it his mission to urge upon them an alternative value-system, a counterpoint to the materialism and competitiveness of the marketplace? Or was the message of self-respect and propriety, aligned with contemporary upper-class American progressivism, the ideological lubricant that kept the wheels of commerce and industry grinding – a short decade after Chicago's Haymarket Riot?

The message conveyed by Rabbi Moses came across yet again in a sermon by his Chicago colleague, Rabbi Bernhard Felsenthal (1822–1908). Felsenthal, rabbi of the Sinai Temple, spoke of the "Jewish home" as a site for fulfilling religious values and enlarged upon the notion of the home as a sanctuary from the social axioms that ruled the outside world:

There are other persons belonging to the family occupying a house, though there are some who maintain that [they] have no claim toward being counted as members of the family. I speak of the class called *servants*. Where religion – I mean *true* religion – has a voice [...] and where man and wife, ruling over the house, honestly endeavor to have their house be a temple of the Lord, there the servant *is* considered a member of the family.[98]

Felsenthal and other rabbis were well aware of their congregants' favored position in society. Risking the ire of some if not most of them, he warned them that "society is in unrest, is in a state of fermentation." He even dared to suggest that "not all the demands of the so-called socialists are unreasonable." However, he was also at pains to put his public's mind at rest, or at least to anaesthetize the patient in advance of the benign procedure to follow. Progressive social reform, attuned to the poorer classes' reasonable demand for equality, consideration, and "true kindness," was not a threat. Class harmony might seem improbable in the present, but "other times will come, and better times – not in the nineteenth century [...] but in the twentieth century."[99]

Again, it is instructive to compare these late nineteenth-century formulations with the earlier sermons by Leeser, whose take on the capitalist

[97] *Sermons*, pp. 55–65.
[98] *Sermons*, p. 364.
[99] *Sermons*, pp. 368–9.

ethic was voiced with greater spleen: "In the very pursuit of wealth there is at all times something so heartless, that the man of feeling, even if we leave religion totally out of view, ought to shrink from it as he would from destruction."[100]

The arc of Jewish religious discourse about money and gain, stretching from the antebellum period to the Silver Age, allows us to see disparities in temperament and worldview, but also some fundamental unities. Men in clerical positions were apt to disparage the preoccupations of the laity (of men in particular), who were stereotypically viewed as prone to materialism and religious delinquency. Religion had often been a vector for processing society's mixed messages about enterprise, individual interest, and virtue. Faced with challenges at the theological level (modernism, scientism, and new philosophies), as well as at the sociological level (the changing demographic and social class composition of the country), American religious life mirrored the nation's disquiet. The emergent Reform Judaism, which achieved the status of the "incumbent" form of American Judaism from the 1860s to the 1890s, was a refraction of the larger national scene.

Yet, it would be too simple to leave it at that, for Jews belonging to Reform synagogues were offered more than just a Jewish version of liberal Protestant religious ideas. They were, quite explicitly, fed on a diet of Jewish "favoritism." Amid the trappings of its universal ethics, Reform oratory was ethnocentric to a fault and emphatically affirmed Jewish pride. Thus, the 1885 Pittsburgh Platform struck an explicit chord of Hebrew primogeniture:

Christianity and Islam being *daughter religions of Judaism*, we appreciate their providential mission to aid in the spreading of monotheistic and moral truth. [...] We extend the hand of fellowship to all who cooperate *with us* in the establishment of the reign of truth and righteousness among men. [emphasis added][101]

The impression of Jewish self-regard was also borne out at the grassroots level, among the laity, in their insular social worlds.[102] It should, indeed, have been surprising had things been otherwise in the 1880s and 1890s, when social exclusivity was prevalent throughout American life.

---

[100] Leeser, *Discourses on the Jewish Religion*, vol. II (Philadelphia, PA: Sherman & Co., 1836), p. 247.
[101] Meyer, *Response to Modernity*, p. 388.
[102] Meyer, *Response to Modernity*, p. 388; Gertel, *Jewish Belief and Practice*; Ariel, "Miss Daisy's Planet."

The Contested Ground of Denominational Judaism

In microcosm, the story of American Judaism around the turn of the twentieth century might be told through the example of Lincoln, Nebraska. Two small synagogue congregations were established there during the 1880s: B'nai Jeshurun (1884) and Tifereth Israel (1885). B'nai Jeshurun followed Reform practice, while its rival was nominally Orthodox. The liturgical and theological divide between them mirrored an ethnocultural difference: the Reform congregation was composed of members with a German-speaking heritage, while those in the Orthodox (in later years, Conservative) synagogue had a Yiddish-speaking, East European heritage.[103]

The nearly simultaneous founding of two separate congregations indicated the degree of separatism in Jewish religious life and social affairs. Despite the heightened appeal of Reform Judaism among native-born American Jews and veteran, well-to-do former immigrants, their aspiration to lead American Judaism into the new century faced strong competition. The greater numbers in the Jewish public were associated with the immigrants from Eastern Europe, most of whom categorically and viscerally rejected the Reform denomination.

In Lincoln, as in many communities, the two groups did not even bury their dead together. In 1892, members of B'nai Jeshurun acquired a small burial section within the Yankee Hill cemetery, southwest of the city, which they designated, with a biblical flourish, "Mt. Lebanon." In 1899, a new cemetery was opened by state and municipal authorities closer to the center of town, and B'nai Jeshurun acquired a section of it. That new "Mt. Lebanon" became, as the local press reported, the regular burial ground for the "reformed Hebrew sect in this city," whereas "the orthodox Hebrews" had their own cemetery, north of city limits, which they called (with correspondingly biblical imagery) "Mt. Carmel."[104]

The disparities between the two groups in cultural background, social class, religious association, and aesthetic perspective were borne out in the material culture of the two burial sites. Mt. Carmel was a visibly Jewish space, marked off by a fence and an entrance gate, with an

---

[103] David Mayer Gradwohl and Hanna Rosenberg Gradwohl, "That is the Pillar of Rachel's Grave unto This Day: An Ethnoarchaeological Comparison of Two Jewish Cemeteries in Lincoln, Nebraska," in *Persistence and Flexibility: Anthropological Perspectives on the American Jewish Experience*, ed. Walter P. Zenner (Albany, NY: SUNY Press, 1988), pp. 229–30.
[104] Gradwohl and Gradwohl, "Two Jewish Cemeteries," pp. 232, 244–6.

identifying sign and visual Jewish symbols. Mt. Lebanon, in contrast, bore no visible Jewish designation. It was set off from the rest of the cemetery only by the bordering pathways meandering through the grounds. Mt. Carmel, used by the city's more traditional Jewish families, featured many bilingual Hebrew–English inscriptions on gravestones; traditional, Jewish funerary art motifs (symbols signifying *kohen* or Levite ancestry, for example); and vertical tombstones in the old, familiar manner. Mt. Lebanon's gravestones, in contrast, were mainly low-profile or horizontal, ground-level markers, mostly bearing only English-language epitaphs, a scarcity of Jewish iconography, and no reference at all to priestly or Levite paternity.[105]

In a nutshell, this division between opposing cultural types reflects the profile of American Judaism for about two generations. Yet, unlike Lincoln, with its neatly juxtaposed division between two factions, in larger cities it was much harder to reduce religious factionalism to a simple binary opposition between German and East European religious styles, or between a unified Reform and a united Orthodoxy. Cultural and religious complexity flowed from the heterogeneous quality of Jewish migration: some of the traditionalists during this period happened to hail from Germany, and there were many other subgroups representing different regions of the Old World: Romania, Hungary, and Balkan and Mediterranean communities. American Judaism may have been divided generically between traditionalists and modernists, but it was polycentered rather than bi-polar.[106]

Examples of this amorphousness might be found in the sphere of rabbinical training. As of the early 1880s, the only center for higher Jewish learning in America was the Reform movement's Hebrew Union College (HUC) in Cincinnati. Two separate groups took parallel initiatives in the mid-1880s to establish new schools for rabbinical studies – both of them in New York City. In 1886, a number of well-to-do lay people active in the Orthodox community in New York established a private academy for Talmudic learning on strictly Orthodox lines, the Etz Chayim Yeshiva. Its name – "Tree of Life," a metaphorical term for the Torah – paid homage to the prestigious Etz Chayim Yeshiva of Volozhin (Valozhyn in today's Belarus), founded in 1803. Etz Chayim offered a comprehensive program

---

[105] Gradwohl and Gradwohl, "Two Jewish Cemeteries," pp. 232–51.
[106] Marsha L. Rozenblit, "Choosing a Synagogue: The Social Composition of Two German Congregations in Nineteenth-Century Baltimore," in Wertheimer, *The American Synagogue*, pp. 327–62.

of religious studies in the traditional East European fashion, beginning at the primary level.[107]

The other group included tradition-minded but liberal-leaning rabbis: Sabato Morais of Philadelphia (1823–97), an Italian-born rabbi of Sephardi-Portuguese descent; his colleague from Baltimore, Hungarian-born Benjamin Szold (1829–1902); Alexander Kohut (1842–94), who was also Hungarian-born and who served the Ahavath Chesed congregation in New York from 1885; Henry Pereira Mendes (1852–1937), the British-born Sephardic rabbi of New York's Shearith Israel; and Bernard Drachman (1861–1945), New York-born and European-trained, whose parents had come from Bavaria and Galicia. The school that they called into existence in New York in 1887 aimed at secondary and university-level studies and they called themselves the Jewish Theological Seminary (JTS) Association. The name echoed that of the modern rabbinical academy in the German city of Breslau (Wrocław, Poland today), founded by Zacharias Frankel in the mid-1850s.[108]

Their New York location placed both of these groups at an advantage. Located amidst a Jewish populace that outnumbered Cincinnati's Jewish community by a factor of about forty to one, they recruited intensively among the youth of the East European immigration. The Etz Chayim Yeshiva, reorganized in 1897 as the Rabbi Isaac Elchanan Theological Seminary (RIETS), became a modern Orthodox rabbinical academy and eventually formed the nucleus of Yeshiva University (founded as Yeshiva College in 1928). The JTS Association was reorganized in 1902 under the leadership of Solomon Schechter (1847–1915), a Romanian-born, German-educated rabbi and Semitics scholar, lately of Cambridge University. As the Jewish Theological Seminary of America, Schechter's school became the intellectual headquarters of Conservative Judaism.[109]

---

[107] Sarna, *American Judaism*, pp. 180–1; Jeffrey S. Gurock, *American Jewish Orthodoxy in Historical Perspective* (New York: Ktav, 1996), pp. 104–5, 107; and *Orthodox Jews in America*, pp. 109–12.

[108] Moshe Davis, *The Emergence of Conservative Judaism* (Philadelphia, PA: Jewish Publication Society, 1963), pp. 159–70, 216–25, 231–41, 335–6, 344–7, 351–6, 360–2; Gurock, *American Jewish Orthodoxy*, pp. 201–31, 112–14; and *Orthodox Jews in America*, p. 124; Sarna, *American Judaism*, pp. 184–5.

[109] Gurock, *Orthodox Jews in America*, p. 119; and *The Men and Women of Yeshiva: Higher Education, Orthodoxy, and American Judaism* (New York: Columbia University Press, 1988), pp. 18–42; Deborah Dash Moore, *At Home in America: Second Generation New York Jews* (New York: Columbia University Press, 1981), pp. 177–99; Michael R. Cohen, "The Travails of Early Jewish Theological Seminary Graduates: Solomon Schechter's Disciples and the Challenges of the Emergent Conservative Movement,

Although divergent in style and institutional culture, these initiatives were not entirely divorced one from the other. Fruitful, sometimes unexpected coalitions persisted at the personal and even at the institutional level. A call to found a "Union of Orthodox Jewish Congregations of America" (1898), for example, was issued by men at JTS. Henry Pereira Mendes was one of them. He was president of the faculty there until 1902, and later (1917–20) served as a professor of homiletics at the Orthodox seminary, RIETS.[110]

One might attribute this sort of religious mobility to the as yet inchoate quality of Conservative Judaism, but it was also due to the ambiguous shape of American Orthodox Judaism. The 1898 call for an Orthodox Union was not the first of its kind. A previous attempt to form an Orthodox congregational association in New York took place in 1887. The short-lived Association of American Orthodox Hebrew Congregations was the collaborative project of fifteen synagogues. Its primary aim was to bring a respected Orthodox rabbinical figure from Eastern Europe to function (as rabbis did in the Old World), not as a congregational pastor based in one synagogue, but as a learned mentor and city-wide authority on religious affairs.

The choice fell on Jacob Joseph (1840–1902), a well-regarded preacher from Vilna (Vilnius, in today's Lithuania). Rabbi Joseph arrived in New York in 1888, strove to create a kind of diocesan office, but could not make a go of it. He died in 1902 in straitened, even pitiable personal circumstances. Ironically, his funeral featured a large public cortege, with tens of thousands of lamenting Jews in tow, perhaps the only time that the late rabbi had ever enjoyed such widespread public distinction. Unfortunately, the procession was marred by a violent melee, sparked when Gentile factory workers clashed with Jewish mourners on the crowded streets. Police constables cleared the streets, beating and arresting disturbers of the peace without discriminating between hooligans and their victims.[111]

1902–1913," *American Jewish Archives Journal* 63(2) (2011): 1–23; and *The Birth of Conservative Judaism: Solomon Schechter's Disciples and the Creation of an American Religious Movement* (New York: Columbia University Press, 2012); Hasia Diner, "Like the Antelope and the Badger: The Founding and Early Years of JTS, 1886–1902," in *Tradition Renewed: A History of JTS*, ed. Jack Wertheimer (New York: Jewish Theological Seminary of America, 1997), vol. I, pp. 1–42; Mel Scult, "Schechter's Seminary," in *ibid.*, pp. 43–102.
[110] Sarna, *American Judaism*, pp. 185–6.
[111] Abraham J. Karp, *Hayei haruah shel yahadut amerikah (The Spiritual Life of American Judaism)* (Jerusalem: The Hebrew University of Jerusalem/Tel-Aviv: Schocken

Several years later, another initiative led to the founding of a board of rabbis, *Agudas harabbonim* (Union of Orthodox Rabbis of America and Canada). This board, in its turn, failed to claim general allegiance, however, and a rival group created another Orthodox Union in 1907. It was, thus, very rare for East European, Orthodox rabbis in America to achieve intramural cooperation, let alone to find common ground with those they considered religious rebels. There were a few noteworthy exceptions, such as Solomon Isaac Scheinfeld (1860–1943), an immigrant rabbi from Lithuania. Scheinfeld was exceptionally well read and comparatively open to worldly views. He achieved something of a consensual status in the Jewish community of Milwaukee during his long rabbinical career at the Beth Israel congregation (1903–43).[112]

Certain prominent lay representatives of Reform Judaism took steps to form bridges to the East Europeans and – in particular – to their children. To men like Jacob Schiff and others in his circle (all of whom were affiliated with Reform Judaism), it seemed like good policy to throw their financial support behind the reorganized JTS, the institution that appeared best positioned to inculcate American cultural values alongside the Judaic traditions practiced by "the masses." The conventional wisdom was that a "halfway house" of this kind was required. Others active in religious outreach believed it was possible to attract young men and women from the immigrant enclaves by offering a moderated version of Reform, along with such activities as Friday evening prayer services and lecture series.[113]

Encounters between Reform rabbis and the burgeoning generation of new Americans of East European descent were not free of stereotypes, but were also not entirely fruitless. Chicago's Rabbi Moses, who was invited (around 1904) to officiate at the wedding of a Jewish couple,

---

Publishing House, 1984), pp. 63–109; Kimmy Caplan, *Ortodoksiah ba'olam hehadash* (Jerusalem: Merkaz Zalman Shazar, 2002), pp. 26–8; and "Harav ya'akov yosef harav hakolel liyehudei nyu-york: hebeitim hadashim" (Rabbi Yaakov Yosef, Chief Rabbi of New York, New Perspectives), *Hebrew Union College Annual* 67 (1996): Hebrew pagination (1–43); Goren, *Politics and Public Culture*, pp. 48–56; Gurock, *American Jewish Orthodoxy*, pp. 212–13; and *Orthodox Jews in America*, pp. 113–15.

[112] Caplan, *Ortodoksiah*, p. 28; Gurock, *American Jewish Orthodoxy*, pp. 213–18; Nir Barkin, "Harav shelomo yitzhak sheinfeld (hashay"ish) bein masoret leshinui, 1860–1943" (Rabbi Shelomo Isaac Scheinfeld Between Tradition and Change, 1860–1943) (MA thesis, Hebrew University of Jerusalem, 2006), pp. 44, 51, 59–60; see also www .cbimilwaukee.org/content.php?I=53.

[113] Davis, *Conservative Judaism*, pp. 322, 324; Miri Gold, "The Absorption of Eastern European Immigrants into the American Reform Movement, 1880–1945" (MA thesis, The Hebrew University of Jerusalem, 1998), pp. 27, 51–3; Sarna, *American Judaism*, p. 196.

arrived at the appointed venue to find himself in the midst of a group of young people of East European origin. He reflected, rather patronizingly: "I was not insulted by any gaudy vulgarity." Instead, he was "delighted" to discover that both bride and groom, who had come from Russia as youths, were working professionals, people with modern educations and favorable prospects in life. The encounter, however, became a two-way transaction, as the groom requested that the Reform rabbi cover his head during the ceremony (as per the traditional custom, but counter to Reform practice at the time), and that he "use as much of the old ritual as possible" in deference to the groom's parents. In this case, as in a host of other encounters – as one scholar has put it – a closer look "reveals a porous weave of personalities, lay and rabbinic, institutions, events, intentions, and decisions which rendered the fortress [of the Reform synagogue] more permeable than imagined."[114]

Sectarianism in the Secular Sphere: Philanthropy and Civic Virtues

Jewish-sponsored charities emerged over the first half of the nineteenth century within the terms of voluntarism offered by the American social system. Jewish philanthropy operated in a semi-public arena, which was decidedly sectarian but, at the same time, increasingly desacralized. Put simply, one did not need to be a devout Christian or Jew in order to organize and support charitable work. In every other instance of the Judaic code of behavior, the act itself (a spoken or performed ritual) could be identified as "Jewish"; charitable works, in contrast, were ambiguous and potentially "secular." A fund for indigent brides is just that; a fund for widows and orphans is transparently a good deed; a hospital is a hospital, and so on.

Indeed, philanthropy opened up a wide field of enterprise and public standing to people who, for various reasons, were not necessarily key players in religious institutions per se. In the Jewish community, that category included affluent but non-observant men (less involved as synagogue-goers), as well as middle-class women (blocked by their gender from leadership in the synagogue). At the same time, it *helped* to

---

[114] Gold, "Absorption of Eastern European Immigrants," pp. 55–6; *CCAR Year Book*, 1904, pp. 66–7; Leon Jick, "The Reform Synagogue," in Wertheimer, *The American Synagogue*, pp. 92–3. On the relations between "Germans" and "Russians" in the Chicago Jewish community, see Brinkmann, *Von Gemeinde zur "Community"*, pp. 331–82.

be either a Christian or a Jew – in terms of one's associations and affiliations – in order to organize charitable activities. Sectarian activity was primary, and by degrees, over time, it was supplemented by non-sectarian or inter-denominational efforts and by programs of public assistance to the needy.[115]

Jewish philanthropy looked inward, but could also perform "good works" in exchange for civic recognition. By extending an umbrella of supervision over their client-group, denominational or congregational bodies were able to assert their influence in the larger social sphere. Thus, philanthropic organization reinforced the self-esteem of groups, such as Catholics and Jews, who felt called upon to ward off the attentions of Protestant missions, which were especially eager to minister to the unfed, the un-churched, the street denizens, and the young children of the meaner quarters of the metropolis.[116] Philanthropy empowered them to assert their own competence in the public realm and thereby to slough off any implication of civic laxness or apathy.

We might take, for instance, the history of the Jewish Orphan Asylum (JOA) established in Cleveland in the wake of the Civil War. The city had been the venue of grassroots charity work as early as the 1830s, based largely within denominational units. As the city developed into a larger commercial center, formal organizations and institutions emerged and, in most cases, men began to replace women in leadership functions. Before the Civil War, the city saw the founding of some of its major welfare institutions, the Protestant Orphan Asylum and two Catholic orphan homes (one for boys, one for girls).[117]

Jews in Cleveland proved similarly ready to support their community. A Hebrew Benevolent Society existed from about 1855 and a Jewish Ladies' Benevolent Society was organized in 1860. A separate (Jewish) Hungarian Aid Society followed in 1863, and five years later it was

[115] Carroll Smith Rosenberg, *Religion and the Rise of the American City: The New York City Mission Movement, 1812–1870* (Ithaca, NY and London: Cornell University Press, 1971).

[116] Sarna, *American Judaism*, pp. 80, 187, 196; and "The American Jewish Response to Nineteenth-Century Christian Missions," *Journal of American History* 68 (1981): 35–51; Rosenberg, *Religion and the Rise of the American City*; see also Yaakov Ariel, *Evangelizing the Chosen People: Missions to the Jews in America, 1880–2000* (Chapel Hill: University of North Carolina Press, 2000), pp. 3, 9–37.

[117] Laura Tuennerman-Kaplan, *Helping Others, Helping Ourselves. Power, Giving, and Community Identity in Cleveland, Ohio, 1880–1930* (Kent, OH and London: Kent State University Press, 2001), pp. 5, 14, 27–9, 30.

augmented by its own Ladies' Aid Society. The founding of the Jewish
Orphan Asylum in 1868 was, however, a more ambitious effort to command regional resources that went beyond local funding. The project
was assigned to a fundraising campaign by "the ladies" of nine cities
(including Cincinnati). The location of the institution – intended to serve
the entire Midwest – was not finally settled until 1868, when a site in
Cleveland was selected. Aside from the women's charity groups, well-
known community leaders like Cincinnati's Rabbi Isaac Mayer Wise and
Cleveland's Benjamin Franklin Peixotto (1834–90), who had been national president ("Grand Sar") of the B'nai B'rith fraternal order, were
heavily involved in promoting the project, as was a blue-ribbon board
of trustees of major businessmen from St. Louis, Cincinnati, Memphis,
Louisville, and Cleveland.[118]

Peixotto's role as a shaper of local communal institutions led him
toward wider civic recognition. Moving to New York and then to San
Francisco, he pursued a career in the law and business until tapped,
in 1870, for an appointment as an honorary United States Consul in
Romania. Romania had yet to grant its Jews full emancipation – one of
the last European countries to do so – and large numbers of Romania's
Jews began to emigrate, mainly to the United States. President Ulysses
S. Grant was prevailed upon to send Peixotto (despite the latter's
Democratic Party leanings) on an unsalaried mission of humanitarian
diplomacy to Bucharest.[119]

Governance was a thorny and perennial issue in the sphere of Jewish
philanthropy. The ethos of voluntarism and free association that fed
the myriad of charitable groups soon ran up against the equally prevalent notions of rationalization and efficiency in resource management.
Moreover, the Jewish population was only a small sector of American
society. That meant that the giving public in the Jewish sector was also
small, and was constantly being asked to contribute its largesse to a growing number of causes; while, at the same time, many of the best-known

---

[118] Gartner, *History of the Jews of Cleveland*, pp. 56–8; Karla Goldman, "The Public
Religious Lives of Cincinnati's Jewish Women," in Nadell and Sarna, *Women and
American Judaism*, p. 116; Gary Edward Polster, *Inside Looking Out: The Cleveland
Jewish Orphan Asylum, 1868–1924* (Kent, OH and London: Kent State University
Press, 1990), pp. 5–8; Swierenga, *The Forerunners*, pp. 252–53, 260–1.

[119] Moore, *B'nai B'rith*, pp. 30–2; Edward E. Grusd, *B'nai B'rith: The Story of a Covenant*
(New York: Appleton-Century-Crofts, 1966), pp. 74–5; Swierenga, *The Forerunners*,
pp. 252–3, 260–1, 302; Lloyd P. Gartner, "Roumania, America, and World Jewry: Consul
Peixotto in Bucharest, 1870–1876," *American Jewish Historical Quarterly* 58(1)
(1968): 24–56, 59–117.

among upper-class Jewish donors took pains to devote some of their generosity to non-sectarian causes and institutions. These issues begged the question of policy-making: by whose authority could (or should) the scarce resources of a small community be organized and prioritized?

At the municipal level, attempts to achieve some degree of coordination between individual charities, at least to combine their annual appeals to the public into one charity drive, attained a substantial degree of success in the form of Jewish philanthropic boards, or "federations." Federations essentially left the original independence of each institution intact while they rationalized fundraising. As wealthy families tended to be involved simultaneously in various worthy causes, however, federations of Jewish philanthropies tended to resemble what in the business world would be called an interlocking directorate. Moreover, the federation system reinforced patron–client relations, granting to the organized elite (and their paid professional staffs) a kind of stewardship in determining social welfare policies, while leaving the lower-class, often immigrant, client population without an effective voice.[120]

A different approach championed transparency and "democratization," which resonated with American liberalism, while also emphasizing Jewish co-responsibility and "peoplehood" in a cross-sectional and anti-elitist style. Advocates of democratization argued that the community was greater than the sum of its philanthropic endeavors and that the Jewish public needed open forums for policy-making. Democracy implied that public affairs ought not to be delegated to charity donors alone; rather, a council representing the large membership organizations active in a given community ought to have a quasi-sovereign role. Power and influence would in this way be shared more equitably and "the people" would have a voice in civic affairs. The community council idea was applied in several American cities during the first quarter of the twentieth century, but with only partial success, at best.

In Cleveland, for example, where the veteran, native-born Jewish leadership had an organized Federation of Jewish Charities, the immigrant sector established its own representative council, the United Jewish

---

[120] H. S. Linfield, "The Communal Organization of the Jews in the United States, 1927," *American Jewish Year Book*, vol. XXXI (Philadelphia, PA: Jewish Publication Society, 1930), pp. 99–254; Daniel J. Elazar, *Community and Polity: The Organizational Dynamics of American Jewry* (Philadelphia, PA: Jewish Publication Society, 1995), pp. 210–19; Philip Bernstein, *To Dwell in Unity: The Jewish Federation Movement in America since 1960* (Philadelphia, PA: Jewish Publication Society, 1983), pp. 3–13; Chaim I. Waxman, *America's Jews in Transition* (Philadelphia, PA: Temple University Press, 1983), pp. 72–4.

Organizations (UJO), in 1906. Based on Jewish clubs, synagogues, and fraternal societies, the UJO voiced its concerns over problems in the civic arena, such as police harassment of Jewish street peddlers, the scheduling of municipal voting on Rosh Hashanah, and the singing of Christmas carols at public schools attended mainly by Jewish pupils. At the same time, it sought to rally Jewish Clevelanders for wider purposes. In 1907, in the wake of anti-Jewish violence in Romania, the UJO held a mass meeting and undertook a collection of relief funds. Yet, the UJO failed to retain the support of some key Jewish constituencies – the city's B'nai B'rith members and the city's two Reform temples. Likewise, it failed in attempts to persuade the local Jewish Federation to provide kosher food for residents of the local Jewish retirement home or the Mt. Sinai Hospital. By 1909, the UJO was defunct. The old-line Federation took over effective leadership by organizing overseas relief for Jews in Europe during World War I. In 1919 it solidified its civic position by becoming affiliated with the new, non-sectarian, Cleveland Community Fund.[121]

A particularly ambitious attempt to create an ethnic democracy was made in New York City, beginning in 1908. Determined to put the huge, polymorphous Jewish population under one "big tent" organization, the *Kehillah*, as it was called (Hebrew for "community"), was led by the charismatic Reform rabbi and Zionist activist, Judah L. Magnes (1877–1948). Resembling a city executive (but without enforcement or taxation powers), the Kehillah established "bureaus" to deal with different realms of Jewish activity. The organization took on the gargantuan task of trying to bring order into Jewish religious life, especially in the realm of religious education and the regulation of the kosher meat industry. Other bureaus were assigned to promoting crime-busting on Jewish "turf," social work, and the coordination of philanthropic activities (insuring the existence of Jewish hospitals and other welfare institutions).[122]

The Kehillah scored certain practical successes, but it failed to recruit large portions of the million-and-a-half-strong Jewish community to its banner. Its education bureau ran up against Orthodox opposition when its staff (mainly non-Orthodox professional men) offered "new-fangled" curricular materials. For its part, the Jewish labor movement was suspicious of the sort of "bourgeois," religio-ethnic solidarity that the Kehillah

---

[121] Gartner, *History of the Jews of Cleveland*, pp. 238–40.
[122] Goren, *New York Jews*, pp. 25–185; Norman Bentwich, "The Kehillah of New York, 1908–1922," in *Mordecai M. Kaplan Jubilee Volume*, ed. Moshe Davis (New York: Jewish Theological Seminary of America, 1953), pp. 73–85.

represented – such "unity" between bosses and workers being a chimerical notion in a class-divided society, as they saw it. Joining forces seemed guaranteed to undercut workers' class-consciousness.[123]

By end of World War I, the Kehillah was scarcely functional, and it finally folded in 1921 when Magnes left for Palestine. It left behind two cohesive bureaus, however, which continued in following decades to function quite effectively: the Board of Jewish Education and the Federation for the Support of Jewish Philanthropic Societies of New York City.[124] Rather than achieving its ideal of an ethnic democracy, the "bureaucratization" of the Kehillah reinforced the separate organizational culture of each separate constituency: the pedagogical professionals, the social workers, and the wealthy managers of the philanthropic purse strings.

A Wartime Consensus in American Judaism?

With America's entry into the Great War in the spring of 1917, over half a million of the nation's civilians were conscripted for the National Army and sent to training camps, mainly located near big cities. Many draftees from New York trained at Camp Upton, Long Island, where they were inducted into the 77th ("Melting Pot") Division. Along with basic training, military authorities tried to ensure "moral hygiene" among servicemen by fighting alcoholism and educating against the spread of venereal diseases.[125]

About one quarter of the enlisted men trained at Upton over the winter of 1917–18 were Jews, but no rabbis were serving as army chaplains at the time. The Jewish Welfare Board (JWB, founded 1917) set itself the task of caring for the needs of the growing numbers of Jews in uniform, but had inadequate resources and very few personnel (Fig. 2.5).

The solitary JWB staffer dispatched to Upton found that he had to handle many requests for a kosher kitchen (which did not materialize, so families sent food from home) and for the conducting of religious services. JWB conducted a major funding campaign over the winter of 1917–18, but the first large wave of draftees was already dispatched overseas by the time a proper budget became available. Meanwhile, Congress ordered the commissioning of twenty Jewish military chaplains.[126]

[123] Goren, *New York Jews*, pp. 57, 76–85, 87–93, 110–33, 186–213.
[124] Moore, *At Home in America*, pp. 149–74.
[125] Christopher M. Sterba, *Good Americans. Italian and Jewish Immigrants During the First World War* (New York and Oxford: Oxford University Press, 2003), pp. 105–21.
[126] Sterba, *Good Americans*, pp. 122–4; Chester Jacob Teller, "The Jewish Welfare Board," *American Jewish Year Book 5679*, vol. XX (1918), pp. 88–102; Slomovitz, *Fighting Rabbis*, pp. 43–62.

FIGURE 2.5. Hanukah greeting card, JWB, 1918. Photo: Beit Hatfutsot Photo Archive, Tel Aviv, courtesy of Shoshana Weber.

In April 1917, representatives of the several denominational streams within American Judaism agreed jointly to provide a prayer book for the men in uniform. The Central Conference of American Rabbis (Reform), the newly established United Synagogue (Conservative, founded 1913), the Union of Orthodox Jewish Congregations (UOJC), Agudas harab-bonim, and the Jewish Publication Society of America delegated the task to a trio of respected and pragmatic men: Cyrus Adler ([1863–1940] a Semitics scholar, president of Philadelphia's Dropsie College, and the new head of JTS); Bernard Drachman (formerly of JTS and now head of the UOJC); and William Rosenau of Baltimore, a Reform rabbi known for his somewhat traditionalist bent and his sympathetic relations with the East European immigrant community.[127]

Producing a prayer book to fit the needs of every Jew in the trenches entailed several expedients. The slim, pocket-sized prayer book opened from the right – the traditional, Hebrew side – and contained facing pages of Hebrew and English, as was common, even in modern Orthodox circles. In order to enable Reform as well as traditional-minded soldiers

[127] *Abridged Prayer Book for Jews in the Army and Navy of the United States*, Prepared and Issued for the Jewish Welfare Board (Philadelphia, PA: Jewish Publication Society, 1918, Cooperating with and under the Supervision of the War Department Commission on Training Camp Activities), Preface; Meyer, *Response to Modernity*, pp. 290, 293; Sarna, *American Judaism*, p. 196.

to feel at home with the text, traditional prayers that had been excised from the Reform movement's Union Prayer Book (such as references to Jerusalem, a future messiah, prayers for God's return to Zion, and prayers for the bodily resurrection of the dead) were set off by an asterisk, so that they might be easily skipped if so desired.[128]

Many men – some of them removed from their family environments for the first time in their lives – encountered in the military a new, "Americanized" form of Judaism. But at the same time, one imagines that for some young men of Reform background, reading this strange prayer book may have been the first and only occasion on which they encountered the more traditional phrases, even as "optional" texts. It may be that this generation of war veterans, upon their return home, played a distinctive role in the dynamics of Jewish denominational blending, mergers, and separations that took place during the interwar period.[129]

At the same time, this episode of cross-denominational cooperation also formalized the until then unofficial, tripartite denominational map. That map now emerged as follows: the Reform movement's influence was still considerable, and though it had ebbed, it still possessed a hard-core base and a dynamism that augured a future comeback. In the camp of the traditional-minded, there had emerged a pragmatic, westernized Orthodoxy, as well as a middle-of-the-road position that represented a theologically Conservative Judaism wedded to Western critical philosophy and scholarship.

The old-guard Orthodox Agudas harabbonim, although sidelined, took an active role in response to the war according to its own agenda. It established a fundraising organization, Ezras Torah, that sent relief to beleaguered rabbis and yeshivas in war-ravaged Eastern Europe. This concern to help maintain the heartbeat of Orthodox Judaism on its home turf bespoke these rabbis' sense that their religious way of life was best preserved via a link with Europe.[130] The persisting bonds of sentiment

---

[128] *Abridged Prayer Book*, Preface; see also Sarna, *American Judaism*, pp. 212–13.

[129] Sarna, *American Judaism*, pp. 213–14. Something similar has been suggested about the Second World War experiences of Jews in the US armed forces: Jack Wertheimer, *A People Divided: Judaism in Contemporary America* (New York: Basic Books, 1993), p. 4; see also Deborah Dash Moore, *To the Golden Cities: Pursuing the American Jewish Dream in Miami and L.A.* (New York: The Free Press, 1994), pp. 12–13; and *G.I. Jews: How World War II Changed a Generation* (Cambridge, MA and London: Harvard University Press, 2004), pp. 153–4, 258–9.

[130] Efraim Zuroff, *The Response of Orthodox Jewry in the United States to the Holocaust. The Activities of the Vaad-Ha-Hatzala Rescue Committee, 1939–1945* (New York: Ktav/ Yeshiva University Press, 2000), pp. 2–10.

and memory were mobilized to counter separation, distance, and the chaos of war.

Memory

Migration cut many family and community ties that normally create links between past and present. Compensating for such losses, one of the fascinating by-products of this era was the self-conscious effort to re-frame a new, American-based, collective Jewish memory. As always, such cultural constructions allocated significance to a selective blend of actual experience and projected ideals.

In 1913, an "Exposition on Jews of Many Lands" was held at the Jewish settlement house in Cincinnati. Placed on exhibit in this Jewish "world's fair" were charts tracing Jewish historical experiences around the world, "a rich collection of different articles for Jewish ceremonial," as well as "samovars, […] women's handiwork, embroidery and crocheting." There were displays exhibiting archetypical costumes worn by Jews of different countries, along with appropriate folklore performances, such as songs and dances from the Spaniola (Sephardic) tradition performed by members of the Turkish Jewish group in Cincinnati. All the figures in the "Russian" tab-leau, including an "Orthodox rabbi, soldier, political prisoner, [and] revo-lutionist," were meant to convey a life of resistance against compulsion and oppression. The United States was represented by a West Point cadet uniform and "the athletic attire of a Vassar maid [student]," indicating the sunny prospects of patriotic citizenship and upper-class aspirations in the free American environment. Jewish masculinity was militarized, while Jewish femininity was updated to include academic achievement.[131]

There was something flagrantly contrived about the choice of West Point and Vassar to represent the lives of Jewish Americans – this being akin to exhibiting a Thanksgiving turkey as an exemplar of Jewish cui-sine. However, the idea of linking American Jewry with something easily recognizable as quintessentially American made perfect sense to the spon-sors of the exhibit, just as it made sense to them, in another way, to situate the American tableau amidst an array of Jewish historical memorabilia from distant Diasporas. They placed America within the longer saga of Jewish history so that America might be cast as its worthy culmination.[132]

---

[131] Bogen, *Jewish Philanthropy*, pp. 253–5.
[132] Beth S. Wenger, *History Lessons: The Creation of American Jewish Heritage* (Princeton, NJ and Oxford: Princeton University Press, 2010), pp. 4, 16.

The need to recount the story of the Jews in new ways found outlets not only in popular pageantry but also in more stable institutional settings. One such instance involved the Jewish Publication Society (JPS), chartered in 1888, though its antecedents went back as far as the mid-1840s. Alongside the JPS, there were other cultural ventures such as an American Jewish Historical Society (1892), a Jewish Chautauqua Society (1893), Philadelphia's Gratz College (1893), and an ambitious *Jewish Encyclopedia*, initiated in 1898 and published between 1901 and 1906.[133] Part of JPS's mission was to connect the public and intellectual discourse of Jews in America to the extant cultural traditions of European Judaism and to current works of popular creativity and erudition, thus putting American Jewry on a recognizable Jewish map. It viewed its goal as rendering American Jewry culturally solvent, "so that Israel in America may proudly claim its literary period, as did our ancestors aforetimes in Spain, in Poland, and in modern Germany."[134]

The American Jewish Historical Society (AJHS) undertook the task of self-documentation in scholarly but accessible form, with particular attention devoted to tracing the earliest evidence of Jews and their lives in North America from colonial times to the American Revolution. The AJHS, like the Publication Society, took a broad view of its brief, with the idea that "gathering the [historical] materials [...] would enable the student of American history to understand the relation of the Jews to the settlement and progress of the American Continent and the student of Jewish history to write a new chapter in the never-ending history of the Jews." Addressing the AJHS on its tenth anniversary in 1902, the association's president, Cyrus Adler, sought to inject another element. Not content with combing the archives for antiquarian data, he had a more ambitious agenda, which included substantiating the Jews' right to call the American heritage their own:

I cannot but feel that political history in the sense of the relation of the Jews to the origin and founding of this Republic [...] through the formation of its political ideals, the maintenance of its cause upon the field of battle, the making of its laws in the halls of legislation, [ought] to be the principal work of this society.[135]

Adler was echoing a sentiment expressed earlier by Oscar Straus, a founder and first president of the AJHS. Straus, a Progressive, served

---

[133] Jonathan D. Sarna, *JPS: The Americanization of Jewish Culture, 1888–1988* (Philadelphia, PA: Jewish Publication Society, 1989), pp. 1–14.

[134] Sarna, *JPS*, pp. 25, 29–32, 34–9.

[135] *PAJHS* 10 (1902): 3–4.

several times as US ambassador to Turkey and, we recall, was to be appointed as Secretary of Commerce and Labor to Teddy Roosevelt's cabinet (1906–09). He had authored a tract that claimed that the biblical Israelite "republic," founded under a written "constitution," was the historical precedent that inspired, as he put it, *The Origin of Republican Form of Government in the United States of America*. Several years later, he commissioned Dr. Meyer Kayserling of Budapest, a rabbi and historian, to author a study entitled, *Christopher Columbus and the Participation of the Jews in the Spanish and Portuguese Discoveries*.[136]

Thus, in an American Jewish community that was being augmented exponentially by a population of new immigrants and their children, the AJHS was keen to distract everyone's gaze from recent events. It wanted not just to establish the antiquity of Jewish settlement in America, but also to lay claim to a "native" ingredient of Judaic spirit and Jewish endeavor, said to lie at the taproot of American heritage. The self-legitimating thrust of this endeavor seemed fairly clear – indeed, it was wholeheartedly embraced.

While the contours of a collective Jewish-American narrative were being sketched out by nascent cultural institutions, more recently arrived Jewish immigrants were intent on quite different projects of memory construction. Idealized memories of Eastern European life were being circulated by immigrant Orthodox rabbis, and much of what they had to say about Old World Judaism was juxtaposed to Jewish religious life in America – to the detriment of the latter.[137] Thus, for instance, one preacher intoned:

We would do well to mark how our fathers lived in Europe, compared to our lives here. [...] People passed their lives [there] in far greater peace of mind and pleasure [...]. Just think of our elders on the Sabbath eve as dusk fell: how their faces shone with beauty, purity, joy, and peace. [...] Who amongst us has not seen and felt [...] the warm, strong love that presided over their homes [at such moments]? All of us, children of Europe, know this for a certainty.[138]

---

[136] Naomi W. Cohen, *A Dual Heritage: The Public Career of Oscar S. Straus* (Philadelphia, PA: Jewish Publication Society of America, 1969), pp. 14–15, 70–3; Oscar Straus, *The Origin of Republican Form of Government in the United States of America* (New York: G. P. Putnam's Sons, 1901).

[137] Jonathan D. Sarna (trans. and ed.), *People Walk on Their Heads: Moses Weinberger's Jews and Judaism in New York* (New York: Holmes and Meier, 1981); and *American Judaism*, pp. 156–7; Annie Polland, "'The Sacredness of the Family': New York's Immigrant Jews and Their Religion, 1890–1930" (PhD dissertation, Columbia University, 2004), pp. 237–40.

[138] Judah L. Levin, *Leveit david (The House of David)* (Baltimore, MD: Rams Press, 1907), p. 79, quoted in Caplan, *Ha'ortodoksiah*, p. 201.

And, again, in the words of another sermon of this genre that cast aspersions on American Judaism:

What do fathers [in America] do? Since on the Sabbath [their children] do not go to [...] *school*, they send them off to sell [news]*papers*, whereas in *Europe* they would educate them to recite the *Kedushah* [a liturgical passage] and to say Amen properly. ["School," "papers," and "Europe" appear in English in the Yiddish original.][139]

Not all of their listeners shared these views, but those who heard such preachers undoubtedly carried away with them a positive image of East European ways of life. This, in turn, fed a stream of post-migration nostalgia.

The popularization of East European memories took place at another level as well. The names of hundreds of Old World communities adorned the myriad prayer-quorums, benevolent fraternities, burial societies, and synagogues that sprouted throughout America. Hometown associations (in Yiddish: *landsmanshaftn*) were vehicles for voluntary activism and social integration at the grassroots level. As such, they were very much invested in the American scene. Still, their European monikers symbolized their identity: *landsmanshaftn* grouped Jewish immigrants by their separate places of origin, not according to their current American neighborhoods, city, region, or state, as was the common pattern among the veteran American (or "German") Jewish population. Among the latter, it was noticeable that B'nai B'rith lodges, Reform synagogues, Jewish organizations (like the National Council of Jewish Women, founded 1893), and innovative cultural endeavors were generally keyed to a national organizational framework, often with city, district, or statewide American subdivisions, mimicking the federal system.

Social activity among the newer arrivals from Europe was more attuned to pre-migration localisms. *Landsmanshaft* members often took pride in their former homes and expressed feelings of homesickness and nostalgia, even as they persevered in making new lives for themselves in the United States. They maintained communication with family relations and compatriots in their old homes, took to heart the distress of those left behind, and channeled financial assistance to their brethren overseas, all in the name of their common heritage.[140]

---

[139] Shaul I. Shochet, *Ahavat shaul (The Love of Saul)*(New York, Chicago, St. Louis: Meites Printers, 1906), vol. II, pp. 40–1, quoted in Caplan, *Ha'ortodoksiah*, p. 201.

[140] Daniel Soyer, *Jewish Immigrant Associations and American Identity in New York, 1880–1939* (Cambridge, MA and London: Harvard University Press, 1997).

That was, perhaps, surprising, for in some cases the old hometowns from which they hailed had only been transit points, where they or their families had lived for little more than a decade, at best. Yet, precisely because local identities were swept up in a changing social landscape, it became necessary to enshrine them as timeless and somehow sacred, and to depict the transition to America as a further chapter in the "continuing" saga of the mother-city or township. *Landslayt* (hometowners) who built new social groups on American shores could, in retrospective inversion, present this as the fulfillment of ideals nurtured for generations in the pre-migration community.[141]

The outbreak of the European war in 1914 presaged a more lasting and tragic severing of ties with old home communities – pushing commemorative nostalgia to its limits but also serving to mobilize public opinion in new ways. The initiative for sponsoring war relief for communities that lay in the path of the German, Austro-Hungarian, and Russian armies was swift and widespread, but wartime communications and restrictions dictated that spontaneous initiatives of families and local communities be coordinated and organized. Various war relief groups became partners in a joint committee formed to expedite the forwarding of relief funds: the American Jewish Joint Distribution Committee (AJDC, or "Joint" for short, founded 1914), a group led mainly by representatives of the established American Jewish leadership and its financial elite.[142]

Rampant destruction of largely Jewish townships, especially by Russian forces, and the ensuing misery of many thousands of Jewish war refugees, was compounded after the war by atrocities committed during the Russian revolutionary and civil war period (1918–21). During those initial postwar years, acts of mass murder against civilian Jews (chiefly in Ukraine, committed generally by anti-Bolshevik militias and insurgents), took place on an unprecedented scale, leaving some 100–150,000 Jews dead and nearly half a million homeless. For many immigrant Jews in the United States, the hometowns of their families and the lives they had known there now appeared thoroughly destroyed. The memorialization of prewar Jewish life in Russia and Poland began to find expression at that time in public discourse and in books, and heightened the Jewish

---

[141] Rebecca Kobrin, *Jewish Bialystok and its Diaspora* (Bloomington and Indianapolis: Indiana University Press, 2010).

[142] On the AJDC, see Naomi W. Cohen, *Not Free to Desist: The American Jewish Committee 1906–1966* (Philadelphia, PA: Jewish Publication Society, 1972, pp. 85–6; Yehuda Bauer, *My Brother's Keeper: A History of the American Jewish Joint Distribution Committee 1929–1939* (Philadelphia, PA: Jewish Publication Society of America, 1974), pp. 3–18.

public's awareness of the dramatic political changes sweeping over Europe at that time.

An early exemplar of war memorial writing, by our New York immigrant poet Alter Brody, was a poem entitled "Kartúshkiya-Beróza," the name of his native town in Ukraine. It began thus:

> It is twelve years since I have been there –
> I was born there,
> In the little town by the river –
> It all comes back to me now
> Reading in the newspaper:
> *"The Germans have seized the bridge-head at Kartúshkiya-Beróza;*
> *The Russians are retreating in good order across the marshes.*
> *The town is in flames."* [Italics in the original.][143]

Another poet mourned the "Destruction of Zvhil," where "The stones are wreathed/ with spattered red blood/ Dogs slobbering/ over the bones of the slain [...]/ Nothing is left/ of my lovely town/ A rusty wire/ holds the rickety gate/ And above it a sign that proclaims/ 'The City of Death.'"[144]

The violent demise of much of this native Jewish landscape, a generation before the Nazi Holocaust, had the effect of permanently anchoring American Jews' identity in their "exodus" out of Europe. Return visits to survey what had survived the war and to determine how humanitarian assistance could rebuild a semblance of normal life underscored the yawning gap that had opened up between American and East European realities.[145] The turn of events between 1914 and 1921 perpetuated the organized community's commitment to "refugeeism," which was now perceived as more urgent than ever before.

---

[143] Alter Brody, "Kartúshkiya-Beróza," in *A Family Album and Other Poems*, p. 13.

[144] The poem by A. Pravatiner is excerpted in *Di yidishe landsmanshaftn fun nyu-york* (*The Jewish Home Town Associations of New York*), ed. Isaac E. Rontch (New York: Works Progress Administration and the I. L. Peretz Association, 1938), p. 214. Zvhil is in Ukraine.

[145] Soyer, *Jewish Immigrant Associations*, pp. 178–89, 199.

3

Finding Space in America, 1920s–1950s

I love the earth on which I tread –
Its freshness, its fruitful plenitude.
A girlish earth, pliant and giving,
Its grasses kiss my steps with cool kisses.
[…]
I know, this ground is not hallowed by my blood –
My father elsewhere lies at rest.
But my child is a grain born of this earth,
Radiant in its light, rejoiced by its good fortune.

          – I. J. Shvarts, dedication (from the Yiddish), *Kentucky*[1]

Only in America, of all the tribes of Jewry,
Did my people eat their fill and sleep securely in their beds […].
Here I became a father, a grandfather,
My loves – for wife, child, grandchild –
Are bound up with love of country,
Though not without attendant doubts,
Of our essence trickling away.
Jew. American. I am both at once, wrapped up together.
How so?
Ask of me no coherent epic, no neatly related narrative.

          – Aaron Leyeles, *Amerike un ikh (America and I)*[2]

Introduction: Immigrants and Natives

Estimated at a little over three million strong by the end of World War I, America's Jewish population was poised to become the largest group

---

[1] I. J. Schwartz, *Kentucky* (New York: Pozy-Shaulson Press, 1936). The work was published in an English translation by Gertrude M. Dubrovsky (Tuscaloosa and London: University of Alabama Press, 1990), but the translations here are mine.

[2] Aaron Leyeles, *Amerike un ikh (America and I)* (New York: 1963), p. 90.

of Jews located in a single country. Tsarist Russia, previously the home of the greatest concentration of Jews, had become Bolshevik Russia at the end of 1917, and its now truncated western boundaries no longer included the Jews living in the newly independent Polish and Baltic states. Similarly, the breakup of the Austro-Hungarian Empire into successor states meant that the formerly large Habsburg Jewry was now subdivided between Hungary, Austria, Czechoslovakia, Poland, and Yugoslavia.

Numerically strengthened and favored with the advantages of American postwar prosperity, America's Jewish community in the 1920s was endowed with new responsibilities and influence in world Jewish affairs. Domestically, however, Jews as a group hardly seemed to dent the surface of US affairs. Jewish organizations took a leading role in lobbying for continued free immigration, but suffered a major defeat when Congress passed severe migration restrictions, selectively targeted to reduce immigration from Southern and Eastern Europe in particular: the demographic Jewish heartland. When, after a lengthy and tangled legislative history, the Quota Act was brought to a vote in early 1921, it passed the House almost perfunctorily in just a few hours. In the Senate it had just one opponent.[3]

No separate Jewish immigration quota existed, since Jews, like all immigrants, were statutorily considered nationals of their prior countries of residence. The low quotas assigned to East European countries applied to all arrivals, regardless of ethnicity or religion. Nonetheless, the historical overrepresentation of Jews in the migrations from Poland had not gone unnoticed, since the number of arriving "Hebrews" was tabulated by US authorities as of 1899. It was not coincidental that the low quotas for Eastern Europe reduced those numbers drastically.[4] A State Department memorandum to the Congressional Committee on Immigration, chaired by Congressman Albert Johnson (Rep., WA), pointed out the undesirability of "the ghetto type" of Jews from Poland, describing them as "filthy, un-American and often dangerous in their habits." The facilities at Ellis Island, it was pointed out, were insufficient to accommodate a further "avalanche of new arrivals; larger cities have not houses for them; work

[3] John Higham, *Strangers in the Land: Patterns of American Nativism, 1860–1925* (New Brunswick, NJ: Rutgers University Press, 2008 [1955]), pp. 277–8, 311. For a recent review of the legislation and enforcement of the immigration quotas, see Libby Garland, *After They Closed the Gates: Jewish Illegal Immigration to the United States, 1921–1965* (Chicago, IL: University of Chicago Press, 2014), pp. 14–42.
[4] Garland, *After They Closed the Gates*, pp. 84–5.

cannot be found for them."[5] Emma Lazarus's premonitions about the limits of America's largesse were belatedly confirmed. With the introduction of immigration quotas (the 1921 quotas were revised downward in 1924), the era of mass Jewish migration ground to a halt. Over the four years from 1921 to 1925, the annual Jewish influx from Eastern Europe fell from 119,000 to under 10,000.[6]

One result was that during the interwar period American Jewry increasingly comprised either veteran immigrants of long standing or their native-born American progeny.[7] Accordingly, the Jewish population became less divided by local Old World identities, languages, accents, and customs and was apt to identify strongly with American nationality, American ideas, and American-produced popular culture. So adept were some of them at handling the new cultural idiom that they easily integrated into the front ranks of cultural producers, such as in the film industry, popular entertainment, popular music, and sports. One need merely recall that Russian-born Irving Berlin (1888–1989, *né* Israel Baline) wrote "God Bless America," along with many of his other iconic American songs; or that George (Cukor) Zukor (1899–1983), born to Hungarian Jewish immigrant parents in New York City, directed such American film classics as *The Philadelphia Story* and *My Fair Lady*, and assisted in the direction of *Gone With the Wind* and *The Wizard of Oz*.[8] Jews gradually became less polarized along class lines, as fewer of them remained employed for very long as industrial workers. By the eve of the Great Depression, most Jews in America could no longer be

---

[5] *Temporary Suspension of Immigration*, Sixty-Sixth Congress, 3rd Session, House of Representatives, Report No. 1109, December 6, 1920; see also Higham, *Strangers in the Land*, pp. 309–10.

[6] Klein, *Population History*, pp. 164–5; Liebman Hersh, "International Migration of the Jews," in *International Migrations*, ed. Imre Ferenczi and Walter Wilcox (New York: Gordon and Breach, 1969), p. 474. A recorded number of 10,292 entries of Jewish immigrants in the year ending June 30, 1925, minus the number of those debarred – 1,137 – or deported (250) yields a figure of 8,905. *American Jewish Year Book*, vol. XXVIII (1926–7), p. 418. There are estimates suggesting that from several thousand to several tens of thousands of Jews entered the US illegally after the onset of immigration restriction, but the numbers are notoriously difficult to ascertain. Garland, *After They Closed the Gates*, pp. 89–117, 145.

[7] Kuznets, "Economic Structure and Life of the Jews," in Finkelstein, *The Jews*, vol. II, p. 1634; Sidney Goldstein, "Jews in the United States: Perspectives from Demography," *American Jewish Year Book*, vol. LXXXI (1981), p. 7; Lestchinsky, "Jewish Migrations, 1840–1956," in Finkelstein, *The Jews*, vol. II, pp. 1536–96; *Jewish Population Studies*, ed. Sophia M. Robison (New York: Conference on Jewish Relations, 1943).

[8] Paul Buhle, *Jews and American Popular Culture*, 3 vols. (Westport, CT and London: Praeger, 2007).

characterized as tenement-dwellers in slum neighborhoods. As we have discussed, a constellation of overlapping factors had helped many Jews – including recent immigrants – to make relatively rapid strides toward economic solvency and even a modicum of success. By no means were all working-class Jews equally adept at moving up, let alone attaining affluence; but in the 1920s there was growing evidence that the second-generation cohort was starting to "make it." A significant portion of the Jewish population was poised to take a leap into the middle classes. Local surveys from that time support an overall picture of an emergent white-collar, professional, and business-based lifestyle. Within the middle classes, of course, there was considerable variation in income levels, home ownership, wage-income vs. self-employment, and the gendering of occupations.[9]

The factors which lay behind this improving economic base included: individual talent; effective family- and group-based support networks; the trial-and-error progress of Jewish parents in working-class jobs and petty trade; and the influx of young women into clerical jobs and public service professions (such as teaching and social work). Even job discrimination against Jews might have had the indirect effect of driving young people toward self-employment or toward jobs in marginal sectors of commerce and manufacturing, where the risks were greater but career advancement more likely.

It should be remembered, too, that beyond the urban throngs of newcomers and their progeny, a Jewish gentry comprising affluent people with native-born pedigrees of two- or three-generations' duration existed well before World War I. In some communities, the business networks of these established families were penetrated by upwardly mobile front-runners from the latest migration wave. Early ventures by well-to-do Jewish families into plush suburbs were tentative signs of what became a wider trend in later generations.[10]

9 Perlmann, *Ethnic Differences*, pp. 154–62; Maurice J. Karpf, *Jewish Community Organization in the United States* (New York: Bloch Publishing Co., 1938), pp. 16–17 (Tables 10 and 11); S. Joseph Fauman, "Occupational Selection among Detroit Jews," in Sklare, *The Jews*, pp. 123, 125, 127.
10 Marshall Sklare and Joseph Greenblum, *Jewish Identity on the Suburban Frontier: A Study of Group Survival in the Open Society* (New York and London: Basic Books, 1967), pp. 9–14; Gerald L. Showstack, *Suburban Communities: The Jewishness of American Reform Jews* (Atlanta, GA: Scholars Press/Brown University, 1988), pp. 32–5; Wertheimer, *A People Divided*, p. 5; Ewa Morawska, *Insecure Prosperity: Small-Town Jews in Industrial America, 1890–1940* (Princeton, NJ: Princeton University Press, 1996), p. 94.

What are we to make of the apparent dissonance between signs of confident enterprise and the context in which this took place: an America that summarily withdrew its welcome mat? How did Jews find space for themselves in America – politically, economically, geographically, and socially? Their foreign heritage did not count in their favor; how did that affect their self-perceptions? What new beginnings did the latest arrivals attempt, even during this era of drastically reduced numbers of Jewish immigrants? Such questions will be addressed in the pages that follow.

Socialism, Suffrage, and Sobriety: Jews and America's Political Culture in the Twenties

Immigration restriction, women's suffrage, the Red Scare, and Prohibition ushered in the first new decade of the interwar period. All of these may be viewed as attempts to tip the balance of American political culture in new ways and, in so doing, to redefine the Republic.

Immigration regulation impinged on Jews in two distinct ways. Obviously, immigration restriction caused the volume of new arrivals to fall sharply and decreased the foreign-born component of American Jewry, while the native-born Jewish population grew. At the same time, however, the release of nativist sentiment into the political mainstream via restrictive immigration laws tended to hinder already resident Jewish citizens in the fulfillment of their aspirations for social equality and that ineffable sense of "at-home-ness." Working to enhance their quality of life and, not incidentally, to underwrite their own social security, Jews did such things as revamp the organizational and physical "look" of their communal establishment (as we shall see later on).

Meanwhile, the cluster of institutions that had developed around Jewish workers, organized labor, and American socialism, which had garnered much momentum from 1908 to 1916, were now sorely tested. The Left and the unions were in an exposed and vulnerable position due to the anti-radical campaign waged by the US Justice Department, beginning in 1919. They also faced a surge of anti-labor organizing on the part of major manufacturers and the business community. Major strikes in the railroads, coal, and steel industries all failed in 1919. In that same year, President Wilson's efforts to bring together representatives of labor, employers, and the public broke up when industrialists balked at labor's demands for collective bargaining rights.

Union membership declined from its war-production crest in 1920 almost down to pre-war levels (see Fig. 3.1). Abetted by the courts,

FIGURE 3.1. US union membership (millions), 1904–29.

which struck down hard-won labor laws in the 1920s, manufacturers organized their own "company unions" under slogans like "the American Plan" and "scientific management," and set wages and work conditions at their plants to improve their employees' welfare, but without the "outside interference" of the large unions. They waged open battle to establish "open shop" plants (i.e. a non-unionized workforce). By 1930, reduced union membership brought the percentage of organized workers in the non-agricultural sector to nearly half of what it had been in 1920.[11]

In the case of workers in the needle trades, structural changes in the industry sometimes left them out in the cold – such changes included jobbing out ("outsourcing" in today's language) by leading manufacturers to producers who could now truck their products from smaller towns, where non-union labor predominated. In 1928, the two flagship unions in the garment industry, the International Ladies Garment Workers' Union (ILGWU) and the Amalgamated Clothing Workers of America (ACWA) – both known for the high proportion of Jews in their leadership and among their veteran members – responded by setting up their own unemployment insurance or guaranteed employment schemes.[12]

[11] *Who Built America? Working People and the Nation's Economy, Politics, Culture and Society*, ed. Stephen Brier et al. (New York: Pantheon Books, 1992), vol. II, pp. 270–2, 290–3; Youngsoo Bae, *Labor in Retreat: Class and Community among Men's Clothing Workers of Chicago, 1871–1929* (Albany, NJ: SUNY Press, 2001); Michael E. Parrish, *Anxious Decades: America in Prosperity and Depression, 1920–1940* (New York: W. W. Norton, 1992), pp. 88–90.

[12] Harry A. Millis and Emily Clark Brown, *From the Wagner Act to Taft-Hartley: A Study of National Labor Policy and Labor Relations* (Chicago, IL and London: University of Chicago Press, 1950), pp. 15–18; Herman Frank, *Tsvishn khurbn un oyfboy: der politisher un sotsialervelt-krizis un di yidishe lage (Between Destruction and Reconstruction: The Political and Social World Crisis and the Jewish Condition)* (New York: Bialystoker Bikur Cholim Center of Brooklyn Educational Committee, 1940), p. 210; Irving Bernstein, *The Lean Years: A History of the American Worker 1920–1933* (Boston, MA: Houghton

Factional splits in the American Left and the labor movement also contributed to the crisis. Militant radicals, emboldened and inspired by the examples set by the Russian Revolution and the initial (but abortive) successes of revolutionaries in Germany and Hungary, sought to capture the leadership of unions, party organs, and press activity.[13]

While radicals busied themselves in ideological splinter groups and in the artistic and literary avant-garde, the center and "right" wing in the labor movement and its associated organizations took anti-Red positions, established new mechanisms for labor – management co-existence, and forged an entente with reform-minded Democrats. Anti-Communists in the ILGWU, for example, fought hard to retain control of their organization throughout the decade. They won a Pyrrhic victory: by 1929 the ILG had only 32,000 members (compared with 105,000 in 1920), and the union was so broke that it had to accept an interest-free loan from financier and later New York State Governor, Herbert H. Lehman (1878–1963), in order to stay afloat.[14]

That was not the only instance in which the convoluted politics of the 1920s produced strange bedfellows. Labor activist Rose Schneiderman (1882–1972), president of the leftist Women's Trade Union League in the 1920s and 1930s, became closely associated with Eleanor Roosevelt and Frances Perkins (Labor Secretary from 1933 to 1945), and assumed a

Mifflin Co., 1960), pp. 51, 57, 62–3, 71, 83–108, 136–89, 242; David Montgomery, *The Fall of the House of Labor: The Workplace, the State, and American Labor Activism, 1865–1925* (Cambridge: Cambridge University Press, 1987), pp. 350–4, 385–424; Eli Ginzberg and Hyman Berman, *The American Worker in the Twentieth Century* (Glencoe, IL and London: Free Press/Collier-Macmillan, 1963), pp. 150, 153–4; Parrish, *Anxious Decades*, pp. 81–2.

[13] Michels, *A Fire in Their Hearts*, pp. 220–56; Irving Howe, *World of Our Fathers*, with the assistance of Kenneth Libo (New York: Harcourt, Brace, Jovanovich, 1976), pp. 330–47; *Socialism and American Life*, ed. Donald D. Egbert and Stow Persons (Princeton, NJ: Princeton University Press, 1952); Montgomery, *House of Labor*; Melech Epstein, *Jews and Communism, 1919–1941* (New York: Trade Union Sponsoring Committee, 1959); John H. M. Laslett, *Labor and the Left* (New York: Basic Books, 1970); Liebman, *Jews and the Left*; Joseph Brandes, "From Sweatshop to Stability: Jewish Labor Between Two World Wars," *YIVO Annual of Jewish Social Science* 16 (1976): 49–60.

[14] Bernstein, *Lean Years*, p. 85; Daniel Aaron, "Some Reflections on Communism and the Jewish Writer," in *The Ghetto and Beyond: Essays on Jewish Life in America*, ed. Peter I. Rose (New York: Random House, 1969), pp. 253–69 (republished from *Salmagundi*, I [Fall 1965]: 23–36); Bat-Ami Zucker, "American Jewish Communists and Jewish Culture in the 1930s," *Modern Judaism* 14 (1994): 175–85; Michels, *Fire in Their Hearts*, pp. 217–50; Edna Nahshon, *Yiddish Proletarian Theatre: The Art and Politics of the Artef, 1925–1940* (Westport, CT: Greenwood Press, 1998); Paul C. Mishler, *Raising Reds: The Young Pioneers, Radical Summer Camps, and Communist Political Culture in the United States* (New York: Columbia University Press, 1999).

government appointment as labor advisor to the New Deal mega-agency, the National Recovery Administration (NRA). Meanwhile, Sidney Hillman (1887–1946), president of ACWA, traveled to Russia in 1921, and signed an agreement with Lenin to help the Russians modernize their clothing industry. A few years later, while the Soviet regime was still unrecognized by the United States, the major Jewish overseas aid agency, the American Jewish Joint Distribution Committee (AJDC), and its cadre of Wall Street-based philanthropists undertook to promote Jewish agricultural colonization in Ukraine, in concert with Soviet government agencies – with State Department approval.[15]

Lillian D. Wald (1867–1940), a social work pioneer and founder of the Henry Street Settlement in Manhattan, was closely associated with leading American Progressives and with Jewish financier and philanthropist Jacob H. Schiff; but her internationalism and anti-war activism led her to evince sympathy for Soviet Russia. She expressed her wish that "Lenin and Trotzky's [*sic*] gallantry could be worked out to something stable." Wald traveled to the Soviet Union in 1924 to discuss public health policies and reciprocal exchanges. Even afterward, under Stalin's rule, Russia continued to elicit her favorable support, and from 1926 to 1930, she (along with John Dewey) served as a leader of the American Society for Cultural Relations with Russia.[16]

The Jewish Left – the unions, the United Hebrew Trades (UHT, the Jewish unions' confederation), the socialist press, the fraternal societies, education programs, and political figures in the Socialist Party – entered the fray, only to discover the perils and confusion of factionalism. Yet, as

[15] Joyce Antler, *The Journey Home: How Jewish Women Shaped Modern America* (New York: Schocken Books, 1997), p. 95; *Jewish Women in America: An Historical Encyclopedia*, ed. Paula E. Hyman and Deborah Dash Moore (New York and London: Routledge, 1998), vol. II, pp. 1209–12, 1341–4; Gary Endelman, *Solidarity Forever: Rose Schneiderman and the Women's Trade Union League* (New York: Ayer Co., 1982); Alice Kessler-Harris, "Rose Schneiderman and the Limits of Women's Trade Unionism," in *Labor Leaders in America*, ed. Warren Van Tine and Melvyn Dubofsky (Urbana and Chicago: University of Illinois Press, 1987); Lewis S. Feuer, "American Travelers to the Soviet Union 1917–32: The Formation of a Component of New Deal Ideology," *American Quarterly* 14(2), Part 1 (Summer 1962): 133–6; Bauer, *My Brother's Keeper*, pp. 57–104; Jonathan L. Dekel-Chen, *Farming the Red Land: Jewish Agricultural Colonization and Local Soviet Power, 1924–1941* (New Haven, CT and London: Yale University Press, 2005); Priscilla Roberts, "Jewish Bankers, Russia, and the Soviet Union, 1900–1940: The Case of Kuhn, Loeb and Company," *American Jewish Archives* 49(1–2) (1997): 9–37.
[16] Marjorie N. Feld, *Lillian Wald, A Biography* (Chapel Hill: University of North Carolina Press, 2008), pp. 126–38; Zosa Szajkowski, *Jews, Wars, and Communism, Vol. I: The Attitude of American Jews to World War I, the Russian Revolutions of 1917, and Communism (1914–1945)* (New York: Ktav, 1972), p. 331.

they and the nation turned the corner to another decade, with the onset of the Depression, organized labor retained a surprising political efficacy. The labor movement was the only instrument within the larger Jewish population that could actually play political hardball. It was, as historian Henry Feingold described it, "the first real power base for East European Jews in America." It controlled a major political asset – a disciplined membership willing to go out on the picket line or make its voice heard at the voting booth.[17]

Much of the innovative work done by those "Jewish" unions in the social field – from medical insurance and pension plans to cooperative housing and credit cooperatives, worker education programs, and professionalized union staff – were anticipations of New Deal programs. Even some of the leading personnel recruited by such political leaders as Al Smith, Frances Perkins, and Franklin D. Roosevelt to frame New Deal-era policies were women and men with prior careers in the Jewish labor and social service sphere, including Sidney Hillman, Rose Schneiderman, Belle Moskowitz (1877–1933), Isaac M. Rubinow (1875–1936), and others.

While Jewish working people and their political representatives were creating a subculture that taught the immigrant generation and its children something about political power and its pitfalls, the women's suffrage movement offered another conduit for confronting the dilemmas of American democracy. It is perhaps apt to mark that parallelism by noting the dual political career of Clara Lemlich Shavelson (1886–1982). The young Clara Lemlich spoke out passionately at a New York strike meeting in 1909, which went on to become the famous "Uprising of the 20,000," a massive strike that changed the garment industry. An immigrant from Ukraine, Clara and her family had settled in New York in 1905, where she became involved in the early development of the ILGWU. In the aftermath of the huge strike she had helped to set off, she found that no employer was willing to hire her again. She enlisted in the new Wage Earners' League for Woman Suffrage and became an agitator for the feminist cause. However, her politics once again rubbed others the wrong way and her middle-class feminist sponsors fired her.[18]

Shavelson's experience was not unique. The American Woman's Movement, intent on winning the support of a majority of citizens (of

[17] Feingold, *Zion in America*, pp. 177–8.
[18] Annelise Orlick, "Clara Lemlich Shavelson," in *Jewish Women in America*, ed. Hyman and Moore, vol. II, pp. 1238–41.

both genders), found it expedient to emphasize national, majoritarian versions of Progressive ideas. Women in leadership positions sought to downplay the efforts made by immigrant, leftist, and African American members, who did much to mobilize support in cities like Chicago and New York. At the same time, Woman's Movement activists sometimes viewed the teeming immigrant tenements as a threat to a reformed, equalitarian America. Newcomers from patriarchal cultures, they thought, usually held women in low esteem and sold their ballots cheaply to party machine ward heelers. The ghettos of the nation hardly seemed to them to be the seeding ground of a great democracy.[19]

Extending the franchise to half of the nation was a vital step in widening the country's democracy, but it meant other things, too. Voting rights for women were narrowly passed into law just as the nation was searching for new formulas for social cohesiveness.[20] A defensive posture against real or imagined threats to America's "way of life" went hand in hand with realigning and strengthening the national consensus. The shrillness of anti-immigrant nativism and the adoption of immigration restrictions in the early 1920s, in tandem with the inclusion of women as voting citizens, formed that kind of double-barreled turning point in American history. As the noted Americanist scholar, Sacvan Bercovitch, put it: "The open-ended inclusiveness of the United States was directly proportionate to America's capacity to incorporate *and exclude*, and more precisely to incorporate by [... closing] everything else out, as being Old World and/or not-yet-America" [emphasis in the original].[21]

A third dimension or sphere in which the general moral and political retrenchment of the early 1920s took place was in the crusade against liquor. Like many of their fellow Americans, Jews were apt to feel uncomfortable about Prohibition. Their discomfort was not religious in nature. The use of wine for religious rituals was not restricted: indeed, it was

---

[19] Elinor Lerner, "American Feminism and the Jewish Question, 1890–1940," in *Anti-Semitism in American History*, ed. David A. Gerber (Urbana and Chicago: University of Illinois Press, 1986), pp. 308–11, 316–26; Gail Bederman, *Manliness and Civilization: A Cultural History of Gender and Race in the United States, 1880–1917* (Chicago, IL and London: University of Chicago Press, 1996), chap. 4.

[20] Karla Goldman, "The Limits of Imagination: White Christian Civilization and the Construction of American Jewish Womanhood in the 1890s," in *Imagining the American Jewish Community*, ed. Jack Wertheimer (Hanover, NH and London: University Press of New England/Brandeis University Press in association with the Jewish Theological Seminary of America, 2007), p. 202, and generally pp. 199–203. See also Louise Michele Newman, *White Women's Rights: The Racial Origins of Feminism in the United States* (New York: Oxford University Press, 1999).

[21] Bercovitch, *Rites of Assent*, p. 14.

explicitly licensed under the law, which accommodated both Catholic and Jewish religious needs. Nonetheless, the national anti-alcohol crusade was hard to ignore. It was in its day the equivalent of the "pro-choice" vs. "pro-life" controversy of later times, pitting two visions of American life against each other and infusing a particularly shrill, adversarial, moralistic note into American politics.

Small-town inhabitants or those with roots in rural America predominated among the "dry" constituency. The first states to go "dry" were in the South and West (but not California) – areas of the country noted for their sparse Jewish population; while New York, Pennsylvania, and New Jersey were among the last to ratify the new law. Prohibition emerged from the agrarian Populist tradition, whereas many Jews identified with organized industrial labor. The missionizing, Protestant, and nativist impulses within the Temperance movement were never far from the surface. If Prohibition found support mainly among native-stock white Protestants, then Jews and other communities of first- and second-generation immigrant stock were apathetic or hostile to the moral and cultural absolutism that it implied.[22]

Prohibition impinged on Jewish-related concerns in two separate ways, one minor and one major. The first – a product of the difficulties in enforcing the Volstead Act – was the involvement of some Jews in the lucrative illegal trade in drink, including bootleggers, "speakeasy" proprietors, mobsters, and even some freelance rabbis – some with bona fide credentials, and some not – who were licensed to stock quantities of sacramental wine and who served as conduits for contraband trade. This was a short-lived phenomenon, but one that nevertheless deeply disturbed the established Jewish communal leadership, which sought to eliminate Jewish criminality. In that connection, it is worth mentioning that one Izzy Einstein was a celebrated Federal law enforcement agent

[22] Richard Hofstadter, *The Age of Reform: From Bryan to FDR* (New York: Knopf, 1955); Andrew Sinclair, *Era of Excess: A Social History of the Prohibition Movement* (Boston, MA: Little, Brown, 1962); James H. Timberlake, *Prohibition and the Progressive Movement 1900–1920* (Cambridge, MA: Harvard University Press, 1963), pp. 4–38; Paul Boyer, *Urban Masses and Moral Order in America, 1820–1920* (Cambridge, MA and London: Harvard University Press, 1978), pp. 191–219; Martin E. Marty, *Modern American Religion, Vol. 2: The Noise of Conflict, 1919–1941* (Chicago, IL and London: University of Chicago Press,1991), p. 236; Parrish, *Anxious Decades*, p. 98; Andrew S. Moore, "Prohibition," in *Encyclopedia of Religion in America*, ed. Charles H. Lippy and Peter W. Williams (Washington, DC: CQ Press, 2010), vol. III, p. 1782; Marni Davis, *Jews and Booze: Becoming American in the Age of Prohibition* (New York: New York University Press, 2012); Sarna, *American Judaism*, p. 218.

who was credited with impressive "busts" against liquor smugglers and purveyors.[23]

The second effect involved a longer-lasting change in American Jewish political affiliations. The 1920s brought many Jews, at least at the national level, into the Democratic Party fold. In 1922, for the first time, more Jewish Democrats were elected to the US Congress than Jewish Republicans. By 1930, six of the eight Jewish members of the House were Democrats. Jews in major centers like New York City, Chicago, and Boston lent considerable electoral support to New York Governor Al Smith in his unsuccessful presidential bid of 1928. "Smith was a 'wet,' a Catholic, and a product of urban, ethnic, working class life," and the campaign against Smith tarred him as the candidate of "foreigners" and "immoral drinkers." Smith's voice came across audibly in the campaign's radio coverage as that of a typical New Yorker, while Hoover, the "dry" candidate, stressed his rural Midwestern roots. When Hoover trounced Smith, the St. Paul *Pioneer-Press* crowed, "America is not yet dominated by its great cities. [...] Main Street is still the principal thoroughfare of the nation."[24] The pro-Democratic trend in American Jewish political culture continued to strengthen, despite Smith's electoral defeat, and in the 1930s Jews in most major cities were a solidly Democratic-voting demographic group.

Quotas, Communities, and Creature Comforts

Immigration quotas were just one aspect of the unfavorable American public disposition on racial, ethnic, and religious difference in the wake of World War I. In the same decade that saw the immigrant quota system established, Jewish Americans began to feel the bite of discrimination in employment and in private colleges.

A survey of commercial employment agencies in one typical community found that just slightly over half were willing to place Jewish job-seekers with employers; others stated their view that it was not worth the effort, as Jewish applicants' chances were slim, or they maintained

[23] Parrish, *Anxious Decades*, pp. 100–1; Joselit, *Our Gang*, pp. 93–105.
[24] Fuchs, *The Political Behavior of American Jews*, pp. 64, 66–7; Breier, *Who Built America?*, vol. II, p. 314; Bernstein, *Lean Years*, pp. 76–80; Hofstadter, *The Age of Reform*, pp. 280–300. The groundswell for the Democrats in 1928 in northern and western cities was also reflected in the dismal showing of Norman Thomas's Socialist Party candidacy: under 270,000 votes (a third coming from New York), as compared to Eugene V. Debs's 900,000 ballots in 1920.

a policy against registering Jewish job-seekers at all. Similarly, the job-referral office of a major university with a 15 percent Jewish student body found that 40 percent of its alumni who were still jobless a year following their graduation were Jewish. Likewise, a study conducted in a large Midwestern city found that the county medical society had never had a Jewish officer; that 60 percent of all retail and manufacturing enterprises did not hire Jews "as a matter of practice"; that Jews were not hired in banking, finance, public utilities, transportation, or insurance companies; that relatively few Jews taught in the public schools; and that Jews were also barred from the Automobile Association of America, Rotary, Kiwanis, and the Athletic Club.[25]

Prestigious institutions of higher learning used discriminatory screening methods or quotas to reduce the statistical "surplus" of Jews on campus. Nationwide, Jews were said to be 10 percent of college enrollment, though at large East Coast universities those estimates were sometimes doubled, or even tripled, especially in particular schools or departments. Selective admissions practices (quotas) were intended to bring Jewish enrollment down to less conspicuous levels.[26]

In practice, many aspiring Jewish students found placement in city and state universities (New York's city colleges were a prime example). Enrollment blockages in professional schools were eased, after a while, by the opening of new medical schools affiliated with Jewish-sponsored hospitals, though this took forward planning and a massive investment of private funds. In one case, this entailed founding an entirely new college under Jewish auspices (Brandeis University, founded 1948), located on the campus of an older, private medical school (Middlesex) in Waltham, MA. In a different case, a former Russian Jewish immigrant, Dr. John

---

[25] Judith R. Kramer and Seymour Leventman, *Children of the Gilded Ghetto* (New Haven, CT and London: Yale University Press, 1961), pp. 43–4; Abraham K. Korman, *The Outsiders: Jews and Corporate America* (Lexington, KY and Toronto: Lexington Books, 1988), pp. 44–5; Leon Sokoloff, "The Rise and Decline of the Jewish Quota in Medical School Admissions," *Bulletin of the New York Academy of Medicine* 68(4) (1992): 497–518; Nathan C. Belth, *A Promise to Keep: A Narrative of the American Encounter with Anti-Semitism* (New York: Times Books, 1979), p. 112.

[26] Klingenstein, *Jews in the American Academy*, pp. 5–7; Marcia Graham Synnott, *The Half-Opened Door: Discrimination and Admissions at Harvard, Yale, and Princeton, 1900–1970* (Westport, CT: Greenwood Press, 1979); Stephen Steinberg, *The Academic Melting Pot: Catholics and Jews in American Higher Education* (New York: McGraw Hill, 1974); Belth, *A Promise to Keep*, pp. 96–110, 185–94; Dan A. Oren, *Joining the Club: A History of Jews and Yale* (New Haven, CT: Yale University Press, 1985); Jerome Karabel, *The Chosen: The Hidden History of Admission and Exclusion at Harvard, Yale and Princeton* (Boston, MA: Houghton Mifflin Company, 2005).

Jacobi Sheinin, took over as dean and president of the Chicago Medical School and guided its upgrade from a low-level, night-school program to a professional training institute. Aimed at future medical practitioners rather than research (and therefore rated as a "Class B" school), about 80–90 percent of its student body was Jewish.[27]

In any event, the academy was not yet, in the interwar period, the sovereign gateway to occupational mobility and economic achievement. The overall patterns of economic performance and mobility of the Jewish population at large were quite favorable, despite discrimination, because they rested more on small- and medium-range businesses than on professional careers. In addition, public employment offered routes to meritocratic advancement and job security. Qualified job-seekers built careers in the postal service, public schools, social work, public health, and law enforcement, while legal and legislative advisors were employed by a myriad of municipal, state, and federal agencies. Thus, patterns of discrimination in certain fields did not cancel out significant integration into the economy and social institutions. Aware of such barriers and openings, people tailored their aspirations to suit job market realities, and such adaptations buffered them from the harsher implications of prejudice.

The significance of student admissions quotas and tacit barriers to Jewish faculty appointments lay not so much in their immediate personal consequences as much as in their symbolic repercussions. An entire generation of the American social, political, and business elite, educated in Ivy League institutions and subsequently able to command policy-making positions in government and major corporations, took for granted the subordinate status of their Jewish fellow citizens. In the mid- to late 1930s, for example, underlying perceptions of Jewish "otherness" buttressed economic and political objections in Congress and the Administration against the admission of Jewish refugees in flight from Nazi Germany. The cultural encoding of Jewishness as a social liability was never enshrined in actual legislation, unlike the infamous Jim Crow system that methodically subordinated and humiliated African Americans; but it had significant consequences nonetheless.

At the subjective level, the disparity between civic equality and relative prosperity on the one hand and the premise that Jewishness was a social liability, on the other, caused considerable fallout. "Not fully accustomed

---

[27] Sokoloff, "Jewish Quota," pp. 508–9; Abram L. Sachar, *Brandeis University. A Host at Last* (Hanover, NH and London: Brandeis University Press/University Press of New England, 1995), pp. 8–16.

to [their] new security," claimed one observer, Jews "alternately revel in it and doubt it." "There are really only two kinds of Jews: those who are consumed by [...] anxiety but succeed in denying it even to themselves [and] those who are troubled [...] but would never dream of denying it," noted another. An insightful religious thinker of the day, Rabbi Milton Steinberg, emphasized the sense of uncertainty: "Only a people of acrobats could preserve a semblance of poise on a footing so unstable." Openly discussed in the Jewish press of the day were questions about the ethics of "passing" in the interests of successful job-hunting, such as "Why should Levy become Lee and Rabinowitz Robins?" Such self-critical questions and assessments became sufficiently familiar and well rooted to persist right down to the 1960s.[28]

The constricted range of socially approved paths for advancement, combined with a characteristically American dose of rashness and sense of self-empowerment, could and sometimes did find alternative expression in criminality. The route of social deviance, as the late sociologist Daniel Bell once argued, could be considered an "American way of life [...] a Coney Island mirror, caricaturing the morals and manners of a society. [...] The coarse gangster elements, most of them from new immigrant families, who were 'getting ahead,' [reflected] the jungle quality of the American business community."[29]

Crime – violent crime in particular – was a major concern during the interwar years. The Jewish population was not egregiously overrepresented in the nation's crime statistics, but neither was it absent. The roll-call of Jewish mobsters, underworld bosses, and bootleggers included the notorious few, the likes of Louis "Lepke" Buchalter, Abe "Kid Twist" Reles, Meyer Lansky, "Dutch" (Arthur Flegenheimer) Schultz, and Benjamin "Bugsy" Siegel, and numerous other petty criminals besides.[30]

---

[28] Stuart E. Rosenberg, *The Search for Jewish Identity in America* (Garden City, NY: Doubleday, 1964), p. 273; Lothar Kahn, "Another Decade: The American Jew in the Sixties," *Judaism* 10 (1961), quoted by Rosenberg; Milton Steinberg, *The Making of the Modern Jew* (New York: Behrman House, 1943 [1934]), p. 247; Riv-Ellen Prell, *Fighting to Become Americans: Jews, Gender, and the Anxieties of Assimilation* (Boston, MA: Beacon Press, 1999), p. 121 (re: "passing"), and generally, on the persistent motifs of cultural anxiety.

[29] Daniel Bell, "Crime as an American Way of Life," *The Antioch Review* 13(2) (1953): 132.

[30] Edwin H. Sutherland and C. E. Gehlke, "Crime and Punishment," in *Recent Social Trends in the United States*, pp. 1144, 1150; Joselit, *Our Gang*, pp. 54–84, 106–39; Albert Fried, *The Rise and Fall of the Jewish Gangster in America* (New York: Columbia University Press, rev. ed., 1993); Anton Hieke, "Frabrekhers in America: The Americanization of Jewish Blue-Collar Crime, 1900–1931," *Aspeers: Emerging Voices in American Studies* 3 (2010): 97–115 (www.aspeers.com/ 2010/hieke).

Neither straitened circumstances nor the ostensible lack of better career options lay behind the most sensational cases of Jewish criminality, however. New York gambling boss and bootlegger Arnold Rothstein (depicted as Jay Gatsby's associate, Meyer Wolfsheim, in F. Scott Fitzgerald's novel *The Great Gatsby*), who was murdered in 1928, came from a "respectable, middle-class, American home." Beyond any remotely picaresque notions of gangster life was the case of Nathan Leopold and Richard Loeb, who committed the "crime of the decade" – the pointless kidnapping and cruel murder of Loeb's fourteen-year-old cousin, Bobby Franks, in 1924. The two killers were University of Chicago-trained, headed for careers in law, and stemmed from the upper-crust, German-Jewish elite in Chicago.[31]

Jews and American Agriculture in the Twenties

Little appreciated today is the fact that in the 1920s and 1930s there was a minor swing of Jewish students toward agricultural colleges – another alternative avenue toward professional mobility. Jewish students represented a fifth of those studying agronomics at New Jersey's Rutgers University (where the department was headed by a Jewish dean, Jacob Lipman, and where other Jews served on the faculty). Agricultural studies attracted job-seeking Jews to careers in experimental farm stations and laboratories.[32]

Jewish farming in the interwar period provided a counterpoint to the mainly urban developments that predominated in Jewish society. An episode worth considering took place in Petaluma, California, not far from San Francisco, the self-styled "Egg Basket of the World." The earliest Jewish farmers in the area had been assisted by a fund established by Fannie K. Haas of the wealthy Haas family of San Francisco, heads of the Levi Strauss Company. About one hundred Jewish families were established there by the mid-1920s, drawn almost entirely from Russia, Ukraine, Bessarabia (today's Moldova), and Poland. Morris Rogin emigrated from the Crimea after the Russian Revolution of 1905, and worked as a cap-maker in New York, Los Angeles, and San Francisco before settling in Petaluma. Basha Singerman went there from Minsk, via a stopover at a Jewish dairy ranch near Nairobi, Kenya, in 1915. Khaya

---

[31] Joselit, *Our Gang*, pp. 140–56; Michael Alexander, *Jazz Age Jews* (Princeton, NJ: Princeton University Press, 2001), pp. 15–54; Simon Baatz, *For the Thrill of It: Leopold, Loeb, and the Murder that Shocked Jazz Age Chicago* (New York: HarperCollins, 2008).

[32] Frank, *Tsvishn khurbn un oyfboy*, p. 264.

Feinstein came from Ukraine after the massacres there during the warfare between Bolsheviks and anti-communist forces in 1919. Yossl Gardner, from Kishinev, Bessarabia, was a factory hand in the needle trades, fought for Britain in the Jewish Legion in World War I, and returned to New York before heading to the West Coast in 1928. Fellow-settler Louis Menuhin also joined the Jewish Legion in 1917 and returned after the war. (Yehudi Menuhin [1916–1999], the celebrated violinist, was his nephew.)

The other farms in the Petaluma area had a mixed population of Italians, Portuguese, Germans, Scandinavians, and native-born Americans. "You had a lot of people growing apples and pears and cherries [but] all the Jewish farmers, they was [*sic*] on little chicken ranches," reported one veteran. Not all went well in Petaluma, however. One disgruntled farm wife deserted home and hearth after three years and headed for the city life in San Francisco. But this community was knit together (and fought together amongst themselves) out of strong ideological loyalties to the radical Left. Active with Communist causes, one resident was tarred-and-feathered by American Legionnaires from Santa Rosa for organizing protest meetings on behalf of striking farm workers.[33]

Community Life in an Age of Affluence

Considering the relative strength of popular anti-Jewish feeling in the twenties, the social distance between Jews and non-Jews may well have reinforced Jewish institutions catering to their own constituency. As an example, between November 1930 and January 1931 meetings were held between various national Jewish organizations to form a National Conference on Jewish Employment, with a view to collecting data to combat job discrimination against Jews.[34]

However, the energies that Jews devoted to their organizational networks seem more than just defensive. They seem, rather, to have drawn upon the positive, activist ethos of America's civic culture. As the

---

[33] Kenneth L. Kann, *Comrades and Chicken Ranchers: The Story of a California Jewish Community* (Ithaca, NY and London: Cornell University Press, 1993), pp. 4–5, 16–17, 19, 23, 37–41, 47–8, 54–6, 84–8, 91–120, 178–220; Levine and Miller, *The American Jewish Farmer*, pp. 60–2; Kenneth Libo and Irving Howe, *We Lived There Too: In Their Own Words and Pictures – Pioneer Jews and the Westward Movement of America, 1630–1930* (New York: St. Martin's/Marek, 1984), pp. 291–3; Eisenberg, Kahn, and Toll, *Jews of the Pacific Coast*, pp. 93–5; Phillip Naftaly, "Jewish Chicken Farmers in the Egg Basket of the World: the Creation of Cultural Identity in Petaluma, California," *Teaching Anthropology: Society for Anthropology in Community Colleges [SACC] Notes* (Fall-Winter 1995–6): 25.

[34] *American Jewish Year Book*, vol. XXXIV (1932), p. 289.

Progressive Era waned and President Warren G. Harding's politics of "normalcy" took its place, America's civic life took on a new set of priorities.[35] The end of mass immigration and the renewed isolationist turn in US foreign policy signaled an embrace of American self-sufficiency. To some extent, we may imagine the lives of Jews living in 1920s America as a minor echo of that theme. Jews applied the logic of self-reliance to their material as well as their spiritual and communal agendas. Some inkling of this positive energy is obliquely conveyed in words that Rabbi Mordecai M. Kaplan (1881–1983) inscribed in his diary in December 1918. Kaplan, who would become a key figure in New York and national Jewish institutions, and was the founder of Reconstructionism, an innovative, American-based Jewish denomination, wrote: "To love America is simply to love myself," indicating that America, for him, meant a certain quality of self-esteem and hardy forthrightness.[36]

"Love of self" – and of the "American" in the self – is a good way to sum up the fundamental positive motive behind the growth of Jewish institutions. The new Jewish communal apparatus, similar to its nineteenth-century precursors but varied and multiplied far beyond nineteenth-century dimensions, seemed to concretize and advertise the American penchant for self-expressiveness and self-boosting.

Partly, the expansion of Jewish communal agencies was a function of the growth of the Jewish population over the course of several decades. Bureaucratic growth followed closely upon demographic growth. Jewish charity federations (described in Chapter 2) were established in some thirty Jewish communities in cities across the country between 1895 and 1920. From 1920 to 1940, the number of such bodies quadrupled to 125. At the same time, the number of special interest or single-constituency organizations outside the purely philanthropic sphere (religious, educational, professional, community service, community relations, Zionist, and social/fraternal associations and institutions) more than doubled from 1910 to the end of the 1930s – some quite small, others boasting memberships in the thousands.[37]

---

[35] Parrish, *Anxious Decades*, p. 9.

[36] *Communings of the Spirit: The Journals of Mordecai M. Kaplan, Volume I: 1913–1934*, ed. Mel Scult (Detroit, MI: Wayne State University Press, 2001), p. 134, entry for Dec. 29, 1918.

[37] Elazar, *Community and Polity*, pp. 211–17, 235–9; Marc Lee Raphael, "Federated Philanthropy in an American Jewish Community: 1904–1948," *American Jewish History* 68(2) (1978): 147–62; Deborah Dash Moore, "From Kehillah to Federation: The Communal Functions of Federated Philanthropy in New York City, 1917–1933," *American Jewish History* 68(2) (1978): 131–46.

The 1920s also saw the mushrooming of American synagogues, even if they appear to have catered mainly to a minority core of active members over the course of a typical year – the annual High Holidays excepted, when attendance was more widespread. Only a quarter of the Jewish population was formally affiliated with a synagogue in the mid-1920s, and in New York City only one Jew in five bothered to attend services. Nonetheless, build they did: there were an estimated 3,120 synagogues in America in 1926 and 3,740 in 1937. Much of the expansion was related to the movement of Jewish residents outward from inner-city quarters to other residential areas. Newly established neighborhood clusters mandated the transfer of old congregations or the founding of new ones.[38]

Some indication of what motivated the building of new synagogues – even into the Depression decade – emerges from a local study, conducted by a team of American sociologists in Newburyport, Massachusetts, in which Jews were one of several subgroups examined. In 1932, their businesses hurting, the Jews in this New England community decided to reduce the salary of the synagogue's Hebrew school instructor, but also decided to raise funds from the membership to build a new synagogue building. The original premises, acquired in 1907, were described as "a plain frame building, fronting on a narrow, unpaved alley-like street [where] families of new [i.e. Southern and Eastern European] ethnic groups lived." The new building, in contrast, was located "on a paved, tree-shaded street whose residents are predominantly middle-class natives [...] in a desirable section of the city [...] one that will make every Jew proud." Members justified the expense and the shift to better quarters, despite the economic turndown, because they no longer wished to resemble "the Salvation Army," as one of them put it. The drive to construct a new edifice, undertaken by younger men and women, was intended to reverse the apathy that had overtaken the religious life of the community, to the point where it had become a residual activity mostly for the elderly.[39]

It should be noted that the Jewish populace behaved more or less in accord with general American trends. While those "not in church" were a substantial part of the national population (30 percent in the South and nearly 70 percent on the West Coast), the property value of church

[38] Abraham J. Karp, "Overview: The Synagogue in America," in *The American Synagogue: A Sanctuary Transformed*, ed. Jack Wertheimer (New York and Cambridge: Cambridge University Press, 1987), pp. 23–4; *American Jewish Year Book*, vol. XXXVIII (1926–7), Preface, p. iv; Moore, *At Home in America*, pp. 123–47.
[39] Warner and Srole, *Social Systems of American Ethnic Groups*, pp. 205–17.

edifices per adult inhabitant in the United States shot up in the 1920s from $7 to nearly $50 and church expenditures more than doubled.[40]

The denominational subdivision typical of American Judaism – a three-way split between Reform, Conservative, and Orthodox streams (virtually exclusive to the United States at that time, albeit with certain German, Hungarian, and British parallels) – took definitive shape during the interwar years. The resultant competition for Jewish souls also helps to account for the multiplication of sectarian institutions. By 1929, the Conservative group (organized nationally as the "United Synagogue") claimed 230 affiliated congregations; the Reform wing (Union of American Hebrew Congregations) claimed 280; and the vast bulk of the remainder were mainly Orthodox congregations – many of which, typical of this era, were very small and led a transient existence. In the late 1930s there were about 900 synagogues affiliated with the Union of Orthodox Jewish Congregations (Orthodox Union), apart from many independent, immigrant-based congregations. The trend, however, was a drift away from Orthodoxy toward the liberal denominations – especially the increasingly popular Conservative movement, which positioned itself in the center of the denominational map.[41]

Other stimuli for synagogue building and the new conventions in synagogue architecture that arose in the interwar years included the conceptual expansion of the synagogue's social function. Apart from being a house of prayer, the modern synagogue offered a venue for a range of social and cultural activities. When Temple B'nai Jeshurun of Newark, New Jersey hired an architect to plan a new building, he thought to equip the main hall with a projection booth and movable screen: "The picture screen is on one side of a revolving partition, the other side being provided with a small cabinet for the [Torah] scrolls when the hall is used for devout services." At a host of other congregations, the laity were happy enough to redesign their synagogues with leisure, socializing, educational, and sport facilities in mind. The design of contemporary, interwar synagogues reflected the concept of a multi-purpose, service institution and often eschewed the orientalist flourishes of the old "Moorish"

[40] C. Luther Fry and Mary Frost Jessup, "Changes in Religious Organizations," in *Recent Social Trends in the United States*, pp. 1025, 1028–9.
[41] Sarna, *American Judaism*, pp. 224–5; Wertheimer, *The American Synagogue*, pp. 63, 116; Henry L. Feingold, *A Time for Searching: Entering the Mainstream, 1920–1945*, The Jewish People in America series (Baltimore, MD and London: Johns Hopkins University Press, 1992), pp. 90–1, 93–9.

style – though, with some modification, the architectural nod toward the Jews' Semitic origins sometimes persisted into the late 1920s.[42]

Such attention to function and style, acknowledging the public's capacity to admire high standards in execution, well suited the tenor of the times. The American generation that had come of age by the First World War, it has been noted, lived in "a time of much greater general activity in the arts and of higher public esteem for them [...], a time when] fewer people gloried in our provincialism."[43] The vogue for large-scale, opulent architecture resonated with the high aesthetics of cathedrals and other public monuments and fitted well with the centrality of institutions to the religiosity embraced during that era.

Ironically, this institutionalism – and the accoutrements of a "club" that added leisure activities to the synagogue center's functions – were precisely what would alienate members of a later generation, whose notions of spirituality were far-removed from the inspirational aids of the 1920s. Casting a backward glance to the interwar years, the investment in large, institutionally complex synagogues (conjuring the droll epithet, "the edifice complex") seemed to some latter-day critics to express an over-compensation for the waning of household observances of Jewish rites.

Taking a less anachronistic, more empathetic approach, we might note that the embellishment of religious expression by means of large buildings and a high aesthetic was in tune with the social experience of the era. It should be recalled that in the 1920s, even motion picture theaters were often built to a scale and with the kind of detailed aesthetic appointments that evoked grandeur, opulence, other climes, and great expectations. Reaching for a visual idiom more suited to the dignity of a religious institution than to a commercialized palace of entertainment, synagogue builders needed to elevate the idea of religion over quotidian affairs. In trying to capture concretely an idea of the sublime, Jews endowed their synagogues with an idealized version of their other aspirations and achievements. At their most prosaic level, those aspirations reflected the improved standards of living of that time.

[42] William G. Tachau, "The Architecture of the Synagogue," *American Jewish Year Book*, vol. XXVIII (1926–7), pp. 190–2; Wischnitzer, *Synagogue Architecture*, pp. 106–32; David Kaufman, *Shul with a Pool: The Synagogue-Center in American Jewish History* (Hanover, NH and London: Brandeis University/University Press of New England, 1999), pp. 242–3, 247–54.
[43] Keppel, "The Arts in Social Life," in *Recent Social Trends in the United States*, p. 962.

Per capita income for occupational groups that closely resembled Jewish employment profiles (men's and women's clothing industry employees, clerks in manufacturing companies, retail sales personnel, and teachers) moved up between 1914 and 1926 by an average of 24 percent. Commenting on the latest trends in private consumption, social researchers at the end of the 1920s wrote: "Science, technology, improved merchandising [...] have created outright, brought into volume production, or raised to the position of necessaries of life, a long list of new goods and services [...] new standards of health, child rearing, comfort, convenience, labor saving, cleanliness, leisure, travel, personal attractiveness, and variety in living." Refrigerator sales jumped by 150 percent during the 1920s, and by 1929, 12 million American families owned at least one radio.[44]

Higher standards of living and the attendant changes in lifestyle provided the means and the goals for new or renewed Jewish organizations and institutions. Organizational life also benefited from the countless hours of labor provided by brigades of volunteer workers, mostly female, who made community service their vocation. The rapidly spreading Jewish federations, less preoccupied now by endemic immigrant poverty, turned their attention to the special needs of those who fell behind in the scramble for getting ahead: those who were handicapped by physical illness, family crisis, or mental disorder. In short, we might describe the sectarian institution-building wave as a social dividend of the rising middle classes' disposable income, tastes, and sense of collective honor. A significant segment of the Jewish population benefited from white-collar employment, entrepreneurship, and professional training; they, in turn, produced the revenue that fueled investment in communal self-organization.

Americanizing the Rabbinate and Fostering Women's Roles

With immigration severely diminished, any further impetus for religious life would necessarily come from mainly indigenous sources. That change was reflected in the emergence, by the 1920s, of a new cadre of American-trained rabbis, not only at the veteran seminary of the Reform movement,

---

[44] Robert S. Lynd and Alice C. Hanson, "The People as Consumers," in *Recent Social Trends in the United States*, pp. 857–8; see also *Recent Social Trends in the United States*, p. 859, Table 1, and 879, Table 8; Ginzberg and Berman, *The American Worker*, pp. 149–50; Parrish, *Anxious Decades*, pp. 30–1.

Cincinnati's HUC, but also at the relatively newer East Coast schools: JTS and RIETS. To these were added, in 1922, the Jewish Institute of Religion (JIR) established in Manhattan by Rabbi Stephen S. Wise as an alternative liberal school of Judaic studies (JIR later merged with HUC in 1950); and the Hebrew Theological College, an Orthodox seminary in Chicago. Fortuitously, the first men of RIETS to be educated entirely in the United States received their ordination in 1919.

Some of the changes this entailed were subtle or invisible to the outside observer. The rabbinical ordination granted to most of the students by the Conservative JTS and the Orthodox RIETS alike was not generally of the most comprehensive kind.[45] Specialized Talmudic expertise had been regarded by traditionalists in Europe as the *sine qua non* of a truly erudite rabbinical scholar, but modern rabbinical seminaries in Central and Western Europe – including Orthodox ones – tended to pare down their curricula (mainly by omitting the realm of civil jurisprudence). This West European practice was grafted onto the American rabbinical schools, even though most of the American students (and their teachers) were of East European birth or descent.[46]

The new crop of American rabbis, who thus acquired a streamlined type of rabbinical training, was groomed for tasks that were not formally part of the rabbi's traditional job description. With an eye to American norms of clerical professionalism, practical and preaching skills were introduced and new attention was paid to pastoral functions vis-à-vis congregants (counseling the troubled, visiting the sick, attending funerals, comforting mourning families). Products of American rabbinical schools also had to have a basic capacity to run an institution while keeping a sovereign lay leadership placated and motivated to renew their rabbinical employees' contracts. The expectations that American rabbis should be all these things gradually meant that American Jewish congregations could no longer rely on imported clergy.[47]

---

[45] Known in Hebrew as *yadin-yadin*, it conferred on those so trained the prerogative of arbitrating civil suits according to rabbinical law.

[46] Victor B. Geller, *Orthodoxy Awakens: The Belkin Era and Yeshiva University* (Jerusalem and New York: Urim Publications), pp. 15–16, 19, 26; Charles S. Liebman, "The Training of American Rabbis," *American Jewish Year Book*, vol. LXIX (1968), pp. 3–112; David Ellenson and Lee Bycel, "A Seminary of Sacred Learning: The JTS Rabbinical Curriculum in Historical Perspective," in *Tradition Renewed: A History of the Jewish Theological Seminary of America, Volume Two: Beyond the Academy*, ed. Jack Wertheimer (New York: Jewish Theological Seminary of America, 1997), pp. 529–30, 535–9.

[47] Liebman, "The Training of American Rabbis"; Gurock, *The Men and Women of Yeshiva*, pp. 50–2, 55–6, 124–5; Ellenson and Bycel, "Seminary of Learning," pp. 544–8, 556–69.

The sense of increased self-sufficiency in religious matters was communicated in other ways, too. Jews in the US directed fewer questions of practical *halakhah* (religious practice according to Talmudic law) to revered rabbis in Europe. Although the links tying rabbis based in America and those in Europe (or Palestine) remained at the core of Orthodox rabbinical discourse, by 1930 the great bulk of practical decisions governing Jewish ritual observance were being rendered locally. Bernard Dov Revel (1885–1940), the head of RIETS, lamented the havoc wreaked upon the great European centers of Torah learning since the Great War, but pointed to America as the foundation stone of a potentially new Judaic center, evidently ordained as such by Providence. As the interwar years advanced, this new Orthodox credo – contrasting European collapse and American peace and growth – took root among some of Revel's peers.[48]

In addition to these denominational changes and pragmatic adjustments, the "woman question" was a key aspect of interwar Jewish communal affairs. As of 1920, there were some half-dozen national Jewish women's organizations.[49] The new ideas about women's unique responsibilities in Jewish communal life were exemplified, to some extent, in the creation of Hadassah, the Women's Zionist Organization, just prior to the First World War. Henrietta Szold and a cadre of like-minded, well-educated, sophisticated women founded this women's club primarily for cultural enrichment and self-education. During the Great War, the group undertook to organize a medical mission whose primary task was to bring modern health care to Palestine, in the wake of Britain's victory over the Turkish imperial regime. One might define their program as a case of applied social feminism: an intervention by women in social improvement, particularly in a field related to the caring professions. Its altruism resembled the ethical impulse of other American-sponsored sectarian missions abroad.[50]

---

[48] Menahem Blondheim, "Harabanut ha'ortodoksit megalah et amerikah: hageiografiah shel haruah bemitvim shel tikshoret" ("The Orthodox Rabbinate Discovers America: The Geography of the Spirit in Communication Networks"), in *Be'ikvot kolumbus: amerikah, 1492–1992 (In the Footsteps of Columbus: America, 1492–1992)*, ed. Miri Eliav-Feldon (Jerusalem: Mercaz Zalman Shazar, 1996), pp. 499–510.

[49] The National Council of Jewish Women (1893), the National Federation of Temple Sisterhoods (1913), the Sigma Theta Pi Sorority (1909), the Women's League of the United Synagogue of America (1918), and Hadassah, the Women's Zionist Organization (1912), all were officered by women. *American Jewish Year Book 5680*, vol. XXI (1919), pp. 304–28.

[50] Donald H. Miller, "A History of Hadassah, 1912–1935" (PhD dissertation, New York University, 1968), pp. 50–104, 244–63; Matthew Silver, *First Contact: Origins of the*

Women like Szold and her colleagues undertook senior executive responsibilities in crucial and sometimes contentious spheres. Hadassah combined cultural activities and self-education in the Jewish heritage along with practical, hands-on projects (sewing clothing for the threadbare households of Palestine pioneers) and raising financial support for the health and social work projects undertaken among both Jews and Arabs in Palestine – particularly in Jerusalem. By the 1930s, Hadassah was able to assume primary responsibility for sponsoring the evacuation of thousands of Jewish teenagers from Nazi-dominated Central Europe, bringing them to live in Palestine.[51]

Another approach to recognizing women's activism and sectarian affinities was via their daughters. Modern, coeducational approaches to rites of passage for youths in the Jewish community had begun as early as the 1840s and continued through the early twentieth century, when Reform rabbis sought to introduce a "confirmation" ceremony for youngsters in their mid-teens, both boys and girls. In this connection, it is also relevant to note that American public high schools, where most Jewish teens were likely to go to school, were overwhelmingly coeducational by the turn of the twentieth century.[52]

Synagogues that identified with the Conservative movement were also not averse to introducing a co-ed confirmation class and an appropriate ceremony, as a supplement to the traditional boys' bar mitzvah. At the same time, a "bas"- (or "bat-") mitzvah, "intended to offer girls an

American-Israeli Connection. Halutzim from America During the Palestine Mandate (West Hartford, CT: The Graduate Group, 2006), pp. 80, 109; Michael Brown, *The American-Israeli Connection: Its Roots in the Yishuv, 1918–1945* (Detroit, MI: Wayne State University Press, 1996), pp. 133–47; Mary McCune, *The Whole Wide World, Without Limits: International Relief, Gender Politics, and American Jewish Women, 1893–1930* (Detroit, MI: Wayne State University Press, 2005), pp. 11–13, 21–8, 37–41, 51–3, 60–2; Mira Katzburg-Yungman, *Hadassah: American Women Zionists and the Rebirth of Israel* (Oxford and Portland, OR: Littman Library of Jewish Civilization, 2012), pp. 11–33.

[51] Miller, "History of Hadassah," pp. 105–15, 134–232, 237–43, 314–21; Brown, *Israeli-American Connection*, pp. 136, 147, 149, 150–5, 159; Aaron Berman, *Nazism, the Jews, and American Zionism, 1933–1948* (Detroit, MI: Wayne State University Press, 1990), pp. 18–19, 28, 34–6; McCune, *The Whole Wide World*, pp. 79–80, 91–111, 136–44.

[52] Meyer, *Response to Modernity*, pp. 50, 140, 175, 237, 241, 286, 298; Regina Stein, "The Road to Bat Mitzvah in America," in Nadell and Sarna, *Women and American Judaism*, pp. 223–4; Jenna Weissman Joselit, *The Wonders of America: Reinventing Jewish Culture, 1880–1950* (New York: Hill and Wang, 1994), pp. 89–119; Melissa R. Klapper, *Jewish Girls Coming of Age in America, 1860–1920* (New York and London: New York University Press, 2005), pp. 93–4, 148–84; Goldman, "Women in Reform Judaism," pp. 118–19; Ruben, *Max Lilienthal*, pp. 85–6.

initiation ceremony in the synagogue in the same spirit as their brothers," was discussed in the 1920s and was tentatively introduced in individual communities. It became more widespread after World War II.[53]

The Orthodox sector typically did not lead the way in gender-egalitarian innovation but a few successful experiments in co-educational school-ing did take root, with long-term implications for the modernized wing of Jewish Orthodoxy. Co-education was introduced in the late 1920s at Brooklyn's Yeshiva of Flatbush, and three more co-educational Orthodox schools were founded in the New York area during the 1930s. In Boston, Rabbi Joseph Ber Soloveitchik (1903–93) and his wife, Dr. Tonya Lewit Soloveitchik (1903–67) – their professional collaboration was significant in itself – introduced co-education at the Torat Israel Yeshiva in 1935. In the next decade, they instituted the same policy at the new, all-day Maimonides School that they co-founded. Particularly surprising was the fact that Maimonides did not distinguish between girls and boys in the advanced grades' religious studies curriculum. Talmud study (historically a male preserve) was standard fare for all junior high and high school pupils. In contrast, the Flatbush Yeshiva practiced a more conservative pedagogy by reserving higher Talmud classes for upperclassmen and offering ethics classes to the young women.[54]

Trans-migrants, Canadians, and Expats

During the mass immigration period, as we saw, there was only a very limited Jewish re-emigration from the United States. Yet, in mapping the entire migration flow of Jews in and out of the US, they should not be entirely dismissed. Two-way traffic was part of the fluid social reality of the migration stream, and émigré Jews who had lived for a time in America and then departed were part of that phenomenon. That contin-ued to be so in the interwar period.[55]

---

[53] Joselit, *Wonders of America*, pp. 131–2, 127–33; Stein, "Bat Mitzvah," pp. 224–6; Paula E. Hyman, "The Introduction of Bat Mitzvah in Conservative Judaism in Postwar America," *YIVO Annual* 19 (1990): 133–46; Sylvia Barack Fishman, *A Breath of Life: Feminism in the American Jewish Community* (Hanover, NH and London: University Press of New England/Brandeis University, 1993), pp. 130–5.

[54] Seth Farber, *An American Orthodox Dreamer: Rabbi Joseph B. Soloveitchik and Boston's Maimonides School* (Hanover, NH and London: Brandeis University Press/University Press of New England, 2004), pp. 41, 68–87, 109–10, 120–1; Gurock, *American Jewish Orthodoxy*, pp. 313–18, 322–4, 332–3.

[55] Ellen P. Kraly, "Emigration: Implications for U.S. Immigration Policy Research," www .utexas.edu/lbj/uscir/binpapers/v2a-4kraly.pdf, p. 587; R. Warren and Ellen P. Kraly,

We should bear in mind that during World War I, New York City was the temporary home of several Jewish political émigrés: Ukrainian-born Bolshevik leader, Leon (Lev) Trotsky (*né* Bronstein, 1879–1940), who would become head of the Red Army following the Russian Revolution of 1917; Polish-born Palestinian Zionist-socialist leader and future first prime minister of Israel, David Ben-Gurion (*né* Grin, 1886–1973); as well as his comrade-in-arms, Ukrainian-born Yitzhak Ben-Zvi (*né* Shimshelevitz, 1884–1963), who later became Israel's second president.

Former Secretary of State and US Senator from New York, Elihu Root, claimed in 1917 that 10,000 émigrés had returned to Russia from the United States – mainly Jewish New Yorkers – in order to participate in revolutionary activity after the fall of the Tsarist regime. Root exaggerated considerably: between 1917 and 1920, the number of Russian "Hebrews" who re-emigrated totaled 3,760, and it is impossible to guess just how many of those were politically active, let alone Bolsheviks. There were simply not that many Trotskys. Still, there were publicized individual cases, such as that of Israel Rubin, the business agent of several locals of the Furriers' union. The union's newsletter, the *Fur Worker*, announced his departure for Russia on May 6, 1917, to take "active part" in the revolution. Among other re-emigrants of the time was Ber Borochov (1881–1917), a leading Marxist theoretician in the ranks of socialist Zionism, who died of illness soon after returning to Russia; and Elias Tcherikover (1881–1943), a historian, though he returned again to America in 1940.[56]

Even after 1921, however, when the volume of Jewish migration to America was radically reduced and native-born American Jews were attaining an ever greater share in the population, a back-channel of two-way traffic persisted. That Jews (whether American-born or foreign-born) should move elsewhere is understandable within the context of overall national American migration patterns in the interwar period. The years from World War I to 1929 – and particularly from 1920 to 1924 – saw

---

The Elusive Exodus: Emigration from the United States. *Policy Trends and Public Policy*, no. 8 (March 1985); Mark Wyman, *Roundtrip to America: The Immigrants Return to Europe, 1880–1930* (Ithaca, NY and London: Cornell University Press, 1993); Sarna, "The Myth of No Return."

[56] Szajkowski, *Jews, Wars, and Communism*, vol. I, pp. 283–314. Borochov's widow and children subsequently resettled in Palestine. Elias Tcherikover, who had first arrived in America in 1915, left after the March Revolution of 1917 and lived in Ukraine until 1921. He later moved to Berlin and, after the rise of the Nazis to power, moved to Paris. A co-founder of the YIVO Institute for Jewish Research in interwar Poland, he continued after 1940 to work under the auspices of the transplanted YIVO in New York. *Encyclopedia Judaica*, 1st ed. (Jerusalem: Keter, 1971), vol. XV, col. 876.

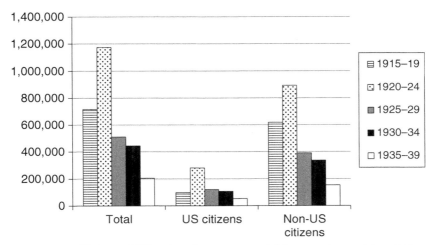

FIGURE 3.2. Estimated US emigration, 1915–39 (citizens and non-citizens).[57]

considerable re-emigration of resident non-US citizens and the emigration of a fair number of citizens (see Fig. 3.2). Re-migration or trans-migration is evidence of the "normalization" of America and of American Jewry as part of an international system, which must be placed alongside regnant myths of America as a "chosen" or "promised land," the ultimate immigrant haven.

American-born Jews, some of whom chose to leave the country permanently, as well as those who left with the full intention of returning, mirrored in their lives some of the more unsettling aspects of life in interwar America. American Jewish students who found they were unable to gain admission to American medical schools, for example, formed one group of expats in the interwar period. Most went to study at universities in Scotland, Switzerland, and Germany. In the early 1930s, more than 90 percent of American citizens studying medicine in Europe were Jews![58]

The closest staging arena for migration and re-emigration was Canada. As the American immigration quotas took hold, European Jewish migration to Canada, as well as other destinations (chiefly Palestine and Argentina), picked up. In 1922, more than 8,000 Jews entered Canada, compared to only 2,760 the previous year. A lower spike occurred again

[57] Warren and Kraly, *Elusive Exodus*, p. 5; Arnold Dashefsky, Jan DeAmicis, Bernard Lazerwitz, and Ephraim Tabory, *Americans Abroad: A Comparative Study of Emigrants from the United States* (New York and London: Plenum Press, 1992), p. 17.

[58] Sokoloff, "Jewish Quota," pp. 504–5.

during the years just after 1924. On average, however, Jewish immigration per year into Canada from 1925 to 1931 was only about 3,680 – lower than pre-1914 rates, owing to Canada's restrictive immigration policies.[59]

As Jewish immigration from overseas began to fall, the interchange of Jewish population between Canada and the United States became proportionally more significant to the migration history of both communities. Twenty-six thousand Jews moved to Canada from the United States from 1926 to 1938; slightly over 10 percent were US-born (second-generation children of East European migrants). In Toronto, there was a Jewish New Yorkers' association – a fraternal society called "Anshe New York." On Canada's Pacific coast, in British Columbia, US citizens made up nearly a third of all the Jewish foreign nationals.[60]

At the same time, Canada was also a source of immigration entering the United States. There were over one million Canadians (one-third of them were French Canadians) living in the US in 1920. Jews formed a small part of this cross-border drift. The official data account for those who entered legally. The country's northern border was notoriously porous, and an unknown number of immigrants – including Jews – entered the United States illegally.[61]

Rose Schneiderman, whose political career we mentioned before, lived in Montreal during 1902–03, before returning to New York. During the 1920s, nearly 25,000 Jews left Canada for the United States, including nine-year-old Saul Bellow, the future author and Nobel laureate, whose family moved from Quebec to Chicago. Another 5,000 entered during the 1930s. Communities relatively close to the border were apt to be primary destinations, such as Buffalo, New York. Some European Jewish migrants arrived in the United States on temporary visas and had to exit to Canada while their papers were processed for re-entry as immigrants – as happened in the case of the Polish-born Yiddish writer, Isaac Bashevis Singer (1902–91).[62]

[59] Hersh, "International Migration," p. 474; Gerald Tulchinsky, *Canada's Jews: A People's Journey* (Toronto: University of Toronto Press, 2008), p. 228; Garland, *After They Closed the Gates*, pp. 73, 79.

[60] Rosenberg, pp. 131, 146, 245, 258; Lestchinsky, "Jewish Migrations," in Finkelstein, *The Jews*, vol. II, p. 1582; Tulchinsky, *Canada's Jews*, pp. 210, 220–1.

[61] Garland, *After They Closed the Gates*, pp. 56, 92, 95, 104; and "Not-quite-closed Gates: Jewish Alien Smuggling in the Post-Quota Years," *American Jewish History* 94(3) (2008): 197–224.

[62] G. E. Jackson, "Emigration of Canadians to the United States," *Annals of American Academy of Political and Social Science* 196 (1923): 25–34; Meinig, *The Shaping of*

Canada was a transit point, as well, because of its political linkage to Great Britain. It served as a convenient conduit for American Jews who volunteered for service in British military units during both World Wars. One episode of this sort involved enlistment of young men from America in the volunteer Jewish Battalions, also called the Jewish Legion, in World War I. The ranks of these North American volunteers included one Nehemiah Rabin (*né* Rubitzov), who had come to New York from Ukraine in 1904. In New York, he was active in the Labor Zionist *Poale Zion* movement. Shipping out with the Legion in 1918, Rabin remained in Palestine after the war; his son Yitzhak (1922–95), born in Jerusalem, twice served as Israeli prime minister until his assassination. Also among this group of trans-migrants was Gershon Agronsky (1894–1959), a Russian-born child of immigrants who grew up in Philadelphia and earned his college degree at Temple University. After graduating, he worked for the Zionist Organization in New York, where he enlisted in the Legion. At the end of the war, Agronsky (who shortened his name to Agron) remained in Palestine after his demobilization, working as a journalist and Zionist spokesman. He founded the *Palestine Post* (later renamed the *Jerusalem Post*) in 1932, and subsequently served as mayor of Jerusalem (1955–9).

During the early years of the British Mandatory government (1921–48), Palestine drew a small but highly qualified group of American-born Zionist immigrants. Henrietta Szold, as a founder of Hadassah, put her organization forward as the major sponsor of the American Zionist Medical Unit (AZMU) – a task force of forty physicians, nurses, technical specialists, and public health officials whose departure for Palestine coincided with that of the Jewish Legion. In 1921, Szold took up the supervision of the AZMU, replacing Alice Seligsberg (1873–1940), a Barnard College graduate and New York social work activist who had accompanied the expedition from its embarkation through its initial running-in phase.[63]

America, vol. IV, p. 126; *American Jewish Year Book (AJYB)*, vol. XXIII, p. 297; *AJYB*, vol. XXV, p. 348; *AJYB*, vol. XXVI, p. 596; *AJYB*, vol. XXVII, p. 404; *AJYB*, vol. XXVIII, p. 421; *AJYB*, vol. XIX, p. 257; *AJYB*, vol. XXX, p. 263; *AJYB*, vol. XXXI, p. 323; Rosenberg, *Canada's Jews*, p. 136, Table 92; Uriah Z. Engelman, "The Jewish Population of Buffalo, 1938," in Robison, *Jewish Population Studies*, p. 39.

63 Silver, *First Contact*, pp. 71–131; Baila R. Shargel, "American Jewish Women in Palestine: Bessie Gottsfeld, Henrietta Szold, and the Zionist Enterprise," *American Jewish History* 90(2) (2002): 141–60; Erica B. Simmons, "Playgrounds and Penny Lunches in Palestine: American Social Welfare in the Yishuv," *American Jewish History* 92(3) (2004): 263–97; Hyman and Moore, *Jewish Women in America*, vol. II, pp. 1227–8.

Szold's close associate in Jerusalem, the New York-raised poet and educator Jessie Sampter (1883–1938), was enraged by the British failure to prevent anti-Jewish violence among Arabs in Palestine in the 1920s. Reflecting on the chances for peaceful coexistence between Palestinian Jews and Arabs, she expressed the hope that small groups of like-minded pioneers from America, who would combine, as she put it, Zionist and "communist" ideals (referring to egalitarian communes), might settle in villages adjacent to those of Palestinian Arab farmers, in order to create niches of personal interaction, understanding, and cooperation.[64]

Like Szold, Judah Magnes, formerly the head of the New York Jewish communal board, the *Kehillah*, resettled in Palestine in 1921, where he was later appointed first president of The Hebrew University of Jerusalem (founded in 1925). Magnes, even more emphatically than Szold, was a pacifist, and both were active in later years in supporting bi-national (Jewish-Arab) political solutions for Palestine. Notable in this coterie was also Deborah Kallen (1888–1957), sister of the American social philosopher, Horace Meyer Kallen (1882–1974). Deborah wrote her brother "Harry" in 1933, describing the school in Jerusalem that she directed, and rejecting his appeal to her to return to the United States.[65]

Agron, Szold, Magnes, Kallen, and Sampter represented what might be called a migration of intellectuals and professionals drawn to service careers in another land (a kind of Jewish "missionary" elite); but they also exemplify a somewhat broader, though numerically select group of idealistic émigrés who personally identified with the social and political

[64] In 1929, in the wake of the particularly savage attacks against Jewish residents in Jerusalem, Safed, and Hebron – all were bi-national cities at that time – Sampter helped draft a letter of protest to Washington, complaining of British negligence: "American citizens in Palestine sent a cable to Washington asking the Government to protest against the criminal negligence of the local [British] administration which, among other horrors, was responsible for the piecemeal butchery [...] of eight American boys, defenseless students in the Academy [yeshiva] of Hebron. Although I contributed a word or two to the cable, I was not able to sign it because I am no longer an American citizen but a Palestinian. Never was I so glad as now of this change of citizenship. I have a right in the protection of my own [Palestine] government [...] and I do not want to be tempted to ask for special privileges." Bertha Badt-Strauss, *White Fire: The Life and Works of Jessie Sampter* (New York: The Jewish Reconstructionist Foundation, 1956; reprint ed. Arno Press, 1977), p. 79 and Appendix B. See also Naomi W. Cohen, *The Year After the Riots: American Responses to the Palestine Crisis of 1929–30* (Detroit, MI: Wayne State University, 1988).

[65] Deborah Kallen to Horace Kallen, February 27, 1933, in *Devorah kallen: hayehah umif'alah* (*Deborah Kallen: Her Life and Work*), ed. Elisha Efrat (Jerusalem: Brandeis Center/Hadassah Educational Publications, 1959), p. 42.

goals of the Jewish national project in Palestine. Between 1919 and 1948, 6,600 Jews born in the United States emigrated to Palestine.[66]

At the time, Winston Churchill remarked that radicalized European Jews were evidently torn between the political poles of Communism and Zionism – and that he rather preferred that they seek a Zionist resolution to the Jewish Question.[67] In America, however, such polarization was buffered by the processes of Americanization then underway among second- and third-generation members of the Jewish population. And yet, even if it was low-key, the political choice between life in America, Palestine, or Communist Russia was freshly posed among some young Jews in the wake of World War I and the Russian Revolution.

Alter Brody, whose lament for the wartime destruction of his old hometown in Ukraine was cited in the conclusion of Chapter 2, dedicated his volume of poems, *A Family Album* (1918), "To Russia." In the book's final poem, he confessed that he had not sufficiently appreciated the epic depths of the Russian soul and regretted that he was not there in Russia's great hour of need, to help usher in the Revolution. The poem registers a reference to the torch of liberty, transposed from New York to the steppes and forests of Russia. Brody, however, like most Jewish radicals in America, chose to stay in the United States.[68]

Some were not given the choice, such as the famous anarchist duo, Emma Goldman (1869–1940) and her partner, Alexander Berkman (1870–1936), who were deported by US authorities. Goldman, a prominent anarchist publicist in America, was widely known for her journal, *Mother Earth*. Berkman, having failed in his attempt on the life of Henry Clay Frick (chairman of the board of Andrew Carnegie's Homestead Steel mills, outside Pittsburgh), was imprisoned for fourteen years in 1892. Goldman and Berkman were part of a group of some 250 radicals deported by the United States to Russia in 1920. The couple found the Bolshevik regime very uncongenial, however (they were anarchists, after all, not communists), and they subsequently wandered between various

---

[66] Lestchinsky, "Jewish Migrations, 1840–1956," vol. XXII, pp. 1572, 1584; Brown, *The Israeli-American Connection*; Joseph Glass, *From New to Old Zion: American Jewish Immigration and Settlement in Palestine, 1917–1939* (Detroit, MI: Wayne State University Press, 2002).

[67] Winston S. Churchill, "Zionism versus Bolshevism," *Illustrated Sunday Herald*, February 8, 1920, p. 5.

[68] "Now I see!/ I will fly to you/ And help you upbear in your arms/ The torch of the new-born Freedom/ That you hold for the world./ I will learn your tongue […]/ And breathe out on your steppes, in your forests/ New York's fever and dust." Brody, "To Russia – 1917," in *A Family Album and Other Poems*, pp. 130–2.

countries. Berkman committed suicide in France. Goldman attempted to move back to America, but her repeated applications were denied, and she lived in Canada until her death. She was buried at Waldheim Cemetery in Chicago, near the graves of the victims of the tragic events at Haymarket Square.[69]

A subsidiary trickle of ideological migrants, drawn from the radical American and Jewish Left, voluntarily made their way in the 1920s and 1930s to the Soviet Union, staying there in some instances for decades. Some apparently remade their lives successfully, while others were deeply disenchanted by their experience, and eventually left.[70]

In some cases, the interplay between divergent ideological choices was uncanny. One such case involved the intertwined stories of Gershon Agron and his friend Louis Fischer (1896–1970). Like Agron, Fischer was a Philadelphian who served with Britain's Jewish Legion in World War I. But while Agron remained in Palestine, Fischer went to live in Bolshevik Russia. There he was a correspondent for *The Nation*, published several books, and became known as an apologist for the Stalinist regime. In the mid-1930s he served in the International Brigade during the Spanish Civil War, fighting Franco, before returning to the US in 1938. Fischer, disenchanted with Stalinism, subsequently renounced his earlier pro-Communist beliefs.[71]

---

[69] Candace Falk, *Love, Anarchy, and Emma Goldman: A Biography* (New Brunswick, NJ: Rutgers University Press, 1990); Marian J. Morton, *Emma Goldman and the American Left: Nowhere at Home* (New York: Twayne Publishers, 1992); Christine Stansell, *American Moderns: Bohemian New York and the Creation of a New Century* (New York: Henry Holt & Co., 2000), pp. 36–8, 120–44, 323–6; Emma Goldman, *Anarchism and Other Essays* (1917; New York: Dover, 1969); *Red Emma Speaks: Selected Writings and Speeches by Emma Goldman*, ed. Alix Kates Shulman (New York: Schocken, 1983).

[70] Nokhem Khanin, *Sovetrusland: vi ikh hob ir gezen* (*Soviet Russia as I Saw It*) (New York: Farlag "Veker," 1929); Daniel Soyer, "Back to the Future: American Jews Visit the Soviet Union in the 1920s and 1930s," *Jewish Social Studies* 6(3) (2000): 124–51. I am indebted to Tony Michels for directing my attention to Khanin's report. See also Paula Garb, *They Came to Stay: North Americans in the U.S.S.R.* (Moscow: Progress Publishers, 1987); Mary M. Leder, *My Life in Stalinist Russia: An American Woman Looks Back*, ed. Laurie Bernstein (Bloomington: Indiana University Press, 2001); Eva Stolar Meltz and Rae Gunter Osgood, *And the Winds Blew Cold: Stalinist Russia as Experienced by an American Emigrant* (Blacksburg, VA: McDonald & Woodward, 2000); Alexander Dolgun, *Alexander Dolgun's Story: An American in the Gulag*, assisted by Patrick Watson (New York: Knopf/Random House, 1975); David Remnick, "The Bitter Pilgrimage of Abe Stolar," *Washington Post*, May 10, 1988. On the "triad of political choice," see Silver, *First Contact*, p. 69.

[71] Silver, *First Contact*, p. 69.

The Great Depression, the New Deal, and the
Jewish Refugee Question

Notwithstanding the tug of ideological alternatives, the main body of American Jewry avoided pitting their Americanism against trans-national commitments of any sort. Rather, they exhibited a strong penchant for their own version of "normalcy." Devoting keen attention to their individual, domestic, and communal welfare, they threw in their lot with America's political progressives: from Teddy Roosevelt's "Square Deal," to Woodrow Wilson's "New Freedom," to Franklin D. Roosevelt's "New Deal."

When the first shocks of the economic crisis were felt, President Hoover voiced his belief that the first line of a citizen's social defense lay in families, communities, and private relief organizations. The Federal government, he warned, ought not to intrude where the private sector, in concert with city and state administrations, exercised primary responsibility. To do otherwise would undermine "the roots of self-government." Yet, by the time Hoover's administration had ended in the winter of 1932–3, he knew that this formula had proven untenable. Indeed, both private and public relief programs had already expanded considerably in the 1920s, paving the way to greater state and Federal funding, essentially blurring the distinctions between public and private welfare. Roosevelt (who was as much opposed as Hoover to a permanent national "dole"), accepted Federal relief as unavoidable.[72]

In light of such systemic change, which impinged on so many individuals, it is difficult to articulate the particular narrative of a small minority like the Jews. In an important sense, that *is* the story of American Jewry in the Great Depression. Historians who have examined a variety of American ethnic groups in the interwar period have characterized the Depression and New Deal era as a time when a broad-based, nationalized approach to government encroached upon formerly distinctive ethnic niches and group-based social functions. As national priorities and a politics of common endeavor came to the fore, particular causes and the constituencies who cared about them were pushed to the margins. This affected the entire gamut of voluntary service agencies, fraternal

[72] Bernstein, *Lean Years*, Hoover quoted on p. 287, and see generally pp. 287–332, 456–74; Parrish, *Anxious Decades*, pp. 240–62, 270–1, 289–300; Jeff Singleton, *The American Dole: Unemployment Relief and the Welfare State in the Great Depression* (Westport, CT and London: Greenwood Press, 2000), pp. 1–13, 27–47, 57–82.

associations, and benevolent societies, both sectarian and non-sectarian. Much the same holds true for the Jews.[73]

As was true of other groups, the private, sectarian communal agencies providing social services and voluntary philanthropy, which Jews had built over the course of generations, continued to function; but they found their resources stretched beyond their limit by the sharply rising demand for relief, caseworkers, and small loans. In New York alone, the Jewish Social Service Association allocated $500,000 for poor relief in 1929. By 1932, faced with the need to spend three times that amount, and having already depleted its own funds, the agency had to draw much of its poverty-relief funding from general community and municipal sources, to which Jews and Jewish organizations had contributed. On the opposite coast, in Los Angeles, the Jewish Social Service Bureau chose to disburse only partial or "supplemental assistance" – that is, aid to poverty-stricken Jewish households already receiving public relief – rather than attempt to assume full responsibility for those Jews' welfare needs. One caseworker stated bluntly, "Perhaps the most important lesson coming out of this emergency is the fact that an unwilling Jewish community has come to realize that relief work can [...] be financed by public funds without detriment to Jewish families."[74]

During those years, many Jewish organizations lost members, as did the nation's synagogues. In part, this was a general American phenomenon, as Federal funding and new public programs took center stage. Private, individual assistance rendered to one's close kin and to one's church or co-ethnic group certainly continued. "I couldn't resist," recorded one well-to-do Florida matron. She helped "two poor Jewish

[73] Bruce Stave, *The New Deal and the Last Hurrah: Pittsburgh Machine Politics* (Pittsburgh, PA: University of Pittsburgh Press, 1970); Lizabeth Cohen, *Making a New Deal: Industrial Workers in Chicago, 1919–1939* (Cambridge and New York: Cambridge University Press, 1990), pp. 219–38, 268–70, 274–7, 362–5; Gary Gerstle, *Working-Class Americanism: The Politics of Labor in a Textile City, 1914–1960* (Cambridge and New York: Cambridge University Press, 1991), p. 195; John Bodnar, *Remaking America: Public Memory, Commemoration and Patriotism in the Twentieth Century* (Princeton, NJ: Princeton University Press, 1992), pp. 37, 42.

[74] Stein, "Jewish Social Work," p. 62; see also Frank, *Tsvishn khurbn un oyfboy*, p. 313; Max Vorspan and Lloyd P. Gartner, *History of the Jews of Los Angeles* (Philadelphia, PA: Jewish Publication Society, 1970), p. 195; Gartner, *History of the Jews of Cleveland*, pp. 290–5, 303–06; Feingold, *A Time for Searching*, pp. 146–52; Tenenbaum, *A Credit to Their Community*, pp. 48–65; Beth S. Wenger, *New York Jews and the Great Depression: Uncertain Promise* (New Haven, CT and London: Yale University Press, 1996), pp. 136–65; Suzanne Wasserman, "'Our Alien Neighbors': Coping With the Depression on the Lower East Side," *American Jewish History* 68(2) (2000): 209–32.

men who begged for work," giving them a day's work of washing windows. But at wider social levels, parochial support groups were no longer regarded as the best model for addressing unemployment and poverty. The crisis spared no one and its rectification, therefore, required systemic rather than case-by-case treatment.[75]

By their voting behavior, a majority of Jews in the 1930s indicated their approval of the governmental interventionist approach and federal activism. They expressed their belief that, by blending everyone (at least hypothetically) into one nationwide constituency, public-based welfare and a regulated economy could become powerful vehicles for ameliorating the lives of the poor and addressing the social exclusion of minorities. In adopting liberal New Deal politics so wholeheartedly, major portions of the Jewish public took an important step from being freshly naturalized citizens toward becoming truly involved in national issues. It was as much a rite of passage as it was the adoption of a political culture. The Jewish lurch to New Deal politics and economics should not be misconstrued as a monolithic verity, however. Jews sometimes remained stalwart Republicans. Prominent among the economic experts who argued heatedly against the new fiscal doctrines were a few influential Jewish professors, like Aaron Director (1901–2004) and Jacob Viner (1892–1970). (Viner taught Milton Friedman [1912–2006], the Nobel laureate and guru of conservative market economics. Director was Friedman's brother-in-law.)[76]

This caveat aside, however, seldom had Jews so overwhelmingly bonded with the political consensus of their neighbors as they did in the 1930s, when they mostly voted Democrat along with other city-dwellers, northerners, and other minority group constituencies. Indeed, even when the broad FDR coalition started to fray, Jews actually increased their

[75] Marc Dollinger, *Quest for Inclusion: Jews and Liberalism in Modern America* (Princeton, NJ and Oxford: Princeton University Press, 2000), pp. 15, 19–35; Jack Wertheimer, "The Conservative Synagogue," in *The American Synagogue*, pp. 122–3; Feingold, *Time for Searching*, pp. 148, 163; Sarna, *American Judaism*, p. 256; Wenger, *New York Jews and the Great Depression*, pp. 166–96; Jason Kaufman, *For the Common Good? American Civic Life and the Golden Age of Fraternity* (New York and Oxford: Oxford University Press, 2002), pp. 8–9, 43–50, 163–76. Quotation from Helen Jacobus Apte, *Heart of a Wife: The Diary of a Southern Jewish Woman*, ed. Marcus D. Rosenbaum (Wilmington, DE: SR Books, 1998), p. 144 (entry for November 11, 1931).

[76] Morawska, *Insecure Prosperity*, pp. 198, 339 n. 6; Don Patinkin, *Essays on and in the Chicago Tradition* (Durham, NC: Duke University Press, 1981), pp. 297–300; Leonard Silk, *The Economists* (New York: Basic Books, 1976), p. 46; Oren Harman, *The Price of Altruism: George Price and the Search for the Origins of Kindness* (London: Vintage Books, 2011), p. 120.

electoral support for the Democratic president. Jewish labor union activists, politicians, and voters who remained loyal to the Social-Democratic left, who reconstituted themselves in 1936 as the new American Labor Party, adopted a solid pro-FDR position, as well. The Labor Party endorsed Roosevelt for President in 1936, 1940, and 1944. Along with significant numbers of other American workers and labor leaders, they tailored their New Deal-era politics to mesh with the new political realities, rather than pursue sectarian ideologies.[77]

So firmly entrenched in the Roosevelt coalition did Jews appear to be, that some opponents of FDR and his policies sneered viciously at his "Jew Deal," alleging that Jews exercised unwarranted political influence in the Administration. On the radical right, disenchanted former Roosevelt-supporters like Father Charles Coughlin, the "radio priest," not only churned out anti-FDR invective from the Shrine of the Little Flower Church in Royal Oak, Michigan, but also spewed virulent Jew-hatred to millions of his listeners across the country.[78]

It was true, indeed, that some Jews were strategically positioned in the inner circle of presidential advisors and senior officials (Bernard Baruch, Felix Frankfurter, Isador Lubin, Henry Morgenthau, Jr., David Niles, and Nathan Straus among them). Irish Catholics, too, figured among FDR's closest advisors and senior appointees (Jim Farley, Ed Flynn, Charles Fahy, and Joseph P. Kennedy). The team of top White House legislative aides, nicknamed "the Gold Dust Twins," was composed of Ben Cohen

---

[77] The ALP, virtually a "Jewish third party" (Feingold, *Time for Searching*, pp. 213–14), was active in New York State and was led by such figures as Jacob Potofsky of the Amalgamated Clothing Workers of America, David Dubinsky of the ILGWU, and Alex Rose of the Hat, Cap, and Millinery Workers Union. See Fuchs, *Political Behavior*, pp. 129–30; Melvyn Dubofsky, "Not So 'Turbulent Years': A New Look at the 1930s," in *Life and Labor: Dimensions of American Working-Class History*, ed. Charles Stephenson and Robert Asher (Albany, NY: SUNY Press, 1986), pp. 221–3.

[78] Alan Brinkley, *Voices of Protest: Huey Long, Father Coughlin, and the Great Depression* (New York: Knopf, 1982), pp. 82–4, 93–100, 119–27, 133–42, 242–8, 266–73; Anthony J. Badger, *The New Deal: The Depression Years, 1933–40* (Basingstoke: Macmillan, 1989), pp. 290–2, 294–5; Benjamin Ginsberg, *The Fatal Embrace: Jews and the State* (Chicago, IL and London: University of Chicago Press, 1993), pp. 104–08, 112–19; Leonard Dinnerstein, *Antisemitism in America* (New York and Oxford: Oxford University Press, 1994), pp. 115–22; Fuchs, *Political Behavior*, pp. 74–9; Marty, *Modern American Religion* 2, pp. 273–81; Michael Kazin, *The Populist Persuasion: An American History* (New York: Basic Books, 1995), pp. 113–33; Parrish, *Anxious Decades*, pp. 325–8; McGreevy, *Catholicism and American Freedom*, pp. 162, 165, 173; Charles R. Gallagher, "A Peculiar Brand of Patriotism: The Holy See, FDR, and the Case of Reverend Charles E. Coughlin," in *FDR, the Vatican, and the Roman Catholic Church in America, 1933–1945*, ed. David B. Woolner and Richard G. Kurial (Basingstoke: Palgrave Macmillan, 2003), pp. 269–77.

and Thomas ("Tommy the Cork") Corcoran. Indeed, the New Deal White House drew much support from among both Jews and Catholics. Yet, political activism and ethnic influence are two separate things, and just as one cannot speak here of an Irish ascendancy, so, too, the impression of "Jewish" influence was deceptive.[79]

The massive social engineering to which many Jews subscribed tended to marginalize all of their parochial concerns within the larger scheme of things. Unable to provide for their own poor-relief needs without public assistance, they were quite willing to ally their interests with the Federal system that was re-engineered to promote the national interest at large. By the very same token, however, Jews were equally unable to enter a forceful claim for their particular needs. This ought not to surprise anyone familiar with the fate of socially based interest group constituencies in that period. Farmers' groups, women's movements, the labor movement, activism among African Americans – all these were characteristically on the rise from post-Civil War Reconstruction to World War I. Then, in the thirties, the New Deal subsumed nearly all prior sectoral interests – farmers, business, and labor alike – under its wing. Disenchantment with this centralistic dispensation was pushed to the political margins, where anti-FDR critics made up in vociferousness what they lost at the polls.

This may help to explain one of the great paradoxes of the Jewish experience in the 1930s – the fact that Jews, many of whom still felt like members of a marginalized minority, were unexpectedly propelled into the very heart of America's political majority, where they were part of a broad consensus. Yet, this integration stood in direct contrast with the resistance Jews personally experienced in everyday life. Racist passions, already flagrant in the 1920s, flared even higher in the United States in the 1930s, and directly targeted black Americans, Mexican migrant workers, and Jews. What advantages Jews might have possessed by virtue of their "whiteness," vis-à-vis other minorities at that time, did not have a significant impact on their ability to defend their separate interests. As a constituency, they felt vulnerable.[80]

[79] Parrish, *Anxious Decades*, pp. 392–3; *Time Magazine*, September 12, 1938 (cover story); Leonard Dinnerstein, "Jews and the New Deal," *American Jewish History* 72(4) (1983): 466–70; Henry L. Feingold, "'Courage First and Intelligence Second': The American Jewish Secular Elite, Roosevelt, and the Failure to Rescue," *American Jewish History* 72(4) (1983): 437; Badger, *The New Deal*, p. 249.

[80] Eric Goldstein, *The Price of Whiteness: Jews, Race, and American Identity* (Princeton, NJ: Princeton University Press, 2006), chap. 6. Meining, *The Shaping of America*, vol. IV, pp. 126–7.

This conundrum would haunt the Jewish leadership's efforts to win adequate support for European Jewish refugee assistance – an issue with both domestic and foreign policy ramifications that became ever more pressing after Nazi Germany enacted its infamous Nuremberg Laws of 1935. Jews with close ties to the Administration raised the issue of refugee assistance, but were not empowered to do very much about it. Felix Frankfurter (1882–1965) – the Harvard jurist, intrepid defender of Sacco and Vanzetti (the anarchist duo convicted of murder and executed in 1927), close advisor to the President and later an FDR appointee to the US Supreme Court – resorted to private channels to try to have his aged uncle released from Nazi incarceration in Vienna in 1938. Frankfurter said he felt it was inappropriate for him to use his connections with the Administration for a personal matter. When the matter of his uncle's release from a Nazi camp was reported in the press, Frankfurter took the trouble to write the President personally in order to deny having curried any special favors in the Administration.[81]

The image that this might convey, of tremulous hesitancy or an exaggerated fear of impropriety, is inaccurate, however, when taken out of context. Frankfurter had very early joined forces with his ally, Labor Secretary Frances Perkins, to formulate the legal means for bringing more asylum-seekers from Germany to the United States, and had discussed the matter with the President himself. Parallel efforts were made by a number of people well placed within or closely tied to the Administration: Henry Morgenthau, Jr. (FDR's Hyde Park neighbor and soon to become his Secretary of the Treasury), Charles Wyzanski (a savvy Labor Department solicitor), and key Democratic political figures like Judge Irving Lehman (1876–1945), and Judge Julian Mack (1866–1943), among others. Those plans and discussions, however, were effectively rebuffed by a combination of senior State Department officials, isolationist America Firsters in public office, and a few powerful Congressional committee chairs, none of whom was willing to relax the extra-stringent post-1930 immigration and naturalization procedures. Procedural and legislative roadblocks prevailed over any serious Jewish lobbying efforts. The Jewish lawyers and advisors in Washington were players within the Administration, but not, in the final analysis, power-brokers in the arena of partisan politics, where votes counted.[82]

[81] Alexander, *Jazz Age Jews*, pp. 69–124; Gulie Ne'eman Arad, *America, its Jews, and the Rise of Nazism* (Bloomington and Indianapolis: Indiana University Press, 2000), pp. 132–3.
[82] Feingold, "'Courage First,'" p. 432; Richard Breitman and Alan M. Kraut, *American Refugee Policy and European Jewry, 1933–1945* (Bloomington and Indianapolis: Indiana

The same was equally true of others, such as James G. McDonald, who as League of Nations High Commissioner for Refugees (1933–5) was in close and constant touch with the White House, American officials, leaders in Latin America and Europe, including Nazi Germany, as well as Jewish leaders in the US. Although strongly committed to refugee aid and thoroughly pessimistic about the ultimate fate of German Jewry, McDonald felt blocked at every turn.[83] It has come to be understood by most scholars that the White House found it expedient to have these issues thrashed out at the inter-office and Congressional level, and, though sympathetic, rarely if ever intervened in any definitive way. As the refugee crisis of the 1930s morphed into wartime cries for rescue in 1942–5, the avoidance of personal political risk on the part of the President took on even greater significance.[84]

Finally, during the war years, the Oval Office had its trump card: making Jewish rescue one of America's war aims would risk the war effort politically. It could cost the lives of US servicemen and women, either directly or indirectly (by prolonging the war, for instance, or by diverting precious resources to humanitarian operations). Could any of the hypothetical ideas being aired – the diversion of troops, ships, and air crews into rescue missions; bombing sorties over Auschwitz; opening negotiations with the Reich, none of which was guaranteed to save anyone – be justified at such cost? Would American soldiers fight for such a cause?

University Press, 1987), pp. 11–27, 34–5, 37, 39, 59–60; Bat-Ami Zucker, "Frances Perkins and the German Jewish Refugees, 1933–1940," *American Jewish History* 81(1) (2001): 35–59. See also David S. Wyman, *Paper Walls: America and the Refugee Crisis 1938–1941* (Amherst, MA: University of Massachusetts Press, 1968); Arad, *America, its Jews, and the Rise of Nazism*; Ariel Hurwitz, *Jews Without Power: American Jewry During the Holocaust* (New Rochelle, NY: MultiEducator Publishers, 2011), pp. 28–69; Richard Breitman and Allan J. Lichtman, *FDR and the Jews* (Cambridge, MA: Harvard University Press, 2013).

[83] See *Advocate for the Doomed: The Diaries and Papers of James G. McDonald 1932–1935*, as well as the sequel volume, *Refugees and Rescue: The Diaries and Papers of James G. McDonald 1935–1945*, ed. Richard Breitman, Barbara McDonald Stewart, and Severin Hochberg (Bloomington and Indianapolis: Indiana University Press in association with the United States Holocaust Memorial Museum, Washington, DC, 2007, 2009).

[84] Feingold, "'Courage First,'" p. 425; *The Politics of Rescue: The Roosevelt Administration and the Holocaust, 1938–1945* (New Brunswick, NJ: Rutgers University Press, 1970), pp. 3–21, 295–8, 301–7; and *Bearing Witness: How America and its Jews Responded to the Holocaust* (Syracuse, NY: Syracuse University Press, 1995), pp. 85–7; David S. Wyman, *The Abandonment of the Jews: America and the Holocaust, 1941–1945* (New York: Pantheon Books, 1984), pp. xiv–xv, 178–205, 311–17; Breitman and Kraut, *American Refugee Policy*; Parrish, *Anxious Decades*, p. 462.

Would this not inflame antisemitism at home? Would American Jews be prepared to bear the consequences? With a few notable exceptions, most Jewish advocates had no adequate answer to give, though they kept up a stream of resolutions and proposals. Those who insisted on a rescue program in real time were considered mavericks on the fringes of Jewish consensus opinion.[85]

At the end of 1943, a damning report by top Treasury Department officials accused the State Department of willful obstruction of refugee assistance and immigrant visa processing, and made the case that the Administration's posture was untenable and immoral. The prospect of a pro-rescue resolution making headway in Congress, combined with the impact of the Treasury report, resulted in the establishment (in January 1944) of a Cabinet-level body, the War Refugee Board (WRB). The WRB sought to intervene in Hungary – the last major European country with a sizeable Jewish population that had not yet been liquidated – in the time remaining before Germany occupied Hungary. The funds placed at the disposal of the WRB were largely drawn from Jewish organizational resources.[86]

The significance and fruits of these efforts are still a matter of debate. The Administration's reputation did not suffer, however, from the appearance of dilatory action on Jewish rescue in wartime. Roosevelt personified the anti-Nazi crusade and he remained the national leader of choice for the vast majority of Jewish Americans. They had responded to him as chief of the New Deal, and they responded, as well, to his explicit moral stance against Nazism. That moral stance mattered a great deal, making it credible to rely on FDR, and seemed to draw a veil over the details of America's refugee policy.

New Americans Starting Over (1930s–1950s)

From the time that Hitler's National Socialist Party took power in Germany (1933) until the aftermath of the Second World War, Jewish refugees in the scores of thousands sought to leave Europe for safe havens abroad. They ended up in a myriad of countries ranging from Cuba, Morocco, Angola, and Turkey, to Australia, China, and Uzbekistan; but three countries in particular absorbed the bulk of them: Britain, Palestine, and the United States (see Table 3.1).

---

[85] Wyman, *The Abandonment of the Jews.*
[86] *Ibid.*

TABLE 3.1. *Jewish refugee immigrants to Britain, Palestine, and the United States**

Years	Canada	United States	Palestine/ Israel	Great Britain
1933–45	<5,000	170,000	280,000	83,000
1945–52	41,000[c] (1945–54)	≈130,000[b] (out of 337,244 total DPs admitted)	490,000	<3,000[a]
Total 1933–54	46,000	300,000	770,000	86,000

* *Britain's New Citizens* (London: Association of Jewish Refugees in Great Britain, 1951); *Memo to America: The DP Story, The Final Report of the United States Displaced Persons Commission* (Washington, DC: United States Government Printing Office, 1952); Moshe Sicron, *Ha'aliyah liyisrael 1948 'ad 1953 (Immigration to Israel 1948 to 1953)* (Jerusalem: Central Bureau of Statistics, 1957), pp. 26–7; Stein, "Jewish Social Work," p. 81; A. J. Sherman, *Island Refuge* (London: Frank Cass, 1973, 2nd ed., 1994); Gerald E. Dirks, *Canada's Refugee Policy: Indifference or Opportunism?* (Montreal and London: McGill–Queens University Press, 1977); Bernard Wasserstein, *Britain and the Jews of Europe* (Oxford and New York: Oxford University Press, 1979 [2nd ed. London: Leicester University Press, 1999]); Lestchinsky, "Jewish Migrations, 1840–1956," p. 1582; Leonard Dinnerstein, *America and the Survivors of the Holocaust* (New York: Columbia University Press, 1982), pp. 251, 288; *Jewish Immigrants of the Nazi Period in the U.S.A.*, ed. Herbert A. Strauss (New York, Munich, London, Paris: K. G. Saur, 1987), vol. VI, p. 197; Dalia Ofer, "Holocaust Survivors as Immigrants," *Modern Judaism* 16(1) (1996): 1–23; Tony Kushner, *The Holocaust and the Liberal Imagination* (Oxford: Blackwell, 1994), esp. p. 331 n. 55; and "Holocaust Survivors in Britain: An Overview and Research Agenda," *The Journal of Holocaust Education* 4(2) (Winter 1995): 147–66; Tony Kushner and Katherine Knox, *Refugees in an Age of Genocide* (Abingdon and New York: Frank Cass, 1999), pp. 126–60, 172–212; Louise London, *Whitehall and the Jews, 1933–1948: British Immigration Policy, Jewish Refugees and the Holocaust* (Cambridge: Cambridge University Press, 2001); Hagit Lavsky, "German Jewish Interwar Migration in a Comparative Perspective: Mandatory Palestine, the United States, and Great Britain," *Ethnicity and Beyond: Theories and Dilemmas of Jewish Group Demarcation. Studies in Contemporary Jewry*, vol. XXV, ed. Eli Lederhendler (New York and Oxford: Oxford University Press, 2011), pp. 115–44; Irving Abella and Harold Troper, *None is Too Many: Canada and the Jews of Europe, 1933–1948* (Toronto: Lester & Orpen Dennys, 1982), p. x.

[a] Precise figures for Holocaust survivors admitted to postwar Britain do not exist. Estimates speak of one or two thousand, or alternatively, "a significant portion" of the 5,600 total admitted under the "Distressed Relatives" scheme (see n. 87).

[b] Postwar US immigration figures grow by another 17,000 if we include arrivals not classified as Displaced Persons (Dinnerstein, n. 87) and refugees residing in America on temporary visas who were later naturalized.

[c] The immigration into postwar Canada included nearly 20,000 trans-migrants or re-emigrants coming from Britain, the US, Israel, and Latin America.

About 280,000 Jews from Poland, Germany, and elsewhere in Central Europe found refuge in Palestine under the British Mandate before 1945; an additional 120,000 Holocaust survivors (including illegal immigrants) arrived there between 1945 and the establishment of the State of Israel in 1948; and about 370,000 arrived in the first four years of Israeli independence (1948–52). The figures for Central European Jewish refugee entry into Great Britain show that some 83,000 arrived between 1933 and 1941, mainly after 1938. The United States permitted entry to about 168,000 Jewish immigrants between 1933 and 1943 (mostly between 1938 and 1941), an additional 2,000–4,000 up to 1946, and some 130,000 from 1946 to 1952.[87]

Those who came to the United States represented only a fraction of those who might have immigrated had it not been for strict immigration controls and, in particular, the administrative stringencies practiced by US consuls abroad since 1930. The German and Austrian yearly immigration quotas (which totaled 27,370) were so strictly hemmed in by constraints aimed at keeping refugees away that they were never filled until a presidential directive freed up the entire quota for the fiscal years 1939–40. In 1935, for example, the year in which Nazi Germany barred Jews from citizenship, schools, and an array of occupations, only 20 percent of the US immigration quota for Germany was used. By 1937, 42 percent of the quota was filled, and in 1938 65.3 percent. The strict immigration regime, which militated against a larger influx of "political refugees" (a euphemism for the victims of Nazi persecution), at least through 1938, was niggardly to a fault. In late 1938, it became possible to enter the United States under a new refugee clause, thus expanding the quota-defined number of legal entrants – albeit under a regimen of strict conditions, including the requirement to have individual financial guarantors who were US citizens.[88]

---

[87] Wyman, *Paper Walls*; Michael R. Marrus, *The Unwanted: European Refugees in the Twentieth Century* (New York and Oxford: Oxford University Press, 1985), pp. 123–207, 296–313, 317–24, 331–9, 343–5; Strauss, *Jewish Immigrants of the Nazi Period*, vol. VI, pp. 190–5, 206–10; Breitman and Kraut, *American Refugee Policy*; Arieh J. Kochavi, *Post-Holocaust Politics: Britain, the United States, and Jewish Refugees, 1945–1948* (Chapel Hill and London: University of North Carolina Press, 2001); Daniel J. Tichenor, *Dividing Lines: The Politics of Immigration Control in America* (Princeton, NJ and Oxford: Princeton University Press, 2002), pp. 150–67, 181–8.

[88] Strauss, *Jewish Immigrants of the Nazi Period*, vol. VI, p. 207; Marrus, *The Unwanted*, p. 137; Breitman and Kraut, *American Refugee Policy*, pp. 11–67; Wyman, *Paper Walls*, pp. 3–39, 67–115, 220–1; Tichenor, *Dividing Lines*, pp. 159–67; Abella and Troper, *None is Too Many*. By 1938, there were some 46,000 recent German immigrants in the United States, including about 27,000 Jews. See Lavsky, "German Jewish Interwar Migration," p. 127.

Controlled entry, often entailing a lengthy and angst-ridden application period and sundry delays in obtaining visas, was, therefore, the common lot of nearly all of the refugees in the 1930s. This in itself colored the immigration experience for these lucky few, and contrasted with the pre-1920s migration narrative of the bulk of American Jews. Veterans of the older migration had plenty of hardships to endure, from cramped steerage berths to the rigors of Ellis Island inspections; but they did not face the labyrinthine "paper walls" – the barriers and bureaucratic procedures – which refuge-seekers of the 1930s had to negotiate over the course of interminable months and even years in order to enter the United States.

The newcomers were special in various other ways. In contrast with the typical Jewish immigrants of earlier eras, those arriving as "political refugees" in the 1930s included individuals professing no religion at all or who were Christians with some Jewish family background (and as such, considered racially non-Aryan under Nazi law), as well as intermarried couples – especially common in the middle-class and professional or artistic occupational categories.[89] Those who came from Germany in the early to mid-1930s were especially apt to include academically trained professionals, scientists, or artists in a variety of fields. Over half of these intellectual émigrés arrived before 1938. Two-thirds of about 2,000 university professors who fled Nazi rule settled in the United States. Overall, the United States and Great Britain, between them, absorbed nearly half of all German Jewish émigré artists, scientists, and professionals. After 1938, however, when the majority of Jewish refugees came, only 6 percent were classified as professionals, academics, or artists. Also, before 1938 the arrivals tended to include many children and adults below age fifty; whereas after 1938, nearly a third of the total were over age fifty and came with far fewer financial or professional assets.[90]

On average, the typical German and Austrian Jewish family had to begin life anew at a much lower social status level. In that sense, despite its somewhat unusual profile, the Central European refugee migration recapitulated certain aspects of earlier Jewish migration experiences. Many entered working-class positions, menial service jobs, petty sales, or lower level white-collar employment occupations – at least while the Depression and the Second World War lasted. Even in a place like Los Angeles, where

[89] Strauss, *Jewish Immigrants of the Nazi Period*, vol. VI, p. 374.
[90] Lavsky, "German Jewish Interwar Migration," pp. 128–9; Strauss, *Jewish Immigrants of the Nazi Period*, vol. VI, pp. 342–65, 377; Judith M. Melton, *The Face of Exile: Autobiographical Journeys* (Iowa City: University of Iowa Press, 1998).

there were more than the usual opportunities for musicians, writers, and artists, some refugees turned to fringe occupations to make ends meet, like making "petit point bags and other novel products."[91]

"Perhaps never before had any people, much less one so prominently situated and so apparently irreplaceable, been so despoiled of its confidence," commented one native son of the German Jewish exodus. "Uprooting and re-integration left many lives permanently diverted," observed another. Like other immigrants before them, they created support groups and clubs. "Among their activities," one study reported, "were women's organizations, sports teams, stamp clubs, and a physicians' training program." Many of them were residentially concentrated in identifiable neighborhood clusters, such as in Manhattan's Washington Heights, north of Harlem (wryly dubbed "the Fourth Reich"), or the neighborhood of Eustaw Place and Druid Hill Park in Baltimore. Trying to make the best of their predicament, they became nose-to-the-grindstone pragmatists, largely focused on regaining middle-class lifestyles. Yet, they made tremendous efforts to "fill in what was missing" from their pedestrian lives and to impart to their children the idea that "a finished education opened gates to a more rewarding life." As was true in earlier times, children and young people experienced an accelerated Americanization process via the public schools, popular culture, employment in established businesses and factories, and – after 1941 – military service.[92]

Certain individuals whose lives bore the indelible imprint of the German trauma were primed to become leaders in religious affairs, scholarship, communal life, and other civic activities, after arriving in America. Joachim Prinz (1902–88) is one case in point. After coming to the United States in 1937, he resumed a public career as a congregational rabbi, Zionist, and a leading figure in the World Jewish Congress

---

[91] Vorspan and Gartner, *Jews of Los Angeles*, p. 197.

[92] William B. Helmreich, *Against All Odds: Holocaust Survivors and the Successful Lives they Made in America* (New York: Simon and Schuster, 1992), p. 76; Walter Laqueur, *Generation Exodus: The Fate of Young Jewish Refugees from Nazi Germany* (Hanover, NH and London: Brandeis University Press/University Press of New England, 2001), pp. 129–60, 295; Strauss, *Jewish Immigrants of the Nazi Period*, vol. VI, pp. 317–33; Steven M. Lowenstein, *Frankfurt on the Hudson: The German Jewish Community of Washington Heights 1933–1983* (Detroit, MI: Wayne State University Press, 1989); Anthony Heilbut, *Exiled in Paradise: German Refugee Artists and Intellectuals in America from the 1930s to the Present* (Berkeley, Los Angeles, and London: University of California Press, 1997 [1983]), pp. x–xi; Strauss, *Jewish Immigrants of the Nazi Period*, vol. VI, p. 332; Laqueur, *Generation Exodus*, p. 295.

(an international organization for defense of Jewish rights, founded in Geneva in 1936). In Prinz, an energetic and passionate supporter of America's postwar Civil Rights movement, we also have the case of a keen participant in American civic life.[93]

Nahum Norbert Glatzer (1903–90), another bridging figure, arrived in the United States in 1938 after a brief sojourn in Palestine. With previous academic teaching experience in Frankfurt, Haifa, and Chicago, Glatzer eventually settled into a faculty appointment at Brandeis University. He not only transplanted to American shores his considerable expertise on the history of the early Rabbinic Judaism, but was also largely responsible for familiarizing English-language readers with Franz Kafka (the darkly eccentric Prague writer was barely known to Americans at the time), as well as the thought of the seminal twentieth-century German-Jewish theologian, Franz Rosenzweig (1886–1929).

Trude Weiss-Rosmarin (1908–89) left Germany in 1931, before the Nazis came to power, armed with a PhD in Semitics, archaeology, and philosophy and a thesis on ancient Arab history. Weiss-Rosmarin brought considerable acumen and her Zionist heritage to bear in the years to come, when she was a well-known publicist (editor and publisher of the *Jewish Spectator* monthly magazine), early advocate of gender equality, and animated critic in the American Jewish community.[94]

"Eclectic" may be a just description of a group of intellectuals as different from each other as Hannah Arendt (1906–75), Erich Fromm (1900–80), and Herbert Marcuse (1898–1979), all of whom made the transition to American shores in the 1930s to early 1940s. Arendt, with her brittle demeanor and brilliance of insight, strove to help Americans make sense of right and wrong as categorical political and ethical qualities, amid the fresh memories and harsh consequences of Nazism and the politics of the Cold War and the nuclear age. Marcuse, a neo-Marxian, anti-Stalinist, and post-Freudian philosopher, embarked on a relentless critique of what he termed the "repressive tolerance" exerted by the mass consumer culture of modern capitalism. Like Glatzer, Marcuse found a berth in the 1950s at Brandeis University, and became a major influence

---

[93] Joachim Prinz, *Joachim Prinz, Rebellious Rabbi: An Autobiography: The German and Early American Years*, ed. and intro. Michael A. Meyer (Bloomington and Indianapolis: Indiana University Press, 2008). See also Prinz, "A Rabbi Under the Hitler Regime," in *Gegenwart im Rückblick*, ed. Herbert A. Strauss and Kurt R. Grossman (Heidelberg: L. Stiehm, 1970), pp. 231–8; and *Wir Juden* (Berlin: E. Reiss, 1934).

[94] Hyman and Moore, *Jewish Women in America, An Historical Encyclopedia*, vol. II, pp. 1463–5.

on both the emergent American New Left and the wider counter-culture movement.[95]

Fromm's response to the derailment of democracy and humanity in Germany was to search for the psycho-social underpinnings of individual commitment to freedom and ethical humanism. Fromm warned the West in the early 1940s: "In our own society we are faced with the same phenomenon that is fertile soil for the rise of Fascism anywhere: the insignificance and powerlessness of the individual." Fromm's demand for a politically and ethically engaged stance by individuals in a free society could be imagined as being in dialogue, from the critical perspective of mid-twentieth century, modern, urban civilization, with Emerson and Thoreau. Perhaps that resonance – and dissonance – with classic American ideals is what made Fromm's teachings so timely and compelling in the 1960s.[96]

As we noted, an estimated 130,000 European Jewish survivors were permitted to enter the United States after the war (1946–52). Initially, some refugees were granted special status by executive order of President Truman (resulting in the immigration of about 28,000); but for the most part, postwar Jewish Holocaust survivors entered the country under the Displaced Persons (DP) legislation of 1948 and its amended version of 1950. The statute aimed to provide visas to specific categories selected from among the millions of European civilians left stranded in Germany, Austria, and Italy.

Of the total of all European nationals displaced by the war (no one ever reached a precise count), most were repatriated fairly quickly by

---

[95] For some representative works: Hannah Arendt, *The Origins of Totalitarianism* (New York: Harcourt, Brace: 1951), *The Human Condition* (Chicago and London: University of Chicago Press, 1958), *Eichmann in Jerusalem: A Report on the Banality of Evil* (New York: Viking Press, 1963), and *Men in Dark Times* (New York: Harcourt, Brace and World, 1968); Herbert Marcuse, *Eros and Civilization* (1955), *Soviet Marxism* (1958), *One-Dimensional Man* (1964), and "Repressive Tolerance," in Herbert Marcuse, Robert Paul Wolff, and Barrington Moore, Jr., *A Critique of Pure Tolerance* (Boston, MA: Beacon Press, 1968 [1965]). On German émigré intellectuals, see Heilbut, *Exiled in Paradise*; Melton, *The Face of Exile*; Lewis A. Coser, *Refugee Scholars in America: Their Impact and their Experiences* (New Haven, CT and London: Yale University Press, 1984); Martin Jay, *Permanent Exiles: Essays on the Intellectual Migration from Germany to America* (New York: Columbia University Press, 1986 [1985]).

[96] Erich Fromm, *Escape from Freedom* (New York: Avon, 1969 [1941]), pp. 265–6. See also his *The Sane Society* (1955) and *The Art of Loving* (1956). On Fromm's influence in American culture, see Andrew R. Heinze, *Jews and the American Soul: Human Nature in the Twentieth Century* (Princeton, NJ: Princeton University Press, 2004), pp. 278–84.

Allied forces and the international refugee welfare agencies: the United Nations Relief and Rehabilitation Administration (UNRRA) and later the International Refugee Organization (IRO). Slightly over one million were resettled in new countries. The United States accepted some 446,600, of whom Jewish Holocaust survivors were between 16 and 25 percent (their proportion varied over different years). The established Jewish communal agencies, including the venerable immigrant aid association, United HIAS (Hebrew Immigrant Aid Society) Service, were joined by newly formed resettlement bureaus, the United Service for New Americans (USNA) and its New York counterpart, the New York Association for New Americans (NYANA). Although the major work of the postwar refugee program was over by the mid-1950s, Jewish refugee assistance continued well into the mid-1960s. A late arriving group of Holocaust survivors came from Hungary in the wake of the Soviet repression of the attempted rebellion there in 1956. Other Jewish populations at risk began to arrive, beginning with Jews escaping from Cuba after the Castro revolution and Jews fleeing from Arab countries.[97]

The relief and resettlement agencies strove to find prospective jobs and homes for them in cities and small towns across the country – repeating, in this fashion, the early twentieth-century population redistribution programs. They engaged in active outreach to prepare local communities to absorb the newcomers and locate work and housing for them: "THIS IS WHERE YOUR MONEY GOES!" read the text of a bulletin distributed to Jewish residents in Montgomery, Alabama in 1948: "Mr. and Mrs. Joseph Rabinovitz and children may move next door to you next week. They speak no English! They spent 4 years in Dachau! They have no money, no job."[98]

Despite dispersal efforts, most of the new immigrants sought out the largest cities. Living where other refugee families lived, they were able to establish zones of attachment. Groups and institutions geared to their particular affinities and shops catering to their tastes were most likely to exist in places like New York, Baltimore, Chicago, and Los Angeles. In

---

[97] Zorach Warhaftig, *Uprooted: Jewish Refugees and Displaced Persons After Liberation* (New York: Institute of Jewish Affairs of the American Jewish Congress and World Jewish Congress, 1946); Dinnerstein, *America and the Survivors*, pp. 251–2, 273–90; Beth B. Cohen, *Case Closed: Holocaust Survivors in Postwar America* (New Brunswick, NJ: Rutgers University Press, 2007), p. 3, Stein, "Jewish Social Work," pp. 79–81; Ilya Dijour, "Jewish Immigration to the United States," *American Jewish Year Book*, vol. LXIV (1963), pp. 77–9.

[98] Helmreich, *Against All Odds*, pp. 68, 205.

some instances, the newcomers breathed new life into old institutions. The veteran Jewish hometown societies, which still abounded in these cities, were no longer as active as they once had been, and they tended to conduct their activities in English. The mainly Yiddish-speaking newcomers often revived these organizations or established entirely new ones.[99]

Such affinities and group-centered activity patterns had been typical of virtually every arriving immigrant cohort, of every nationality. Yet, the postwar survivors' case was more complex. These were people whose entire previous lives had been effaced. There was no one left to write home to. Orphaned of an entire world – parents, former spouses, children, siblings – it was evident that webs of mutual support, the familiarity of speech and culture, and above all the uniquely shared knowledge of what they had been through would play a distinctive role in the way they rebuilt their lives. Sometimes, these relationships acquired the in-grown intensity of an extended, surrogate family.

Given its modest proportions (perhaps 5 or 6 percent of the whole US Jewish population),[100] the Nazi-era and post-war refugee stream was less consequential than had been the case for previous immigrant waves. However, in certain specific facets of Jewish life, the mid-twentieth-century arrivals left a mark well beyond their numbers. As we saw, pre-war refugees from Central Europe had included a uniquely endowed subgroup of savants – the professionals, scientists, artists, and intellectuals. The postwar refugee newcomers similarly included a small but special minority (perhaps 10 percent of the whole): the strict or sectarian traditionalists, popularly known in English as "ultra-Orthodox" (or in Yiddish: *frum* [pious]), and today commonly grouped together under the Hebrew term, *haredim*. Subdivided amongst themselves into smaller, rival sects, they hailed from different regions of Poland, Lithuania, and Hungary and owed fierce allegiance to a variety of Hasidic rabbinical dynasties or particular yeshivas, which propagated their own codes of conduct and worldviews (see Chapter 5).

The wartime or postwar cohort also exerted some qualitative influence in American colleges and universities, especially in the developing field

---

[99] *Ibid.*, pp. 60–1, 75; Hannah Kliger, *Jewish Hometown Associations and Family Circles in New York: The WPA Yiddish Writers' Group Study* (Bloomington and Indianapolis: Indiana University Press, 1992), pp. 119–31.

[100] Jews born in Germany in LA, 1950: 3,900 = 1.2% of total Jewish population, and 3.8% of all foreign-born Jews. Austrian-born: 5,400 = 1.6% of total, 5% of the foreign born. Figures for Poland: 15,000 = 4.7% of total, 14.5% of the foreign-born. *AJYB* 1953, p. 21.

of Jewish Studies. Canvassing key figures in such disciplines as Yiddish language and literary studies, European Jewish history, Holocaust research, philosophy, and religion, we find over thirty prominent individuals who derive from this small migration stream. Some of them left Germany or Poland in the 1930s and early 1940s, either as mature adults or as children, and came to the United States directly or via a third country (Britain, Canada, Palestine/Israel, and Cuba). The youngest among the postwar scholars were born in DP camps in Europe just after the war, or else were born in North America and Israel to refugee parents. They did much to put American Jewish scholarship in the front ranks of Jewish intellectual endeavor, and helped establish post-biblical Jewish history and culture as part of the humanistic tradition of the American academy.[101]

Starting Over on the Farm

Approximately 1,500 Jewish war refugees and Displaced Persons, augmented by about 1,000 returning US war veterans, settled on farms in the period just after World War II. Among the Holocaust survivors, one factor promoting employment in agriculture was the provision in the 1948 Displaced Persons Act that offered farmers a priority status, according to which they were to receive 30 percent of all immigrant visas.[102]

There was, in fact, a small renewal of Jewish farming in the years just before the Second World War. At the end of the 1930s, Jewish refugees from rural areas in western Germany set up as cattle dealers in four adjacent counties near Binghamton, New York. Some of these families had carried on local traditions as cattle-dealers for generations. The Jewish

---

[101] In Yiddish studies, Max and Uriel Weinreich (father and son), Mordkhe Schaechter, Ruth R. Wisse, David G. Roskies (the latter two are brother and sister), and Anita Norich; in European and Jewish history: George Mosse, Peter Gay, Selma Stern, Ismar Schorsch, Michael A. Meyer, Henry L. Feingold, Jehuda Reinharz, Marion Kaplan, Michael Stanislawski, David Engel, Samuel Kassow, Jack Wertheimer, Steven Lowenstein, Marsha Rozenblit, and Robert Lieberles; in religion, philosophy, and theology: Nahum N. Glatzer, Abraham Joshua and Susannah Heschel (father and daughter), Jakob Petuchowski, Michael Wyschogrod, and David Weiss-Halivni; the pioneers of Holocaust research in America: Philip Friedman, Isaiah Trunk, Jacob Robinson, and Raul Hilberg; Jewish economic history: Arcadius Kahan; librarianship: the near-legendary Dina Abramowicz, former librarian of the YIVO Institute for Jewish Research. From 1945 to 1965 the number of American universities (not including Jewish theological colleges) that offered Jewish Studies courses at either undergraduate or graduate levels expanded sevenfold. Arnold J. Band, "Jewish Studies in American Liberal-Arts Colleges and Universities," *American Jewish Year Book*, vol. LXVII (1966), pp. 3–30.

[102] Helmreich, *Against All Odds*, pp. 37, 63–5, 87, 117–19, 161–2.

Agricultural Society reported that in 1937 eleven refugees from Nazi Germany applied for farm loans, while just one year later the number of such applicants rose to 600, and increased again to 741 in 1940.[103]

New Jersey, New York, Connecticut, and California proved the most attractive to pre- and postwar Jewish farmers. In Petaluma, California, 300 Holocaust survivors and their families added a new element to the aging (and fraying) prewar community of Jewish poultry farms. Back east, in south Jersey's Vineland area, there were perhaps 1,000 such new immigrant farmers in the 1950s, specializing in poultry and egg production. In Connecticut, immigrant farmers settled around Norwich and Colchester, and in an all-Jewish, Holocaust-survivor community called Danielson.[104]

Although a second generation and even a small group of third-generation Jewish farmers appeared on the postwar scene, they were so marginal in quantitative terms that they seem almost anecdotal trivia. Even with the small postwar influx, the Jewish farming population dwindled from about 85,000 in 1945 to around 35,000 in 1965. The motivational drive for integration was best answered by means other than agrarianization.[105]

On that note, however, it is worth mentioning the less obvious ways in which postwar Jewish refugees and survivors – most of them city dwellers – were conscious of the countryside. Holocaust survivors who were interviewed about life in America in the 1950s reported that their social lives included communal gatherings at parks, lakes, and beaches.[106] One

---

[103] Robert H. Ruxin, "The Jewish Farmers and the Small-Town Jewish Community: Schoharie County, New York," *American Jewish Archives* 29(1) (1977): 3–21; Rhonda F. Levine, *Class, Networks, and Identity: Replanting Jewish Lives from Nazi Germany to Rural New York* (Lanham, MD: Rowman and Littlefield, 2001); Levine and Miller, *American Jewish Farmer*, p. 74; Françoise Ouzan, "New Roots for the Uprooted: Shoah Survivors as Farmers in America," in *Holocaust Survivors: Resettlement, Memories, Identities*, ed. Dalia Ofer, Françoise Ouzan, and Judy Tydor Baumel-Schwartz (New York: Berghahn Books, 2012), pp. 234–57.

[104] Levine and Miller, *The American Jewish Farmer*, pp. 28–34, 77–81; Teasdle, "Jewish Farming in Michigan," pp. 7–8; Arthur Goldhaft, *The Golden Egg* (New York: Horizon Press, 1957), p. 269; Beatrice Parsons, "Starting from Scratch," *The National Grange Monthly* (October 1956). For the trend in American agriculture away from small individual farms toward large farm management corporations, see Meinig, *The Shaping of America, vol. 4: Global America, 1915–2000*, p. 264.

[105] Levine and Miller, *The American Jewish Farmer*, pp. 22–39, 49–50; United States Department of Agriculture, *The 20th Century Transformation of U.S. Agriculture and Farm Policy* (electronic report, June 2005: www.ers.usda.gov/publications/EIB3), pp. 2–3.

[106] Helmreich, *Against All Odds*, pp. 164–5.

author's account of "finding America," as the child of Holocaust survivors, living in New York City, underscored the great value of spending time in countryside:

The space, the absence of enclosure, relaxed my parents like a drug. They began to sing [...] Czech folksongs [...]. "Hory, jsou hory," [my father] began to repeat as we left flat ground: "Mountains are mountains." [...] A sense of well-being pervaded the car; it was like a party, self-contained and happy, flying through the countryside unconstrained. My mother smiled, threw back her head and laughed, even though she often said that she had forgotten how to laugh since the war.[107]

Jews in Search of America

That fragment of memory suggests that the urban environment of most Jews was nonetheless apt to become the portal into a pastoral imagination. The city's familiar sights of endless row houses and tenements, peopled by anonymous strangers – constituted one kind of "wilderness." Its perfect foil was the prairie wilderness: a social and physical space which could be imagined as open and inviting, imbued with sentimental longing, a spatial aesthetic, and – above all – a national, American mystique.

In that vein, we might note the significance of Aaron Copland's musical oeuvre. Copland (1900–90), the Brooklyn-raised son of Jewish immigrants from Russia, composed a number of major works in the spirit of rural Americana, including a wartime paean to American virtues, *Lincoln Portrait* (1942); *Appalachian Spring* (1945) – the ballet he composed for Martha Graham (later a suite for full orchestra); two sets of *Old American Songs* (1950 and 1952); and the opera, *The Tender Land* (1952–4). Copland used themes from revivalist hymns, such as "Zion's Walls" (in *The Tender Land*), and the Shaker hymn, "Simple Gifts" (in *Appalachian Spring*).[108]

Moving from the concert hall to mass-marketed popular music, it may not be irrelevant that during the 1950s, independent recording firms (about 40 percent of them owned by Jews) took the lead in promoting the "ethnic" music of America's hinterland. Jack Holtzman, founder of Electra Records, along with his musical manager Paul Rothschild, specialized in folk. Sid Nathan's King Records (in Cincinnati) promoted Black

---

[107] Helen Epstein, *Children of the Holocaust* (New York: Putnam, 1979), pp. 137–8, quoted also by Helmreich, *Against All Odds*, p. 165.
[108] Howard Pollack, *Aaron Copland: The Life and Work of an Uncommon Man* (Urbana: University of Illinois Press, 2000).

performers. Jerry Wexler, one of the key names in the trade (vice-president of Atlantic Records), later recalled the "universal appeal" and "diverting" freshness that helped to sell the sounds of the "other" America, despite the racial segregation that still held sway in the 1950s.[109]

Some background perspective is useful, for these encounters were not entirely unprecedented. There had been a long-standing, traditional linkage between America's racial history and European representations of American life and culture. The natural and rural landscapes were associated with the land's aboriginal inhabitants and with the history of Southern slavery, themes conveyed in American literary classics that were most familiar to European readers via translations (Longfellow, Cooper, Stowe) and – in more recent times – in motion pictures. Encountering the vast American countryside, whether directly or by fanciful projections, inevitably brought into view the subject of those presumed to possess an "innate" relatedness to the soil: the African slaves who had tilled the earth in bondage to "the white man" and whose descendants still were primarily southern and rural in 1920s, or those peoples who had inhabited the forests and plains before "the white man" came.

Aspects of this romantic representation of America's racial history were carried over into Jewish culture in America in the first half of the twentieth century. Yiddish author and playwright, Dovid Pinski (1872–1959), had the protagonist of his novel, *Arnold Levenberg, Portrait of a Torn Man* (*Arnold levenberg, der tserisener mentsh*), visit a wealthy Hudson Valley manor, where he reflected:

Once upon a time this was a thick forest, with footpaths left by Indians making their way down to the Hudson. The Indians gloried in its density, which enfolded them and sheltered them from the sun and from their foes, rejoiced in its greenness, spring and summer, its many-hued beauty in autumn.[110]

---

[109] I am indebted for these notes on the music industry to my student, Ari Katorza, and his doctoral dissertation, "Hayehudim shel harok: musikat rok, hamaavak lema'an tsedek hevrati beartsot haberit, vehakonflikt seviv hahegemoniah hatarbutit be'idan habtar-milhamti" (Rock Jews: Rock Music, the Struggle for Social Justice in the USA, and the Conflicts over Cultural Hegemony during the Postwar Era) (Hebrew University, 2007), esp. pp. v, 13, 107–14; and *Hamahar le'olam eino yode'a: rok bame'ah ha-20* (*Tomorrow Never Knows: Rock Music in the Twentieth Century*) (Tel-Aviv: Rimon, 2012), pp. 88–100.

[110] Dovid Pinski, *Arnold levenberg, der tserisener mentsh* (Warsaw: Farlag Ch. Brzoz, n.d.), p. 230; and *Arnold Levenberg*, trans. Isaac Goldberg (New York: Simon and Schuster, 1928), pp. 196–7. The quotation is my slightly modified version of Goldberg's translation. On this topic generally, see Rachel Rubinstein, *Members of the Tribe: Native America in the Jewish Imagination* (Detroit, MI: Wayne State University Press, 2010).

Similar preoccupations with authenticity and aboriginality animated Hebrew poetry written in America. Hebrew poets often invoked the biblical archetypes of both "wilderness" and "promised land." The ancient Israelite wilderness motif of "tents," for instance, figured in American Hebrew poets' depictions of both Blacks and Indians. The tent – in its guise as "tent of meeting" or "tabernacle," but also connoting a dwelling place – appears in Ephraim E. Lisitzky's Hebrew representation of African American folk religion, *Beohalei khush* (In the Tents of Cush, 1953).[111] Lisitzky (1885–1962), a Lithuanian-born Hebrew poet and educator, lived in New Orleans for fifty-four years. The characteristics he found attractive in Black culture, as he portrayed it, included its fervent, "unadorned" religiosity. Lisitzky's translations of the singsong gospel sermons evoked East European Jewish Hasidic pietism and Hasidism's rusticity. *Beohalei khush* represents Black religiosity as folkloric, vocal, uninhibited, and collective – and it nowhere mentions the word "Christian." Lisitzky also wrote a long "Indian" epic, *Medurot do'akhot* (Dying Campfires, 1937).[112]

To configure an American landscape that, in its metaphysical essence, could be seen as pre-Christian, or rooted in a generically biblical idiom that was not necessarily Christian (Old Testament-based and not explicitly reminiscent of European Christendom), was to imagine a country that might be hospitable, as well, to Jews and Judaism. There seems to have been an inter-textual conversation going on among Jews about nativity and identity and about America in its imagined "pristine" form.

In the moral universe that such Jews constructed, the notional "Indian" or "Negro" figured in a distinctive manner. Their presence in the culture was not a matter of "achievements," but of destiny and soul. Like Jews born into a Gentile world, Indians and Blacks were born into a predicament that defamed them, but, in their own estimation, ennobled them. The Gershwin brothers' *Porgy and Bess* (first performed in 1935) was, in that sense, a Jewish folk opera.

Reading into these texts a programmatic concern for the underdog is plausible. There were those in the Jewish community who were haunted by the menace encroaching upon the rural "innocence" of life in the South.

---

[111] Cush is a biblical word (Gen. 10: 6–7), conventionally identified as Ethiopia, but generically connoting Africa.

[112] Alan Mintz, *Sanctuary in the Wilderness: A Critical Introduction to American Hebrew Poetry* (Stanford, CA: Stanford University Press, 2012), pp. 138, 426–43. See also E. E. Lisitzky, "So Miriam Spoke of Moses," translated and commentary by Stephen Katz, *CCAR Journal* 55(4) (2008): 59–89.

We find blunt expression of this in a 1923 volume of Yiddish short stories, called *Rasse* (Race), written by Joseph Opatoshu (1887–1954). In the first story, entitled *"Lintcheray"* (Lynching), a mob is gathering to chase down a suspected rapist who has fled to the nearby swamps. The town's iron-monger, Mr. Levy, forbids his son from taking part in the posse:

You're not going! [...] A Jew has no business getting involved in this. [...] I'll tell you this for sure: if they lynch a Negro today, they'll do it to a Jew tomorrow.[113]

Years afterward, when another Yiddish writer, Itzhok (Isaac) Ronch, looked for a way to express the horrors of what Jews had experienced at the hands of the Germans, he wrote: "They were tortured at Auschwitz and Drancy, lynched like the Negroes of Georgia."[114]

What is most striking about the Black-Indian-Jew triangle is not its political ramifications, however, or the theme of oppression, but rather the fact that it offered a powerful, alternative way to talk about quali-ties of mind and spirit, especially those that departed from the popu-lar American mainstream. There, in the realm of the imagined cultural "other," Jews were able to envisage the possibility of their own persistence. This was not always very nuanced or sophisticated. Native Americans, for instance, could be reduced to a stereotype of stoic persistence. In one of his "Western" poems, Ronch, for example, fell into this vein: "Indian women, dancing, dancing," the dancers' heavy, rhythmic steps prompting him to paint them as timeless figures of passive resistance, with "faces full of mystery" and eyes like "black fires gleam through looks of steel."[115]

The obverse of this image of persistence and fortitude was a discourse of assimilation. Just as Jews themselves were beginning to voice their con-cern about identity erosion, we find this theme cropping up in Jewish por-trayals of cultural displacement and social maladjustment among Indian reservation dwellers:

Almost the same situation [of psychological difficulties] takes place among the Indians born on reservations [...]. Under similar conditions of pressure, when individuals are punished to make them unlike their parents, the personality con-flicts engendered tend to be similar [...] to those of the Jews, the Italians, and

[113] Joseph Opatoshu, *Rasse. Lintcheray un andere dertseylungen (Race: Lynching and Other Stories)* (Warsaw: Farlag Peretz-bibliotek, 1923), pp. 25–6. My thanks to Gali Drucker Bar-Am for this reference.

[114] Robert G. Weisbord and Arthur Stein, *Bittersweet Encounter: The Afro-American and the American Jew* (New York: Schocken Books, 1970), pp. 32–3; Itzhak E. Ronch, *A loyb un a dank/ Poems* (Los Angeles, CA: Isaac E. Ronch, 1981), p. 7 (English side).

[115] Ronch, *A loyb un a dank/ Poems*, English p. 27.

other children of immigrants, to whom Americanization implies the complete taking over of both the viewpoint and the culture of the urban and Protestant native [white] middle class.[116]

One may read these texts as an antidote to "plain white bread" America: a plea for Jewish visibility in American culture, pitted against the powerful discourse of cultural homogenization. A quest for cultural visibility, perhaps inevitably, led to symbolic references to America's "visible" minorities.

Intimate (if limited) experience of the countryside, beyond inner metropolitan counties, filtered into American Jewish life in other ways. Resort areas in the lake- or hill-districts which catered to Jewish weekenders, summer bungalow colonies, and summer camps for children (quite a number of which were established on the grounds of Jewish-owned farms) were the primary rural experience of most city-dwelling Jewish vacationers. These summertime exposures to the "other" America became a staple part of Jewish popular culture.

Active wartime service, especially during the Second World War, was another factor that brought Jewish city dwellers into outlying parts of the country, where another America confronted them. Most US military training bases were located in the South and Southwest. One Jewish recruit, who had previously lived in New York City, Chelsea, Massachusetts, and Washington, DC, later recalled his trip to basic training in Mississippi, describing the rustic Kentucky hills as resembling "the choppy ocean," crowned by "rock and dead grass." Alabama, near the Gulf coast, was "swampy," crossed here and there by "a wide, muddy river." Another Jewish GI, southward-bound from New York, was as impressed by the exotic sight of palm trees.[117]

The migration of Jewish households from cities of the Northeast and Midwest to the West Coast and south Florida, which accelerated after 1945, altered the visual and social environment of many thousands of Jewish Americans. Even the accepted categories of urban space changed. Los Angeles as it appeared at mid-twentieth century, for instance, could be described as "the first major city that was not quite a city, that is, not a crowded industrial metropolis [but] a garden city of backyards and quiet

---

[116] David Rodnick, "The Effect of Culture Change upon the Personalities of Second-Generation Reservation Indians," *YIVO Annual of Jewish Social Science* 2–3 (1947–8): 252–61, originally published in Yiddish in *Yivo bleter*, 1941.

[117] Meinig, *The Shaping of America, vol. IV*, pp. 166–7, 173; Moore, *G.I. Jews*, pp. 63–4.

streets, a sprawling small town magnified a thousand-fold and set among palms and orange trees under a sunny sky." As historian Deborah Dash Moore put it, the "promise" of places like Miami and Los Angeles lay in "an almost rural innocence, the intimacy of a small town, coupled with the glamour of movies and tourism [...] a leisurely paced life [...] and sportswear fashions."[118]

Taking Stock

These new beginnings by Jewish immigrants of the 1930s and 1940s and postwar veterans and their families, seemed to change prewar realities. The 1950s seemed to attest to the completion of an entire migration cycle – marking a "definitive" stage of "homecoming" for the great European outpouring that had lasted over the previous 100 years. As Americans were told that their country had arrived at an unprecedented moment of national fulfillment – embodied in the phrase, "the American century" – so, too, the roughly five million Jews in the United States were informed that they were now the largest and most affluent national community of Jews the world had ever known. European Jewry was decimated by the Holocaust, with only about one-third of its pre-1939 population remaining. Jews in the Soviet Union, estimated to be about two million in number, seemed irretrievably lost behind the Iron Curtain. The new State of Israel, which absorbed many new immigrants and doubled its population within its first years of existence, still was home to barely two million: equivalent to the number of Jews residing in New York City alone.

Characteristically, the notion of a journey that had reached its destination and its climax was endorsed and feted by communal spokesmen. In 1954, when they marked the 300th anniversary of the settlement of early Jewish colonists in New Amsterdam, Jewish publicists invested the postwar attainments of US Jewry with a sense of historic significance. The special effort they took to do so – a hint of the still-contested nature of their status – reflected anxieties stirred by the Depression, by antisemitic agitation and discrimination, and by the traumatic destruction of European Jewry by the Nazis. Another source of discomfort may have been the past or current association of some Jews with the radical Left – a

---

[118] Kenneth T. Jackson, *Crabgrass Frontier: The Suburbanization of the United States* (New York and Oxford: Oxford University Press, 1985), p. 189; David Brodsly, *L.A. Freeway: An Appreciative Essay* (Berkeley: University of California Press, 1981), p. 4, 137, quoted by Meinig, *The Shaping of America, vol. IV*, p. 172; *To the Golden Cities*, p. 52.

sensitive issue that loomed in the foreground in the early Cold War years. They allayed these concerns in public rhetoric that historicized the Jewish experience in the United States. Jews of the 1950s took pride in marking their own well-being as the ultimate vindication, as it were, of colonial-era Jews' decision to go to America, and claimed this – alongside their own families' separate and more recent migration history – as their own heritage. Seen in this light, that experience possessed a single, integral arc of development, native to America since the colonial era, and thus sketched out its own teleology.[119]

With perhaps a greater sense of verisimilitude, I. J. Shvarts and Aaron Leyeles, the Yiddish poets quoted in this chapter's epigraph, did not indulge in quite the same sort of epic imagination. It was enough for them to assert that they loved America in the same sense that they loved their family. The country was not theirs by inheritance, but it became the soil of their existence, allowing them to beget a second generation and witness the advent of a third. It was not the "Land where my fathers died," but the land of their fatherhood. *Dayenu*, as the Jews' tradition puts it: surely that ought to suffice.

Thus far, we have explored Jews' lives as newcomers in America. The touchstone of that part of the story is the fact that it seems so familiar. It often parallels the histories of other migrant groups and, indeed, of the American nation at large. The Jews' gestures toward a better life for themselves and their children were recognizably American. As we have seen, even in their religious distinctiveness, Jews followed paths leading toward Americanization. Yet, in tracing the narrative of migration and integration, we have seen its counterpoint: circumstances in which Jews departed from widely accepted patterns.

Before proceeding to examine the history of the most recent decades, therefore, we will pause for a kind of intermezzo, to go back and try to understand why Jewish difference persisted. The abiding sediment of the Jews' diasporic involvements, which set them apart from other Americans, constitutes the bedrock of this qualitative difference.

---

[119] Wenger, *History Lessons*, pp. 210–22; Arthur A. Goren, "A 'Golden Decade' for American Jews: 1945–1955," in *A New Jewry? America Since the Second World War. Studies in Contemporary Jewry*, vol. VIII, ed. Peter Y. Medding (New York and Oxford: Oxford University Press, 1992), pp. 10–14.

4

The European Nexus

Spain, Germany, and Russia

"Europe has a set of primary interests which to us have none, or a very remote relation. Hence [...] it must be unwise in us to implicate ourselves by artificial ties in the ordinary vicissitudes of her politics, or the ordinary combinations and collisions of her friendships or enmities."
– George Washington's "Farewell Address," 1796

"With Europe devastated, there falls upon us here in the United States a far greater share of the responsibility for carrying forward, in a creative way, our common Jewish cultural and spiritual heritage. [...] Surely, we who have survived catastrophe can survive freedom, too."
– Elliot Cohen, *Commentary* editor, 1945

Introduction

While George Washington's admonition to the nation was more honored in the breach, his view of foreign affairs nonetheless retained a long-term, sustained resonance for many Americans. In contrast, among many Jews – not all, by any means, but not just a select few – the "vicissitudes" and "collisions" of Europe have been an abiding, perturbing, and personally significant concern. Jews could rarely take for granted the patriotic license to avoid involvement in foreign passions.

We might well ask: have not most immigrant groups been caught up for at least one generation with the affairs of their former communities and homelands? Is the Jewish case so very different? For that matter, from a religious point of view, were Jews so qualitatively different in this respect from other religious groups? Might we not discern a distinct "offshore" or foreign aspect in the history of quite a number of American churches, as indicated by their involvements with foreign missions or their commitments to ecclesiastical ties abroad?

I shall argue, in response, that for American Jews there have been lingering engagements abroad that defy exact analogies with either their fellow immigrant groups or other religious communities. American Jewry's ties abroad have been multiple, rather than tethered to one particular former homeland, as is the common situation in other migrant populations. Jews have related equally as much to countries and communities where they personally remembered languages, people, and places, as to those places where they had no direct family ties or memories. Jews' expressions of solidarity with Jews elsewhere do not appear dependent on consanguinity of a first- or second-generation order, or indeed any direct kinship at all.

At the same time, American Jews' attention has not been projected outward toward a global human arena, in the manner of universal churches, but rather has been directed to a more specific geography of collective memory. As for ecclesiastical ties, there were and are no formal, hierarchical relations between Jewish rabbis and congregations in the United States and those abroad. Such ties of religious dependency that occasionally developed were ephemeral and apt to atrophy quickly. On both of these counts, then – the Jews' concerns for Jewish issues abroad, regardless of shared language or kinship ties, as well as the Jewish departure from world-service models of universal religious missions or world clerical confederations – the foreign aspect of American Jewry's history is different. Indeed, this difference is an essential attribute of Jews' "otherness."

The foreign dimension of American Jewish history finds expression in the way their community life is structured. In their *domestic* affairs, no single office or committee has ever united all American Jews from separate cities, regions, religious outlooks, political philosophies, social classes, and ancestral lands of origin. Unlike some other modern Jewish communities around the world – those of Britain and France, for example – American Jewry has never had a chief rabbi or national communal council. The closest approximations to a domestic Jewish establishment in the United States are the denominational assemblies that deal with education and synagogue affairs, and the municipal and regional conferences or philanthropic federations that coordinate social welfare programs for their affiliated agencies. In sharp contrast to the localism and pluralism that holds sway in American Jewry's domestic activities, however, when it came to Jews' needs overseas, particularly in instances of actual (or potential) distress, American Jewry has spawned quasi-centralized consultative bodies and leadership committees, spanning the denominational divide and other internal differences. Driven by crisis, the lifespan of these committees has sometimes been brief, their mandates lapsing when the particular crisis has abated. In some cases, they devolved into yet another specialized or sectoral organization, only to be replaced in turn by a new, centralized organization when crisis has struck anew.

Examples include the Board of Delegates of American Israelites, established in the wake of a bitter confrontation with the Vatican in 1858 over a child baptized in Italy against its Jewish family's wishes;[1] the B'nai B'rith fraternal order's nationwide activity on behalf of Jews abroad, including the posting of Benjamin Franklin Peixotto as honorary US Consul to Bucharest (1870); and the American Jewish Committee, founded in 1906, which undertook a leadership role in a time of grave crisis for Jews abroad (at the time, mainly Russian Jewry), and which continued to act on the political scene throughout the twentieth century. Similarly, we could enumerate here the American Jewish Joint Distribution Committee (AJDC, founded 1914 for European Jewish war relief); the American Jewish Congress (1916), organized to coordinate the activities of the various representative Jewish groups in anticipation of a world peace conference; and the American Jewish Conference (1943), which brought most (though not all) representative Jewish groups under one big tent at a time of unprecedented emergency.

In contrast with general civic or church groups that sponsor humanitarian or political action on behalf of foreign nationals, American Jewish emergency committees and foreign relief agencies rarely depicted Jews abroad as essentially foreign, but rather as fellow Jews. That is, they asserted kinship ties (even in the abstract sense), rather than a purely altruistic humanitarian concern. Moreover, such agencies generally worked together with Jewish organizations in other lands to pursue common aims and facilitate the delivery of relief. Thus, while channeling voluntarism into civic associations fits readily into familiar American models,

---

[1] On the Edgardo Mortara Affair, in which an Italian Jewish child was baptized by a household servant and then raised as a Christian, enforced by Church authorities, see Bertram W. Korn, *The American Reaction to the Mortara Case 1858–1859* (Cincinnati, OH: American Jewish Archives, 1957); Sarna, *American Judaism*, pp. 100–1. On the Board of Delegates and other American Jewish interventions in European affairs, see Davis, *The Emergence of Conservative Judaism*, pp. 101–8; Gerald Sorin, *A Time for Building: The Third Migration 1880–1920. The Jewish People in America* (Baltimore, MD and London: The Johns Hopkins University Press, 1992), pp. 201–4.

the trans-national Jewish organizations were also constitutive bodies of another public arena: that of world Jewry.[2]

Apart from these structural features, the foreign dimension of American Jewish public life entails a set of peculiarly Jewish concerns. Three of the major European arenas that elicited Jewish concern – Spain, Germany, and Russia – represent more than just former homelands. Rather, they have haunted American Jews in a way that is unparalleled by other American groups' folk memories. Spain, Germany, and Russia were once the sites of large, flourishing Jewish communities, each one embedded in its native soil for centuries, and each one sustaining an amazingly productive culture. Each one abruptly ended its career as a major Jewish center under dire circumstances. ("Germany" in this context refers to all parts of historically German-speaking Central Europe, including Austria). The cautionary tales of these Jewish Diasporas' rise, great promise, and calamitous demise cast a shadow over American Jews' sense of their history, and endowed them with a mission peculiarly their own: to dodge history's bullet, to prove America to be the exception, to become the Jewish Diaspora that "made it," and to inherit the mantle of all previous diasporas. That is why the perennial recurrence of these three lands in American Jewish public life endows them with a singular, emblematic meaning.

Moreover, Spain, Germany, and Russia represent axial cultures in the larger orbit of world Jewry: they were hubs of wider influence, beyond the confines of their own territory and history. Iberian Jewish traditions in rabbinic jurisprudence, mysticism, philosophy, and Hebrew poetry continued to influence Jewish culture for centuries throughout the Mediterranean basin, and beyond. Further, the Iberian Jewish experience of living in close relations with both Muslim and Christian cultures is a potent, almost mythic, symbol of multiculturalism. What is known in Spanish today as *La Convivencia* (co-existence) is held up as an ideal of cultural cross-fertilization, with explicit implications for today's world.

German-speaking habitats were important for both medieval and modern Jewish languages, liturgy, and scholarship. They served as launching pads for early pietistic Orthodoxy as well as later trends toward

[2] Lawton Kessler, Aaron Alperin, and Jack J. Diamond, "American Jews and the Paris Peace Conference," *YIVO Annual of Jewish Social Science* 2–3 (1947–8): 222–42; Cohen, *Not Free to Desist*, pp. 102–3, 110–21; Oscar I. Janowsky, *The Jews and Minority Rights, 1898–1919* (New York: Columbia University Press, 1933); Carole Fink, "Louis Marshall: An American Jewish Diplomat in Paris, 1919," *American Jewish History* 94(1–2) (2008): 21–37.

religious reformation. The German cultural orbit, finally, is also regarded as the paramount site of secular Jewish interventions in modern science, philosophy, literature, and the performing arts, and thus it provided a standard by which Jewish secular achievements in other lands might be measured – including the United States.

Russia – having absorbed the main body of Polish-Lithuanian Jewry of earlier times – was the forcing ground of Hasidism and later saw the emergence of modern Yiddish and Hebrew literatures, theater, music, as well as all the major political trends of modern times, including both Jewish socialism and Zionism.

Each of these geographic and cultural centers has been related to American Jewish history in somewhat different ways. Spain (along with Portugal) figured as a land of emigration during the Colonial period, and thereafter retained its resonance mainly as a site of memory. Indeed, Spain and its after-image continued to figure in American Jewish public life long after there were no Jews living there at all. There would have been no Moorish-style synagogues in nineteenth-century America had there been no intended evocation of Spain and its *Convivencia*. Likewise, there would have been no American Jewish academies, libraries, hospitals, or social clubs named "Maimonides," in recognition of the illustrious medieval Spanish Jewish savant. And there would, today, not be any trendy groups devoted to popular kabbalistic philosophy (kabbalism having sprouted mainly from Spanish soil), nor would there be any Jewish ethno-tourism today to historic Jewish sites in Toledo, Barcelona, and Cordoba.

The Spanish connection also reappeared in American Jewish history, at one remove, when immigrants bearing the Judeo-Spanish (Sephardi) heritage began to arrive in the United States from the eastern Mediterranean, starting in the late nineteenth century. Finally, in the late twentieth century, the encounter between Jewish and Hispanic cultures in the United States took a new twist when Jewish residents of Mexico, Cuba, and elsewhere across Latin America – most of them of recent Ashkenazi descent, but Spanish-speaking nonetheless – began to immigrate to North America, bringing into being a new Jewish subgroup that was Latino in terms of its native tongue and cultural ambience.

Germany and Russia both functioned as lands of ongoing emigration throughout American history, and both contained large Jewish communities, alongside of which American Jewry took shape. However, the significance of the German Jewish heritage transcends the arc of German Jewish migrations to the United States. A German Jewish trace

in American Jewish life includes, for example, modern rabbinical seminaries and Jewish studies at the university level, as well as the intellectual legacy of German literature, philosophy, social science, and the arts.
Russia and its heritage, similarly, reverberated among American Jews
in a variety of ways, not only during the era of mass migration from
Europe, but also during the long decades, from the 1920s to the 1970s,
in which virtually no Jews were leaving Russia for the United States.

Finally, Spain, Germany, and Russia are also representative of three
powerful ideologies with international connotations, with which
Jews have had fateful encounters: Roman Catholicism, Fascism, and
Communism.

In the previous chapters, American Jewish history appeared as a
facet of American migration history – multiple entry events, bracketed
by America's colonial, national, and urban development. The history
recalled in those chapters was intermittent, composed of various frag-
ments, a digest of events occurring in the lives of individuals and families.
The Euro-centric part of American Jewish history, in contrast, supports
a view of the *longue durée*: an arc that may be tracked across many
decades, even across centuries, and that assumes a symbolic universe of
meaning, rather than a prosaic tale of everyday affairs.

We could in principle extend this chapter to cover other lands (Romania
and Hungary, for instance), which have also figured in American Jewish
foreign "entanglements." It is not our purpose here, however, to conduct
a comprehensive survey, but rather to illustrate the qualitative distinctiveness of the American Jewish experience. For that purpose, our symbolic
trio of paradigmatic countries should suffice.

Spain: Old and New Inquisitors

Two weeks after US Commodore George Dewey demolished Spain's
Pacific fleet at Manila Bay (May 1, 1898), the Russian Jewish immigrant
author and journalist, Abe Cahan, published one of his regular columns
in Lincoln Steffens's New York *Commercial Advertiser*. "The God of
Israel is Getting Even with Them," proclaimed Cahan's headline. The
article offered readers a taste of popular opinion on Manhattan's Lower
East Side:

"Serve them right!" said a patriarchal old tailor, speaking of Manila. "They [the
Spanish] tortured the Jews and banished them from their land, and now the God
of Israel is getting even with them." [...] The younger and more educated part
of the East Side population are against Spain because they are Americans and

because they sympathize with the cause of free Cuba, but to the older folks [...] a victory like Dewey's is as much of a triumph to the Jewish race as it is to the American people.[3]

Cahan framed his description of Jewish satisfaction upon hearing of the Spaniards' military defeat, citing the Jewish people's grievances against the Spanish throne ever since 1492, as a vestige of what the "old folks" had to say on the matter. A nearly biblical retribution had taken place: God acts in His own good time, which may be 400 years "late" but, nonetheless, is just. In contrast to the "patriarchal" types, Cahan portrayed "younger and more educated" Jews as taking a less tribal, more politically informed position. Such a construction suited Cahan, a socialist and an atheist, who prided himself on his realism. Nevertheless, the "old tailor" stole the headline. Cahan went on to assert: "When the first report of Dewey's victory reached the ghetto, the joy expressed in the streets, tenement houses and sweatshops reached a pitch of excitement the like of which was perhaps unknown in any other part of the city."

Neither Cahan nor the other East-Siders who figured in his report were descended from Spain's Jewish exiles. Not Iberian ancestry, but rather a pan-Jewish solidarity, prompted these Yiddish-speaking Jews born in Eastern Europe to recall the monarchy of Ferdinand and Isabella with righteous anger and to indulge in a moment of *Schadenfreude* (gloating at another's comeuppance).[4]

Cahan's vignette, however, was hardly just an innocent ethnic tableau: it was a political statement. None of the Jews depicted in Cahan's sketch would have ranted about Spanish crimes four centuries old, were it not for the war that was being fought between their newly adopted country and the Spanish crown. In 1898, American politics were fraught with polarizing domestic issues that spilled over into foreign policy. The years from 1893 to 1900 were marked by financial panics and recessions and the stirrings of popular opposition to continued immigration. Conflicting opinions about America's Pacific and Caribbean ambitions were produced in a pressure-cooker of divided interests, derived from Progressive, imperial, high finance, and even socialist agendas.

When the Cuban revolution broke out in 1895, moderate forces of opinion in America, including William McKinley (who would take office

---

[3] Quoted by Wenger, *History Lessons*, pp. 101–2; *Commercial Advertiser*, May 14, 1898, reprinted in *Grandma Never Lived in America: The New Journalism of Abraham Cahan*, ed. and intro. Moses Rischin (Bloomington: Indiana University Press, 1985), pp. 7–9.
[4] Wenger, *History Lessons*, pp. 102–3.

as US President in 1897), were increasingly hard-pressed to maintain a non-interventionist position. The press, in particular, with few exceptions, was pro-war. The anti-jingoist coalition, on the other hand, included important public voices, such as that of Carl Schurz (1829–1906, the former US Senator and Secretary of the Interior, anti-imperialist Mugwump, and journalist), and Oscar Straus who, we recall, was a leading Jewish communal figure, former US Ambassador to Turkey, presidential advisor, and future cabinet secretary. At the same time, a cluster of left-wing and liberal intellectuals, including Eugene V. Debs (1855–1926), the socialist leader with whom Cahan was most closely allied, believed that ending Spanish rule over Cuba and Puerto Rico (and the annexation of Hawaii) was good for social democracy and good for the international working class. Indeed, although Debs objected to the American annexation of the Philippines, he viewed the Cuban revolutionaries as comrades-in-arms across the "Florida channel."[5] In that context, the apparent ethnocentrism in Cahan's East Side tableau was secondary to the issues of American priorities and the war enthusiasm that had divided America's elite. Cahan portrayed the Jewish tenement dwellers' war-fever as an amplification of a generally accepted American point of view.

There were others in the Jewish community, however, who counseled peaceful steps to defuse the Spanish conflict. Perhaps surprisingly, in light of Cahan's assertions of universal Jewish consensus, these pacific voices included the rabbi of New York's venerable Spanish and Portuguese synagogue, Shearith Israel, not very far uptown from Abe Cahan's Lower East Side. Rabbi Henry Pereira Mendes (1852–1937), a scion of Sephardi Jewry, advocated arbitration by an international tribunal during the weeks following the sinking of the USS *Maine* in Havana. When war was declared, however, his congregation raised an American flag every day until the fighting ceased. Mendes's further reactions are not recorded.[6]

The editors of the influential *American Hebrew* also initially opposed the clamor for war; but by April 1898, they fell into line with the tenor of opinion, declaring: "As Americans, [Jewish soldiers] will stand by the flag

---

[5] Jonathan M. Hansen, *The Lost Promise of Patriotism: Debating American Identity, 1890–1920* (Chicago, IL and London: University of Chicago Press, 2003), pp. xiv–xviii, 17–22, 135–6, 149–51; Harold U. Faulkner, *Politics, Reform and Expansion, 1890–1900* (New York: Harper Torchbooks, 1959), pp. 163–259; Cohen, *A Dual Heritage*, pp. 48–54.

[6] Marc Saperstein, *Jewish Preaching in Times of War, 1800–2001* (Oxford and Portland, OR: Littman Library of Jewish Civilization, 2008), pp. 262–5.

that knows no difference of faith, while as Jews they will be urged on by the memories of the Inquisition."⁷

Likewise, Rabbi Joseph Krauskopf of Philadelphia initially supported arbitration and negotiation, until he became convinced that Spain had forfeited peaceful approaches to resolving the conflict. When he spoke on May 1, 1898, he invoked Spanish crimes of the past, sandwiching the Jewish persecution narrative together with other notorious episodes of tyranny and perfidy:

[Spain] continued her outrages upon Cuba, trampled upon justice, throttled every liberty [...]. It was the old story of her brutality in former centuries against the Jew and the Moor, against the Peruvian and Mexican, against the Protestants of the Netherlands.⁸

Yet, Krauskopf's fellow Philadelphian, Solomon Solis-Cohen, a community leader in his own right, denounced that line of thought: "History [...] will condemn the Cuban war. But whether or not we hold this view, let us not drag our religion into disgrace by allusions to Spain's conduct toward the Jews as justifying the present war."⁹

This was hardly the first occasion on which the question of Spain and its historical associations with Jewish affairs had intruded into American Jewish discourse. Mordecai Noah, the early nineteenth-century New York journalist, playwright, and noted political figure, was wont to recall his maternal grandmother's Spanish ancestry and the harrowing escape of his great-grandfather, Dr. Samuel Nuñez. Noah took certain liberties with his family tree, suppressing his (presumably less exciting) Ashkenazic heritage in order to stress his Iberian ancestors' courtly past.¹⁰

Somewhat after that, President Buchanan's offer in 1858 to appoint Louisiana's Senator Judah P. Benjamin as US ambassador to Spain (a post that he declined) sent a satisfied pulse of gratification through the Jewish community, reaching even beyond American shores. The American correspondent for the German-Jewish newspaper, the *Allgemeine Zeitung des Judenthums*, saw poetic justice in the proposed "return" of a scion of banished Sephardic Jews as the honored representative of his country: "[T]he United States are sending out a Jew as their representative to the Spanish government! O! The old God of Israel is still alive!"¹¹

⁷ *The American Hebrew* 62(23) (April 8, 1898).
⁸ Saperstein, *Jewish Preaching*, pp. 269–76.
⁹ *Ibid.*, pp. 268–9.
¹⁰ Sarna, *Jacksonian Jew*, p. 3.
¹¹ Ben-Ur, *Sephardic Jews in America*, p. 87; Eli N. Evans, *Judah P. Benjamin, The Jewish Confederate* (New York: The Free Press, 1987), p. 96; *Allgemeine Zeitung des Judenthums*

In the 1870s, as we saw previously, Emma Lazarus made a point of invoking her Iberian lineage. At the behest of Gustav Gottheil, rabbi of New York's Temple Emanu-El, she undertook to translate (from the German version) several hymns (*piyyutim*) written by medieval Spanish Hebrew poets. To Lazarus, who had imbibed what her biographer describes as a "sense of entitlement" from her socially elite family, the courtly image of these classical medieval poets represented a high Jewish aesthetic. Elaborating on these conventions, she extolled the Sephardic background of British statesman Benjamin Disraeli, calling it the source of his "fiery Castillian pride [befitting] the descendant, not of pariahs and pawnbrokers, but of princes, prophets, statesmen, poets, and philosophers." Lazarus adhered to popularized romantic traditions of Iberian Jewish sensibility and nobility of spirit (though mediated through her turn toward Germanic romanticism and Heinrich Heine's lyric poetry in particular).[12]

Other Jewish writers, in contrast, dispensed entirely with the images that Lazarus treasured, and stressed instead the destruction of Spanish Jewry during the fifteenth-century Catholic *Reconquista*. In 1910, the Russian-immigrant Hebrew poet, Benjamin Silkiner (1882–1933), published an epic poem, *Mul ohel timurah* (Before the Tent of Timmura), a complex, dense, tragic ballad about the demise of Native American tribes and their cultures, set in the time of the Spanish *conquistadores*:

Rivers and rivers of blood and tears the men of Spain have already spilt – by day clouds of smoke mounting skyward from the debris of ruins, by night the light of pyres built for their god, who demands victims by the thousands.[13]

Images like rivers of spilled blood and the pyres lit on behalf of the Spaniards' God referred the average Hebrew reader back to the

---

22(40) (1858): 553, cited by Sonja L. Mekel, "'Salvation Comes from America': The United States in the *Allgemeine Zeitung des Judenthums*," *American Jewish Archives Journal* 60(1–2) (2008): 9.

[12] "Heine, the modern, cynical German Parisian, owns a place among these devout and ardent mystics who preceded him by fully eight centuries. [Heine's] *Intermezzo*, so new and individual in German literature, is but a well-sustained continuation of the *Divan* and *Gazelles* of Judah Halevi, or the thinly veiled sensuousness of Alcharisi and Ibn Ezra." Quoted by Sol Liptzin, "Attitudes Toward Heine's Jewishness in England and America," *YIVO Annual of Jewish Social Science* 2–3 (1947/8): 76, from *Century Magazine* 7 (1884): 215. See also Schor, *Emma Lazarus*, pp. 26, 73–4, 76–8, 130; Young, *Emma Lazarus in Her World*, pp. 36–7. On Disraeli and the Sephardic myth, see Todd Endelman, "Benjamin Disraeli and the Myth of Sephardi Superiority," *Jewish History* 10(2) (1996): 21–35.

[13] Michael Weingrad, *American Hebrew Literature. Writing Jewish National Identity in the United States* (Syracuse, NY: Syracuse University Press, 2011), p. 83.

Inquisitorial *autos da fé*, where Judaizers were burned at the stake. The pillars of cloud and fire in this verse were an explicit biblical reference (Exodus 13: 21), intended to highlight the Spaniards' violent perversion of divine purposes.

The greatest popular resonance in American Jewish discourse was achieved, however, by the long-rumored connections between Christopher Columbus and the Jews of Spain. This was occasioned by the coincidence between the wholesale expulsion of the Jews from Castile and Aragon carried out on August 2, 1492 and the departure of the *Niña*, *Pinta*, and *Santa María* on the following day. "After the Spanish monarchs had expelled all the Jews from all their kingdoms and lands [...] they commissioned me to undertake the voyage to India," as Columbus's journal put it.[14]

That historical coincidence carried inordinate weight in American Jewish letters: namely, the idea that the fortuitous discovery of a new continent, destined to serve in the future as a haven for the ever-wandering Jews, was uncanny and, somehow, foreordained. This twist of fate, then, placed the entire narrative of America into the service of Jewish survival. Much significance was imputed to the presence on board Columbus's ships of New Christian crewmembers, including Luis de Torres, who, baptized shortly before the departure, was appointed the mission's interpreter; and the ship's physician, Maestre Bernal, who had done public penance for Judaizing at Valencia in 1490. Other embellishments of these materials have asserted that Columbus himself was a crypto-Jew.[15]

---

[14] Meyer Kayserling, *Christopher Columbus and the Participation of the Jews in the Spanish and Portuguese Discoveries*, trans. Charles Gross (New York: Hermon Press, 1968, originally published 1894, 1907); see also Simon Wiesenthal, *Sails of Hope: The Secret Mission of Christopher Columbus*, trans. Richard and Clara Winston (New York: Macmillan, 1973); Lewis A. Tambs, "Expulsion of the Jewish Community from the Spains, 1492," in *Religion in the Age of Exploration: The Case of Spain and New Spain*, ed. Bryan F. Le Beau and Menachem Mor (Omaha, NE: Creighton University Press and New York: Fordham University Press, 1996), p. 51; Jonathan D. Sarna, "The Mythical Jewish Columbus and the History of America's Jews," in *Religion in the Age of Exploration*, ed. Le Beau and Mor, pp. 81–95. See also Wenger, *History Lessons*, pp. 14, 47–8, 51, 60–3, 68, 152–3, 216.In a sonnet that Emma Lazarus wrote in 1883, several days after penning "The New Colossus," she noted the two coinciding events of 1492: "Thou two-faced year, Mother of Change and Fate/ Didst weep when Spain cast forth with flaming sword/ The children of the prophets of the Lord[...]. Then smiling, thou unveil'dst [...] A virgin world where doors of sunset part/ Saying "Ho, all who weary, enter here!" Schor, *Emma Lazarus*, pp. 192, 289–95.

[15] Kayserling, *Columbus and the Jews*, p. 90.

The lingering popularity of these Columbian tales assuredly stemmed from a wish to locate the Jewish drama at the very genesis of the American saga, as a corrective to the regnant Anglo-Protestant foundational traditions of Jamestown and Plymouth Rock – also matching, in equal measure, Italian-Americans' claim on Columbus's nationality. Columbus, of course, did not really lay America's national foundations. However, the notion of Columbus as America's first "founding father" (with Jewish help, if not actual Jewish roots) was so pervasive that it even inspired parodies, as in the sarcastic Yiddish ditty about the rigors of immigrant life, *Di grine kusine* (My Greenhorn Cousin), whose punchline was: "Columbus's country be damned!" – *brenen zol kolombeses medine*.[16]

As much as the "Columbus myth" was promoted to confer on Jews the imagined prestige of quasi-native or "co-founder" status (a status that was not colloquially granted to them by anyone else), it was, at the same time, a measure of Jewish difference in the contemporary American urban landscape. In the context of the late nineteenth and early twentieth century, Jews were pitting their narrative of flight from persecution against someone else's narrative: namely, Catholic opinion in America. While Jews took it for granted that Catholic Spain and Portugal symbolized the worst of Old World fanaticism, the contemporary Catholic press played down the severity or questioned the veracity of such notions.[17]

Minor examples abound in which Jewish articulations of strident anti-Catholicism were coupled with anti-Spanish propaganda and grandstanding boasts of Jewish super-patriotism, as in the following front-page item in a typical Jewish communal weekly, the Pittsburgh *Jewish Criterion*, in March, 1898:

A Contrast: We had occasion recently to be present [...] in the dedication of a modest room to [Jewish] religious worship and the instruction of children. The walls of the place were liberally decorated with the Stars and Stripes. [...] Contrast with this the [...] church dignitary [who] ordered the removal of unblessed insignia, emblems of our country, from the church wherein services for the [USS] *Maine* victims were held.[18]

Readers were likewise informed that Spanish troops sent to Cuba were accompanied by "papal blessings, to take effect at the scene of pillage and carnage."

[16] "Di grine kusine," music by Abe Schwartz, lyrics by Khayim Prizant.
[17] Egal Feldman, *Catholics and Jews in Twentieth-Century America* (Urbana and Chicago: University of Illinois Press, 2001), pp. 19–21.
[18] *Jewish Criterion* 7(6) (March 11, 1898) (http://pjn.cmu.edu).

The Cincinnati *American Israelite*, edited by Isaac Mayer Wise, chimed in with its own anti-Catholic tirade, going so far as to proclaim a joint Jewish-Protestant triumphalism. Here, Wise highlighted the idea that various recent events, such as the anti-Jewish lynch-mob atmosphere manifested during the Dreyfus Affair in Paris and the election of an openly anti-Semitic mayor in Vienna, were only to be expected, given that both France and Austria were predominantly Catholic countries:

Anglo-Saxonism [*sic*], Protestantism, Americanism, Freemasonry and Judaism are common objects of hatred in [non-Protestant] Paris and Vienna [...], just as they are in Madrid and Havana. *It is the lower civilization against the higher.* [Emphasis added][19]

American Jews, we might recall, were at this time overwhelmingly residents of big cities where immigrants made up large proportions of the population: notably, Catholics of Irish, Italian, Austro-Hungarian, and Polish origin. Hence, the clashing of diametrically opposed religio-cultural discourses bristled with street-level pugnacity, bred between strangers crowded into adjacent neighborhoods.

As events unfolded, Jews in America were embroiled in new ways in affairs of the Spanish state. In one bizarre episode, in 1912, twenty years after the Columbian quadricentennial, the Spanish government decided to encourage the "repatriation" of Jews of Sephardic ancestry. This initiative was directed toward Jews hailing from the eastern Mediterranean, including those who had in the meantime migrated to the United States. A few American Jewish notables, including Oscar Straus, engaged in tentative talks with the Spanish embassy in Washington. But the Federation of Oriental (i.e. eastern Sephardic) Jews, composed of Sephardic immigrants in the US, hastened to quash such an initiative. Joseph Gedalecia, head of the Federation, stated: "Jews of the orient, though they have no feelings of resentment or animosity against Spain, have not forgotten the sufferings of their ancestors." Likewise, Moise Gadol (1874–1941), editor of the New York Ladino (Latino-Jewish) newspaper, *La America*, wrote that Sephardim in America would not "return to a country that left us with such sad memories." Those voices represented the mainstream Jewish consensus. However, one Jew who did "return" to Spain – a certain José M. Estrugo, a Turkish Jew and a founding member of the

---

[19] Jeanne Adams, "Remembering the Maine: "The Jewish Attitude toward the Spanish-American War as Reflected in *The American Israelite*," *American Jewish History* 76(4) (1987): 441–2.

Sephardic congregation in Los Angeles – wrote, "For the first time in my life I felt truly aboriginal, native [...], much more than in the Jewish quarter where I was born!"[20]

For most Jews, however, the archetypal foe of the medieval past (Spain) was paired with all contemporary antisemites, on the one hand, while America was cast in the role of providential refuge, on the other. "Listen [...] you drunkards, hooligans, pogrom-makers!" – thus began a diatribe, written by the celebrated Yiddish author, Sholem Aleichem (pen name of Sholem Rabinovich, 1859–1916), in his last work of fiction, *Motl peyse dem khazns* (Motl, the Cantor's Son):

Were it not for you and your persecutions and oppressions and pogroms, we should not have known about Columbus, and Columbus would not have heard of us! [...] You'll have a bitter end, just like the Spaniards did.[21]

Two decades later, the Spanish Civil War of 1936–9 brought many of these threads together once again, as Jews in the United States, along with many others, reacted to the bloody struggle between the Republican Loyalists and Francisco Franco's rebel *Falangistas*. Support for Franco's forces by Mussolini's Italy, Hitler's Germany, and Romanian "Iron Guard" fascist volunteers, and the atrocities committed against Spanish civilians, such as the indiscriminate bombing at Guernica by German and Italian warplanes, turned the Spanish Civil War into an ominous dress rehearsal for World War II.[22]

In line with anti-Fascist opinion elsewhere in the 1930s, the radical Left in Depression-era America rallied to the Spanish Republican cause. One expression of support for the anti-Fascist cause was the recruitment of an international army of 40,000 volunteers, the *Brigadas Internacionales*, to join the Loyalist forces. Nearly 3,000 young men and women came from the United States – this, at a time when Congress was passing Neutrality Acts to keep America out of Europe's conflagrations. They were mostly recruited to a unit dubbed the Abraham Lincoln Battalion (sometimes

[20] Ben-Ur, *Sephardic Jews in America*, pp. 10, 160; Albert J. Amateau, "The Sephardic Immigrant from Bulgaria: A Personal Profile of Moise Gadol," *American Jewish Archives Journal* 42(1) (1990): 57–70.

[21] Sholem Aleichem, *Motl peyse dem khazns*, from *In amerike: letste shriftn* (New York, 1918), pp. 58–9, cited by Khone Shmeruk, "Sholem Aleichem and America," *YIVO Annual* 20 (1991): 224.

[22] Raymond L. Proctor, *Hitler's Luftwaffe in the Spanish Civil War* (Westport, CT and London: Greenwood Books, 1983); Judith Keene, *Fighting for Franco: International Volunteers in Nationalist Spain During the Spanish Civil War* (New York and London: Hambledon Continuum, 2001), pp. 7, 11, 215–44.

fancifully enhanced to a "Brigade"). About a third of this American contingent was Jewish, and among the female volunteers, Jews were a majority. The highest-ranking officer in the Lincoln Battalion, Lt.-Col. John
Gates (*né* Sol Regenstreif), was Jewish, as was the unit's last commander,
Maj. Milton ("El Lobo") Wolff. There were also those, like volunteer
pilot Ben Leider, shot down near Madrid in the spring of 1937, who had
no connection to the Battalion.[23]

   The historical conjunction of Jews and Spanish history was not at
the top of the volunteers' list of motivations. Fighting Franco, Hitler,
and Mussolini was far more significant. As "internationalists" (mostly
Communists), they eschewed ethnocentrism of any sort. Many had
adopted non-Jewish-sounding *noms de guerre*: Bill Harvey (*né* Horwitz),
Joe Gordon (*né* Mendelowitz), Dave Doran (*né* Dransky), Reuben Barr
(*né* Bacofsky), the above-mentioned John Gates, or the super-WASP-
sounding Yale Stuart (*né* Skolnik).[24]

   However, one young man, Hyman Katz (who retained his distinctly
Jewish name), wrote home from a hospital bed in Spain: "Don't you realize that we Jews will be the first to suffer if fascism comes?" As he put it
in another letter (no doubt trying to appeal to parental conscience), his
mother was partly "to blame" for his decision to volunteer to fight, since

---

[23] Allen Guttman, *The Wound in the Heart: America and the Spanish Civil War* (New York:
The Free Press of Glencoe, 1962); Vincent Brome, *The International Brigades: Spain,
1936–1939* (London: Heinemann, 1966); Robert A. Rosenstone, "The Men of the
Abraham Lincoln Battalion," *Journal of American History* 54(2) (1967): 327–38; David
Diamant, *Yidn in shpanishn krig, 1936–1939* (Paris: Yidish Bukh – Oyfsnay, 1967);
Cecil Eby, *Between the Bullet and the Lie: American Volunteers in the Spanish Civil
War* (New York: Holt, Rinehart and Winston, 1969), see re: Ben Leider, pp. 99–100;
Michael Jackson, *Fallen Sparrows: The International Brigades in the Spanish Civil
War* (Philadelphia, PA: American Philosophical Society, 1994); Peter N. Carroll, *The
Odyssey of the Abraham Lincoln Brigade: Americans in the Spanish Civil War* (Stanford,
CA: Stanford University Press, 1994), esp. pp. 17–18; Kenyon Zimmer, "'The Whole
World is Our Country': Immigration and Anarchism in the United States, 1885–1940"
(PhD dissertation, University of Pittsburgh, 2010), pp. 436, 440; *African Americans in
the Spanish Civil War*, ed. Danny Duncan Collum (New York: G. K. Hall, 1991).

[24] Carroll, *Odyssey*, pp. 18, 20–1; Eby, *Between the Bullet and the Lie*, pp. 5, 10, 53, 174.
The Socialist Party, the radical IWW movement ("Wobblies"), and American Communist
groups all afforded foreign-language groups the possibility of associating under the
Leftist umbrella, but emphasized the desirability of Americanizing their leadership and
sought to shed the image of a movement based on foreigners. This spurred Jewish political activists to assume American-sounding names. See Sally M. Miller, "For White Men
Only: The Socialist Party of America and Issues of Gender, Ethnicity, and Race," *Journal
of the Gilded Age and Progressive Era* 2(3) (2003): 283–302; Harvey Klehr, "Immigrant
Leadership in the Communist Party of the United States of America," *Ethnicity* 6(1)
(1979): 41–3.

she had "sacrificed to give me a good Jewish education, and the whole history of our people has taught me to admire the [...] fighters who died for liberty."[25]

The interplay between contemporary politics, historical consciousness, and ethno-national memories was mirrored in Franco's ideology, which harked back to the "glory days" of the *Reconquista*, of Ferdinand and Isabella, who had "triumphed over malignant foreign powers" – meaning the historic Moslems and Jews. It was perhaps more than mere coincidence, then, that another Jewish volunteer wrote home: "Today Jews are returning, welcomed by the entire Spanish people to fight the modern inquisition." In all, the number of Jewish volunteers who came from Poland, Belgium, France, Germany, Austria, Romania, Palestine, Britain, North America, and Latin America is estimated at about 5,000 (over 12 percent of the total – a conspicuously disproportionate number). They represented a microcosm of leftist Jews from across the world.[26]

The ill-fated Spanish Republican battle reverberated in Jewish circles in America well beyond the ranks of the radical Left. The Jewish ethnic press at large was consistent in identifying Franco with Fascism and, in addition, it signaled that a Spanish Loyalist victory was vital for the free world and for the Jewish people, in particular. In 1937, the national rabbinical association of Reform Judaism, the Central Conference of American Rabbis, endorsed a resolution in support of the anti-Franco forces. By 1938, when Hitler annexed Austria to the Third Reich and Italy proclaimed new racial decrees similar to Germany's anti-Jewish Nuremberg Laws, European Fascism and antisemitism had become

[25] Carroll, *Odyssey*, pp. 17–18.
[26] Michael Richards, *A Time of Silence: Civil War and the Culture of Repression in Franco's Spain* (Cambridge: Cambridge University Press, 1998), p. 9; Josef Toch, "Juden im Spanischen Krieg 1936–39," *Zeitgeschichte* (April 1973); Albert Prago, "Jews in the International Brigades," *Jewish Currents* (February 1979): 15–27; Alan S. Rockman, "Jewish Participation in the International Brigades in the Spanish Civil War 1936–1939" (MA thesis, California State University, Fullerton, 1981); Binyomin Lubelski, *Yidn in shpanishn birgerkrig* (Tel-Aviv: Leivick Farlag, 1984); Arno Lustiger, "German and Austrian Jews in the International Brigade," *Leo Baeck Institute Year Book* 35 (1990): 297–320; Colin Shindler, "'No pasaran': The Jews who Fought in Spain," *Jewish Quarterly* 33(3) (1986): 34–41; G. E. Sichon, "Les volontaires juifs dans la guerre civile en Espagne: chiffres et enjeux," *Les temps modernes* 44(507) (1988): 46–62; Gerben Zaagsma, "'Red Devils': The Botwin Company in the Spanish Civil War," *East European Jewish Affairs* 33(1) (2003): 83–99; Isabelle Rohr, *The Spanish Right and the Jews, 1898–1945* (Brighton and Portland, OR: Sussex Academic Press, 2007), pp. 65, 73–4, 78–82; Feldman, *Catholics and Jews*, p. 55.

the pervasive filter through which Jews gauged their relations with the world – including other Americans.[27]

Once again, this occasioned the airing of religious and ethnic tensions in American cities. Parts of the Catholic public seemed particularly susceptible to seeing the Spanish Civil War in terms quite different from their Jewish neighbors. Some 53 percent of American Catholics claimed to favor neither side in the Spanish conflict and 39 percent sympathized with Franco, while only 20 percent supported the Loyalists. Nearly half of the Irish respondents from New York City said they favored Franco, as did half of Italians (although Italian anti-Fascist volunteers were conspicuous in the ranks of Spanish Republican units, including almost 300 Italian-Americans – about 10 percent of the American contingent). Conservative Catholics tended to view the Soviets, rather than the Fascists, as the more dangerous threat to humanistic, Christian, and democratic values. The Spanish Republicans had, after all, abolished state funding for the Church and allegedly committed atrocities against nuns and priests.[28]

Atlanta-born Jane Anderson, a pro-Franco propagandist, toured the United States in 1937 and 1938, speaking at over a hundred public events, virtually all of them before Catholic audiences.[29] In May 1938 a mass meeting was held at Boston's Symphony Hall, sponsored by Boston's William Cardinal O'Connell, where supporters of "White [i.e. "anti-Red"] Spain" demanded that the United States recognize Franco's regime. Patrick Scanlan, editor of the mass-circulation *Brooklyn Tablet*, the influential paper of the Brooklyn archdiocese, wrote in February 1939: "The lining up of Jews [...] with the loyalist anarchists and Communists [...] is a more fearful indictment [against the Jews] than any Father Coughlin [the well-known antisemitic propagandist] ever uttered."[30]

---

[27] Robert Singerman, "American-Jewish Reactions to the Spanish Civil War," *Journal of Church and State* 19 (1977): 261–78; Ronald H. Bayor, *Neighbors in Conflict: The Irish, Germans, Jews, and Italians of New York City, 1929–1941* (Urbana and Chicago: University of Illinois Press, 1988), pp. 78–81, 92–3.

[28] Dinnerstein, *Antisemitism in America*, pp. 113–17, 120–21; Fraser Ottanelli, "Anti-Fascism and the Shaping of National and Ethnic Identity: Italian American Volunteers in the Spanish Civil War," *Journal of American Ethnic History* 27(1) (2007): 9–31.

[29] Anderson afterward went to Berlin to become one of Goebbels's English-language radio propagandists. Like the infamous "Lord Haw Haw," the moniker given to several male English-language broadcasters, Anderson was a "Lady Haw Haw." See Keene, *Fighting for Franco*, pp. 260–3.

[30] Feldman, *Catholics and Jews*, pp. 53–8; Bayor, *Neighbors*, pp. 91, 194 n. 28; Stephen H. Norwood, "Marauding Youth and the Christian Front: Antisemitic Violence in Boston

One outstanding Catholic voice that was raised against Franco was that of Father Michael O'Flanagan (1876–1942), an Irish Republican priest and socialist, who went on a speaking tour in the United States in 1937. His chagrin at the pro-Franco trend in Catholic opinion was shared by others. Writing in the prominent Catholic journal, *Commonweal*, George N. Shuster (1894–1977), a Wisconsin-born graduate of Notre Dame, questioned whether Catholics could in good conscience ignore or support "the manifest brutality, reactionary political method and intellectual simplicity of the Francoites?" Slammed by overwhelmingly negative reader response, Shuster was taken aback and resigned from *Commonweal*: "It now dawned on me that for Catholic New York the world outside was either Communist or Fascist and that therefore they opted for Fascism." Even the popular mayor of New York City, Fiorello LaGuardia, was smeared as a "Jewish communist warmonger" for speaking out forcefully against European Fascism.[31]

In that embattled atmosphere, neutrality seemed to appeal to most other Americans. President Roosevelt, who otherwise chafed at Congressional restrictions on his foreign policy options, actually outdid Congress's isolationist intent by imposing an arms embargo on both sides fighting in Spain, even though the Neutrality Laws at that time did not yet apply to civil wars. It has been suggested that, among other things, he was wary of adverse reaction among the Catholic electorate. The State Department declined to issue passports to American volunteers seeking to drive ambulances in Spain.[32]

By and large, many Jews looked at the Spanish conflict differently: through the eyes of the Jews of Europe. Even those whose political consciousness was not guided by parochial Jewish concerns but, rather, by "internationalist" (Communist) principles were, by definition, staking out a position that placed them well outside the American consensus. Closer to home, they were in direct conflict with some of their neighbors from around the block.[33] These asymmetries were fed by the undertow of racism that marked American domestic life during the Depression.

and New York City During World War II," *American Jewish History* 91(2) (2003): 247; see also *Boston Globe*, May 4, 1938.
31 Ottanelli, "Anti-Fascism," p. 20; Marty, *Modern American Religion* 2, pp. 283–4; Parrish, *Anxious Decades*, p. 451.
32 Parrish, *Anxious Decades*, pp. 453–4.
33 The close encounter of Jews and Catholics was not just a function of neighborhood proximity in the major cities, but also extended to university campuses. In the 1920s and 1930s, when major Protestant institutions of higher learning limited Jewish enrollments, Catholic universities had a higher-than-average proportion of Jewish students: about

Anxious Jewish community-relations agencies discerned a politicized "Jewish question," and they were not at all pleased. In polls taken between March 1938 and April 1940, between 26 and 31 percent of Americans believed Jews to be "less patriotic" than other citizens. Similar or higher percentages believed that Jews wished to drag the United States into a foreign war. As some analysts concluded, Jews were thought of as non-conformists "with a self-centered morality of their own [...] that supposedly permitted them to undercut the patriotism of the larger society."[34]

Jewish groups attempting to deflect anti-Jewish stigmas looked for ways to de-politicize the image of American Jews and to make their cause appear benign. They worked to enhance inter-faith dialogue, partnered with non-Jewish liberals and anti-Fascists in the German-American and Italian-American communities, cooperated with non-sectarian humanitarian and refugee agencies, and distanced themselves from any association with the radical Left. The "establishment" organ, the *American Jewish Year Book*, studiously avoided reporting on the involvement of Jews in the fighting in Spain, and made only a brief reference to the anti-Jewish tones in Spanish Nationalist propaganda.[35]

In sum, the Spanish motif in Jewish history prevailed across several centuries of migration, literature, and politics. As we have seen, some Jews saw their presence in America as a vindication of old grievances against Spain, and they reveled in Spain's political reversals. Sometimes American Jews celebrated the glories of the Spanish Golden Age, when Jewish life and art flourished under both Christian and Moslem rulers. That medieval Spanish precedent of cultural symbiosis (exaggerated as the notion may have been) symbolized the ideals of acceptance and achievement – and portended the same for a free life under an American "Golden Age" of liberty. At other times, Spanish motifs also served as portents of calamity.

Perhaps most of all, the Spanish theme reflects one of the long-running fissures in the landscape of Jewish-Gentile relations in the United States: the historical friction between Jews and Catholics. With

---

15 percent at the top 25 Catholic colleges, and reaching a remarkable majority of 56.7 percent at one Catholic university in New York City. See Claris Edwin Silcox and Galen M. Fisher, *Catholics, Jews and Protestants: A Study of Relationships in the United States and Canada* (Westport, CT: Greenwood Press, 1934), pp. 228–9.

34 Charles Herbert Stember et al., *Jews in the Mind of America* (New York: Basic Books, 1966), pp. 116–19.

35 *American Jewish Year Book*, vol. XL (Philadelphia, PA: Jewish Publication Society, 1938), p. 187, and vol. XLI (Philadelphia, PA: Jewish Publication Society, 1939), p. 353; Dollinger, *Quest for Inclusion*, pp. 62–76.

one noticeable respite during the late 1920s, when Alfred E. Smith ran for the US presidency and the two religious minorities were more or less in political alignment, the tensions between them were seldom far from the surface. This would substantially change only much later, during the 1960s, in the era of the Second Vatican Council, when interfaith understanding gained wider support and when racial conflict in American society was perceived as far more pressing than religious issues.

Germany: From "Civic Betterment" to the Holocaust

From the start, the Jewish–German nexus took shape quite differently from the Jews' Spanish connection. Until the Nazi period, Germany never loomed as the Jews' great nemesis. The permanent, wholesale banishment of Spain's Jews in 1492 and the subsequent persecutions of New Christian *conversos* had no close Austro-German parallels, even though anti-Jewish massacres and regional or local expulsions did take place in Central Europe at various times during the Middle Ages. True, in his day, Martin Luther had broadcast virulent hostility to Jews and Judaism, which filtered into the culture of the Lutheran Church and, later, into German nationalism. But from the mid-seventeenth century on, state policies in the historic lands of German and Austrian rule tended to favor the selective integration of Jews into the local economy – namely, those with financial capital or high-level commercial and manufacturing.

In the late eighteenth century, large numbers of Jews were unexpectedly brought under Prussian and Austrian rule by the annexations of former Polish territories. Many of those Jews were subsequently naturalized and culturally "Germanized" within the expanding imperial system. In a process that culminated close to a century later (1870) in the virtually complete Jewish (male) political emancipation, the policy of "civic betterment" (*bürgerlicher Verbesserung*)[36] of the Jews gained ground, despite anti-Jewish bigotry in various quarters. Germany and Austria-Hungary in the nineteenth century were, in their stodgy, inconsistent, bureaucratic way, archetypes of enlightened pragmatism and toleration, when compared with the onerous policies and outbreaks of anti-Jewish violence that characterized the Russian Empire and Romania.

---

[36] The eighteenth-century German liberal thinker, Christian Wilhelm von Dohm, published a tract in 1781 entitled *Über die bürgerlicher Verbesserung der Juden* (Concerning the Amelioration of the Civil Status of the Jews) (Berlin: F. Nicolai, 1781–3). He argued that only by emancipating the Jews from their legal disabilities could the state hope to attract Jews to a rationale of full integration into German society and culture.

Jews in America who hailed from Germany and Austria-Hungary saw
those lands not only as their patrimony, but also as integral parts of their
contemporary world, not scenes and landscapes abandoned long ago.
They had not been expelled from their homes. Jews from Central Europe
emigrated in high proportions, compared to their non-Jewish neighbors, and they had certain extra motivations to leave (especially prior
to 1870) because of irksome restrictions on residence permits, marriage
licenses, and commercial or professional opportunities.[37] Still, their
decision to seek their fortunes abroad was no less voluntary than similar
choices made simultaneously by thousands of other, non-Jewish, émigrés.

There was, therefore, no single, galvanizing issue or historical griev-
ance that divided Austro-German Jewish immigrants in America from
their non-Jewish compatriots. As we noted in Chapter 1, there was some
degree of social distance and exclusivity along denominational lines that
divided German-speaking immigrants amongst themselves, but there
were also opportunities for cross-denominational fraternization. As
Edna Ferber recalled in her memoirs, an American-born young woman
from a German-speaking Jewish family around the turn of the twentieth
century might enjoy the hospitality of a non-Jewish, German-speaking
boarding house in Milwaukee. The profoundly German atmosphere
cohabited lightly with American civic propriety in a neighborhood where
shops hung out signs to assure potential customers: "Hier wird Englisch
gesprochen" (English is spoken here).[38] Even when Jews established their
own, separate social groups – like B'nai B'rith and its parallel women's
organization, the Treue Schwestern (Faithful Sisters) – these groups
combined genteel camaraderie with "civic improvement" in the classic
German-liberal and American fashion.[39]

The fact that a Jew in America might interact with fellow-citizens of
Austro-German background in an environment where all of them shared

[37] Barkai, *Branching Out*, pp. 9–10, 20.
[38] Ferber, *A Peculiar Treasure*, p. 132.
[39] There were important regional distinctions, including a greater tendency toward inter-
denominational fraternization in Midwestern communities – Milwaukee is the best
example – as compared to New York, Philadelphia, and Baltimore. See H. G. Reissner,
"The German-American Jews," *Leo Baeck Institute Year Book* 10 (1965): 94–6; Glanz,
Studies in Judaica Americana, pp. 132–5, 193, 203–55; Barkai, *Branching Out*, pp. 175–
9; Nadel, *Little Germany*, pp. 60–1, 99–103; Michael A. Meyer, "German-Jewish Identity
in Nineteenth-Century America," in *Toward Modernity: The European Jewish Model*,
ed. Jacob Katz (New Brunswick, NJ: Transaction, 1987), pp. 247–52. On B'nai B'rith
and the True Sisters, see Cornelia Wilhelm, *The Independent Orders of B'nai B'rith and
True Sisters: Pioneers of a New Jewish Identity, 1843–1914* (Detroit, MI: Wayne State
University Press, 2011); Moore, *B'nai B'rith*.

an identical civil status was (for the Jews, at least) a novel improvement. Moreover, the extent to which Jewish people chose to engage in close so-cial relations with other German-speakers (and, along with them, to eat alike, dress alike, and school their children alike) was no longer of any consequence for the Jews' status as citizens.[40]

A concrete example of the guarded but respectful interface between German gentiles and Jews in America is provided in the case of the Lorelei Fountain, a monument erected to honor the memory of the poet, Heinrich Heine. In the late 1880s, the German city of Düsseldorf refused to accept a sculpture commissioned to immortalize its illustrious native son, the Jewish-born expatriate writer with the magnificent but acid-dipped pen, whose memory still evoked local rage and contempt. After the city of Mainz also rejected the sculpture, it was purchased for New York City by a German-American club, the Arion Society. Neither Heine's anti-monarchist political views nor his Jewish descent appeared to bother the Arion Society in the least. After several years of controversy (politics and disagreements in the art commission), the Heine monument was installed at a public site in the southwest Bronx in 1899 – known today as Joyce Kilmer Park.[41]

In the final analysis, Jews' notions of "belonging" to or sharing in German-language culture did not depend on the mutuality of feeling between Jews and non-Jews. Rather, it was a subjective affair, evinced by certain ethno-cultural behaviors: accents and cadences of speech, prefer-ences of cuisine, reading habits, musical repertoires, loyalties to ethnic and religious associations, the names given to children, and the endearments used for "Mother" and "Father." The Jewish–German nexus in America, at least prior to World War I, was clearly a variant of the homeland-based ethnicities that prevailed among first- and second-generation Americans of European extraction.

That would not go far enough, however, toward a full understand-ing of the German connection and its importance for American Jewish

---

[40] Gregory Kupsky, "Germanness and Jewishness: Samuel Untermyer, Felix Warburg, and National Socialism, 1914–1938," *American Jewish Archives Journal* 63(2) (2011): 26–30.

[41] Rischin, *Promised City*, p. 264; see also www.nycgovparks.org/parks/ X028/highlights/ 11363; Paul Reitter, "Heine in the Bronx," *The Germanic Review: Literature, Culture, Theory* 74(4) (1999): 327–30; William Steinway, "The Heine Fountain Controversy," *The Forum* (February 1896), pp. 739–46; Jeffrey L. Sammons, "Jewish Reception as the Last Phase of American Heine Reception," in the *Jewish Reception of Heinrich Heine*, ed. Mark H. Gelber (Tübingen: Niemayer Verlag, 1992), pp. 197–207; and "The Restoration of the Heine Monument in the Bronx," *Germanic Review: Literature, Culture, Theory* 74(4) (1999): 337–9.

life. American Jewry in the nineteenth century mainly followed customs and liturgies that were derivations of practices in synagogues in Central and East-Central Europe. The Jewish community in the United States structurally resembled the decentralized pattern of small congregations that was typical in many parts of Germany. What American Jewish religious life chiefly lacked was a rationale – a theology. In a country where there had been no ordained Jewish clergy at all until the 1840s, the influx of German-speaking immigrant rabbis had tremendous impact. In the 1840s, 1850s, and 1860s, men like Abraham Rice, Isaac Mayer Wise, Max Lilienthal, David Einhorn, and Bernard Illowy (see Table 4.1) endowed the religious populism of American Jewry with a Central European demeanor and highbrow polish.[42]

Austro-German Jewry was numerically larger in the 1800s than its American offshoot, and it was also the foremost example of upward Jewish mobility at the time. By the 1870s, many Austro-German Jews nurtured an idealized self-image as the foremost modern Jewish community (though this was patriotically contested by their French and British coreligionists, who had equally firm notions about their own countries). German-speaking Jewry in Europe boasted a well-heeled class of theater- and opera-lovers, coteries of literati, a growing class of legal and medical professionals, a financial elite class that sponsored ambitious philanthropic projects, and a post-traditional younger generation that had left the "ghetto" behind but was not averse to nostalgia for family traditions – especially for a sentimentalized motherhood.[43]

Jews in America, aware of all this, built their opulent new synagogues in the so-called "Moorish" style in order to keep up with the Jewish Joneses in Berlin and Budapest whence the style had been had adopted. Jewish peddlers from Bavaria and merchandising tyros from Posen (today Poznań, Poland) sought to fulfill in America the bourgeois ideal that they

---

[42] Meyer, *Response to Modernity*, pp. 226, 235–95; Naomi W. Cohen, *Encounter with Emancipation: The German Jews in the United States 1830–1914* (Philadelphia, PA: Jewish Publication Society, 1984), pp. 159–94; Silverstein, *Alternatives to Assimilation*, pp. 94–103, 114–28.

[43] David J. Sorkin, *The Transformation of German Jewry, 1780–1840* (New York and Oxford: Oxford University Press, 1987; 2nd ed. Detroit, MI: Wayne State University Press, 1999); Marion A. Kaplan, *The Making of the Jewish Middle Class: Women, Family, and Identity in Imperial Germany* (New York and Oxford: Oxford University Press, 1991); Ismar Schorsch, *From Text to Context: The Turn to History in Modern Judaism* (Hanover, NH and London: Brandeis University Press/University Press of New England, 1994), pp. 93–117; Richard I. Cohen, *Jewish Icons: Art and Society in Modern Europe* (Berkeley and London: University of California Press, 1998), pp. 155–85.

TABLE 4.1. *Central European rabbis in America**

Name, lifespan	Birthplace	Academic training	Rabbinical training
Samuel Adler, 1809–91	Worms	Bonn, Giessen	Frankfurt
Bernard Drachman, 1861–1945	New York City[a]	Columbia University, Breslau, Heidelberg	Breslau
David Einhorn, 1809–79	Bavaria	Erlangen, Munich, Würzburg	Fürth
Bernhard Felsenthal, 1822–1908	Rhineland-Palatinate	Munich	Munich
Gustav Gottheil, 1827–1903	Posen	Berlin, Halle	Berlin
Emil G. Hirsch, 1851–1923	Luxembourg	Berlin, Leipzig	Berlin
Samuel Hirsch, 1815–89	Prussia	Bonn, Berlin, Leipzig	Berlin
Henry Hochheimer, 1818–1912	Middle Franconia	Munich	Ansbach, Munich
Bernard Illowy, 1812–71	Bohemia	Budapest	Pressburg (Bratislava)
Marcus Jastrow, 1829–1903	Posen	Halle	Breslau
Kaufmann Kohler, 1843–1926	Bavaria	Berlin, Erlangen	Fürth, Frankfurt
Alexander Kohut, 1842–94	Hungary	Leipzig	Breslau
Max Lilienthal, 1815–82	Bavaria	Munich	Munich
Leo Merzbacher, 1809/10–56	Bavaria	Erlangen, Munich[b]	Pressburg
Morris Raphall, 1798–1868	Stockholm	Giessen, Erlangen	Copenhagen, London
Abraham Joseph Rice (Reiss), 1802–62	Bavaria	–	Fürth, Würzburg
Henry Schneeberger,[c] 1848–1916	New York City	Columbia University, Jena	Berlin
Benjamin Szold, 1829–1902	Hungary	Vienna, Breslau	Pressburg, Breslau
Aaron Wise, 1844–96	Hungary	Berlin, Leipzig, Halle	Pressburg, Eisenstadt
Isaac Mayer Wise,[d] 1819–1900	Bohemia	Prague, Vienna	Prague

TABLE 4.1 (*cont.*)

---

* Silverstein, *Alternatives to Assimilation*, p. 115; Meyer, *Response to Modernity*, pp. 237–40, 245; Sarna, *American Judaism*, pp. 91–102; Davis, *Conservative Judaism*, pp. 335, 356, 344–5, 365–6; Gurock, *American Jewish Orthodoxy*, pp. 3–4.
a Drachman's parents were from Bavaria and Habsburg Galicia, respectively.
b Some question exists regarding Merzbacher's doctoral degree.
c Schneeberger's father was an immigrant from Central Europe.
d Isaac Mayer Wise did not complete his academic training, nor (apparently) did he receive formal rabbinical ordination. His published work, however, indicates a high proficiency in modern German philosophy and theology.

had witnessed and internalized on native ground – long before having glimpsed New York, Philadelphia, the towns of the Ohio or Mississippi River valleys, or the boom towns of the California gold rush. Indeed, it was *because* the bourgeois German ideal was so familiar, yet beyond the grasp of so many ordinary Jews in Europe, that America beckoned them so strongly.

The trail of German influence extended far beyond the immediate circles of émigré populations, however. It touched the lives of Americans with no direct ties to the *Vaterland*. As we have noted, Emma Lazarus – with her ancestral Sephardic pride – nonetheless found her métier as a poet as much through translating and imitating German verse as through immersing herself in American letters of the Gilded Age, or Hebrew literature of the Golden Age in Spain. Starting with "reams of blank verse on the Germanic legends of Lohengrin and Tannhäuser," as well as a novel with a twist on Goethe's romanticism (*Alide: An Episode from Goethe's Life*), Lazarus's best literary accomplishments may have been her translations of Heine. Some of her impassioned poems on Jewish themes were based on her gleanings from the German-Jewish historian, Heinrich Graetz (1817–91). She also needed the filter of German translation, we recall, in order to read the Hebrew poetry of her Iberian forebears.[44]

---

[44] Schor, *Emma Lazarus*, pp. 32, 44–5; Julian Levinson, "Brooklyn Am Rhein? The German Sources of Jewish American Literature," in *Jewish Literatures and Cultures: Context and Intertext*, ed. Anita Norich and Yaron Z. Eliav (Providence, RI: Brown University Press, 2008), pp. 233–5; Robert Lieberles, "Conflict over Reforms: The Case of Congregation Beth Elohim, Charleston, South Carolina," in *The American Synagogue: A Sanctuary Transformed*, ed. Jack Wertheimer (New York and Cambridge: Cambridge University Press, 1987), pp. 274–96; Meyer, *Response to Modernity*, pp. 228–33.

German literary culture, science, music, and medicine were bellwethers for many upper-class Americans and members of the intelligentsia – fully compatible with and quite as influential, at that time, as that other great "entitling" culture of the American elite, that of England and Scotland. German schools of sociology, anthropology, and political economy were finding outlets in contemporary social criticism – not least in the form of Marxism, which soon reverberated in the working-class districts of urban America. In the 1880s, the German-led immigrant Left in America nurtured the first wave of Russian-Jewish immigrant socialists and anarchists.[45]

Having nourished its spiritual, domestic, aesthetic, and political sensibilities on German cultural products, American Jewry was alert to events in the German-speaking parts of Europe. Due attention was paid to seemingly trivial items along with weightier matters. Thus, readers of the Pittsburgh *Jewish Criterion* learned in the fall of 1895 that the theology faculty of the University of Berlin had awarded its annual prize to a Jewish doctoral candidate, eliciting the comment: "This is [...] quite an honor, as the trophy is rarely won by a Jewish student." Meanwhile, the paper editorialized against the notorious judeophobe, Adolph Stoecker (1835–1909), whose Christian Social movement had been active in Germany since 1878. Stoecker, the paper claimed, had finally run afoul of decent opinion in Germany and was losing popularity.[46] Such over-optimistic forecasts were fully in keeping with the integrationist mood that animated Jewish opinion throughout much of the Western world: progress and humanism must certainly triumph over irrational fears and incitement to hatred.

(Of parenthetical interest in this regard is the fact that the African-American intellectual and political leader, W. E. B. Du Bois [1868–1963], who spent time in Berlin in the early 1890s on a graduate studies

---

45 Robert Ernst, *Immigrant Life in New York City, 1825–1863* (Port Washington, NY: Ira J. Friedman, Inc., 1965 [c. 1949]), pp. 118–21; Frankel, *Prophecy and Politics*, p. 123; Michels, *A Fire in Their Hearts*, pp. 41–9. On the background of German immigrant socialism in America, see Stanley Nadel, "From the Barricades of Paris to the Sidewalks of New York: German Artisans and the European Roots of American Labor Radicalism," in *Immigration to New York*, ed. William Pencak, Selma Berrol, and Randall M. Miller (Philadelphia, PA: The Balch Institute Press and London and Toronto: Associated University Presses, 1991), pp. 56–80.
46 *Jewish Criterion* 2(12) (October 25, 1895), and 2(18) (December 6, 1895) (http://pjn. cmu.edu). The prize was awarded to Felix Coblenz for his thesis, *Über das Betende Ich In den Psalmen. Eine Beitrag zur Erklärung des Psalters* (Frankfurt a/M: J. Kaufmann, 1897).

fellowship, applied his sensitivity to race-related issues to the question of social relations in Germany, and saw the situation more pessimistically than did many American Jews at the time. He later recalled having been struck by the distinct pattern of discrimination against Jews as well as Poles, seeing this as confirmation that hatred and prejudice cut across racial lines to "reach all sorts of people.")[47]

At about the same time, the Viennese journalist, Theodor Herzl (1860–1904), published a pamphlet called *Der Judenstaat* (The Jewish State). Far from being on the wane, a militant new antisemitism was on the rise, Herzl declared. That was true in Herzl's own city, where an openly anti-semitic mayor, Karl Lueger, held sway. It was true, as well, in Tiszaeszlár, the Hungarian town where in 1882 Jews were accused of ritual murder (a stock item of medieval antisemitic lore, revived in the 1800s); in Moscow, where the authorities expelled Jewish residents en masse in 1891; and in Paris, where Captain Alfred Dreyfus of the French general staff had been framed and convicted for espionage amid a lynch-atmosphere of anti-Jewish incitement.

Herzl reasoned that Jews could only integrate successfully into European society by winning a place in the upper bourgeoisie, where they might marry and intermingle with a dominant social class. But they were thwarted by social stigma and hatred, and therefore they could never achieve such a goal. Hence, their complete integration and equality was a chimera and Jews must, therefore, embrace a political solution to resolve their perennial minority status, once and for all. Herzl's call to affirm Jewish nationhood, with a road map leading toward self-government in one, single territorial entity (ideally, though not necessarily, in ancestral Palestine or thereabouts), heralded a great parting of the ways in modern Jewish political opinion.

Herzl's Zionist manifesto may have seemed appropriate to his supporters on the Continent (where he also faced many opponents), but it posed significant challenges to most American Jews, because it questioned the commitment of Western countries to Jewish civic equality – implicitly including the United States. An older generation of American Jews, many of whose members were raised on concepts of Jewish religious universalism alloyed with American patriotism, now confronted a new, secularized intelligentsia of Jewish activists in a post-liberal Europe. The mainstream, native-born Jewish consensus in America, as voiced in the

[47] George Bornstein, *The Colors of Zion: Blacks, Jews, and Irish from 1845 to 1945* (Cambridge, MA and London: Harvard University Press, 2011), pp. 5, 26.

American Hebrew, rejected Jewish nationalism and denigrated Herzl and his associates. We recall that, even before Herzl, Emma Lazarus's call for Jewish restoration to Palestine met with Jewish opposition, and that the Reform movement's denominational platform of 1885 explicitly rejected Jewish nationhood.[48]

Zionism did win adherents in America, however, and it was, in some respects, a "post-German" movement. Although many rank-and-file Zionists in America were Yiddish-speaking migrants recently arrived from Europe, most of the leadership were American-born figures with German or Central European roots and considerable social and professional status. They included Henrietta Szold, the educator and publicist, and her cousin, attorney Robert Szold (1889–1977); Harry Friedenwald (1864–1950), a Baltimore ophthalmologist and a close friend of the Szolds; Richard Gottheil (1862–1936), a Semitics professor at Columbia University and son of Gustav Gottheil, rabbi of New York's Reform Temple Emanu-El; Horace Kallen, Harvard alumnus and liberal philosopher, critic of "melting pot" rhetoric and exponent of ethno-cultural diversity; Max Heller (1860–1929) of New Orleans, one of the early presidents of the Central Conference of American Rabbis; Stephen S. Wise (1874–1949), a younger Reform rabbi and a zealous promoter of various Progressive causes; and Julian Mack of Chicago (1866–1943), a law professor, judge, Progressive activist, and influential public figure.

Most notably, this blue-ribbon group also included the prominent jurist and Progressive crusader, Louis D. Brandeis (1856–1941), who joined the American Zionist movement in 1914 and was instantly catapulted to the position of its national leader. When President Wilson appointed Brandeis to the Supreme Court in 1916, the new Justice resigned his formal affiliation with the Zionist Organization, but he continued to exert considerable influence from behind the scenes through his lieutenants: Wise, Mack, and a young, Viennese-born jurist, Felix Frankfurter.[49]

Why this "revolt" by members of a privileged class, favored by high professional and cultural status and fairly well integrated in America?

48 *The American Hebrew* 61(3) (May 21, 1897).
49 Melvin I. Urofsky, *American Zionism from Herzl to the Holocaust* (New York: Anchor Press/Doubleday, 1975), pp. 81–163; and *Louis D. Brandeis*, pp. 399–459, 515–44; Ben Halpern, *A Clash of Heroes: Brandeis, Weizmann, and American Zionism* (New York and Oxford: Oxford University Press, 1987), pp. 83–90, 94–108, 109–23; Gary P. Zola, "Reform Judaism's Pioneer Zionist: Maximilian Heller," *American Jewish History* 73(4) (1984): 375–97; Mark A. Raider, *The Emergence of American Zionism* (New York and London: New York University Press, 1998), pp. 5–29; Jonathan D. Sarna, "Two Jewish Lawyers Named Louis," *American Jewish History* 94(1–2) (2008): 1–8, 14–18.

In part, theirs was a generational rebellion against the Germanized American Judaism their fathers and mothers had so avidly promoted, but which they saw as hackneyed. In a letter to Stephen Wise, Henrietta Szold outlined her impatience with the ideas, institutions, and discussions then current in American Jewry – an impatience that animated her turn to Zionism: "It [Zionism] is the only living thing in Judaism of to-day. Reform and Orthodox squabbles, public Seders and Synods, and all the rest of the palaver, is on dead issues."[50]

By hoisting the banner of Jewish nationality, these sons and daughters of mostly Austro-Hungarian and German immigrant families also caught the rising tide of opposition to intramural sectionalism within the Jewish public. As we have seen, there was considerable inter-communal tension at the time between the veteran, naturalized Austro-German Jewish social set and the newly arriving East European immigrants. Those representing the established or "native" part of American Jewry felt a sense of stewardship over their less fortunate "eastern" cousins, but were also apt to sense an estrangement (at least) from them.[51] Their Germanophilic ethnicity was undercut, however, by the Zionist activists, who reframed the issue around what was common to all Jews, rather than what separated them into subgroups of European derivation.

The Zionist incursion into Jewish discourse in America thus leveraged the separation of Jewish and German identities, even before World War I, and it enhanced the popularization of a new, American-Jewish identity, amalgamating and transcending the "Germans," "Russians," and "Sephardim." This "post-German" group, then, posed a politically trenchant response to developments both at home and overseas.

While leading American Zionists went about reconstructing Jewish identity along modern, national lines, another of their "post-German" contemporaries, the Columbia University anthropologist, Franz Uri Boas (1858–1942), was pursuing a course that would relativize *all* differences between nations, cultures, tribes, and races. Boas is credited with (at least) two innovations with respect to notions of human diversity. First, in a counter-thrust against the regnant evolutionary and racialist models of his day in Germany and the United States, he set out to demolish the

[50] Henrietta Szold to Stephen S. Wise, March 26, 1899, quoted by Baila Round Shargel, *Lost Love: The Untold Story of Henrietta Szold. Unpublished Diary and Letters* (Philadelphia, PA: Jewish Publication Society, 1997), p. 321.
[51] Brinkmann, "Exceptionalism and Normality," pp. 316–19, 327; Kupsky, "Germanness and Jewishness," 26.

entire armory of ideas that arranged populations according to a hierarchy from "primitive" to "advanced."

Second, he refashioned a theory of anthropology in which race was not the master key. Rather than viewing group characteristics and behaviors as flowing from quasi-biological, "racial" forms pre-set and congenitally determined within populations, Boas contended that group traits and cultural codes were socially, environmentally, and historically constructed, and that, in any case, individuals always varied from group norms in significant ways. By these two strokes, Boas began to un-couple American anthropology from German "racial science" (*Rassenwissenschaft*) and studies of collective character, or "national psychology (*Völker-* or *Rassenpsychologie*). Instead, Boas pointed toward the study of "cultures."[52]

The Great War

The process by which Jewish Americans of Austro-German background began to assume new positions and identities in which the German factor was fading was further catalyzed by the Great War. Ethnic affinities which had for a long time been reinforced by active cultural engagement would quickly fall victim to the politicization and stigmatizing of anything Germanic.

Over the winter of 1914, German-Americans campaigned for an arms embargo to offset Britain's advantage in American arms procurement and to ensure America's neutrality. The response in Washington and in American public opinion was swift and unforgiving. The neutrality of the United States in the conflict until the spring of 1917 was not a neutrality of thought, word, and deed. Public opinion generally, as well as American naval, commercial, and strategic interests tended to favor Britain and,

---

[52] Amos Morris-Reich, *The Quest for Jewish Assimilation in Modern Social Science* (New York and London: Routledge, 2008), pp. 20–33, 34–9, 42–6, 49–50, 58; Franz Boas, *The Mind of Primitive Man* (New York: Free Press, 1963 [c. 1911]); and "Changes in the Bodily Form of Descendants of Immigrants," *American Anthropologist* 14(3) (1912): 530–62; Carl Degler, *In Search of Human Nature: The Decline and Revival of Darwinism in American Social Thought* (New York and Oxford: Oxford University Press, 1991), esp. p. 61; *Volksgeist as Method and Ethic: Essays on Boasian Ethnography and the German Anthropological Tradition*, ed. George Stocking (Madison: University of Wisconsin Press, 1996); Mitchell B. Hart, "Franz Boas as German, American, Jew," in *German-Jewish Identities in America*, ed. Christof Mauch and Joseph Salomon (Madison: Max Kade Institute for German-American Studies, University of Wisconsin-Madison, 2003), pp. 88–105; Thomas F. Gossett, *Race: The History of an Idea in America* (New York: Oxford University Press, 1963, new ed. 1997), p. 418.

by extension, its allies. Germany's repeated breach of a crucial national asset – the security of America's shipping – involving significant American losses at sea, signaled America's growing involvement in the war.[53]

At the same time, however, for many American citizens, the war aroused deep ambivalence. Many Irish-Americans, Austro- and German-Americans, socialists from diverse ethnic backgrounds, religious pacifists of various churches, and an assortment of other war objectors comprised a loose coalition of dissident opinion opposed to American military involvement. Irish-Americans were less than enthusiastic about US support for Britain, to say the least. Conscientious objectors and the Left alike were convinced of the futility and sheer wickedness of the awful carnage and appalled by the drive to war to support imperial interests.

Many American Jews viewed Britain and France quite favorably, but they were bothered by the Anglo-French alliance with Russia, because they considered the tsar of Russia the scourge of their people. Earlier memories, punctuated by the malignant turn of Russian antisemitism after 1881, were now exacerbated by bloodcurdling reports of the havoc wreaked by Russian troops on Jewish populations in towns and villages in occupied Galicia. Given that background, the anti-Russian tide in American Jewish public opinion would turn only in March 1917 (just prior to the US entry into the war), when the Romanov dynasty was overthrown and a provisional government, committed to equal rights for all, came to power.[54]

Some Jews took principled, anti-war positions, such as Lillian Wald (1867–1940), founder of the settlement house on Henry Street in New York, or the publisher, Ben W. Huebsch (1875–1964), the executive head of the American Neutral Conference (and the son of Rabbi Adolph Huebsch). Judah Magnes, the San Francisco-born rabbi and head of the New York Kehillah, held staunchly pacifist views throughout the

[53] Higham, *Strangers in the Land*, pp. 195–212.
[54] J. S. Hertz, *Di yidishe sotsialistishe bavegung in amerike* (New York: "Der Veker," 1954), pp. 161–3; Maxim Vinaver, D. O. Zaslavskii, and G. M. Erlikh, "Iz 'chernoi knigi' rossiiskogo evreistva: Materialy dlia istorii voiny 1914–1915 g." (From the 'Black Book' of Russian Jewry: Materials for the History of the War in 1914–1915), *Evreiskaia starina* 10 (1918): 195–296; S. Ansky [Rapoport], *The Enemy at His Pleasure: A Journey Through the Jewish Pale of Settlement During World War I*, ed. and trans. Joachim Neugroschel (New York: Henry Holt & Co., 2002), pp. 63–110; Eric Lohr, "The Russian Army and the Jews: Mass Deportation, Hostages, and Violence During World War I," *Russian Review* 60(3) (2001): 404–19; Feld, *Lillian Wald*, pp. 107–13.

war – a posture that he transplanted to Palestine politics, when he moved to Jerusalem in 1921.[55]

Likewise, Maurice Harris, rabbi of Temple Israel in Harlem (a largely German-Jewish congregation) preached against war in September 1914:

> The old standard set in the Crimean war, "Theirs not to reason why, theirs but to do and die," must be rejected by the people. They are not pawns, but living beings. Theirs is to reason why. They must ask what right has a Government to plunge the land into war.[56]

His British-born colleague, J. Leonard Levy (1865–1917), rabbi of Pittsburgh's Rodeph Shalom Temple, went even further. Having adopted pacifism in the wake of the Spanish-American War (only fitting, perhaps, for one who led a congregation named "Pursuit of Peace"), Levy asserted that, notwithstanding his natural sympathy for Britain, "if the United States government had the right to draft me today into an army, I would refuse to serve." He denounced those who would "arouse the ire of this nation against all things German," and reminded his public not to forget what "German art, and German culture, and German research, and German science, have done for the world."[57]

However, the notion that neutrality was tantamount to a pro-German posture became increasingly common as America's drift toward war gained momentum. In effect, all other positions were denied legitimacy by the argument that only one side in the conflict – the Central Powers – was eager for the Yanks to stay home. The chilling effect of this argument was felt in ever-widening circles, from academia (where German influence had been at its height) to local politics and organizational life. The Yiddish socialist paper, *Der Forverts*, was nearly muzzled for its anti-war stance, judged to be seditious. Morris Hillquit (*né* Hilkowitz, 1869–1933), a Socialist Party stalwart who ran for the New York mayoralty in 1917, was beaten at the polls, partly because he was outspokenly against the war.[58]

[55] Szajkowski, *Jews, Wars, and Communism*, vol. I, pp. 79–102; Goren, *New York Jews and the Quest for Community*, pp. 231–5; *Dissenter in Zion: From the Writings of Judah L. Magnes*, ed. Arthur A. Goren (Cambridge, MA: Harvard University Press, 1982); Silver, *First Contact*, pp. 189–328; Daniel Kotzin, "An American Jewish Radical: Judah L. Magnes, American Jewish Identity, and Jewish Nationalism in America and Palestine" (PhD dissertation, New York University, 1998).

[56] Saperstein, *Jewish Preaching*, p. 301.

[57] Saperstein, *Jewish Preaching*, pp. 324–45. Levy apparently changed his mind one last time, following Wilson's declaration of war on April 2, 1917 – just three weeks and two days before he died.

[58] Higham, *Strangers in the Land*, p. 219; Lucy Dawidowicz, "Louis Marshall and the *Jewish Daily Forward*: An Episode in Wartime Censorship, 1917–18," in *For Max*

There was no clear-cut line, however, aligning the entire Yiddish immigrant world or even just its labor-Left section with pacifism, anti-militarism, and neutralism. When Samuel Gompers, head of the American Federation of Labor, formed an anti-pacifist group in July 1917, he included such well-known Jewish labor movement figures as Joseph Barondess (1867–1928, popularly styled as the "people's tribune"); William Edlin (1878–1947, editor of a Yiddish daily, *Der Tog*, and co-founder of the Jewish fraternal order, *Arbeter Ring* [Workmen's Circle]); and Nachman Syrkin (1868–1924, a leading Zionist socialist). Calling itself the American Alliance for Labor and Democracy, the group met in Minneapolis and adopted a manifesto. An entry in Edlin's diary for November 1917 registered his exasperation with his fellow Jews and the anti-war camp generally:

Jews [...] glory in their pacifism, ascribing it to mental superiority, little thinking that it's a product of their 'goluth' ["exilic" mentality, deficient in patriotic virtues] – a stamp [of] their inferior position [...]. Peace! Peace! I hear that all around me [...]. My only consolation is that somewhere in this vast country there must be a few dozen million Americans who think and talk otherwise.[59]

Perhaps most poignantly, the case of Mary Antin (1881–1949) illustrated the personal dilemmas aroused by the war and the steep price to be paid. Antin, daughter of a Russian-Jewish immigrant family in Boston, had married Amadeus Grabau (1870–1946), a Columbia University scholar of paleontology and son of a German Lutheran minister. Antin, the author of the well-known immigrant memoir, *The Promised Land* (1912), had committed herself to thoroughly suppressing her Russian-Jewish roots in favor of an unhyphenated American identity. She adopted a pro-Allied, patriotically American view of the war. Her husband, in rather stark contrast, adamantly stood by his German roots. Antin experienced a painful domestic crisis, as she felt her husband wanted to foist his ideas on her. Their marriage broke up, Grabau was fired from his Columbia post (friends found him a job in China), and Antin remained emotionally incapacitated for most of the rest of her life.[60]

Weinreich on his Seventieth Birthday: Studies in Jewish Languages, Literature, and Society, ed. Lucy Dawidowicz et al. (The Hague: Mouton, 1964), pp. 29–43; Irwin Yellowitz, "Morris Hillquit: American Socialism and Jewish Concerns," *American Jewish History* 68(2) (1978): 163–85; Goren, *New York Jews and the Quest for Community*, pp. 217, 229; Sorin, *A Time for Building*, pp. 198–9; Sterba, *Good Americans*, pp. 58, 63–9, 72–8, 153–69; Brandes, "From Sweatshop to Stability," 24–6.
[59] Szajkowski, *Jews, Wars, and Communism*, vol. I, pp. 162–90, esp. 164–8 (quote on 167–8).
[60] *Selected Letters of Mary Antin*, ed. Evelyn Salz (Syracuse, NY: Syracuse University Press, 2000), pp. 87–90, 95–8; Werner Sollors, "Introduction," to Mary Antin, *The Promised Land* (New York: Penguin Books, 1997), pp. xli–xlv.

Conscription for military service threw young men of various Jewish backgrounds together, despite some of the earlier misgivings they might have harbored. Reflecting on the possible ironies and complexities, one woman's diary recorded the impressions she took away from a weekend visit to a training camp near Atlanta:

We were at Camp Gordon last Sunday [...]. So many Jewish faces among the soldiers one sees; some have only been here from Russia or Austria a few years. Some have to fight against their own brothers in the German Army.[61]

Wartime politics also penetrated deep into Jewish organizational and philanthropic politics. Felix Warburg (1871–1937) and Jacob Schiff, the Wall Street magnates who were the effective leaders of Jewish philanthropic networks in America, retained very close family ties in Germany. Perhaps for that very reason, they took care to hew closely to a patriotic American course, but they also made common cause with those in Washington who desired peaceful relations with Germany's ally, Ottoman Turkey. (The United States refrained from declaring war against Turkey when it went to war with the other Central Powers.)[62] Accordingly, they sought to avoid making any overtures to Britain or France (which were already secretly engaged in planning how to divide up Turkish imperial possessions in the Middle East between them), and they distanced themselves from the beleaguered Zionist establishment in Palestine, which the Turks considered seditious.

Following a course advised by Henry Morgenthau, Sr. (1856–1946), the US ambassador to Constantinople, they steered American Jewish relief funds in the Holy Land to the religiously Orthodox, apolitical, non-Zionist charities and health institutions. In turn, this "Turcophilic" group squared off against their rivals, the pro-British Zionists (led by Brandeis, Frankfurter, Wise, Gottheil, Mack, and Horace Kallen), who sought a diplomatic entente with Britain. Kallen conducted back-channel communications between Brandeis in Washington and Chaim Weizmann, the rising Zionist statesman, then living in the UK, who was pursuing a pro-Zionist demarche in British diplomacy.

Meanwhile, the American Red Cross, guided by its War Council in Washington, agreed to send a relief mission to Palestine (to be headed by two Protestant representatives plus a Catholic and a Jew). The man selected for the Jewish appointment, in a compromise between the

---

[61] Apte, *Heart of a Wife*, p. 77 (entry for November 29, 1917).
[62] Naomi W. Cohen, *Jacob H. Schiff: A Study in American Jewish Leadership* (Hanover, NH: Brandeis University Press, 1999), pp. 189–205.

Zionists and the Schiff–Warburg faction, was Israel Friedlaender (1876–
1920), a Polish-born professor at the Jewish Theological Seminary in
New York, who was an expert in both Arabic and Hebrew. With his
non-German background and his English wife, Friedlaender's pro-Allied
credentials should have been above reproach; but he was pulled out of
the mission on the eve of its departure when the New York press (following innuendo spread by Wise and Gottheil, apparently), falsely accused
him of harboring pro-German views.[63]

Yet, even then, the crucial role that German high culture had played in
many American Jews' self-perception was not entirely erased. One of the
more mercurial figures in the world of American (and American-Jewish)
letters, Ludwig Lewisohn (1882–1955), was teaching German literature
at Ohio State University in 1916. Well into the days of the anti-German
campaign in American academia, he was still worshipping at the shrine
of the modern German *"Geist"* (spirit), citing Germany's devotion to
"naturalism, cultivation of science, social organization for the collective
welfare and practical efficiency – *Tuechtigkeit.*" He celebrated what he
called Germany's "individualistic humanism" and the "tireless spiritual
striving" of its cultural elite, whose values "shall make life [...] deeper,
richer, more reasonable and more beautiful."[64]

Lewisohn lost his job at Ohio State. Later in life, in the wake of the
Second World War, he published a volume of translations of the poetry
of Rainer Maria Rilke (the Prague-born German writer and poet, 1875–
1926). There, Lewisohn articulated his double-edged relationship with
that part of modern German culture that he still identified as beautiful

[63] Shlomo Yotvat, "Hamas'a shelo histayem: yisrael fridlender be'ikvot yehudei hamet-
sukah veerets yisrael, 1917–1920" (The Unfinished Journey: Israel Friedländer's Path
to Oppressed Jewries and the Land of Israel, 1917–1920), unpublished manuscript,
in author's possession; Halpern, *Clash of Heroes*, p. 180; Cohen, *Not Free to Desist*,
pp. 87–8; Frankel, *Prophecy and Politics*, pp. 537–8; Mark A. Raider, "The Aristocrat
and the Democrat: Louis Marshall, Stephen S. Wise and the Challenge of American
Jewish Leadership," *American Jewish History* 94(1–2) (2008): 103–8.
[64] Ludwig Lewisohn, *The Spirit of Modern German Literature* (New York: B. W. Huebsch,
1916), p. 118–19, quoted by Stanley F. Chyet, "Ludwig Lewisohn: The Years of
Becoming" (MA thesis, Hebrew Union College – Jewish Institute of Religion, March
1957), pp. 151–6; see also his "Ludwig Lewisohn: The Years of Becoming," *American
Jewish Archives* 11(2) (1959): 125–47; Levinson, "Brooklyn Am Rhein?," pp. 235–7.
Coincidentally or not, Lewisohn's 1916 lectures on German literature were published by
Ben W. Huebsch, who had adopted anti-war and radical views. Huebsch has been called
"first of the new publishers," and published the works of James Joyce, Maxim Gorkii,
Eduard Bernstein, August Rodin, and Mahatma Gandhi. See Bornstein, *The Colors of
Zion*, p. 165.

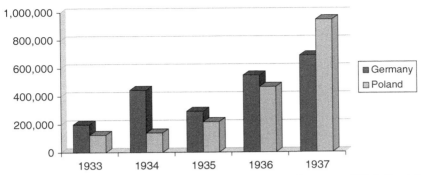

FIGURE 4.1. AJDC expenditures in Germany and Poland, 1933–7 (US dollars).[66]

and true: "All those who [...] awaken with a yearning for purity and oneness will seek out the work of Rainer Maria Rilke, because they will come upon that nostalgia for it in their hearts."[65] But this was no longer an identification in the present tense. It had become an elegy for the past.

The New European Crisis in the 1930s

The major organizational innovation in Jewish public life spawned by the Great War was the establishment of a united umbrella group for overseas relief, called the American Jewish Joint Distribution Committee (AJDC). In the war's aftermath, and for more than a decade thereafter (right through the outbreak of World War II), the "Joint," as it was dubbed in popular parlance, funded programs of occupational and health-care rehabilitation for the three million Jews in the newly reconstituted Polish Republic, including many war refugees. In the early 1930s, with the rise of Hitler's party to power in Germany, the AJDC found itself confronted simultaneously with multiple humanitarian crises. It stepped up its welfare expenditures in Europe during the 1930s, even though these were the Depression years and philanthropic dollars were harder to solicit (see Fig. 4.1).

During the first weeks of Nazi rule in Germany in 1933, there was much initial confusion in American Jewish ranks. Jewish agencies were somewhat slow to shift gears in order to focus on German Jewry. In this they were partly guided by voices coming from within the Jewish

[65] Ludwig Lewisohn, *Thirty-one Poems by Rainer Maria Rilke* (New York: The Beechhurst Press/Bernard Ackerman, 1946), Introduction.
[66] Bauer, *My Brother's Keeper*, pp. 127, 190.

communal leadership in Germany, some of whom believed (initially) that German Jews could fight their own battles.[67]

Similar confusion plagued the planning of emigration and refugee assistance. Officially, there were about 500,000 Jews in Germany in 1933, but under the Nazis' racial policy, that number expanded to include children of Jews who were not registered in any Jewish community, Christians who were regarded in Nazi terms as "half-Jews," and other "non-Aryans," adding about 250,000 persons. An emigration panic during 1933 prompted the departure of as many as 50,000 people, but some Jewish spokesmen in Germany opposed a mass exodus at that point, arguing that the regime's intention to de-nationalize them was illegitimate and ought to be deplored and opposed, rather than acceded to. Similar counsel was heard in parts of the American Jewish philanthropic establishment, where some not only opposed giving Hitler any "concessions," but also argued that emigration could not provide a blanket solution for all the Jews in Germany. The needs of those who would remain behind would still have to be provided for.[68]

Given the simultaneous pressures being mounted against Jews in Poland, especially after the mid-1930s (pressure that took the form of officially sponsored employment and academic discrimination, commercial boycotts, and other forms of agitation), the Jewish immigrant aid agencies in America – chiefly HIAS (Hebrew Sheltering and Immigrant Aid Society, founded 1909) – did not consider the plight of German Jewry to be the sole, overriding emergency. Residual ethnic rivalries in the Jewish organizational world, dividing the "Germans" from the "Poles," might have played a background role in these arguments over priorities, since HIAS was by and large run by former East European immigrants. Yet, such frictions at the sub-ethnic level did not carry weight for very long.[69]

---

[67] Bauer, *My Brother's Keeper*, pp. 3–56, 105–13; Cohen, *Not Free to Desist*, pp. 156–60; Shlomo Shafir, "American Jewish Leaders and the Emerging Nazi Threat, 1928–1933," *American Jewish Archives* 31(2) (1979): 150–83; Arad, *America, Its Jews, and the Rise of Nazism*, pp. 97–8.

[68] Bauer, *My Brother's Keeper*, pp. 115–17; Avraham Barkai, *From Boycott to Annihilation: The Economic Struggle of German Jews, 1933–1943*, trans. William Templer (Hanover, NH and London: Brandeis University Press/University Press of New England, 1989 [*c.* 1987 by Fischer Taschenbuch Verlag]), pp. 55–6.

[69] The JDC was perceived as the agency most suited to deal with the German crisis, while HIAS retained its image as an arm of the East European immigrant community in America. One indication of this is the comparison between the two agencies in terms of fundraising. Until 1934–5, HIAS's annual income was about a third of the Joint's,

The new situation also spawned new organizations that hoped to promote practical solutions and spread the anti-Fascist cause. One such initiative was the Jewish Labor Committee (JLC). The formation of the JLC was sparked at an AFL convention in San Francisco in 1934, where a Labor Chest was formed to assist German labor movement members who were being victimized by the Nazi regime. The JLC was an offshoot of the Labor Chest. Established by leaders of the Jewish-affiliated labor unions, including Baruch Charney Vladeck (1886–1938) and David Dubinsky (1892–1982), the JLC viewed its work primarily as a partnership with other social-democratic and labor movement groups in America and Europe. They publicized Nazi persecution of German labor figures (Jews and non-Jews alike) and, in addition, worked to help comrades escape from Germany (and, later on, all German-held territories).[70]

One of the first acts of the Nazi regime was to institute a massive boycott against Jewish-owned businesses and Jewish professionals. The initiative to respond with a counter-boycott against German goods sold in the United States got off to a rocky start. Irving Lehman (1876–1945, brother of New York Governor Herbert Lehman) and Judge Joseph M. Proskauer (1877–1971), representing the American Jewish Committee, fearful that Jews in Germany might have to pay the price for American Jewish anti-Nazi activism, implored other Jewish organizational representatives not to approve militant steps. Their stance was

---

but from 1936 on HIAS could rely on only about a tenth of the funds that stood at the JDC's disposal. From 1936 to 1939 JDC's fundraising for overseas and domestic refugee work rose from 2.5 million dollars to 7.65 million dollars. See Karpf, *Jewish Community Organization in the United States*, pp. 124–5; Mark Wischnitzer, *Visas to Freedom: The Story of HIAS* (Cleveland, OH and New York: World Publishing Co., 1956), pp. 135–57; Zosa Szajkowski, "Budgeting American Jewish Overseas Relief (1919–1939)," *American Jewish Historical Quarterly* 59(1) (1969/70): 83–114; and "Relief for German Jewry: Problems of American Involvement," *American Jewish Historical Quarterly* 62(2) (1972): 111–46; Ze'ev Deutsch, "Hias: hahevrah hayehudit lemahaseh ve'ezrah lamehagrim 1909–1939 (HIAS: The Hebrew Sheltering and Immigrant Aid Society 1909–1939)" (PhD dissertation, Hebrew University of Jerusalem, 2003), pp. 197–9, 225–9. See also Arad, *America, Its Jews, and the Rise of Nazism*, pp. 97–9; Szajkowski, "Relief for German Jewry," p. 112.

70 Henry Cohen, "Crisis and Reaction," *American Jewish Archives* 5(2) (1953): 105–6; Jack Jacobs, "A Friend in Need: The Jewish Labor Committee and Refugees from the German Speaking Lands, 1933–1945," *YIVO Annual* 23 (1996): 391–417; Gail Malmgreen, "Comrades and Kinsmen: The Jewish Labor Committee and Anti-Nazi Activity, 1933–41," in *Jews, Labor and the Left, 1918–48*, ed. Christine Collette and Stephen Bird (Aldershot: Ashgate, 2000), pp. 4–20; *Archives of the Holocaust, vol. 14: Robert F. Wagner Labor Archives. Records of the Jewish Labor Committee*, ed. Arieh Liebowitz and Gail Malmgreen (New York: Garland Publishers, 1993).

derived, in part, from communications received from prominent Jewish business leaders in Germany. A counter-boycott of German goods was supported, however, by J. George Fredman (1895–1958), head of the US Jewish War Veterans, by movie mogul Louis B. Mayer (1884–1957), and by the Yiddish press. The boycott campaign was spearheaded by Samuel Untermyer (1858–1940), an attorney active in New York public life and Jewish organizational work, previously known for his close personal identification with German culture.[71]

With little initial support from established Jewish communal groups, the boycott also ran counter to a quite different strategy that was being pursued by the Zionist leadership in Palestine. In August 1933, the German government and the Anglo-Palestine Bank (the main Zionist financial institution) arrived at an agreement that would allow German Jews to emigrate to Palestine, while transferring some of their assets (confiscated by the German regime) in the form of German machinery and manufactured goods. Thus, they would arrive in their new country with some means at their disposal – a criterion making them eligible for a larger quota of immigration certificates, as specified by the British government in Palestine. This so-called Ha'avarah (Hebrew: Transfer) Agreement remained viable until 1938 and, while it lasted, it facilitated the exit of German Jews via Palestine. The Zionist leadership thus prioritized rescue-by-emigration over the boycotting of German commerce and industry.[72]

After November 1938, the American government, through the Intergovernmental Committee on Refugees (ICR), pursued financial negotiations with the German government that would, in turn, have entailed some guaranteed form of capital transfer in lieu of former

[71] Moshe R. Gottlieb, *American Anti-Nazi Resistance, 1933–1941: An Historical Analysis* (New York: Ktav, 1982), pp. 30, 42–64; Bayor, *Neighbors in Conflict*, p. 68; Cohen, *Not Free to Desist*, pp. 162–3; Kupsky, "Germanness and Jewishness," pp. 30–4; see also www.criticalpast.com/video/65675028554_J-George-Fredman_Madison-Square-Garden_German-Boycott.

[72] The total value of German goods transferred in this manner for sale in Palestine from mid-1933 to the end of 1937 was about 4.4 million pounds. Bauer, *My Brother's Keeper*, pp. 128–9; Yoav Gelber, *Moledet hadashah: 'aliyat yehudei merkaz eiropah uklitatam 1933–1948 (A New Homeland: The Migration and Absorption of the Jews from Central Europe, 1933–1948)* (Jerusalem: Yad Yitzhak Ben-Zvi, 1990); Avraham Barkai, "German Interests in the Haavara-Transfer Agreement 1933–1939," *Yearbook of the Leo Baeck Institute* 35 (1990): 245–66; and *From Boycott to Annihilation*, pp. 51–3, 76, 100–04; David Yisraeli, "The Third Reich and the Transfer Agreement," *Journal of Contemporary History* 6 (1972): 129–48; Feingold, *Bearing Witness*, pp. 189–90.

German citizens' assets. Again, the purpose was refugee rescue. These negotiations broke down, however, at the beginning of the war.[73]

Thus, there was no true coordination of boycott policy at either the national or the trans-national level. Nevertheless, during the 1930s, the boycott campaign in the US slowly gathered steam. It was finally adopted and supported by, among others, the American Jewish Congress, leading retail corporations, the Jewish Labor Committee, and major national labor unions. Even the American Jewish Committee was prepared to quietly countenance it. Four years into the boycott effort (March 15, 1937), a major rally was held at Madison Square Garden and broadcast by radio. Its aim was to present the struggle against Hitler as an American, non-sectarian cause, and among the speakers there were several prominent public figures as well as high-profile representatives of anti-Nazi opinion in the German-American community.[74]

Cooperation between German-American opponents of Nazism and their Jewish counterparts had grown gradually since 1933. One of the most principled, consistent, and outspoken American political leaders in the effort to bring Jewish refugees (children in particular) to the United States was New York's four-term Democratic senator, German-born Robert F. Wagner, Sr. (1877–1953). The State Department's Raymond Geist was a staunch anti-Nazi, and in the early 1930s, after the Nazi takeover, George S. Messersmith, the US Consul in Berlin, tried (without success) to persuade the Administration to halt the shipment of raw materials to Germany. Among German writers and intellectuals living in America in exile from Nazi Germany, there existed relationships of friendship and cooperation between those of Jewish descent and their non-Jewish compatriots.[75]

---

[73] Wyman, *Paper Walls*, pp. 52–6; Breitman and Kraut, *American Refugee Policy*, pp. 67–70; Feingold, *Bearing Witness*, pp. 76–7.

[74] Among the key speakers, apart from the organizers, were Erika Mann (playwright, actress, and daughter of the celebrated, exiled German author, Thomas Mann); John L. Lewis, chairman of the CIO; Dr. Frank Bohn, a distinguished economist and (like Erika Mann) a representative of anti-Nazi opinion in the German-American community; and New York Mayor Fiorello LaGuardia. See Bauer, *My Brother's Keeper*, pp. 112–13; Barkai, *From Boycott to Annihilation*, pp. 13–53; Gottlieb, *American Anti-Nazi Resistance*, pp. 92–103, 125–42, 169–236; Arad, *America, Its Jews, and the Rise of Nazism*, pp. 109–14, 121–4, 168; Cohen, *Not Free to Desist*, pp. 164–6.

[75] Wyman, *Paper Walls*, pp. 75–92, 96, 157; Breitman and Kraut, *American Refugee Policy*, pp. 43–5, 66, 73, 107, 232; Deborah Lipstadt, *Beyond Belief: The American Press and the Coming of the Holocaust 1933–1945* (New York: Free Press, 1986), pp. 15, 24–6, 32; Cohen, *Not Free to Desist*, p. 162; Guy Stern, "German-Jewish Writers and

Other German-Americans, who had not themselves been exposed to Hitler's regime and were native-born Americans of two or more generations' standing, were less likely to be involved in anti-Nazi activity. But by the late 1930s there was a pressing need to disassociate mainstream, democratic Americans of German heritage from the taint of Hitlerism that dogged their community. A pro-Nazi group, the National Socialist Teutonia Society, was founded in Detroit in 1924. It tended to attract members from among the most recent immigrants from Germany, and by 1930, it had chapters in Cincinnati, Chicago, Milwaukee, and New York. In October 1933, German-Americans in St. Louis organized a group called the Friends of New Germany, often referred to locally as the "Hitler Club." In December of that year a German-American Business League (DAWA) was organized in New York, which encouraged German-American merchants to import German goods and fomented an anti-Jewish boycott. The group with the greatest pro-Nazi impact from the mid-1930s was Fritz Kuhn's German-American Bund.[76]

The Jewish engagement with friendly German-Americans and with other allies in liberal public opinion was matched by an equal insistence that an anti-German trade boycott was intended as a means of preventing war, not warmongering. At the 1937 rally at Madison Square Garden, Dr. Joseph Tenenbaum, chair of the Joint Boycott Council, called the campaign a "peaceful weapon which will lead Hitlerism to its doom" and an alternative to war, "which we dread, loathe, and fear."[77] The non-violent, anti-militarist note was similarly sounded by Rabbi Stephen Wise, whose rhetoric was politically correct to a fault (if less than prophetic):

German-Christian Writers: Cooperation in Exile," in *The Jewish Response to German Culture, from the Enlightenment to the Second World War*, ed. Jehuda Reinharz and Walter Schatzberg (Hanover, NH and London: Clark University/University Press of New England, 1985), pp. 154–8.

[76] According to one estimate, just before World War II there were about eighty street meetings a *week* (!) in New York City alone at which anti-Jewish hate speech was promoted by the Christian Front, German-American Bund, and allied groups. For George Washington's birthday in 1939, the German-American Bund brought 19,000 people to Madison Square Garden, along with Nazi flags, a corps of 400 uniformed "troopers," and banners reading "Stop Jewish Domination of Christian America!" and "Smash Jewish Communism." See Bayor, *Neighbors in Conflict*, pp. 57–76; Cohen, *Not Free to Desist*, pp. 215–18; Dinnerstein, *Antisemitism in America*, pp. 112–23, 121–2; Burton Alan Boxerman, "Rise of Anti-Semitism in St. Louis, 1933–1945," *YIVO Annual of Jewish Social Science* 14 (1969): 251–69.

[77] *Hitler A Menace to World Peace. Addresses and Messages Delivered at the Peace and Democracy Rally at Madison Square Garden, March 15, 1937* (New York: Joint Boycott Council, American Jewish Congress, and Jewish Labor Committee, 1937).

We again offer to the world a substitute, peaceful and non-violent, in the place of war. [...] We would not even, if we could, wage physical, violent, destructive, murderous war against Hitlerism. [...] Our moral and economic boycott means the governments may continue their official relations with one another, but we [...] indicate that we American citizens have nothing in common with the Nazi government. [...] The boycott [...] is a warless war against the war makers.[78]

Wise, who had been an anti-militarist before the First World War, was associated in the early 1930s with a non-sectarian, anti-war coalition called the Emergency Peace Campaign. He was also undoubtedly concerned to distance himself, as a high-profile Jewish public figure, from charges of warmongering – which, by 1937, at the height of the civil war in Spain, were already rife.

(The idea that Jews were hoping to drag the United States into war was not just Nazi propaganda, in the eyes of some Americans. One of their spokesmen, Charles Lindbergh, the famous aviator, delivered a speech on behalf of the America First Committee in Des Moines on September 11, 1941 in which he scored Britain, Roosevelt, and the Jews for "pressing this country toward war" – the climax of a long-simmering and very disturbing propaganda campaign.[79])

Jews, by and large, were apt to keep a low profile in this regard. Yet, their overwhelming electoral support for FDR and the moral support they gave to anti-German boycotts, for example, definitely placed them in the pro-active, anti-Nazi wing of American opinion, rather than in the isolationist camp. In retrospect, knowing how instrumental President Roosevelt was in forging the Atlantic alliance (the Atlantic Charter, jointly declared by the US and Great Britain on August 14, 1941, called for full

---

[78] *Hitler A Menace*. At the same rally, Dr. Frank Bohn, a former President of America's German-Speaking Societies, was more forthright than Wise. Declaring that Hitler was preparing for an imminent war, he reminded the public of how Americans had had to fight Germany in the previous war, and predicted that, once Spain was secured, Hitler would not hesitate to strike at France and Russia. The boycott was necessary, he argued, in order to deny Germany's military machine any additional power.

[79] Lindbergh inveighed against American Jews as the "principal war agitators" when he spoke out against the Lend-Lease legislation over the winter of 1940–1. See Parrish, *Anxious Decades*, pp. 470–71; Dinnerstein, *Antisemitism in America*, pp. 129–30.

Wise was among other eminent Americans who sponsored an Emergency Peace Campaign in the 1930s, that urged "Prevent [world war] from happening again! Keep the United States out of war and work for world peace!" Other members included writer Kathleen Norris; Charles G. Fenwick, president of the Catholic Association for International Peace; William Green, president of the AFL; Fanny Fliegelman Brin, president of the National Council of Jewish Women; and Paul B. Kern, Bishop of the Methodist Episcopal Church, South.

collaboration until the "final destruction of Nazi tyranny"), makes it possible to view the Jewish community's activities in America in the 1930s as
part of a larger, civic activism that provided essential political support for
the Administration. In real time, however, the matter was not quite that
simple. It was more plausible at the time to believe that a real struggle
was being waged for America's national identity, the outcome of which
was by no means certain. Americans who saw their country's involvement in the coming war as inevitable and just were pitted in fierce debate
against others who feared that a new world war was being too readily
accepted, and who sought to forestall its consequences.

Unlike the First World War, there were no grounds this time to suspect
Jews of harboring sympathies for the German side. Yet, on the far Left, the
issues were framed rather differently and there were points at which Jewish
socialists and Communists confronted a conflict in values. The Socialist
Party (SP), led by Norman Thomas, pursued a hardline, anti-war platform,
arguing that only capitalist-imperialist interests would be served by a new
round of war. Thomas even shared speaking platforms with notorious
America-Firsters like Lindbergh. The socialist slogan "Keep America Out
of War" had its Jewish supporters, but for the majority it simply became
intolerable. Jews in large numbers began to sever their ties with the SP,
which was left in dire straits. By 1939 only about 150 dues-paying members were left in New York City, and the votes received by the party in
New York State plummeted from 87,000 in 1936 to just 19,000 in 1940.[80]

The small Communist faction within the Jewish populace supplied
the only real platform for sudden and bizarre shifts of political tactics.
When the Communist Party directed its rank-and-file to rally around
anti-Fascism, the members dutifully did so. Indeed, after 1936 the
Communists increasingly made the point that they were fighting antisemitism by embracing the anti-Fascist struggle, and they won an increasing
number of Jewish adherents and sympathizers (as was the case with many
of the Spanish Civil War volunteers). The crisis came, however, when
Moscow ordered the Party to fall in line behind the Molotov-Ribbentrop
agreement of August 23, 1939, which pledged the Soviet Union and Nazi
Germany to mutual non-aggression and opened the way for both countries to jointly dismember and occupy Poland just over one week later.[81]

[80] Daniel Bell, *Marxian Socialism in the United States* (Princeton, NJ: Princeton University
Press, 1967 [c. 1952]), pp. 178–82; Liebman, *Jews and the Left*, pp. 489–91.
[81] Bell, *Marxian Socialism*, pp. 182–4; Irving Howe and Lewis Coser, *The American
Communist Party: A Critical History 1919–1957* (Boston, MA: Beacon Press, 1957), pp.

The American Communist Party then began to hemorrhage many of its Jewish members, although a hard core of loyal Stalinists remained. Paul Novick (1891–1989), editor of the Yiddish Communist daily, the *Morgen frayhayt*, stuck with the Party and threw out of his office a distraught union official who remonstrated with him: "What has Stalin done to us? Why did he sign the Pact? Everything we have built up in the last twenty years has been destroyed!"[82]

Another leftist activist recalled:

Incredible as it seemed [...], the Communists were able to survive even the Nazi-Soviet pact. They were able, even, to hold on to many of the Jews [...], the really tough party people plus those who were so involved psychically with the idea of being Communists that they had to rationalize away all their doubts.[83]

Espousing the new, anti-war, anti-British, and anti-Roosevelt propaganda, the Stalinist die-hards remained on the far fringes of American (and American Jewish) opinion, until the start of the Soviet-German war on June 22, 1941. In this case, Russia was, as ever, fated to be enmeshed with the politics of Jewish foreign sensibilities.

Russia: The Long Trek

In the first half of the nineteenth century, relations between America and imperial Russia had been cordial. In 1832, America and Russia contracted a mutual commercial treaty to facilitate trade. Alaska had been acquired by the United States from the Russian government in 1867 (at 2¢ per acre). Unlike Spain and (later) Germany, there was no history of military confrontation between Russia and the United States, at least until America's participation in the British-led military intervention

---

387–94; Benjamin Gitlow, *The Whole of Their Lives: Communism in America – A Personal History* (Boston, MA: Western Islands, 1965), pp. 309–13; Liebman, *Jews and the Left*, pp. 507–9; Alan Wald, *The New York Intellectuals: The Rise and Decline of the Anti-Stalinist Left from the 1930s to the 1980s* (Chapel Hill and London: University of North Carolina Press, 1987), pp. 193–9; Guenter Lewy, *The Cause That Failed: Communism in American Political Life* (New York and Oxford: Oxford University Press, 1990), pp. 63–5; Harvey Klehr, *The Heyday of American Communism: The Depression Decade* (New York: Basic Books, 1984), pp. 400–3; Harvey Klehr, John Earl Haynes, and Kyrill M. Anderson, *The Soviet World of American Communism* (New Haven, CT and London: Yale University Press, 1998), pp. 71–83.

[82] Liebman, *Jews and the Left*, pp. 507–8.
[83] Paul Jacobs, *Is Curly Jewish? A Political Self-Portrait Illuminating Three Turbulent Decades of Social Revolt, 1935–1965* (New York: Atheneum, 1965), pp. 100–1.

against the Bolsheviks in northern Russia in 1918–19.[84] Russia impinged on American affairs up until the First World War chiefly in two sensitive areas: the migration of Russian nationals to the United States and the ambitions of both countries in the Far East. Jews were involved in both contexts.

The Jews who lived between the banks of the Vistula and the Dniepr (including today's Poland, Belarus, Lithuania, Ukraine, and the western and southern portions of European Russia) had formed the largest of all concentrations of Jewish population in modern times. This was the great human reservoir that supplied most of the transatlantic Jewish migrants from the last quarter of the nineteenth century to the mid-1920s. Most Americans by and large were hardly cognizant of Russian affairs. (The exceptions were, like the Jews, other emigrants from the Russian Empire: Poles, Finns, and Ukrainians.)

Russia had tried, over the course of the nineteenth century, to revamp its government somewhat akin to Prussia's police-bureaucracy system. But in the vast and poorly administered Russian Empire, these efforts sagged lamentably, rarely achieving their stated aims. The exacerbation of Russian Jewry's condition toward the end of the nineteenth century can be considered one more aspect of prevailing Russian norms of misrule. Although a policy intended to incorporate Jews (at least, selectively) within the autocracy's system of administration had officially existed at least since 1804 – with periodic revisions in nearly every decade up to the 1880s – that strategy did not offer reasonable options for social and economic security for most of the nearly five million Jews, whose residence was restricted to the empire's western borderlands.

A wave of agitation and violence against Jews in 1881 (mainly in Ukraine) followed the assassination of Tsar Alexander II and the transition to the reign of his son and heir, Alexander III. Residential and occupational restrictions on Jewish inhabitants already in force were substantially reinforced in 1882, in line with the regime's belief that Jews (rather than being the victims) were an aggravating factor in the social and political disruptions in the southern provinces. As a result, Russia's

---

[84] George F. Kennan, *Soviet-American Relations, 1917–1920, Vol. II: The Decision to Intervene* (Princeton, NJ: Princeton University Press, 1958); Eugene Trani, "Woodrow Wilson and the Decision to Intervene in Russia: The North Russian Expedition, 1918–1919," *Diplomatic History* 6 (1982): 45–67; Benjamin D. Rhodes, "The Anglo-American Intervention at Archangel, 1918–1919," *International History Review* 8(3) (1986): 367–88.

Jewish policies deteriorated to levels no longer deemed tolerable elsewhere in Europe.

This social and human-rights crisis, which did much to boost the outflow of Jews from a small trickle to a steady stream, cast the United States – the primary receiver-nation – in the unbidden role of being the solution to Russia's "Jewish problem." In just two years from 1880 to 1882, Jewish emigration from Russia to America more than tripled (from 4,300 to 13,200). After receding temporarily, the volume of Jewish immigration soon rose again to an average of 25,000 to 30,000 per year during the late 1880s, and spiked to over 76,000 a year early in the 1890s.[85]

The impact of these events on American public life was reflected in President Benjamin Harrison's third annual message to Congress, in December 1891:

> This government has found occasion to express in a friendly spirit, but with much earnestness to the government of the Czar its serious concern because of the harsh measures now being enforced against the Hebrews in Russia. [...] Great numbers of those unfortunate people have been constrained to abandon their homes [...]. It is estimated that a million will be forced from Russia within a few years.[86]

While he took care to strike a note of tolerance, even admiration – "the Hebrew is never a beggar, he has always kept the law, he lives by toil" – Harrison nevertheless concluded that "the sudden transfer of such a multitude under conditions that tend to strip them of their small accumulations and to depress their energies and courage is neither good for them nor for us."

That was more or less in keeping with similar anxieties expressed in American Jewish opinion (we recall Emma Lazarus's reaction, which was not an isolated example). Initial contacts between Jewish organizational leaders in the United States and their counterparts in Western and Central Europe, during the critical year of 1881–2, had quickly established that an uncontrolled refugee migration was not desirable. The migration

---

[85] *Migration from the Russian Empire: Lists of Passengers Arriving at the Port of New York*, ed. Ira Glazier (Baltimore, MD: Genealogical Publishing Co., 1995–8), vol. I, pp. xv–xvi; Kuznets, "Immigration of Russian Jews to the United States," pp. 36–9; Alroey, *Hamahapehah hashketah*, p. 60.

[86] "Benjamin Harrison's 3rd Annual Message," in *A Compilation of the Messages and Papers of the Presidents*, ed. James D. Richardson (New York: 1897), vol. XII, 5623; Ann E. Healy, "Tsarist Anti-Semitism and Russian-American Relations," *Slavic Review* 42(3) (1983): 409; Elias Tcherikower, "Jewish Immigrants to the United States, 1881–1900," YIVO *Annual of Jewish Social Science* 6 (1951): 169–70.

nonetheless continued to swell, eventually growing far beyond even President Harrison's fears.[87]

As philanthropic groups, grassroots immigrant associations, and Jewish labor organizations went about the job of dealing with the difficult circumstances of immigrant life in America, the Jewish ethnic press and the stewards of wider Jewish interests sought ways to publicize Russia's policies, characterized as not merely unjust but downright brutal. Public rallies were held, one of the largest of which was attended by Secretary of State William Evarts and former President Ulysses S. Grant. This event, held in New York on February 1, 1882, paralleled a similar protest meeting organized at London's Mansion House (which was, in turn, attended by leading public dignitaries). Resolutions protesting Russian antisemitism were introduced in Congress.

American Jews continued to propagate the image of despotic Russia as inimical to American values over the course of the following years. In 1904, following anti-Jewish atrocities in cities like Kishinev and Gomel during the previous year, the Jewish Publication Society published a denunciation of tsarist policies and outrages, entitled *The Voice of America on Kishineff.*

The Kishinev pogrom of 1903 and subsequent, widespread outbreaks of anti-Jewish violence in 1905–6 also formed the backdrop to the most popular Jewish contribution to the American stage prior to World War I: Israel Zangwill's 1908 production, *The Melting Pot.* The play assumed its place as a key text in the formulation of American attitudes to European immigrants and the notion of America as the first "universal nation." Zangwill posed the question of America's unique destiny in an unsubtle, melodramatic formula: could American freedom succeed in bringing together in holy wedlock a Russian-born Jewish orphan (his parents murdered in Kishinev) with an enlightened young Russian (non-Jewish) woman, the daughter of a benighted Russian official who had personally supervised the bloodshed? (The answer in the play, of course, was "yes.")

---

[87] *Protokole der Internationalen Conferenz in Wien am 2–4 August 1882 zu Gunsten der Russisch-Jüdischen Flüchtlinge* (Vienna, 1882); *Report of the President for 1882* (New York: HEAS, 1882); *Ninth Annual Report of the Board of Relief of the United Hebrew Charities of the City of New York* (New York: United Hebrew Charities, 1883); Wischnitzer, *Visas to Freedom,* pp. 30–2; Esther Panitz, "The Polarity of Jewish Attitudes Towards Immigration, 1870–1891," *American Jewish Historical Quarterly* 53(2) (1963): 99–130; Charles Wyszkowski, *A Community in Conflict: American Jewry During the Great European Migration* (Lanham, MD: University Press of America, 1991), pp. 1–21.

The Russian crisis left an indelible imprint on American Jewry and did much to redefine the Jewish community's sense of its identity. It was not just the fact that imperial Russia furnished the bulk of Jewish immigrants to America, creating in the process a new Jewry in the United States, some three million-strong by 1914. It was also the fact that Jews in America – the recently arrived as well as the long-time veterans among them – formulated the possibilities of life in America as the antithesis of Russian autocracy, antisemitism, and fecklessness. The Russian crisis also furnished Jews in America with a cause to champion in the White House, the halls of Congress, and in the court of public opinion. This contributed a great deal to the coalescence of organizations and institutions within the loosely defined American Jewish community.

An opportune chance to act politically in America against Russian interests presented itself when Russia went to war with Japan in 1904. An initiative undertaken by financier Jacob Schiff among sympathetic circles in the international money market sought to deny the Russian government ("the Northern Goliath" in Schiff's words) access to loan credits, while furnishing ample credit to the Japanese ("the Far-Eastern David"). Anglo-American loans in which Schiff's help was a significant factor were critical to Japan's victory in 1905. The Japanese regarded Schiff as a true friend and an important asset.[88]

Over the immediate short term, however, Schiff's campaign against Russian financial interests did little, if anything, to ameliorate conditions for the Jews of Russia. Rather, it was the outbreak of revolutionary uprisings in 1905, followed by the tsar's insincere promises of parliamentary reforms, which raised the hopes of many of Russia's subjects, including its Jews. Mark Twain offered his opinion at the time that most Americans remained apathetic to the situation in Russia – with one notable exception: the Jews. Reacting to Nikolai Tchaikovsky's US fundraising tour

---

[88] Jacob H. Schiff, "Japan After the War," *North American Review* 183(597) (August 1906): 161–8; Gary Dean Best, "Financing a Foreign War: Jacob H. Schiff and Japan, 1904–1905," *American Jewish Historical Quarterly* 61(4) (1972): 313–24; and "Jacob Schiff's Early Interest in Japan," *American Jewish History* 69(3) (1980): 355–9; Cohen, *Jacob H. Schiff*, pp. 33–8, 134, 136, 147, 161, 208; A. J. Sherman, "German-Jewish Bankers in World Politics: The Financing of the Russo-Japanese War," *Leo Baeck Institute Year Book* X (1983): 59–74; Roberts, "Jewish Bankers"; Michiko Nakanishi, *Heroes and Friends: Behind the Scenes of the Treaty of Portsmouth* (Portsmouth, NH: Peter E. Randall, 2005), pp. 4, 79–80, 97, 99. Schiff was decorated by the Japanese emperor in recognition of his services. When Lillian Wald traveled to Japan in 1910, Schiff, her friend and chief benefactor, gave her tips on where to visit and provided letters of introduction to highly placed figures. Feld, *Lillian Wald*, pp. 96–7.

conducted on behalf of the radical populist movement in Russia, Twain commented: "That money [collected in the United States] came not from Americans, it came from Jews."[89]

The Russian regime nevertheless took the Schiff affair of 1904 very seriously and, at the outbreak of the Great War nearly ten years afterward, sought to avoid similar machinations against it. When the question of a large American loan to Russia was raised, Schiff, together with Louis Marshall (Schiff's partner at the helm of Jewish political affairs), insisted that Russia first relax or abolish entirely its system of discriminatory regulations aimed at the Jewish population. At that time, indeed, there was some positive compliance.[90]

The steady migration of Jews now attained the full-fledged dimensions of a mass movement, nearly half a million making the trek to America between 1903 and 1907. This was nearly seven times the magnitude (on an average annual basis) of the Russian Jewish emigration of twenty years earlier.

The wave of anti-Jewish pogroms in Russia during 1905–6 entailed mass violence and atrocities far in excess of the earlier looting rampages of 1881–2. From October 1905 to September 1906 alone, the number of Russian Jews murdered totaled about 3,000. An additional 2,000 sustained serious wounds and injuries, and 15,000 more were treated for less critical injuries.[91]

Under the impact of these events, elements of the American Jewish community, including Judah Magnes (an arch-pacifist in later years), organized a Jewish Defense Association, which raised funds for Jews in Russia to acquire firearms. This marked one of the first joint efforts linking Jews from across the communal spectrum. More crucially, the 1905-era also saw the establishment of two longer-lasting Jewish organizations: the American Jewish Committee (AJC, founded in 1906) and

[89] Zosa Szajkowski, "Impact of the Russian Revolution of 1905 on American Jewish Life," *YIVO Annual* 17 (1978): 109–10.

[90] Hans Rogger, "Russian Ministers and the Jewish Question, 1881–1917," *California Slavic Studies* 8 (1975): 43; Frankel, *Prophecy and Politics*, p. 522; *Prologue to Revolution: Notes of A. N. Iakhotonov on the Secret Meetings of the Council of Ministers, 1915*, ed. Michael Cherniavsky (Englewood Cliffs, NJ: Prentice Hall, 1967), pp. 56–72; Cohen, *Not Free to Desist*, 89–90; Roberts, "Jewish Bankers," pp. 18–19.

[91] Shlomo Lambroza, "The Pogroms of 1903–1906," in *Pogroms: Anti-Jewish Violence in Modern Russian History*, ed. John Klier and Shlomo Lambroza (Cambridge: Cambridge University Press, 1992), pp. 226–31.

HIAS, which was reorganized in 1909 as a partnership between two older aid committees, and bankrolled by Schiff.

In early 1906, both houses of Congress passed a unanimous joint resolution, "That the people of the United States are horrified by the reports of the massacre of Hebrews in Russia, on account of their race and religion." Theodore Roosevelt appointed Oscar Straus as his secretary of Commerce and Labor – the first Jew to hold a cabinet post in the United States (apart from Judah P. Benjamin's cabinet career in the Confederacy) – a post which included responsibility for immigration. It was Straus, apparently, who persuaded Roosevelt to write to Count Sergei Witte, Chairman of the Russian government's Council of Ministers, to underscore America's interest in matters related to Russia's Jewish policy, which impinged on the two countries' commercial and diplomatic relations. This was one step in a wider initiative that led, several years later, to the abrogation of the 1832 commercial treaty with Russia.[92]

Quiet diplomatic activity by American officials had been undertaken as early as 1881, when Russia's Jewish policies began to have a direct impact on American citizens. At that time, the US Minister to St. Petersburg, John W. Foster, remonstrated with senior Russian officials over the fact that American citizens of the Jewish faith were being barred from freely traveling in some parts of the Russian Empire, in contravention of the commercial treaty that guaranteed "reciprocal liberty of commercial intercourse." In some cases, visiting American Jews were expelled from Russia, and in other cases they found themselves subject to arrest and imprisonment. A certain Jacob Schneider, a Russian-born US citizen, was prosecuted in Odessa in 1892 on the charge of having been "naturalized in another country without prior Imperial consent." In 1895, President Grover Cleveland castigated these actions as "obnoxious invasions" of American jurisdiction.[93]

Unlike Schiff's intervention in financial markets at the time of the Russo-Japanese War, which did not implicate the US government, the campaign over the "passport question" (equal protection for the rights of all US passport-bearers) and the commercial treaty with Russia, which was coming up for review, required leading Jewish representatives to obtain an American political consensus. By 1910, however, when the Russian treaty became an urgent matter, Jewish groups urging abrogation faced a reluctant State Department and an equally unwilling president, William Howard

[92] *American Jewish Year Book 5667*, p. 91; Cohen, *Not Free to Desist*, chap. 4.
[93] Healy, "Tsarist Anti-Semitism," pp. 411–13, 415.

Taft. Schiff and his associates at the American Jewish Committee set out to "build a fire in the rear of the President" by mobilizing public opinion.[94]

The American political climate was susceptible to the argument that foreign regimes that discriminated between US citizens of different faiths should not be rewarded with favorable commercial concessions. The abrogation of the 1832 treaty with Russia was probably the first instance of economic sanctions imposed by the US government in the interests of human-rights diplomacy, and as such, a significant milestone for American foreign policy. (It also cost the American economy very little, as exports to Russia in this period represented less than 2 percent of the American total.[95])

The abrogation of the 1832 treaty boosted the reputation of the American Jewish Committee, which had taken the issue to the public and had scored an important victory. Unfortunately for the AJC, in 1911, virtually at the very moment of this endorsement of Jewish equality as a matter of principle, Congress adjourned its four-year Immigration Commission, the massively documented investigation that recommended discontinuing free immigration. Although (as noted earlier) no Jewish quota was ever enacted, there was no mistaking the purpose of monitoring Jewish ("Hebrew") immigrants as a separate statistical category, as practiced since 1899 and as set down in the authoritative *Dictionary of Races or Peoples* that the Immigration Commission published in 1911. American nativism, which was soon reinforced by World War I, the Bolshevik Revolution in 1917, and the Red Scare of 1919, proved to be the dominant interest in American domestic politics of that era. Jewish lobbying in favor of continued free immigration was no match, in this case, for the overwhelming groundswell of American opinion.

Russia Under the Soviets

In principle, a number of factors ought to have distanced most American Jews from taking any special interest in Russian affairs after 1917, and

---

[94] Cohen, *Jacob H. Schiff*, pp. 144–52, 166; Roberts, "Jewish Bankers," p. 16.

[95] Kendalle E. Bailes, "The American Connection: Ideology and the Transfer of American Technology to the Soviet Union, 1917–1941," *Comparative Studies in Society and History* 23(3) (1981): 423–5. The United States continued to export goods to Russia, mainly raw cotton, farm equipment, and other machinery. American exports to Russia increased dramatically during World War I, when Russia was cut off from its main industrial goods supplier, Germany. In 1917 General Electric contracted to re-equip Russia's electricity industry and an American-led commission took over the operation of the Trans-Siberian Railroad.

would certainly have militated against any affinity with Communism. First, the American Jewish population apparently felt most at home politically in the Progressive or reformist wings of either of the major parties, although it also offered significant support for local political machines. A growing proportion among the Jewish population had its sights squarely on bread-and-butter attainments that were within reach of America's industrial working class, small-business owners, and white-collar employees. This in itself would have deflected the attractiveness of radical causes.

Second, the majority of the Jewish Left at that time had been radicalized primarily by their experience of American industrial relations rather than by Russian revolutionary activism, and had, moreover, accumulated enough experience on picket lines and election campaigns to prefer workplace pragmatism, consumer cooperatives, and "scientific" management–employee arrangements, to militant Marxist doctrines. The force field that held their interest most consistently was that of American domestic affairs.

Finally, a fair proportion of the Jewish public – perhaps as much as a third in the adult population – held conservative religious convictions. They favored a traditionalist (in some sense, almost quasi-puritan) mind-set and a temperate demeanor – not flamboyant provocation and anti-religious material philosophies – and their religious convictions also underwrote an abhorrence of political violence. If, despite all these factors, the Russian Revolution produced a strong ripple effect in American Jewish public life, this calls for some explanation.

While the overthrow of the tsarist regime was, at least in theory, all that was required to right all the injustices of the past and, therefore, to release the tension from the Russian-Jewish encounter, this proved not to be the case. The chaos unleashed in 1917 held sway with little respite until 1921. As if the horrors of the First World War had not been sufficiently ghastly, fighting raged on across the territories of the former Russian Empire during nearly four years following the Revolution. In Ukraine and along the new Russo-Polish border, the fighting was accompanied by outrages of mass brutality and massacre committed against the civilian Jewish population, mainly at the hands of anti-Bolshevik forces – outrages that cost about 150,000 Jewish lives. The Red Army, in most cases, shielded the Jewish populace from these depredations and appeared capable, ultimately, of imposing its power and restoring a semblance of order. Here, in the first instance, was a powerful motivation for

Jews to view the Soviet regime with a degree of latitude, if not outright admiration.[96]

The impulse to intervene with humanitarian assistance during this period and in subsequent years, providing funds and programs to reha-bilitate the social and economic fabric of Jewish life, was very much alive for the American Jewish aid agencies. Israel Friedlaender, whose wish to take part in a foreign aid mission to Palestine in 1917 had been mali-ciously thwarted, attached himself to an AJDC aid delegation that pen-etrated the Ukrainian front in early July 1920, where the Jewish populace was caught in the crossfire between Polish troops, Ukrainian partisans, and Red Army forces. There, near Kamenets-Podolsk, the young Semitics scholar and father of six met a violent and untimely death (at age forty-four), along with two other representatives of the AJDC. They were apparently shot at close range by a small Bolshevik patrol, which may (or may not) have mistaken the men for Poles.[97]

Beyond the general commitment to help Jews in trouble, which con-tinued to motivate the social service and philanthropic organizations right through the 1920s, and apart from gratitude to the new Russian regime for having swept away the Romanovs, some account must also be taken of the mesmerizing power projected by the Revolution. The spec-tacle of men and women from humble backgrounds, rallying to seize power, putting paid to a 300-year-old imperial dynasty, beating back an array of domestic and international enemies, and claiming mastery over a vast country, presented Bolshevism as a nearly invincible force propel-ling its way into human history. It was a Russian apocalypse, seeming to divide all things straight down the middle: one could be either for the Revolution or against it. It was difficult to find an alternative that was wholly satisfactory.

Moreover, the idea of a people's revolution against despotism, war, ser-vitude, and poverty touched sufficiently upon radical themes in American history, so that it seemed (at least to some) entirely plausible to imagine these two revolutionary traditions as forming two parts of a single, inex-orable, historic continuum. In this, there was nothing peculiarly related

---

[96] Eliyahu Tcherkikower, *Di ukrayner pogromen in yor 1919 (The Ukrainian Pogroms of 1919)* (New York: YIVO Institute for Jewish Research, 1965).

[97] Yotvat, "Hamas'a shelo histayem," pp. 133–6; Michael Beizer, "Who Murdered Professor Israel Friedlaender and Rabbi Bernard Cantor? The Truth Rediscovered," *American Jewish Archives Journal* 55(1) (2003): 63–112. Eighty years later, the graves of Friedlaender and his comrades were discovered by JDC representatives. Friedlaender's remains were reburied in Jerusalem, on the slopes of Mt. Scopus.

to Jewish sensibilities: the same ideas were widespread throughout the American radical Left and avant-garde.

Beyond radical ranks, however, the luster of the Bolshevik Revolution was regarded with far greater circumspection, if not downright alarm. Leading Jewish public figures (Jacob Schiff, Louis Marshall, Oscar Straus, and Stephen Wise) supported the anti-Bolshevik Russian Information Bureau, both financially and politically – at least until late 1919, when they became convinced that the anti-Bolshevik ("White") forces in Russia were directly implicated in anti-Jewish atrocities. Another key figure in the Jewish financial elite of the day, Felix Warburg, gave funds to garment union leader David Dubinsky in the 1920s to help the ILGWU expel its pro-Communist "fifth column."[98]

In those years, ongoing Jewish interests in Russia became part of a tacitly approved de facto system of commerce and cooperation with the new Russian regime. Normalization of American business and other relations with the stabilized Communist regime after 1921 was slow and gradual, and it was only in 1933, in the first Roosevelt Administration, that full diplomatic relations between the United States and the Soviet Union were established. Soviet authorities were, for much of this period, interested in upgrading their relationship with the United States, including an avid interest in the mechanization of agriculture. Russian desires to cultivate the Americans were barely reciprocated in Washington. Nevertheless, the United States became a major exporter to Soviet Russia in the 1920s (furnishing a quarter of Russian imports by 1930) and there were various technical aid agreements that facilitated the modernization of Soviet industry and agriculture. The General Electric Corporation extended credits to the Soviets even though the US government refused to guarantee them, and 40,000 American-made tractors were being used in Russia by 1930.[99]

As early as 1921, representatives of the AJDC were present in Russia as members of the American Relief Administration, headed by Herbert Hoover, which focused on postwar famine relief and operated in Russia

---

[98] Roberts, "Jewish Bankers," pp. 22–5.

[99] Hans Rogger, "Amerikanizm and the Economic Development of Russia," *Comparative Studies in Society and History* 23(3) (1981): 382–420; Jonathan Dekel-Chen, "An Unlikely Triangle: Philanthropists, Commissars, and American Statesmanship Meet in Soviet Crimea, 1922–37," *Diplomatic History* 27(3) (2003): 353–76; Bailes, "The American Connection," pp. 427–36. "[Lenin] hoped that by involving the United States economically, in Siberia especially, he would [...] help preserve Siberia from Japanese conquest" (*ibid.*, 427). See also Deborah Fitzgerald, "Blinded by Technology: American Agriculture in the Soviet Union, 1928–1932," *Agricultural History* 70(3) (1996): 459–86.

until 1923. The reluctance of the American government to fully normal-
ize its relations with the Soviets left the Jewish "channel" in a somewhat
special position, but flexibility in Washington made it possible for Jewish
communal agencies to operate in Russia.

The major Jewish philanthropic venture in Soviet Russia, starting
in 1924, was the development of Jewish agricultural colonies in the
Crimea and southern Ukraine. By 1937, when Soviet authorities finally
closed the door on AJDC work in their country, there were about 250
such farming communes, founded on state-provided land and populated
by Russian Jews who otherwise would have faced very bleak prospects.
As former petty traders, many had been stripped of civil and political
rights during the early years of the Communist regime. Farming provided a livelihood as well as a way to achieve civil rehabilitation. The
AJDC, through a subsidiary called Agro-Joint, funded the costs to the
tune of $16 million dollars (in today's worth, in excess of $200 million),
major portions of which were donated by some of America's wealthiest
business magnates, like Julius Rosenwald of Sears, Roebuck Company
(1862–1932) and the Rockefeller Foundation. Some 200,000 Jewish
farmers were involved in this massive social-engineering project, whose
demise was partly a function of Stalinist xenophobia in the late 1930s
but, more tragically, by the German occupation of the region in the
Second World War.[100]

Cultural Russian Echoes
The Russian connection marked not only the public or civic dimension of
Jewish life in America, but also the cultural world of self-representation,
aesthetics, artistic and literary creativity. When Abe Cahan wrote his
celebrated novel, *The Rise of David Levinsky* (1917), which dealt with
the *anomie* of urban industrial life and the spiritless chase after material success, he was drawing not only on his American mentor, William
Dean Howells's *The Rise of Silas Lapham* (1885), but also on one of his
favorite Russian authors, Nikolai Gogol', whose *Tales of St. Petersburg*
(1842) portrayed "a world deprived of grace, where only human greed
and vanity can thrive." Yiddish playwrights and theatrical directors in
New York similarly took Russian aesthetics as their benchmark when

---

[100] Dekel-Chen, "Unlikely Triangle"; see also his *Farming the Red Land*; Jerome C.
Rosenthal, "Dealing with the Devil: Louis Marshall and the Partnership Between the
Joint Distribution Committee and Soviet Russia," *American Jewish Archives* 39(1)
(1987): 1–22.

reaching for highbrow, art-theater standards. That was the case with Jacob Gordin (1853–1909), who immigrated to America in 1891 and became famous as a standard-bearer for quality art theater in Yiddish. An analogous trend took hold again during the early Soviet period, when the radical Yiddish *Artef* theater in New York looked to the Russian stage for avant-garde styles.[101]

To take the measure of this aesthetic and literary dimension it is important to note that the immigrant stream from Eastern Europe, similar in this respect to the arrivals from German-speaking lands, included a portion of the Jewish intelligentsia – products of Russian *gymnasii* (advanced secondary schools) and other institutions of higher education. A fair number of them were fully conversant with the cosmopolitan music, art, and literature of *fin-de-siècle* Europe. Some could speak or read several languages, including Russian, German, Polish, or French, before they had mastered English. By the time they had arrived in America, such people had attended theaters or even been exposed to that wonderful new medium, moving pictures, shown in the years before World War I in major Lithuanian, Russian, and Polish cities like Vilna (Vilnius), Moscow, Odessa, Łódź, and Warsaw.[102]

These men and women, youngsters for the most part, did not wait very long before setting out to replicate the heady cultural and intellectual atmosphere of the student "circles" they had belonged to in Europe. The freedom from censorship that they enjoyed as Americans and the prospect of engaging with the world of science, culture, and philosophy without the constricting apparatus of Russian laws were conducive to the founding of clubs and journals, women's reading groups, and publishing ventures, in addition to an ambitious array of after-hours lectures, "lyceums," and institutes.[103]

[101] Nahshon, *Yiddish Proletarian Theater*; Nahma Sandrow, *Vagabond Stars: A World History of the Yiddish Theater* (New York: Harper and Row, 1977); Orlando Figes, *Natasha's Dance: A Cultural History of Russia* (London: Penguin, 2002), p. 160.
[102] Yuri Tsivian, *Early Cinema in Russia and its Cultural Reception*, ed. Richard Taylor, trans. Alan Blodger (London: Routledge, 1994); Yael Ohad-Karny, "Hitkablut hakolno'a bekerev yehudei artsot haberit bein shtei milhamot ha'olam" (The Reception of American Cinema among United States Jews between the Two World Wars) (PhD dissertation, Hebrew University of Jerusalem, 2011), p. 55; J. Hoberman, "Cinema," in *YIVO Encyclopedia of Jews in Eastern Europe* (www.yivoencyclopedia.org/article .aspx/Cinema).
[103] Hagit Cohen, "The Demands of Integration – The Challenges of Ethnicization: Jewish Women's Reading Circles in North America Between the Two World Wars," *Nashim: A Journal of Jewish Women's Studies and Gender Issues* 16 (2008): 98–129; and "Min haloer ist sayd ve'ad sinsinati: max n. maisel ve'itsuvah shel zehut yehudit amerikanit"

It is difficult to overestimate, in terms of popular cultural consumption, the sensational impact of a virtuoso musical performer like Jascha Heifetz (1901–87), son of a violin teacher and concert-master, trained at the legendary St. Petersburg Conservatory, who took America by storm at age sixteen after he and his family arrived via the Far East and San Francisco. (During the last years of the Russian Empire, roughly one out of every three university-level Jewish students was a musician at the St. Petersburg Conservatory.[104])

Ten years later another Jewish star, the Kiev-born pianist, Vladimir Horowitz (1903–89) arrived from the Soviet Union and quickly established himself on the American and Western concert stage. More than simply prodigies or musical celebrities, they were venerated as folk heroes in many Jewish homes, where hapless youngsters were apprenticed to violin or piano lessons. The remarkable phenomenon of star-performers as accessible cultural icons was closely related to the mass-marketing of their recordings for home listening and to the influence of radio broadcasting.

At a later stage, the impact of Marc Chagall (1887–1985), the avant-garde artist from Vitebsk, whose American period was relatively brief (from 1941 to 1948), was similar. Chagall's work was showcased in 1946 at a major exhibit at New York's Museum of Modern Art. It reformulated the reception of modern art forms in Jewish visual culture and, equally, achieved wide popularization for a new Jewish iconography in modern art: a fanciful iconography, worldly and witty, replete with flying goats, levitating brides, and fiddlers on roofs.

In conclusion, we may say that Spain, Germany, and Russia, either separately or in tandem, limned the political and cultural imagination of American Jews and provided a foreign dimension that anchored their collective consciousness. Whereas American national myths celebrated "independence" – the detaching of the New World from the Old – Jewish myths worked to retain Old World engagements.

At the same time, the foreign entanglements of America's Jews spurred some of them to thicken and complicate the repertoire of their civic activities, which rooted them more firmly in the American public square. When American foreign interests expanded, during and after the

(From the Lower East Side to Cincinnati: Max N. Maisel and the Construction of American Jewish Identity), *Zion* 75(4) (2010): 427–61.
[104] James Loeffler, *The Most Musical Nation: Jews and Culture in the Late Russian Empire* (New Haven, CT and London: Yale University Press, 2010), esp. pp. 2, 7, 11, 95–8, 200.

Spanish-American War, for instance, many Jews were more than willing to chime in with the general air of patriotic fervor. Sometimes they were also willing to join in the anti-Catholic chorus of their Protestant neighbors.

In general, Jewish overseas activities were visible signs of their domestic energy. The public virtues of voluntarism and civic consciousness were evident in the committees they established, in the ways that they mobilized public support both within and beyond Jewish ranks, and in the fundraising drives for overseas relief that they undertook. They articulated their goals with explicit reference to American foreign and domestic political agendas. They were able, in that sense, to forge for themselves a position mid-way between sectarian Jewish activism and the civic responsibility expected of an American citizenry.

Crisis tended to put that equilibrium to the test. In times of war, some Jews risked their personal interests, their reputations, or even their lives, as they pursued their overseas agendas. During World War II, however, many Jews chose to put America's interests (as the political leaders of the nation defined them) ahead of sectarian ones – persuaded that, by doing so, they were eminently helping to defeat the great enemy of both the Jewish people and the United States. With their sons and daughters risking their lives as soldiers and sailors along with other citizens, America's Jews found compelling reasons not to break ranks.

It was during peacetime, in contrast, that the Jewish concern with other Jews in foreign lands stood out in comparison with the domestic orientation – at times the isolationist cast – of their fellow Americans. Most striking, perhaps, was the fact that those who were involved included members of the recent immigrant cohorts as well as second-generation, American-born Jews; wealthy financiers and philanthropists as well as working men and women; people with filial attachments and memories of their historic homelands, as well as those who lacked such personal memories or family heritage.

5

Recapitulations and More Beginnings, 1950s to the Twenty-first Century

> While the West takes pride in itself, most of the rest of the world lives in shame.
>
> – Orhan Pamuk, *The Museum of Innocence*

As we noted at the conclusion of Chapter 3, more Jews were living in America in the 1950s – an estimated 5.5 million souls – than in any other country in the world. That was due primarily to the history of European migration to the United States. Comprising mainly first- and second-generation Americans, the US Jewish population was augmented in the postwar years by third- and fourth-generation descendants. Jews constituted about 3 percent of the US national population (about twice their proportion today).

The numerical dominance of American Jewry in the postwar Jewish world was also the indirect by-product of the extermination of two-thirds of European Jewry by the Nazis and their accomplices. With most of Europe's Jews decimated, only the Soviet Union still harbored a postwar Jewish population upwards of two million, second in size after US Jewry. After 1948, the newly established State of Israel absorbed the greatest part of the remaining Jewish survivors and, in addition, provided new homes for close to a million Jewish refugees and emigrants displaced from Arab lands. By the early 1960s, Israel had some two million Jewish residents – roughly equivalent to the number of Jews living in New York City at the time.

Jewish families in America expanded along with other American households in those "boomer" years – though a bit less so – which made the postwar birth cohort especially large in comparison with older age

248

groups. Along with a small surplus of new foreign immigration, these growth factors offset losses due to aging, to Jews marrying non-Jews and raising their children as Christians, as well as other forms of disaffiliation.[1]

Substantial portions of American Jewry moved house in the postwar years, as they moved into more affluent social sectors. As we will see, this was not true for a significant minority, including workers, small independent shopkeepers, new immigrants, the elderly, and families in distress. Their lower social profile and special needs, however, did not alter the stereotypical image that, increasingly, characterized the rest of the Jewish population. Many members of the younger generation, in particular, were able to make their way through life without the close-knit support structures of organized self-help agencies. As affluence tended to diminish the need for a communal infrastructure, especially in the sphere of health care and social welfare, Jews as a group faced the challenge of redefining the nature and purpose of their community-backed institutions.

Gentrification

By 1945, many Americans had considerable savings in the form of war bonds and other assets, totaling $140 billion (three times the entire national income for 1932). Such privately held capital was augmented by veterans' benefits on an unprecedented scale. The GI Bill offered Veteran Administration (VA) mortgages with no down payment and affordable rates to young families of demobilized servicemen. In addition, over 400,000 war veterans were the beneficiaries of occupational training programs and 318,000 were helped to start their own businesses or professional practices. Federal benefits also included free tuition and a stipend for college-bound veterans. Half a million Jewish men and women had served in the US armed forces during World War II. For those among

---

[1] Sidney Goldstein, "American Jewry, A Demographic Analysis," in *The Future of the Jewish Community in America*, ed. David Sidorsky (Philadelphia, PA: Jewish Publication Society/New York: Basic Books, 1973); *Yearbook of American Churches, 1941 Edition*, ed. Benson Y. Landis (Jackson Heights, NY: Yearbook of American Churches Press, 1941), p. 37; Wilbur Zelinsky, "An Approach to the Religious Geography of the United States: Patterns of Church Membership in 1952," *Annals of the Association of American Geographers* 51 (1961): 139–93. For methodologies, see Uriah Zvi Engelman, "Sources of Jewish Statistics," in *The Jews: Their History, Culture, and Religion*, ed. Louis Finkelstein, 3rd ed. (Philadelphia, PA: Jewish Publication Society of America, 1966), vol. II, pp. 1510–35.

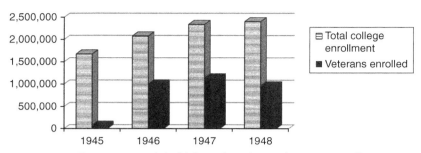

FIGURE 5.1. Postwar growth in higher education and veteran enrollment.[4]

them who returned to establish new lives, the unprecedented veterans' benefits were a palpable advantage (see Fig. 5.1).[2]

As America entered the Cold War era, there was an urgent demand for trained experts in science, technology, and math, as well as foreign cultures and languages. The doors of universities, including those in the Ivy League, were now more open to students who heretofore had had fewer opportunities for higher education, such as Jews, Catholics, women, and the children of the working class. This not only created a more welcoming atmosphere for Jewish students but also a more open hiring environment for new Jewish faculty members.[3]

The relative accessibility, public subsidy, and popularization of higher education made a college degree an important asset in securing employment. Higher education became the basic standard of competency in an increasing number of fields, including some that had not traditionally been seen as academic, such as business management, journalism, teaching, and public service.

The effects of employment and educational training trends in the interwar years, combined with the boost provided by postwar benefits, made for especially striking results in the Jewish population. Between 1948 and 1953, Jewish communal and welfare agencies in fourteen cities (outside of New York City) conducted social and demographic surveys of their areas. They found that the proportion of Jews in non-manual occupations (proprietors, managers, officials, clerks,

[2] Michael J. Bennett, *When Dreams Came True: The GI Bill and the Making of Modern America* (Washington, DC and London: Brassey, 1996); Joseph C. Goulden, *The Best Years: 1945–1950* (New York: Atheneum, 1976); Keith W. Olson, *The G.I. Bill, the Veterans, and the Colleges* (Louisville: University Press of Kentucky, 1974).

[3] Bennett, *Dreams Came True*, pp. 2, 15–16, 23–5, 155–7, 201–2; Moore, *G.I. Jews*.

[4] Bennett, *Dreams Came True*, pp. 18, 201.

salesmen, and professionals) now ranged from 75 to 96 percent, compared to just 38 percent for Americans at large. Even in New York City, where working-class Jews had predominated in the early twentieth century, less than a third of the Jewish workforce was now employed in manual trades.[5]

The subgroup of professionals, in particular, had grown appreciably. In addition, a small but highly visible coterie of Jewish artists, performers, scriptwriters, and athletes were active in concert and opera halls, on radio, on stage and screen, and in professional sports. To these we must add all those who were in the business side of music production, art galleries, theater, radio, TV, film, and sports. Around 1 percent of economically active Jews were farmers.[6]

Public employment – vastly expanded during the 1930s and 1940s – remained a secure occupational niche for some Jews in the postwar period. Civil servants enjoyed job security and regular opportunities for promotion. Apart from Jews in active military service, Jewish men and women were also postal service employees, teachers, legal and paralegal professionals (working in public prosecutors' offices, as judges, in federal agencies, or as court stenographers), health-care professionals and technical workers (public hospitals, the VA), social workers, labor relations experts, economic analysts, police, and firefighters.[7]

[5] Nathan Glazer, "The American Jew and the Attainment of Middle-Class Rank: Some Trends and Explanations," in Sklare, *The Jews*, pp. 138–9. The communities were Camden, NJ; Charleston, SC; Gary, IN; Indianapolis, IN; Los Angeles, CA; Miami, FL; Nashville, TN; New Orleans, LA; Newark, NJ (and its suburbs, considered as a separate community); Passaic, NJ; Port Chester, NY; Trenton, NJ; and Utica, NY. See also Kuznets, "Economic Structure," p. 1640.
[6] Ben Seligman with assistance of Aaron Antonovsky, "Some Aspects of Jewish Demography," in *The Jews: Social Patterns of an American Group*, ed. Marshall Sklare (New York: Free Press, 1958), pp. 76–7; Glazer, "The American Jew," pp. 138–40; Liston Pope, "Religion and Class Structure," *Annals of the American Academy of Political and Social Science* 256 (1948): 84–92; Jonathan Z. S. Pollack, "Success from Scrap and Secondhand Goods," in Kobrin (ed.), *Chosen Capital*, pp. 93–112; Calvin Goldscheider, "Immigration and the Transformation of American Jews: Assimilation, Distinctiveness, and Community," in *Immigration and Religion in America*, ed. Richard Alba, Albert J. Raboteau, and Josh DeWind (New York and London: New York University Press, 2009), pp. 205–10.
[7] Stephen D. Isaacs, *Jews and American Politics* (Garden City, NY: Doubleday, 1974), p. 70. A third of the men and women who passed the police academy entrance exam in New York City in 1939 were Jewish. "Most of them were college graduates out of work: teachers, lawyers, accountants, and even two doctors" (www.nypdshomrim.org/shomrim.html). "Shomrim" policemen's benevolent associations were established for Jewish law enforcement personnel in New York City, Philadelphia, Chicago, and eventually in most major metropolitan areas.

Public service at senior levels was sometimes a springboard to executive positions in the corporate sector. Emanuel Ruben Piore (1908–2000), an immigrant from Lithuania, became head of the Office of Naval Research (the Navy's chief scientist). He was later hired as the first director of research at IBM. Irving S. Shapiro (1916–2001), a Minneapolis-born son of immigrants from Lithuania, pursued a legal career in the federal Office of Price Administration and the Criminal Division of the Justice Department before becoming the first Jewish chairman of the DuPont Corporation.[8]

In terms of income, in New York City, the highest-earning bracket (over $10,000 annually) represented 12 percent of all Jewish residents. This was a relatively larger elite sector than the 5 percent that such top earners represented in the general population. By the same token, those at the lowest end of the scale (earning under $4,000 annually) accounted for nearly half the general population, but only about 30 percent among Jews. Jews in smaller cities and suburban townships were likelier to be better off economically than those in the metropolis, since the largest cities tended to house more recent immigrants, salaried employees, and retirees – populations known to have lower incomes. In the Chicago suburb of Highland Park, for instance, most of the Jewish residents earned over $10,000 per year, with nearly half in the $10–20,000 bracket. Regardless of their income bracket, level of educational attainment, and place of residence, Jews as a group were overwhelmingly reliant on income-generating jobs, rather than on estate ownership and other capital earnings.[9]

The rise of a mass-based middle class, accompanied by the exodus from cities to suburbs, suggested a major social realignment in America. The evenness and look-alike physical surroundings of streets and houses in the new developments and the apparently homogenous, middle-class social profile of the residents were thought to blur older distinctions between class, religious, and other group identities (Jewish, Catholic, etc.) that had been inbred in ethnically dense city neighborhoods.[10]

[8] *Science and Academic Life in Transition: Emanuel Piore*, ed. Eli Ginsberg (New Brunswick, NJ: Transaction Publishers/Rutgers, 1990); Charles E. Silberman, *A Certain People: American Jews and their Lives Today* (New York: Summit Books, 1985), p. 86; Harman, *Price of Altruism*, p. 150.

[9] Glazer, "Middle-Class Rank," p. 141; Sklare and Greenblum, *Jewish Identity*, p. 29. Data for 1980 showed that the five metropolitan areas of New York, Los Angeles, Chicago, San Francisco, and Miami represented altogether 12.6 percent of the national population, but contained 38.7 percent of the nation's immigrants. Elizabeth Bogen, *Immigration in New York* (Westport, CT: Praeger, 1987), Table 5.1, p. 61.

[10] David Riesman, "The Suburban Dislocation," *Annals of the American Academy of Political and Social Science* (November 1957): 133, 138; see also Max Lerner, *America as a Civilization* (New York: Simon and Schuster, 1957), pp. 173–4.

That was not always the case. Jewish young marrieds who resettled in the suburbs may have imagined that they were escaping the social claustrophobia of their old city neighborhoods, but many of them ended up living in communities that closely resembled their own social profiles, with a considerable percentage of Jewish residents. As one observer has put it, "Jews went to the suburbs to become Americans and found themselves back in Jewish neighborhoods."[11]

The postwar trend toward upward mobility and suburbanization had its counterpart in a new cycle of synagogue construction. In a single two-year period in the mid-1950s, the centrist-moderate traditional denomination, Conservative Judaism, gained 131 new congregations. Altogether, there were a thousand more synagogues in America at the end of the 1950s than there had been in the 1930s. Enrollment in Jewish educational programs for schoolchildren went from 190,000 in 1940 to 488,000 in 1956.[12]

New synagogues built to suit the needs and tastes of young suburban families were often less stately or imposing than those erected before the Depression. Some sported a trim one-story design and the requisite grassy lawn that echoed the popular domestic "ranch" style. They could also be marked by features such as tan- or red-brick construction, a parking lot, and a marble facade over a lobby entrance, as well as a well-appointed classroom wing, carpeting, modern pews, modern stained-glass windows in the sanctuary, and often a pitched roof or another skyward-sweeping gesture.[13]

Immigration

In 1965 the Johnson Administration, following up on a decade of White House policy deliberations, pushed through new immigration legislation

---

[11] Riv-Ellen Prell, "Community and the Discourse of Elegy: The Postwar Discourse of Elegy," in *Imagining the American Jewish Community*, ed. Jack Wertheimer (Hanover, NH: Brandeis University Press, University Press of New England, and the Jewish Theological Seminary of America, 2007), pp. 70–81, 85 (quotation on p. 85).

[12] Wertheimer, *A People Divided*, p. 5; and "The Postwar Suburban Synagogue in Historical Context," in *Text and Context: Essays in Modern Jewish History and Historiography in Honor of Ismar Schorsch*, ed. Eli Lederhendler and Jack Wertheimer (New York: Jewish Theological Seminary, 2005), pp. 580–9; Susan G. Solomon, *Louis I. Kahn's Jewish Architecture: Mikveh Israel and the Midcentury American Synagogue* (Waltham, MA: Brandeis University Press, 2009).

[13] Lance J. Sussman, "The Suburbanization of American Judaism as Reflected in Synagogue Building and Architecture, 1945–1975," *American Jewish History* 75(1) (1985): 31–47.

and ushered in a new wave of migration to the United States, mostly from Asian and Latin American countries. The new migration, following decades of strictly administered national-origins quotas and quasi-racial bars, boosted American population growth. Over the course of the next thirty years (1970–2000), some twenty million people immigrated to the United States and the ratio of the foreign-born in the national population more than doubled, from 4.7 to over 11 percent.[14]

A modest volume of Jewish immigrants also arrived at this time from various parts of the world: refugees from postwar Europe; Jewish transmigrants – originally hailing from Europe – who came now from their interim homes in Cuba and elsewhere in Latin America; and Jewish émigrés from Syria and other Moslem countries, compelled to leave their homes in the 1950s and 1960s. In the late 1960s, following the new immigration legislation, about 39,000 foreign Jews entered the United States as permanent residents.[15]

In the 1970s, the Soviet government permitted some of its Jewish citizens to apply for permission to leave the USSR. The destination of most of them was Israel, but among those who did not resettle in Israel, many went to America. Between 1980 and 1986, 5,600 Soviet Jews resettled in New York City alone – representing nearly 20 percent of the assisted-refugee influx into the city in those years, and second in rank only to Vietnamese immigrants.[16] This presaged an even larger contingent that entered the United States after 1989, following the fall of the Soviet regime, at which point about 35,000 such arrivals occurred each year. They came chiefly from Russia, Belarus, and Ukraine (areas with the largest Soviet Jewish population), but they also included members of ethnically distinct, close-knit communities from former Soviet republics in the

---

[14] Public Law 89-236 – October 3, 1965: An Act to Amend the Immigration and Nationality Act, Sec. 2: "No person shall receive any preference or priority or be discriminated against in the issuance of an immigrant visa because of his race, sex, nationality, place of birth, or place of residence." See also Klein, *Population History of the United States*, pp. 202–4, 226; Donald W. Meinig, *The Shaping of America: Volume 4: Global America, 1915–2000* (New Haven, CT and London: Yale University Press, 2004), pp. 233–44; Barkan, *From All Points*, pp. 446–8.

[15] Goldstein, "American Jewry"; Waxman, *America's Jews in Transition*, pp. 189–202; Henry A. Green, "Transnational Identity and Miami Sephardim," and Margalit Bejarano, "From Turkey to the United States: The Trajectory of Cuban Sephardim in Miami," both in *Contemporary Sephardic Identity in the Americas: An Interdisciplinary Approach*, ed. Margalit Bejarano and Edna Aizenberg (Syracuse, NY: Syracuse University Press, 2012), pp. 124–58.

[16] Bogen, *Immigration in New York*, Table 9.1, p. 122.

Caucasus region and Central Asia. Altogether, these former Soviet Jewish immigrants totaled about 300,000.[17]

Following the 1979 Islamic revolution in Iran, a substantial number of Iranian Jewish émigrés resettled in Los Angeles and other parts of the country. Like the former Cuban Jews living in Florida in close proximity to other Cubans, Iranian Jews shared much in common with their fellow Iranian émigrés, such as language, political posture, and an active entrepreneurial class. There was also a steady trickle of new arrivals from Israel, who brought with them a new type of national-Jewish, Hebrew-speaking culture that contrasted with the denominational Judaism of the native-born Jewish community. By the end of the twentieth century, foreign-born Jews constituted at least 8 percent (or one in thirteen) of Jewish American adults. These helped the Jewish community to stabilize its numbers and to restock its roster of associations, synagogues, and schools. However, the overall growth of the US national population, especially after the post-1965 immigration policies took effect, gradually reduced the *proportional* share of Jews in the national population, which had declined to below 2 percent by 2010.[18]

Incoming foreign immigrants, in contrast to the suburbanization trend among native-born Jews, were apt to establish clusters in big city neighborhoods. Indeed, Jewish immigrant neighborhoods of this period were frequently located within or adjacent to the historical staging areas of previous Jewish generations. This *déjà vu* effect was compounded when parts of these old-new enclaves came to be populated by traditionalist Jews attired in Old World garb: the ultra-Orthodox or *haredi* Jews, whose arrival we have briefly noted before. Albeit a small part within the overall Jewish public, they were conspicuous in their appearance. Those who viewed them as anachronistic vestiges of past ages were surprised over the years by their cultural resilience and their persistent numerical growth, as we will see.

---

[17] Uziel O. Schmelz and Sergio DellaPergola, "World Jewish Population, 1994," *American Jewish Year Book* 96 (1996): 438; *National Jewish Population Survey 2000–1: Strength, Challenge, and Diversity in the American Jewish Population* (New York: United Jewish Communities, 2003), pp. 32–3; *Current Jewish Population Reports*, ed. Arnold Dashefsky, Sergio DellaPergola, and Ira Sheskin, No. 1 (2010): "Population in the United States, 2010," www.jewishdatabank.org/Reports/Jewish_Population_in_the_United_States_2010.pdf.

[18] Bejarano and Aizenberg, *Contemporary Sephardic Identity in the Americas*.

Foreign Affairs and Domestic Issues

Migration and resettlement represented but one motif, familiar from earlier times, which reverberated anew in this period. Other "recapitulations" occurred with regard to assistance for Jews overseas. At such times, it seemed natural to recall lessons from the past and to deploy some of the same organizational resources.

In the postwar decades, American Jews' concern for the welfare of Jews in other lands benefited from a positive environment. Indeed, there was direct and indirect support by successive American administrations and significant portions of American public opinion. The United States was heavily involved in the postwar reconstruction of Europe, which it viewed as a strategic national interest, and took the lead in establishing the United Nations. This contrasted with the isolationist posture that had dominated the nation's affairs during the 1920s and 1930s. Jewish organizations that sponsored refugee relief, migration and resettlement, and foreign aid derived confidence from their sense that the national interest and the Jewish situation appeared to be more in sync than ever before. Offering succor to Jewish people abroad – in Israel in particular – also seemed to anoint American Jewish prosperity with higher purpose: affluent means matched altruistic ends, and giving to the cause became a rite of entry into Jewish fellowship.

However, things did not remain quite so straightforward or simple. Almost before World War II was concluded, former colonial states in Asia, Africa, and the Middle East entered a prolonged struggle for their independence. Israel's emergence in the post-colonial Middle East was only one such instance, and a particularly complicated one at that, since all its immediate neighbors vehemently opposed its existence and continued to boycott its normalization. What role would the United States play in these struggles, given the lingering and sometimes violent final chapter of the European powers' imperial ambitions – chiefly those of Britain and France, America's closest allies? The United States, with its own interests at stake (some of America's largest corporations were based in precisely those parts of the world), inherited some of the international role once played by France and Britain – and with it, a difficulty in explaining just why it was intervening in the affairs of countries far from its borders. The US framed its foreign involvements in terms of the strategic need to forestall Communist influence.

In that atmosphere, Jewish engagements abroad could not long retain their purely apolitical, humanitarian character. Beginning with Israel and postwar Eastern Europe, eventually embracing Soviet Jewry as well as the Jewish communities of Argentina and Chile during the years of military dictatorship (the "dirty war"), few American Jewish overseas interventions remained insulated from politicized discourse and conflict. (A more detailed discussion of pro-Israel and pro-Soviet-Jewry activities is included later in this chapter.) There was wisdom, perhaps, in seeking to promote Jewish causes as bi-partisan and human-rights issues, but it was equally tempting to frame Israel and other Jewish issues in Cold War terms, as the Soviets turned increasingly pro-Arab and, in their domestic policies, continued to severely curtail cultural and religious freedoms.

The postwar years could, thus, hardly be characterized as benign. At the very least, an anxiety hovered over the material comfort that Americans experienced at home, which contrasted sharply with the deprivation and conflict suffered by most of the world's population. These tensions, in turn, echoed and reshaped the nation's responses to an array of domestic issues, which pitted the "affluent society" against the "other America." "The times they are a-changin'" declared an iconic bard of the new era. The slogan was as much a warning and a challenge as it was a swaggering note of self-confidence.[19]

Questions of race, which had always deeply furrowed the ground of American democracy, now emerged as the country's most polarizing domestic issue. Broad-based awareness of this "American dilemma"[20] followed the redistribution of the nation's Black population northward to the Northeast and Midwest after World War I. The trend continued in the post-1945 period: between four and five million African Americans relocated out of the South from 1940 to 1970. Racial diversity and racial inequality redefined urban realities across the country and, in contrast to earlier times, racial issues became primarily associated with cities. Moreover, now there was not just one "racial question," since the expanding population of Hispanic residents in the Southwest, Florida, and the Northeast complicated the old, binary "black/white" formula.[21]

---

[19] The title track of Bob (Robert Allen Zimmerman, b. 1941) Dylan's famous record album, Columbia Records, 1964. *The Affluent Society* was the title of the famous book by Harvard economist John Kenneth Galbraith (1958), who warned against the growing disparity in income and economic opportunity between Americans. *The Other America* was the name of American socialist Michael Harrington's book of 1962, also devoted to the topic of poverty in the United States.

[20] Gunnar Myrdal, *An American Dilemma: The Negro Problem and Modern Democracy* (New York: Harper, 1944).

[21] Nicholas Lemann, *The Promised Land: The Great Black Migration and How it Changed America* (New York: Vintage, 1991); Klein, *Population History of the United States,*

The heavily northern and, for the most part, still mainly urban Jewish population lived astride one of the major fault-lines of American political and social ferment. Their hospitals, social welfare institutions, synagogues, property holdings, and businesses were often heavily concentrated in neighborhoods where Jewish residents had once predominated but now were growing scarce. In a semantic switch, these aging Jewish tenement neighborhoods became the nation's "ghettos," and that word's older Jewish connotations were displaced or forgotten. Between 1940 and 1980, the number of cities containing such racial ghettos more than tripled (from 55 to 179). Inter-group relations remained high on the Jewish public agenda. One upshot was an "ethnic turn" in American Jews' point of view about their group in relation to others.[22]

Urban Crucibles

The great bulk of the American Jewish population was contained within fewer than a dozen metropolitan areas around the nation's perimeter. Greater New York was in a class of its own, with over two million Jewish residents. The other large Jewish hubs, each with over 150,000 Jewish residents, were Los Angeles, Philadelphia, Chicago, Boston, Washington, DC, and Miami (including their metropolitan areas). Baltimore and Detroit were not far behind, each with close to 100,000 Jewish residents. Altogether, these nine cities accounted for over 60 percent of all American Jews. In contrast, the ten largest metropolitan areas of the United States contained barely a quarter of the national US population.[23]

pp. 167, 191; Alan Brinkley, "World War II and American Liberalism," in *The War and American Culture: Society and Consciousness During World War II*, ed. Lewis A. Erenburg and Susan E. Hirsch (Chicago, IL and London: University of Chicago Press, 1996), p. 315; Meinig, *Global America, 1915–2000*, pp. 180–5; James Grossman and Albert J. Raboteau, "Black Migration, Religion, and Civic Life," in Alba, Raboteau and DeWind, *Immigration and Religion in America*, p. 308.

[22] Klein, *Population History of the United States*, p. 192; William H. Chafe, *Unfinished Journey: America since World War II* (New York: Oxford University Press, 1991), pp. 117–19; Moore, *Golden Cities*, pp. 38–9; Matthew Frye Jacobson, *Roots Too: White Ethnic Revival in Post-Civil Rights America* (Cambridge, MA: Harvard University Press, 2005).

[23] Sarna, *American Judaism*, pp. 358–9 (map); *American Jewish Year Book 1979* (New York and Philadelphia, PA: American Jewish Committee/Jewish Publication Society, 1978), pp. 177–89; C. Morris Horowitz and Lawrence J. Kaplan, *The Jewish Population of the New York Area, 1900–1975* (New York: Federation of Jewish Philanthropies of New York, 1959); Eli Lederhendler, *New York Jews and the Decline of Urban Ethnicity, 1950–1970* (Syracuse, NY: Syracuse University Press, 2001), pp. 11–12; United States Census Bureau, "Population of the 100 Largest Cities and Other Urban Places in the United States," www.census.gov/population/www/documentation/twps0027.

The density of Jewish population in certain parts of the country indicated how most Jews had adapted economically to American ways of life, with an intensive, even disproportionate, participation in urban trade, consumer goods manufacturing, and services. The clustering that characterized the Jewish population also fostered among them a coherent set of lifestyles, which extended even to such intangibles as the newspapers and magazines they read, the places where they vacationed, and the range of local and regional accents noticeable in their speech. Geographic and occupational concentration of the Jewish population also favored the chances for in-group socialization and in-marriage between Jews.[24]

Distinctive Jewish residential patterns also boosted their visibility and magnified their social impact beyond the meager share they held in the national population. This granted them a certain political bonus, particularly in presidential voting, for a relatively high proportion of Jewish voters cast their ballots in states that had unusually large, high-density populations and (therefore) the largest blocs of Electoral College delegates. Perhaps for this reason, many Americans tended to think that the Jewish population was larger than it actually was.[25]

Cities were the crucibles of American Jewish culture, in its widest sense. Works written by Jewish authors and featuring a Jewish social landscape were invariably city-based narratives: Saul Bellow's and Isaac Rosenfeld's Chicago, Philip Roth's Newark, and the New York of (to cite just a few) Henry Roth, E. L. Doctorow, Grace Paley, Paul Auster, Isaac Bashevis Singer, and Cynthia Ozick. In film, too, Jewish characters were nearly exclusively portrayed against urban backgrounds: *The Last Angry Man* (Daniel Mann, 1959), *The Pawnbroker* (Sidney Lumet, 1964), *Funny Girl* (William Wyler, 1968), *An American Tail* (Don Bluth, 1986), *Brighton Beach Memoirs* (Gene Saks and Neil Simon, 1986), *Crossing Delancey* (Joan Micklin Silver, 1988), and Barry Levinson's Baltimore trilogy, *Diner, Avalon,* and *Liberty Heights* (1982, 1990, 1999). Some of the most memorable of Woody Allen's cinematic oeuvre, including *Annie Hall* (1977), *Manhattan* (1979), and *Broadway Danny Rose* (1984), featured New York as a favored backdrop.[26]

[24] Calvin Goldscheider and Alan S. Zuckerman, *The Transformation of the Jews* (Chicago, IL and London: University of Chicago Press, 1986), pp. 181–4.

[25] Stember et al., *Jews in the Mind of America*, p. 77.

[26] Paul Auster, *The Invention of Solitude* (New York: Penguin, 1988); and *The New York Trilogy* (London: Faber and Faber, 1987); Saul Bellow, *The Adventures of Augie March* (New York: Viking Press, 1953); E. L. Doctorow, *Ragtime* (New York: Random House, 1975); *World's Fair* (New York: Ballantine Books, 1985); and *City of God*

Such cultural artifacts created an image of coherency. The middle-class, urban Jewish "type," as disseminated in the cultural output by Jews and about Jews, rested on broad generalizations, whereas in fact the social terrain was much more complex. In the 1950s and 1960s, although many Jews enjoyed higher-than-average incomes, a quarter of them across the country (and nearly a third in New York City) earned less than $3,000 a year. Blue-collar Jewish families were mainly a big city phenomenon: adult Jews who had less than a secondary education were more likely than their more educated, younger, and better salaried peers to remain in the city.

Caseworkers of Jewish and non-sectarian social agencies knew well enough that the urban Jewish population included the elderly, the mentally and physically infirm or incapacitated, immigrant refugees with little to carry them through initial hard times, single-parent households requiring welfare assistance, families trying to cope with business failure, juvenile offenders, and inmates of correctional facilities. Mutual self-help, labor unions, free loan services, and institutionalized social services – augmented in the postwar era by benefits from Social Security and public health-care subsidization programs – made it possible for a significant portion of the urban Jewish population to scrape by.[27]

(New York: Plume/Penguin, 2001); Faye Kellerman, *The Ritual Bath, A Novel* (New York: Arbor House, 1986); and *The Quality of Mercy* (New York: W. Morrow, 1989); Cynthia Ozick, *The Puttermesser Papers, A Novel* (New York: Vintage, 1997); Grace Paley, *The Little Disturbances of Man* (New York: Doubleday, 1959); Chaim Potok, *The Chosen* (New York: Simon and Schuster, 1967); and *The Promise* (London: Heinemann, 1969); Isaac Rosenfeld, *Passage from Home* (New York: Dial Press, 1946); Henry Roth, *Call it Sleep* (New York: R. O. Ballou, 1934); and *Mercy of a Rude Stream* (London: St. Martin's, 1994–6); Philip Roth, *The Facts: A Novelist's Autobiography* (New York: Farrar, Straus, and Giroux, 1988); *Patrimony* (New York: Vintage, 1992); and *The Plot Against America, A Novel* (New York: Vintage, 2004); Isaac Bashevis Singer, *Enemies, A Love Story* (New York: Farrar, Straus, and Giroux, 1972); and *Shadows on the Hudson* (New York: Farrar, Straus, and Giroux, 1998).

[27] Goldstein, "American Jewry," pp. 120–1; Nathan Glazer and Daniel Patrick Moynihan, *Beyond the Melting Pot: The Negroes, Puerto Ricans, Jews, Italians and Irish of New York City* (Cambridge, MA: MIT Press, 1963), pp. 143–4; Sidney Goldstein and Alice Goldstein, *Jews on the Move: Implications for Jewish Identity* (Albany: State University of New York Press, 1996), pp. 139, 149–52; Martha K. Selig, "Changes in Child Care and Their Implications," *Journal of Jewish Communal Service* 33(1) (1956): 73–86; Milton Goldman, "Characteristics of the Jewish Poor Served in a Family Agency: A Case Study," *Journal of Jewish Communal Service* 43(3) (1967): 249–52; Morris Zelditch, "Trends in the Care of the Aged," *Journal of Jewish Communal Service* 34(1) (1957): 126–40; Samuel Lerner, "The Jewish Family Agency and the Problem of Poverty among Jews," *Journal of Jewish Communal Service* 53(3) (1976): 293–300.

Consider the following notation describing social workers' interventions, contained in a report on the activities of the Federation of Jewish Welfare Agencies (subsequently renamed the Jewish Service Agency) in Memphis, Tennessee:

Except for new immigrants, most financial problems encountered after 1945 were due to an inability to live on what was available [...]. Budget planning thus became an essential aspect of family counseling. Caseworkers would very carefully go over all family expenses: food, clothing, education, recreation [...], insurance, health, rent, fuel, utilities [...]. A budget plan would then be worked out.[28]

Memphis was a relatively small community of about 9,500 Jewish residents. The larger social reality may be comprehended when we consider that analogous operations on a grander scale were applied in larger urban centers. Indeed, the larger the city, the greater was the share of communally raised funds that were apportioned to local welfare needs, rather than being forwarded to overseas assistance. City-based Jewish services included such standard items as health, family and child care, refugee aid, care for the aged and vocational services. These were funded by a combination of Jewish community fundraising in tandem with supplemental assistance from non-sectarian community chest funds.[29]

Still, there remained a hardcore of Jewish households living on lower incomes. Data from New York City in the late 1950s showed that in Williamsburg – a Brooklyn neighborhood mainly populated at the time by white residents with a 30 percent Jewish concentration, on its way to becoming a Hasidic stronghold – the median income of neighborhood residents stood at $2,630. At that time, the median household income for the US as a whole was $4,800. Not far away, in Bedford-Stuyvesant – in the throes of becoming a notorious poverty-stricken ghetto, where African American residents comprised two-thirds of the population – the median household income was just slightly lower than in Williamsburg: $2,317.[30]

---

[28] Lawrence Charles Meyers, "Evolution of the Jewish Service Agency in Memphis, Tennessee, 1847 to 1963" (MA thesis, Memphis State University, 1965), p. 86 (in author's possession).

[29] Meyers, "Evolution of the Jewish Service Agency," pp. 83–8; S. P. Goldberg, "Jewish Communal Services: Programs and Finances," *American Jewish Year Book 1965* (New York and Philadelphia, PA: American Jewish Committee/Jewish Publication Society, 1965), pp. 230–9, 257–78.

[30] Horowitz and Kaplan, *Jewish Population of New York*, pp. 208–9, 216–7, Appendix D, Table 2; US Department of Commerce, Bureau of the Census, "Current Population Reports: Consumer Income," Series P-60, no. 26, September 9, 1957, www2.census .gov/prod2/popscan/p60-026.pdf. An income of $4,800 in 1956 was equivalent to about $30,000 in the year 2000.

In 1972, about 15 percent of the Jewish population in New York was still poor or nearly poor. Over half of these were elderly, and another third consisted of young singles, young families, and single-parent households. On the opposite coast, in Los Angeles, 18 percent of Jewish households were reported to be poor (at least half were in the over-fifty age bracket), and similar data appeared in studies on Philadelphia, Boston, Miami, Chicago, San Francisco, Baltimore, and Detroit.[31]

It was in the cities that the Jewish public's liberal self-image was subjected to the litmus test of concrete issues: the relocation of synagogues and other community installations away from inner-city neighborhoods; the integration of non-white workers in Jewish-led labor unions, now that only a fraction remained of the old Jewish working class; the setting of budgetary priorities in Jewish-sponsored philanthropic programs; and racial profiling in the peripheral urban residential areas with substantial Jewish clustering.[32]

[31] Nationally, estimates pointed to an average of 10 to 15 percent of poor people within the total Jewish population. Dorothy Rabinowitz, *The Other Jews: Portraits in Poverty* (New York: American Jewish Committee, 1972); *New York's Jewish Poor and Jewish Working Class* (New York: Prepared for the Federation of Jewish Philanthropies of New York by the Center for New York City Affairs, New School for Social Research, 1972); Chaim I. Waxman, "Bringing the Poor Back In: Jewish Poverty in Education for Jewish Communal Service," *Forum on the Jewish People, Zionism and Israel* 35 (1979): 133–43; Jack S. Cohen, "A Coordinated Response to Jewish Poverty," *Metropolitan Council on Jewish Poverty* (1973), www.bjpa.org/Publications/details.cfm?PublicationID=11674; Samuel Lerner, "The Jewish Poor: Do We Help? Should We? Can We?," *Journal of Jewish Communal Service* 62(1) (1985): 49–56.

[32] Paul Jacobs, "David Dubinsky: Why His Throne is Wobbling," *Harper's* (December 1962): 75–84; and *Is Curly Jewish?*, pp. 311–3; Arthur Hertzberg, "Changing Race Relations and Jewish Communal Service," *Journal of Jewish Communal Service* 41(4) (1965): 324–33; Jonathan Rieder, *Canarsie: The Jews and Italians of Brooklyn against Liberalism* (Cambridge, MA and London: Harvard University Press, 1985); Hillel Levine, *The Death of an American Jewish Community: A Tragedy of Good Intentions* (New York: Free Press, 1993); Peter B. Levy, *The New Left and Labor in the 1960s* (Urbana and Chicago: University of Illinois Press, 1994), pp. 20–1, 78–82; Roger Waldinger, "When the Melting Pot Boils Over: The Irish, Jews, Blacks, and Koreans of New York," in *The Bubbling Cauldron: Race, Ethnicity, and the Urban Crisis*, ed. Michael Peter Smith and Joe R. Feagin (Minneapolis: University of Minnesota Press, 1995), pp. 269–70; Nancy L. Green, "Blacks, Jews, and the 'Natural Alliance': Labor Cohabitation and the ILGWU," *Jewish Social Studies* 4 (new series)(1) (1997): 79–104; Gerald H. Gamm, *Why the Jews Left Boston and the Catholics Stayed* (Cambridge, MA and London: Harvard University Press, 1999); Lederhendler, *New York Jews*, p. 137; Wendell Pritchett, *Brownsville, Brooklyn: Blacks, Jews, and the Changing Face of the Ghetto* (Chicago, IL and London: University of Chicago Press, 2002); Michael E. Staub, *Torn at the Roots: The Crisis of Jewish Liberalism in Postwar America* (New York: Columbia University Press, 2002), pp. 76–111; *Strangers and Neighbors: Relations between Blacks and Jews in the United States*, ed. Maurianne Adams and John Bracey (Amherst: University of Massachusetts Press, 1999), pp. 495–9, 511–21, 524–63, 596–636.

Both formal and informal social organizations – not necessarily under Jewish auspices but including significant Jewish membership – were coping with physical, social, and economic instability in the major cities. There were, for instance, merchant associations in ghetto areas, old lower-middle-class commercial zones, where Jewish-owned businesses had proliferated. There were neighborhood "boys' clubs" and similar social centers for adolescents, located in residential areas once predominated by Jewish families and staffed by Jewish personnel. There were Parent-Teacher Associations (PTAs) embroiled in bitter controversies over school desegregation in middle-class neighborhoods bordering on black ghettos. Probably the most visible instance of open, rancorous tension between a predominantly Jewish civic and professional group and ghetto-bred anger was the conflict over teachers' employment rights, defended by the New York union, the United Federation of Teachers, against a community school board in Brooklyn led by militant Black Nationalists. The crisis erupted over the summer of 1968 and resulted in a three-month, citywide strike against the entire public school system.[33]

Bucking trends of white flight and suburbanization, these organizations and institutions saw themselves as holding the line against social fragmentation. Neighborhoods like Boyle Heights in Los Angeles – home to a mix of Jewish, Mexican, Japanese, and Black residents from the 1930s to the 1950s – or parts of South and East Bronx in New York City fell into economic and social decline when intervention by civil government (highway construction, in both these cases) sliced through viable communities and displaced thousands of former residents. Other external factors included layoffs in manufacturing jobs that left swaths of impoverished households in inner-city neighborhoods.[34]

[33] Vorspan and Gartner, *History of the Jews of Los Angeles*, pp. 243–4; Gerald Sorin, *The Nurturing Neighborhood: The Brownsville Boys' Club and the Jewish Community in Urban America* (New York: New York University, 1990); Jonathan Kaufman, *Broken Alliance: The Turbulent Times between Blacks and Jews in America* (New York: Simon and Schuster, 1995 [1988]), pp. 136–8, 171–93; Lederhendler, *New York Jews*, pp. 170–81; Naomi Levine and Richard Cohen, *Ocean Hill-Brownsville: Schools in Crisis* (New York: Popular Library, 1969); Diane Ravitch, *The Great School Wars: New York City 1805–1973* (New York: Basic Books, 1974), pp. 338–78; *Confrontation at Ocean Hill-Brownsville*, ed. Maurice R. Berube and Marilyn Gittell (New York and London: Praeger, 1969); *The Jewish Sixties: An American Sourcebook*, ed. Michael E. Staub (Waltham, MA and Hanover, NH: Brandeis University Press/University Press of New England, 2004), pp. 92–115; David Jay Merkowitz, "The Segregating City: Philadelphia's Jews in the Urban Crisis, 1964–1984" (PhD dissertation, University of Cincinnati, 2010).
[34] Ira Katznelson, *City Trenches: Urban Politics and the Patterning of Class in the United States* (Chicago, IL and London: University of Chicago Press, 1981), pp. 89–110; Moore,

When elderly ghetto residents fell victim to violent street crimes and small merchants' shops were robbed, vandalized, or boycotted, a ritual of mutual blame took place, with hard feelings all around. During the mid-1960s, major riots engulfed inner city areas in Philadelphia, Newark, Detroit, and Los Angeles. American Jews – as employers, merchants, property owners, municipal employees, residents, and voters – were ineluctably implicated in the nation's racial politics. An increasing proportion among them felt that not only race relations in general, but also Black-Jewish relations in particular, had become an issue in its own right.[35]

More than one Jewish commentator thought it best to remove Jewish merchants and property owners from friction-prone encounters in ghetto areas. Tenement owners ("slumlords") and other commercial interests in ghetto areas were accused of exposing the Jewish community at large to moral taint and collateral political damage. The Jewish public was urged by some vocal critics to denounce such individuals and even to bar them from synagogue leadership or other communal honors. Such fractures in their positive self-image were urgently "exposed" in a moralizing discourse about justice and social obligation.[36]

Many Jews simply left, but some would not or could not. The issue of social stratification within the urban Jewish communities retained its salience. In the early 1970s, just a few years after Philadelphia's ghetto streets exploded and burned, and when most of the city's Jewish families were generally considered to be well off and well out of reach of urban decay, the Jewish population's mixed-status character persisted. It was legible in the embittered words of some young people, students at Philadelphia's Community College, who compared their lives with their well-heeled peers:

The Jews who live in slum neighborhoods, whose parents are truck drivers, short order cooks, waitresses and longshoremen. The small store owner who busts his

To the Golden Cities, pp. 56–7; Robert A. Caro, *The Power Broker: Robert Moses and the Fall of New York* (New York: Knopf, 1974), pp. 843–94; Joel Schwartz, *The New York Approach: Robert Moses, Urban Liberals, and Redevelopment of the Inner City* (Columbus: Ohio State University Press, 1993).

[35] See Louis Harris and Bert E. Swanson, *Black–Jewish Relations in New York City* (New York: Praeger, 1970), pp. 4, 45, 80, 185–96; *Black Anti-Semitism and Jewish Racism*, ed. Nat Hentoff (New York: Schocken Books, 1970); Murray Friedman, *What Went Wrong? The Creation and Collapse of the Black–Jewish Alliance* (New York: Free Press, 1995); Ben Halpern, *Jews and Blacks: The Classic American Minorities* (New York: Herder and Herder, 1971).

[36] Judd Teller, "Negroes and Jews: A Hard Look," *Conservative Judaism* 21(1) (1966): 13–20; Weisbord and Stein, *Bittersweet Encounter*, pp. 80–4; Lederhendler, *New York Jews*, p. 184.

ass 7 days a week to send his kid to college. The Jews who go to a Community College, work, and do charity work [...]. No, we don't drive Cadillacs, nor do we have grand homes.[37]

The persistence of a relatively small but not insubstantial class of less affluent Jews seemed like a surprising relapse to earlier times when immigrant Jews, recently arrived from Eastern or Central Europe, had stood out in the public mind as examples, if not the very personifications, of urban poverty. The transient and flimsy nature of the livelihoods earned by pushcart peddlers, saloonkeepers, and small-scale sweatshop employers in the old, mass immigration period bore some comparison with their latter-day sequels: small storefront operations in seedy surroundings, second-hand dealerships, household repair services, struggling tailors' and dry cleaners' shops, gypsy taxicab services and the like. The foreign accents discernible in the speech of the elderly poor were clear reminders that not all Jewish immigrants of the previous half-century had managed to move up into the middle classes.

The differences, however, between the contemporary situation and historical analogies were also instructive. Poor Jewish immigrants at the turn of the twentieth century had often had the option of factory labor in manufacturing plants and workshops close to home in their urban ghettos. By the 1960s, America's big cities did not offer quite so many alternatives for blue-collar job-seekers or to small, independent operators. Further, the immigrant poor of yesteryear got by with family support networks, private charities, and, in time, labor union-backed health-care and housing programs. Until the Depression, those remedies had often been effective. By the 1960s, a generation after the massive government interventionism of the New Deal, federally backed welfare programs were the main instrument by which America tried to manage its social crisis. While offering a minimal safety net to households in trouble, public welfare programs and unemployment benefits fell short of ensuring adequate housing and health care, let alone a springboard to economic and occupational viability. Further, they similarly lacked the community-building, neighborly functions that older forms of social support had performed.

---

[37] "Street Jews," *Network* 3(10) (May 12, 1972), p. 4, quoted by Linda Maizels, "'Charter Members of the Fourth World': Jewish Student Identity and the 'New Antisemitism' on American Campuses, 1967–1994" (PhD dissertation, The Hebrew University of Jerusalem, 2009), pp. 86–7. On the marginality of some "Jewish" parts of north Philadelphia and Jews' roles in responding to the changes in their neighborhood, see Merkowitz, "The Segregating City," pp. 168–93.

Finally, among the Jewish poor in more recent decades there were those who lacked educational or professional credentials. For the most traditionally religious among them (men in particular), that stemmed from a conscious avoidance of career-oriented professional training in favor of religious seminaries. No generalizations are adequate to summarize any group, including these *haredi* ("ultra-Orthodox") Jews. Their communities include households with significant incomes from wages and entrepreneurship, and some of them have become well known in lucrative commercial niches such as electronics and the diamond trade. However, substantially more *haredi* families cope with economic distress than is true of other sectors of the Jewish population. Here, perhaps for the first time in American Jewish history, was a sub-class of Jewish households in which a choice was made to prefer spiritual equity at the expense of material prosperity. For the first time, as well, dependency in some form was considered a legitimate way of life, bearing no stigma.

A combination of factors made such a life-style practicable: a basket of basic welfare services provided by both government and private social agencies; a thick, intra-communal web of religious self-help and barter programs – a veritable second economy of free or cut-rate goods and services; a post-industrial economy that put at the disposal of such households an array of service jobs, especially for women (who often serve as the main breadwinners in this community), demanding minimal clerical or technical training; and a wider political discourse that, on the Left, enshrined cultural diversity as legitimate and, on the Right, asserted an appreciation of traditionalism. It is in this context that a handful of American cities witnessed the formation of dense neighborhoods of so-called "black-hatted" Jews.

"Extreme Jews"

About 200,000 men were members of various types of Orthodox synagogues in the mid-1960s. That number has to be tripled, at least, in order to account for other household members. Within that total, the traditionally clad sectarians constituted a comparatively small proportion, but they had attained a visible presence in New York, Baltimore, Los Angeles, Boston, and Chicago.[38] A generation later, the overall numbers of Orthodox Jewry

---

[38] Solomon Poll, "The Persistence of Tradition: Orthodoxy in America," in Rose, *The Ghetto and Beyond*, pp. 118–19, 125–36; Chaim I. Waxman, "From Institutional Decay to Primary Day: American Orthodox Jewry since World War II," *American Jewish History* 91(3–4) (2003): 405–21.

were similar. In 1990, there were still about 500,000 Jews in the United States belonging to various types of Orthodox congregations, but the sectarian *haredim* had grown disproportionally and were now estimated at around 40 percent (200,000) of the Orthodox community. Youthful age at marriage and high fertility rates gave this sector a demographic advantage and indicated a trajectory of possible further growth in the future.[39]

In their strict piety and fastidious, retro attire (reiterating the "native" Jewish costume of Poland, Ukraine, and the Carpathian region of Slovakia and Hungary), *haredim* constitute a veritable counter-culture, lodged awkwardly but firmly in the contemporary world. Committed to stringent religious dietary regulations and a regimen of highly specific prescriptions for keeping the Sabbath, *haredi* Jews tended to cluster together in dense neighborhoods to be within walking distance of their synagogues and other services catering to their religious needs. Subdivided into individual sects, they eat only what their own particular rabbis have sanctioned (including certified meat, dairy products, and baked goods); use Yiddish at home and for much of their daily communication (though liberally sprinkling their vernacular with both English and rabbinic Hebrew); read their own newspapers; encourage large families and uphold arranged marriages for their eligible children. Their staunchly traditional outlook includes an acute sense of sin, just as it embraces an equally palpable sense of the sacred. They live by a strictly gendered moral code that, in their minds, has existed since time immemorial. Their social ethic does not sanction individualism as an autonomous value, and they consider some of the values of modern society (especially related to sexuality) to be shameful, licentious or downright pathological.[40]

---

[39] Charles S. Liebman, "Orthodoxy in American Jewish Life," *American Jewish Year Book 1965* (New York and Philadelphia, PA: American Jewish Committee/Jewish Publication Society of America, 1965), pp. 23–5, 30–6, 67–85, 93–7; Samuel C. Heilman, "Orthodox Jews, the City and the Suburb," in *People of the City: Jews and the Urban Challenge. Studies in Contemporary Jewry*, vol. XV, ed. Ezra Mendelsohn (New York: Oxford University Press, 1999), pp. 19–34; Waxman, "From Institutional Decay to Primary Day." At the most recent count (2011), the ultra-Orthodox concentration in Greater New York's eight counties (Westchester, Nassau, Suffolk, and the five city boroughs) gave them a 22 percent share of the entire Jewish population of the city – outnumbering the non-sectarian Orthodox two-to-one. See "New York Jewish Population Grows to 1.5M: Study," http://forward.com/articles/157654/nyjewishpopulation-grows-to-m-study/.

[40] Poll, "Persistence of Tradition," pp. 136–45; Samuel Heilman, *Defenders of the Faith: Inside Ultra-Orthodox Jewry* (New York: Schocken Books, 1992); Egon Mayer, *From Suburb to Shtetl: The Jews of Boro Park* (Philadelphia, PA: Temple University Press, 1979); Jerome R. Mintz, *Hasidic People: A Place in the New World* (Cambridge, MA and London: Harvard University Press, 1992); Sarna, *American Judaism*, pp. 296–304.

While much of the rest of the contemporary Jewish community immersed itself in moral wrangling over racism, poverty, urban politics, and business ethics, these "extreme Jews" (as the celebrated Yiddish author and Nobel laureate, Isaac Bashevis Singer [1902–91], once called them) demonstrated a blithe unconcern with others. Indeed, they are fairly insulated from intimate contact even with other Jews. The one notable exception are the outreach programs of the Chabad (Lubavitcher) Hasidic community, which missionizes energetically within the wider Jewish population, taking their inspiration from their late leader, "the Rebbe," Menahem Mendel Schneerson (1902–94).[41]

Aside from viewing the liberal forms of American Judaism as heretical, many *haredim* also dissent from American Jews' pro-Zionist consensus, because they look askance at the idea of a secular Jewish state governed by man-made laws and civil courts. (A hardcore of militant anti-Zionists among them is even more vociferous in their fundamentalist opposition to Israel. They have sent representatives as far as Teheran to make their feelings known to leaders of the Islamic Republic.)[42]

The particularistic worldview cultivated in *haredi* communities has not sat very well with the mainstream of American Jewry. In the non-Orthodox denominational camp (representing the vast majority of American Judaism), among progressive rabbis, student radicals, and rank-and-file members concerned with social issues, it became almost second nature, especially from the late 1960s, to refer to "repairing the world" (in Hebrew: *tikkun 'olam*) as a sacred duty of social conscience imposed by Judaism on its adherents. By this they meant social action on behalf of non-Jews in distress. Even within the rabbinical establishment in the mainline, non-sectarian, Orthodox community, voices were being raised in the 1960s on behalf of civil rights for Black people and the welfare of working men and women.[43]

Yet, for *haredim*, the "world" that needed repair the most was their own. Blasted nearly to non-existence by the Holocaust, their entire way of life could be considered an endangered cultural species. They have been bent on reconstituting as far as possible the sort of traditionalist Jewish milieu that once proliferated throughout Eastern Europe. In the midst of American society, they perceive themselves to be alone in striving

[41] Liebman, "Orthodoxy," pp. 67–85; Lederhendler, *New York Jews*, pp. 75, 80–5; Isaac Bashevis Singer, "The Extreme Jews," *Harper's* (April 1967): 56–62.
[42] www.washingtonpost.com/wpdyn/content/article/2006/12/13/AR2006121130229.html.
[43] Liebman, "Orthodoxy," p. 44; Marc Lee Raphael, *Judaism in America* (New York: Columbia University Press, 2003), p. 92.

to attain a state of holiness, and cannot fathom the pride in Jewish secular achievements, Jewish social conscience, and Jewish religious identity that other American Jews have cultivated – except as props required by those who live without Torah.

Moral Imperatives and the Smallness of Humanity

As new challenges mounted in an era that had promised tranquility and prosperity but delivered these only selectively, if at all, a renewed intellectual discourse emerged that dealt with the limitations of progress and the perils of the unaided moral imagination. Inevitably, these points drew particular responses from Jewish thinkers and commentators.

Louis Finkelstein (1895–1991), a Cincinnati native who headed the Jewish Theological Seminary, headquarters for the Conservative Jewish movement, wrote one of the better known mid-century descriptions of Judaism. In that essay, he described the Jewish heritage as a blend of "religion and morality":

Justice to all, irrespective of race, sect or class is the inalienable right and inescapable obligation of all. The state and organized government exist in order to further these ends. [...] Judaism seeks [...] the elimination of man-made misery and suffering, of poverty and degradation, of tyranny and slavery, of social inequality and prejudice, of ill-will and strife. [...] It champions the cause of all who work and of their right to an adequate standard of living, as prior to the rights of property.[44]

First published in 1949 and re-issued in popular editions for decades thereafter, Finkelstein's *The Jews* painted an image of what he wished Americans to think about their Jewish neighbors. It need hardly be pointed out that this programmatic declaration was prescriptive, rather than empirically accurate.

Although his statement on social ethics echoed some key points of the mid-century American liberal program ("justice to all," "inalienable rights," the elimination of prejudice, working-class protections), careful scrutiny of Finkelstein's text reveals that he skirted some of the basic conventions of classical American liberalism. For instance, he offered no justification of the state in terms of republican values, such as self-government, the constitutional heritage, or the safeguarding of persons and property. He portrayed "organized government" as legitimate on a

---

[44] Louis Finkelstein, "The Jewish Religion: Its Beliefs and Practices," in Finkelstein, *The Jews*, vol. II, pp. 1757–8.

contingent basis only, insofar as it served the instrumental purposes of secular, social salvation.

Moreover, the concept of economic and social justice that Finkelstein defined as being "prior to the rights of property" (rather than dependent upon them), and predicated on a notion of "adequate standards of living" (not determined by free enterprise or market values) – cannot be equated with either conventional liberal capitalism or radical socialism. Nor, yet again, did the seminary leader's social vision share common ground with the kind of enlightened self-interest that motivates philanthropists (such as those who funded his institution). Rather, it derived from a kind of conservative (small "c"), religious, and communitarian worldview that was uncomfortable with capitalism, but also afforded no aid and comfort to radical politics or historical materialism.

Kindred ideas that blended liberal and conservative impulses had been floated in lay circles and clergy in the Catholic community as well as among Jewish intellectuals close to Finkelstein's milieu.[45] That mix of religious conservatism, a critique of modern nation-states, and a communitarian-liberal politics also bears comparing with the views of Protestant theologian Reinhold Niebuhr (1892–1971), Finkelstein's eminent neighbor and colleague from just across the street at the Union Theological Seminary. Indeed, the tone and substance of Finkelstein's remarks owe something to Niebuhr's philosophy. In the context of the late 1940s, rhetoric that avoided validating the political nation as the apotheosis of "the people" must be read as a firm repudiation of both fascism and communism as well as of the "imperial" American state.[46]

Despite the implied shadows underlying Finkelstein's liberalism, in the Jewish public at large Judaism was often generically associated with a uni-dimensional liberalism. Public opinion polls in the late 1940s and data on voting patterns suggested that most Jews, like many Catholics

---

[45] Eli Lederhendler, "A Jewish Third Way to American Capitalism: Isaac Rivkind and the Conservative-Communitarian Ideal," in *Chosen Capital: The Jewish Encounter with American Capitalism*, ed. Rebecca Kobrin (New Brunswick, NJ: Rutgers University Press, 2012), pp. 234–51; McGreevy, *Catholicism and American Freedom*, pp. 127–65; Dolan, *The American Catholic Experience*, pp. 334–46. See also Milton Steinberg, *Basic Judaism* (New York: Harcourt, Brace, Jovanovich, 1947), p. 174.

[46] Avihu Zakai, "The Irony of American History. Reinhold Niebuhr and the American Experience," *Revue LISA/LISA e-Journal, Media, Culture, History, World War II*, online 2008, accessed June 16, 2011 (http://lisa.revues.org/915); Martin E. Marty, *Modern American Religion, Vol. 3: Under God, Indivisible, 1941–1960* (Chicago, IL and London: University of Chicago Press, 1996), pp. 51–3, 122–4, 128; James T. Fisher, "American Religion since 1945," in *A Companion to Post-1945 America*, ed. Jean-Christophe Agnew and Roy Rosenzweig (Oxford: Blackwell, 2002), pp. 47–8, 49–50, 51.

and Baptists, were inclined to favor government-sponsored, redistributive economic justice. Unlike their Christian confreres, however, many Jews tended to embed these New Deal ideas ever deeper in their operative definition of their religious heritage. The waning of liberalism in later years among voters belonging to other religious groups was not replicated in the Jewish community. An early inkling of the continuing liberal tilt in the predominantly Jewish sections of America's cities was demonstrated by the disproportionately large minorities in those districts who voted for Henry Wallace, the presidential candidate of the third-party Progressives in 1948 (whom President Truman had tarred with the brush of pro-Communist leanings), and the warm support given by Jewish voters in 1952 to the Democratic presidential candidate, Adlai Stevenson.[47]

Indeed (quite unlike Finkelstein in this matter), a substantial number of Jews rated liberal-democratic ethics above everything else in their scale of religious values, including faith in God and ritual observance. In doing so, perhaps, they bore in mind the recent past, when bigotry and discrimination were openly directed at Jewish Americans. Jews were, by and large, less subjected to significant discrimination, but they were ready to formulate their liberal agendas in terms of others' needs.[48]

This sidelong, "horizontal" glance at the secular world as the proper sphere of religious conscience bespoke a this-worldly outlook, in which men and women were viewed as competent to change things; in which Judaism was conceived as a universal religion, albeit anchored in a community that prided itself on its particularity; and in which metaphysical ("vertical") aspects of theology and spirituality were all but effaced. The

---

[47] Lawrence H. Fuchs, "American Jews and the Presidential Vote," *American Political Science Review* 29(2) (1955): 387–93; Kenneth D. Wald, "Toward a Structural Explanation of Jewish-Catholic Political Differences in the United States," in *Jews, Catholics, and the Burden of History. Studies in Contemporary Jewry*, Volume XXI, ed. Eli Lederhendler (New York: Oxford University Press, 2005), p. 111.

[48] Stember et al., *Jews in the Mind*; Dennis H. Wrong, "The Psychology of Prejudice and the Future of Anti-Semitism in America," *European Journal of Sociology* 6(2) (1965): 311–28, reprinted as "The Rise and Decline of Anti-Semitism in America," in *The Ghetto and Beyond: Essays on Jewish Life in America*, ed. Peter I. Rose (New York: Random House, 1969), pp. 313–34; Sklare and Greenblum, *Suburban Frontier*, pp. 89–94, 321–9; Charles S. Liebman, *The Ambivalent American Jew: Politics, Religion, and Family in American Jewish Life* (Philadelphia, PA: Jewish Publication Society of America, 1973), pp. 135–59; Dinnerstein, *Antisemitism in America*, pp. 150–74; Dollinger, *Quest for Inclusion*, pp. 129–90; Stuart Svonkin, *Jews Against Prejudice: American Jews and the Fight for Civil Liberties* (New York: Columbia University Press, 1999), pp. 41–112; see also David H. Bennett, *The Party of Fear: From Nativist Movements to the New Right in American History* (Chapel Hill and London: University of North Carolina Press, 1988), pp. 282–5.

popularization of such propositions fared particularly well in the early postwar years, as exemplified by the inspirational text, *Peace of Mind*, written by a Reform rabbi, Joshua Loth Liebman (1907–48). The book sold a million copies in its first three years and by 1968 it went through forty-three printings. *Peace of Mind* was devoted to what the author called a "life-affirming" faith in human beings and to a philosophy of self-acceptance. The supportive "relatedness" function of community-based living, embedded in the Jewish tradition, was portrayed as a model for psychic health. "There is a chance here in America," Liebman wrote, "for the creation of a new idea of God; a God reflected in the brave creations of self-reliant social pioneers; a religion not based on surrender or submission, but on a new birth of confidence in life and in the God of life."[49]

In this brave, new, sinless world of optimism and self-assurance, some different voices were nonetheless raised in both secular social thought and in theology, which seemed haunted by the ghosts of the post-Holocaust, nuclear age. Without forfeiting for a moment their right or obligation to act in the world, some thinkers of this era were skeptical of mankind's mastery over the mechanisms of social and political relations. They questioned our ability to fathom the meaning of human existence – much less draw comfort from the state of the world and American society – in an age when human lives in their millions were squandered without mercy.

Not all of their ideas were completely congruent; indeed, any selection among them must appear somewhat arbitrary. Nonetheless, people such as Sidney Hook and Hannah Arendt (in political philosophy), Joseph Ber Soloveitchik and Abraham Joshua Heschel (in Jewish theology), Stanley Milgram (in social psychology), and Raul Hilberg (in Holocaust scholarship), among others – representing different semantic fields and diverse political worldviews – were participants in the development of a different kind of Jewish discourse in postwar America: a discourse that offered no "peace of mind."

Sidney Hook (1902–89) belonged to the second-generation cohort of Jewish Americans, born to immigrant parents of East European background. A pragmatist philosopher and, for a while, a devoted Marxist, he was one of a larger group of ex-radicals who, when confronted with the egregious crimes of Stalinism in the late 1930s, could

---

[49] Joshua Loth Liebman, *Peace of Mind* (New York: Simon and Schuster, 1946, 1968), esp. pp. 159–62; Heinze, *Jews and the American Soul*, pp. 195–6, 217–31; Sarna, *American Judaism*, pp. 272, 282; Fisher, "American Religion since 1945," p. 46.

find no further justification for Communism. He taught philosophy at New York University and later became a fellow at the Hoover Institution in Stanford, California, a leading right-wing think-tank. Hook was a formidable polemicist and one of the most preeminent and most militant of the Cold Warriors. Unlike some of his former comrades, who took the path of a reformed, social-democratic, anti-Communist liberalism, Hook immersed himself in a single-minded holy war against Soviet despotism and its apologists (of whom he believed there were many). He authored such works as *Marx and the Marxists: The Ambiguous Legacy* (1955), and *Determinism and Freedom in the Age of Modern Science* (1961).[50]

Stanley Milgram (1933–84), on the other hand, was a political liberal. A brilliant, unconventional social psychologist, Milgram was trained at Harvard, did research work at Yale, and taught at Harvard and at the City University of New York (CUNY) Graduate Center. He performed his famous "obedience experiments" at Yale between 1961 and 1962. In those experiments, the subjects – unaware of the true object of the study – were instructed by a "project leader" to "teach" other participants by punishing them when they gave wrong answers: they were to deliver to the unseen "pupils" what they believed were electric shocks of increasing voltage. They did so readily and in amazing numbers.

The readiness of individuals from all walks of life to obey an authority figure was not the truly innovative crux of Milgram's work; rather, it was the extreme degree to which they were willing to go. The majority of people in the study were likely to pursue their instructions to the point (so they believed) of placing another person's life at risk with lethal voltage shocks. Milgram's methods and the ominous results of his work raised a clamor of debate about research ethics, human morality, democratic values, and civil disobedience. His first results were published in 1963, coinciding closely with Hannah Arendt's published coverage of Adolf Eichmann's war crimes trial in Jerusalem.[51]

[50] Sidney Hook, *Marx and the Marxists: The Ambiguous Legacy* (Princeton, NJ: D. Van Nostrand, 1955); *Political Power and Personal Freedom: Critical Studies in Democracy, Communism, and Civil Rights* (New York: Criterion Books, 1959); *Determinism and Freedom in the Age of Modern Science* (New York: Collier Books, 1961); *The Quest for Being, and Other Studies in Naturalism and Humanism* (New York: St. Martin's Press, 1961); *Religion in a Free Society* (Lincoln: University of Nebraska Press, 1967); and *Out of Step: An Unquiet Life in the Twentieth Century* (New York: Harper and Row, 1987). See also Stephen J. Whitfield, *The Culture of the Cold War* (Baltimore, MD and London: Johns Hopkins University Press, 1991), pp. 24, 102, 179.
[51] Stanley Milgram, "Behavioral Study of Obedience," *Journal of Abnormal and Social Psychology* 67 (1963): 371–8; and *Obedience to Authority: An Experimental View*

Arendt (1906–75), whom we briefly considered earlier, came originally from Koenigsberg in what was then eastern Germany (today Kaliningrad, Russia). She escaped from occupied France to the United States in 1941, along with her mother and her husband. Trained in German philosophy, her postwar career was mainly devoted to political and social studies, in which she addressed questions of authoritarianism and individual conscience. A formidable critic and widely published essayist, she became best known for her work in modern political theory – *The Origins of Totalitarianism* (1951) – and contemporary reportage: mainly her *Eichmann in Jerusalem* (1963).[52]

In 1961, just prior to Milgram's obedience study and Arendt's *Eichmann*, Raul Hilberg (1926–2007) published his magisterial study of the genocidal machinery that made possible Nazi Germany's destruction of European Jewry.[53] Hilberg had fled Nazi Vienna with his family in April 1939 and arrived in America, via Cuba, on the day that Germany invaded Poland. After serving in the US Army during the war, he later studied at Brooklyn College and Columbia University. Hilberg based his fine-tooth-combed reconstruction of the Third Reich's extermination of the Jews on massive German documentation. It demonstrated the complexity of the process at each step of its development, as well as its implacability. Despite controversy sparked by Hilberg's nearly exclusive focus on the perpetrators (the victims remained, for Hilberg, passive objects), the book has remained a standard study of the Holocaust.

(New York: Harper and Row, 1974); Thomas Blass, *The Man Who Shocked the World: The Life and Legacy of Stanley Milgram* (New York: Basic Books, 2004), esp. pp. 62–3, 65, 99–101, 110, 123, 260–1, 264, 268–70, 283; Kirsten Fermaglich, *American Dreams and Nazi Nightmares: Early Holocaust Consciousness and Liberal America* (Hanover, NH and Waltham, MA: Brandeis University Press and University Press of New England, 2006), pp. 83–123.

[52] Arendt, *The Origins of Totalitarianism* and *Eichmann in Jerusalem*. See also Stephen J. Whitfield, *Into the Dark: Hannah Arendt and Totalitarianism* (Philadelphia, PA: Temple University Press, 1980); Elisabeth Young-Bruehl, *Hannah Arendt: For Love of the World* (New Haven, CT and London: Yale University Press, 1982); Dagmar Barnouw, *Visible Spaces: Hannah Arendt and the German-Jewish Experience* (Baltimore, MD and London: Johns Hopkins University Press, 1990); Steven E. Aschheim, *Scholem, Arendt, Klemperer: Intimate Chronicles in Turbulent Times* (Bloomington: Indiana University Press and Hebrew Union College/Jewish Institute of Religion, 2001); Richard Wolin, *Heidegger's Children: Hannah Arendt, Karl Löwith, Hans Jonas, and Herbert Marcuse* (Princeton, NJ: Princeton University Press, 2001); Patricia Owens, *Between War and Politics: International Relations and the Thought of Hannah Arendt* (Oxford: Oxford University Press, 2007).

[53] Raul Hilberg, *The Destruction of the European Jews* (Chicago, IL: Quadrangle Books, 1961, 1967).

In some respects, Hilberg, Arendt, and Milgram – each in his or her distinct discipline and style – reinforced one another's work. All three were fixated upon the menace posed by impersonal, amoral, bureaucratic systems and the damage caused by ready compliance. Hilberg and Arendt controversially extended their theory of political compliance in the Third Reich to include the behavior of the victims as well. As for Milgram, his work was strongly informed by a sense of Germany's historical guilt, but was most convincing in its argument that human behavior *anywhere* could swing wildly beyond normative moral restraints, given the proper circumstances.

What these postwar secular intellectuals had in common was their ability to look over the precipice of political complacency and to draw for the American (and Jewish) public an agitated sketch of what might lie in store for modern society. What they also shared was a quality of mind: power, originality, and special urgency in their convictions about the human condition.

The two religious scholars in our small sample may also be said to have looked into an abyss, and their gaze was informed by the same historical traumas; but theirs was a different gaze. The abyss that they looked into was that of radical, individualist, anomie. Their contributions to postwar discourse lay not just in the contemplative realm alone, however, but also in their follow-through; for both drew certain conclusions based in the real, empirical, political world.

Joseph Ber Soloveitchik, Russian-born scion of a distinguished line of rabbinical scholars, immigrated to the United States with his wife, Tonya, in 1932 after completing a doctorate in philosophy in Berlin. Rabbi Soloveitchik served as a communal leader and educator in Boston, where he and his wife founded the co-educational Maimonides school. He was also for many years head of the yeshiva at RIETS, the Orthodox rabbinical seminary at New York's Yeshiva University. Soloveitchik published very sparsely, but compilations of his work are considered essential reading.

In the quest for self-knowledge, he argued, it was necessary to acquire a form of knowing that went beyond the self. Only an "objective" point of view, outside the self (*halakhah* – "the way," often translated as "Jewish law"), could enable the individual to withstand moral relativism and spiritual solipsism. Soloveitchik also refused to be satisfied with a religious life of surface compliance and conformity. Religiosity had, rather, to be transformative. In his system, religious integrity lay in acknowledging the soul's isolation in this world, but acting decisively against it by actively choosing a life-long discipline and discipleship, and by rooting that choice in real, corporeal behavior. By a semantic stretch, we might call this an "obedience experiment" of a different sort, except that this one was wholly inner-directed. Soloveitchik's theological dilemmas were related at their root to the same background and context that we saw in Milgram's project: it was all about making choices in a morally perilous world:

Judaism declares that man stands at the crossroads [...]. Before him there is an awesome alternative – the image of God or the beast of prey, the crown of creation or the bogey of existence [...], the image of the man of God or the profile of Nietzsche's "superman" – and it is up to man to decide and choose.[54]

Soloveitchik's reference (in a text originally written in the 1940s) to the "superman" (*Übermensch*) and to the German philosopher most revered among the Nazi leadership could not have been clearer. The demons of the age were Soloveitchik's witnesses, as it were, to the theological case he was arguing.

The quest to transcend spiritual anomie and moral isolation was central, as well, in the teachings of Abraham Joshua Heschel (1907–72). Born into the illustrious Hasidic dynasty of Apt (Opatów, Poland), Heschel had gone, like Soloveitchik, to study at the university in Berlin. He was deported in 1938 by the Nazi regime and the next year was able, via London, to reach sanctuary in the United States. He taught briefly at Hebrew Union College in Cincinnati, and in 1945 he moved to New York's Jewish Theological Seminary. Unlike Soloveitchik, however, he did not teach rabbinics (Talmudic jurisprudence). His role at JTS was more akin to that of a resident philosopher.[55]

Both men were religious gurus, but also modern academic scholars, schooled in the North European vein of modern religious philosophy. Soloveitchik took his point of departure from the role of self-discipline as a means for realizing the ideal in concrete acts; whereas Heschel felt that to achieve illumination, a person must fling open an inner door,

---

[54] Joseph B. Soloveitchik, *Halakhic Man*, trans. Lawrence Kaplan (Philadelphia, PA: Jewish Publication Society of America, 1983, originally published in Hebrew as *Ish hahalakhah*, 1944), p. 109.

[55] Abraham Joshua Heschel, *Man is Not Alone: A Philosophy of Religion* (Philadelphia, PA: Jewish Publication Society of America, 1951); *The Prophets* (Philadelphia, PA: Jewish Publication Society of America, revised ed., 1962); *God in Search of Man: A Philosophy of Judaism* (New York: Farrar, Straus and Giroux, 1978 [1955]); and *The Earth is the Lord's: The Inner World of the Jew in Eastern Europe* (Woodstock, VT: Jewish Lights, 1995 [1949]); Raphael, *Judaism in America*, pp. 137–40.

resisting the inbred inhibitions of secular thinking. In that way, he argued, the anomie of abandonment in the world – the manifest smallness of humanity – could become the counterintuitive portal for a deeper appreciation and "wonder" at existence itself. Thought of in this way, the life of the spirit was not so much about integrity as it was about cultivating an alert hopefulness.

Of the two, Heschel was the better known for taking ethical-political stands outside the classroom. He was active in interfaith dialogues with the Vatican, marched in civil rights demonstrations alongside Martin Luther King, Jr., opposed the Vietnam War, and stirred up American Jewish activism on behalf of Soviet Jewry in the 1960s. Thus, the transcendental ("vertical") explorations of his faith were matched by the "horizontal" element of his ethical approach to the realm of politics.[56]

In that connection, it is telling that both Soloveitchik and Heschel viewed Israel's existence in the same light. Israel, for them, was situated at the intersection of the vertical and the horizontal axes. They argued that Israel's existence and survival, in the wake of the Holocaust, indicated that "despair is not man's last word [and] hiddenness is not God's last act," as Heschel put it. In Christian terms, Heschel was describing Israel as a moment of grace – indeed, the crucial moment of grace for Judaism in modern times.[57]

In one form or other, all of these postwar thinkers were concerned with the problem of secular evil and what could be done about it. Informing everything they wrote about Nazism and Communism, bureaucracy and authority, moral autonomy and moral passivity was a conviction about the sacred – but vulnerable – aspects of personhood.

Postwar Jewish thought – in the widest sense – might be compared, then, to a wobbly compass needle, caught between two poles: the one, a therapeutic liberal ethic of tolerance, whose counterpart was a liberal politics of social reform; and the other, a sober sensitivity to the potential – indeed, the likelihood – of recurring suffering and injustice. The liberal-therapeutic mode posited predictable outcomes for positive actions. The less ebullient "risk" paradigm placed far less emphasis on

---

[56] Abraham Joshua Heschel, *The Insecurity of Freedom* (New York: Noonday, 1967), p. 273; Sarna, *American Judaism*, p. 311; Lederhendler, *New York Jews*, pp. 187–8; Staub, *Torn at the Roots*, pp. 60–1, 111.

[57] Yosef Dov (Ber) Soloveitchik, *Kol dodi dofek* (Jerusalem: Ministry of Defense, 1976); Abraham Joshua Heschel, *Israel, An Echo of Eternity* (New York: Farrar, Straus and Giroux, 1967), pp. 112–13, 115, 134–5, 137, 145.

our ability as human beings to prevail, but much more on the worthiness of our persistence, even in the face of our seeming lack of consequence.

Although Jews in the public sphere were in some ways very close to mainstream American ideas, we can discern some daylight between some of their discourse and the more important strains in the national arena. What Jewish discussants on issues of conscience and society shared with broad currents in American postwar thought could be summarized as a common concern with freedom and democracy. Indeed, over the course of the 1960s this concern was acted upon by droves of young Jews who joined the effort to ensure equal civil rights for all Americans. But there was no perfect match between what Jews worried and wrote about and what their Christian peers had to say. Repeatedly, the Jewish compass swayed slightly off the axis drawn in American culture at large, exposing fault-lines of difference and particularity.

From Denominational Diversity toward a New Folk Religion?

The institutionalization of a three-pronged denominational diversity in American Judaism – Reform, Conservative, and Orthodox – as we have seen, was largely accomplished by the interwar years. That pattern substantially persisted during the 1950s and accompanied the proliferation of new synagogues in the postwar period of suburbanization (the Conservatives outstripping the others, initially). Yet, by the end of the "baby boom" years, only 45 percent of Jewish heads of household were members of a synagogue at any given time. It therefore might be best to refer to American Judaism as being "semi-denominational." This less structured feature of American Jewry's religious culture became the norm over time and leads us to the notion that a "folk Judaism" was once again becoming a way of life for many people. Little more than a generation ago, that seemed less obvious, but a closer look would reveal how this came to be.

The non-Orthodox practices – Reform and Conservative – had proved particularly adept at organizational techniques that corralled large constituencies. People signed up as members – most often, families with children – only a minority of whom actively participated in congregational life. Local congregations, though independent of one another, functioned substantially as "franchises" of their national networks, so that membership in a single congregation granted access to nationally sponsored men's, women's, and youth associations, and summer camps. Each denomination maintained a national lay league of synagogue members, a professional rabbinical association, a rabbinical seminary, several publications and other media outlets, women's and men's clubs, and councils or commissions to recommend practical religious guidelines for observing the rites of Judaism. In contrast, the Orthodox, as before, retained a more fractious and independent spirit that resisted unifying all congregations under a single roof organization. However, their dwindling numbers (up until a turnaround took place after the 1960s) offered little challenge to the regnant pattern.[58]

The tripartite denominational division seemed so "enshrined" that even the "un-synagogued," when asked to define themselves religiously, readily named a denominational affinity.[59] The popular three-way split remained largely in place through the end of the 1980s. Some 85 percent of Jewish adults identified at that time with one of the three major denominational rubrics; 12.4 percent recorded their preference as "just Jewish," "other," or claimed to be non-participating. Over half of those who were "just Jewish" (i.e. without specific denominational affiliation) said that they had been raised in denominationally identified families. This drift away from organized religion indicated that denominational Judaism was showing some erosion. Only a small minority (3 percent) had gone the other way, from having been raised "just Jewish" (or "other Jewish") to claiming a particular denominational identification in adult life.[60]

An incipient crumbling around the edges of denominationalism could be discerned, too, in the emergence of a small, fourth Jewish

[58] Wertheimer, *A People Divided*, pp. 3–17; Sarna, *American Judaism*, pp. 274–9, 282–93; Raphael, *Judaism in America*, pp. 75–96.

[59] Eighty-two percent of survey responders in 1970 volunteered a denominational self-definition. Only 13 percent called themselves "just Jewish" or "other Jewish," and 1.5 percent averred that they were "atheist or agnostic." Fred Massarik, *Jewish Identity: Facts for Planning* (New York: Council of Jewish Federations, 1974), pp. 2–3, at www.jewishdatabank.org/Archive/ NJPS1971-Jewish_Identity.pdf; Sidney Goldstein and Calvin Goldscheider, *Jewish Americans: Three Generations in a Jewish Community* (Englewood Cliffs, NJ: Prentice Hall, 1968), pp. 171–205.

[60] Barry A. Kosmin, Sidney Goldstein, et al., *Highlights of the CJF 1990 National Jewish Population Survey* (New York: Council of Jewish Federations in Association with the Mandell Berman Institute-North American Jewish Data Bank, The Graduate School and University Center, CUNY, 1991), pp. 32–37. Adults who had converted to Judaism were very slightly more apt than born-Jews to identify with one of the three main Jewish denominations – a characteristic that probably reflected their recent or current involvement with a particular rabbi and synagogue as part of their conversion process – and they particularly leaned toward Reform Judaism.

denomination: Reconstructionism, which claimed the allegiance of
1.4 percent of adult Jews (and 2.6 percent of adult synagogue members)
by 1990. Mainly composed of Jews from Conservative or non-religious
backgrounds, the inspiration for this type of congregation, which first
began to emerge in the 1920s and 1930s, was Mordecai M. Kaplan, long
regarded as one of American Jewry's major interpreters, along with a coterie of like-minded religious intellectuals. Kaplan espoused a naturalistic
religious worldview: that is, he saw religion (any religion) as a social and
cultural product that led its adherents toward higher values, rather than
as a divinely revealed system of eternal, cosmic truths, handed down by a
personalized, supernatural God. Kaplan proposed to "reconstruct" a coherent Jewish way of life that would be focused around institutions like
the synagogue and the community center; would identify broadly with
all forms of Jewish culture and aesthetic endeavor; would stress the unity
of Jews all over the world; and would affirm central Jewish symbols and
customs ("sancta") while freely revising their interpretation. Seeking to
transcend the theological constraints of Orthodoxy, Kaplan was equally
opposed to a universalistic ethical humanism shorn of communal intimacy or ritual content.[61]

Centered initially around one synagogue in New York (the "Society
for the Advancement of Judaism"), Reconstructionism was propagated
in small group settings until it was organized in a national association in
the early 1960s. The Reconstructionist Rabbinical College, established
to institutionalize the new denomination, was founded in Philadelphia
in 1968 by Ira Eisenstein (1906–2001), Kaplan's son-in-law and intimate
collaborator. From about ten affiliated congregations across the United
States in 1968, Reconstructionism grew to include about one hundred
around the turn of the twenty-first century; but its delayed establishment,
combined with its relatively highbrow religious philosophy, militated
against its becoming a large, popular movement.

Other breakaways in this period included an inchoate collection of
post- or trans-denominational Jewish Renewal groups that emerged under

---

[61] Charles S. Liebman, "Reconstructionism in American Jewish Life," *American Jewish Year
Book*, vol. LXXI (New York and Philadelphia, PA: American Jewish Committee and
Jewish Publication Society of America, 1970), pp. 3–99; Wertheimer, *A People Divided*,
pp. 160–9; *The American Judaism of Mordecai M. Kaplan*, ed. Emanuel S. Goldsmith,
Mel Scult, and Robert M. Seltzer (New York: New York University Press, 1990); Mel
Scult, *Judaism Faces the Twentieth Century: A Biography of Mordecai M. Kaplan*
(Detroit, MI: Wayne State University Press, 1993); Raphael, *Judaism in America*, pp. 94–
6; Sarna, *American Judaism*, pp. 244–7.

the influence of American youth culture in the 1960s, New Age spirituality, Eastern religions, and heightened religious individualism. At the same time, some Jews referring to their religion as "Secular Humanistic Judaism" organized themselves under the tutelage of a Reform rabbi, Sherwin T. Wine (1928–2007), who founded a Society by that name in 1969. A further split in the denominational structure occurred in 1990 with the departure of a select group of more traditionalist rabbis and their congregants from the Conservatives' ranks. Their Union for Traditional Judaism dissented from the Conservative Seminary's latter-day policies, such as the decision (in 1983) to enroll women for rabbinical ordination.[62]

Arthur Green (b. 1941), a Newark-born rabbi, exemplified some of this religious drift. Ordained at the Conservative JTS, Green became in 1968 a founder of Havurat Shalom (Peace Fellowship) in Somerville, Massachusetts, one of the first of the renewal-style, gender-egalitarian, non-denominational Jewish "fellowships." Green's subsequent career included a stint as dean of the Reconstructionist Rabbinical College, before he moved on yet again to establish a post-denominational rabbinical ordination program at Boston's Hebrew College.

Non-structured learning-and-ritual fellowships like Havurat Shalom, in which a formal leadership structure (lay or otherwise) was absent, were typically made up of college students and young adults. Such independent groups began to sprout across the United States in the 1970s, often forming alternative prayer groups alongside established synagogues. Fostered by people – often the alumni of Conservative-sponsored youth groups and summer camps – who were dissatisfied with the spiritual fare offered in their parents' synagogues, *havurot* offered members a young, trendy Judaism along with a sense of intimate interpersonal bonding. They became known for experimenting with meditation, song, and celebration (and, sometimes, illegal substances). They embraced an ideology of "self-empowerment" (in contrast with the passive mode of most conventional congregational behavior in modern synagogues).

By the turn of the twenty-first century, it was increasingly likely for respondents in public opinion surveys to identify themselves as "just

---

[62] Wine, "Humanistic Judaism"; Yaakov Ariel, "Hasidism in the Age of Aquarius: The House of Love and Prayer in San Francisco, 1967–1977," *Religion and American Culture: A Journal of Interpretation* 13(2) (2003): 139–65; Wertheimer, *A People Divided*, pp. 67–72, 77–80; Sarna, *American Judaism*, pp. 345–55; Dana Evan Kaplan, "Judaism, Sectarian Movements," in *Encyclopedia of Religion in America*, ed. Charles H. Lippy and Peter W. Williams (Washington, DC: CQ Press, 2010), vol. II, pp. 1151–2.

Jews," rather than select a particular denominational affiliation, or for adults born and raised as Jews to claim no "current religion" at all (that is, no congregational affiliation and no affinity for articulated theological beliefs).[63]

Home, Family, and Religion

Considering the importance attached to inter-generational transmission in Judaism, the relationship between religious institutions and the home could be seen as necessary and complementary. Rabbis and congregants, women in particular, often spoke of the sacredness of the home and strove to upgrade religious sentiments born of close family relations. Yet, as younger adults continued to rate themselves as more religiously lax than their elders, this tended to undercut the primacy of the home as an authentic site of religious meaning.[64]

Religious professionals, therefore, sought to create in and around the synagogue a sense of religious community as a counterfoil to religious non-observance at home. "Surrogacy" of this sort seemed attractive to Jews who saw the institutional setting as the proper venue to express their religion (in keeping with other Americans' notion of "church"). In contrast to more traditional patterns of Jewish life, in which a Jew would come to the synagogue to continue doing what one also did at home (e.g. pray, study, wear religiously appropriate headgear and other pre-scribed garments), Jews using the "surrogate" model often went to the synagogue to perform acts that they would hardly ever perform at home on their own. Similarly, one could bring one's children to the synagogue (or more precisely, its pre-school or school-age programs) to be exposed to what they were not exposed to at home. Home-based religious cere-mony could, in this fashion, be reduced to a handful of ceremonial prac-tices, conducted once a year, for the most part. These few observances

---

[63] *National Jewish Population Survey 2000–1: Conservative Jews* (New York: United Jewish Communities, 2004, available at www.bjpa.org/Publications), pp. 5, 11; Barry A. Kosmin, Egon Mayer, and Ariela Keysar, *American Jewish Identity Survey 2001* (New York: The Graduate Center of the City University of New York, 2001), esp. pp. 12, 21–2, 43; and *American Religious Identification Survey* (New York: The Graduate Center of the City University of New York, 2001); Sarna, *American Judaism*, p. 367.

[64] Marshall Sklare, *Observing America's Jews* (Hanover, NH and London: University Press of New England/Brandeis University Press, 1993), pp. 38–43; Kramer and Leventman, *Children of the Gilded Ghetto*, p. 151; Goldstein and Goldscheider, *Jewish Americans*, pp. 177–205; Waxman, *America's Jews in Transition*, p. 81. See also Gerhard Lenski, *The Religious Factor* (Garden City, NY: Doubleday, 1963).

were favored – especially if they were child-oriented – and even became reinforced over time.[65]

Some of the post-1960s experimentation we have referred to arose in opposition to precisely this style of practice, which young dissidents saw as catering to indifference, perpetuating dull and formalized repetition, and over-reliance on clergy (rabbis and cantors) to provide Judaic essentials. The oppositional fringe Judaism this inspired has not, however, displaced the synagogue-surrogacy mode. In moving toward an amalgam of privatized and congregational religiosity, American Jews have gradually evolved a few discernible approaches that cut across denominational subdivisions. To simplify an admittedly complex phenomenon, I will distinguish between *residual, recuperative,* and *embedded* types of ethno-religious engagement.

"Residual" religiosity entails a pro forma adherence to certain religious behaviors, without much reflection or justification. This may apply, in the first place, to a few practices that are considered very widespread, such as male infant circumcision (a procedure that became a norm in American pediatrics in the twentieth century and, thus, nearly ceased to mark Jews out as a distinct religious group). At the other end of the life cycle, Jews also typically continued to choose Jewish cemeteries for their burial rites.

Residualism applies, as well, to household practices that may be traditional in origin but have lost much of their original meaning. Affixing a *mezuzah* (a small cylinder containing scrolled-up parchments inscribed with passages from the Torah) to the doorframe of one's home, for instance, has acquired the character of an ethnic or an aesthetic, decorative gesture for many people. Minimal – though not merely perfunctory – rites also might include reciting the filial prayer of commemoration in honor of one's deceased parents, which many residualists make an effort to do on Yom Kippur.

Residual religiosity may occur, perhaps surprisingly, not just among religious minimalists, but also among some Jews who maintain an intensive

---

[65] Steven M. Cohen and Arnold M. Eisen, *The Jew Within: Self, Family, and Community in America* (Bloomington and Indianapolis: Indiana University Press, 2000), pp. 73–99; Kosmin and Lachman, *One Nation Under God,* pp. 46–7; Sklare, *Observing America's Jews,* pp. 37–54; see also Charles S. Liebman, "Ritual, Ceremony and the Reconstruction of Judaism in the United States," in *Art and Its Uses: The Visual Image and Modern Jewish Society. Studies in Contemporary Jewry,* vol. VI, ed. Ezra Mendelsohn (Oxford: Oxford University Press, 1990), pp. 275–82; Bernard Susser and Charles S. Liebman, *Choosing Survival: Strategies for a Jewish Future* (New York and Oxford: Oxford University Press, 1999), pp. 68–89.

regimen of religious practice. With such Jews, it is the formal character of religious practice that appears to count most, rather than their theological rationale. Hillel Halkin (b. 1939), the American-born Israeli author, translator, and critic, used the term "orthoprax" in this regard, in reference to his father, Abraham S. Halkin (1904–90), who was an eminent Judaic scholar. Practicing religious precepts, but acknowledging no ultimate "truth" or belief system behind them, the senior Halkin nonetheless took religious culture quite seriously and thought it ought to be maintained.[66]

Residualist affiliation and practice were widespread in the Orthodox orbit in the early to middle decades of the twentieth century. The 1960s seem to have been a watershed period. Since then, there has emerged a significant countervailing trend, particularly noticeable in the Orthodox public, and especially among its younger members. The point seems to be a "recuperation" of traditionalist ideas and behavior. This has entailed greater efforts to infuse ritual behavior with conscious belief, a heightened and consistent attention to studying sacred texts, and the assumption of a wider range of personal religious commitments.[67]

If the latter-day momentum toward a more "orthodox" Orthodoxy may be labeled "recuperative," this phenomenon is also discernible well beyond the confines of the Orthodox community. In another anecdotal testimony about a father, anthropologist Harvey E. Goldberg related that his father, an attorney, had had minimal connection to or curiosity about Judaic tradition until, in mid-life, he rediscovered a keen interest in his heritage. His early retirement in the mid-1960s was followed by his enrollment for studies at the JTS Rabbinical School.[68]

[66] Hillel Halkin, *Letters to an American Jewish Friend: A Zionist's Polemic* (Philadelphia, PA: Jewish Publication Society, 1977), pp. 149–50.
[67] Howard W. Polsky, "A Study of Orthodoxy in Milwaukee: Social Characteristics, Beliefs, and Observances," in Sklare, *The Jews*, pp. 325–35, 651 n. 3; Gurock, *Orthodox Jews in America*, pp. 199–209; and *American Jewish Orthodoxy*, pp. 299–312; Wertheimer, *A People Divided*, pp. 36, 43–65; see also Theodore I. Lenn et al., *Rabbi and Synagogue in Reform Judaism* (New York: Union of American Hebrew Congregations, 1972), p. 396; Marshall Sklare, *Conservative Judaism: An American Religious Movement* (New York: Schocken Books, 1972), pp. 261–76. On religious standards among nominally Orthodox men and women in the New York community in the 1980s, see Samuel C. Heilman and Steven M. Cohen, *Cosmopolitans and Parochials: Modern Orthodox Jews in America* (Chicago, IL and London: University of Chicago Press, 1989).
[68] Harvey E. Goldberg, "A Tradition of Invention: Family and Educational Institutions among Contemporary Traditionalizing Jews," in *National Variations in Jewish Identity: Implications for Jewish Education*, ed. Steven M. Cohen and Gabriel Horenczyk (Albany, NY: SUNY Press, 1999), pp. 86–9.

One of the more engaging personal stories about recuperative Judaism stems from someone born and raised outside the Jewish fold entirely. The African American social activist, Julius Lester (b. 1939), son of a Protestant minister, related in his memoirs how he came to revert to the religion of his maternal great-grandfather – an itinerant peddler from Germany with the surname of Altschul, who married a former slave, Maggie Carson. Lester eventually became a professor of Jewish Studies at the University of Massachusetts as well as an active member of his local Conservative synagogue.[69]

Along with such individual cases, in recent decades there have been several instances of group-based reclamations of Judaic traditions. Here we might cite the embrace of religious ritual by some feminist activists, who have reshaped Jewish customs in a gender-egalitarian spirit. Much of the Jewish feminist ferment is geared toward synagogue performance, an area in which women of past generations tended to be passive onlookers more than direct participants. By putting women front and center in a public arena, feminist Jews thus make a stronger point about gender egalitarianism; far less feminist attention has been directed to private, home-based Judaism.[70]

One by-product of that development has been the introduction in many communities of a new ceremony, known as "adult bat-mitzvah." The recuperative twist involved in adapting this puberty-related rite of passage for use among adults relates to the notion that these women (and some men) in mid-life or older may now celebrate their religious "coming of age" to compensate for what they missed as adolescents. In this innovative rite, they wish to stress their newfound competence in reading Hebrew prayers, or in lending a more active hand in religious ceremonies.[71]

---

[69] Julius Lester, *Lovesong: Becoming a Jew* (New York: Henry Holt and Co., 1988).

[70] Blu Greenberg, *On Women and Judaism: A View from Tradition* (Philadelphia, PA: Jewish Publication Society of America, 1981); Ellen Umansky, "Females, Feminists and Feminism: A Review of Recent Literature on Jewish Feminism and a Creation of a Feminist Judaism," *Feminist Studies* 14 (Summer 1988): 349–65; Fishman, *A Breath of Life*, chapters 6–7; Rachel Adler, *Engendering Judaism* (Philadelphia, PA: Jewish Publication Society of America, 1998); Pamela S. Nadell, *Women Who Would Be Rabbis* (Boston, MA: Beacon Press, 1990); and "A Bright New Constellation: Feminism and American Judaism," in *The Columbia History of Jews and Judaism in America*, ed. Marc Lee Raphael (New York: Columbia University Press, 2013), pp. 385–405.

[71] Stuart Schoenfeld, "Integration into the Group and Sacred Uniqueness: An Analysis of Adult Bat Mitzvah," in *Persistence and Flexibility: Anthropological Perspectives on the American Jewish Experience*, ed. Walter Zenner (Albany, NY: SUNY Press, 1988), pp. 117–35; and "Ritual and Role Transition: Adult Bat Mitzvah as a Successful Rite

Interestingly, a nearly opposite reaction to second-wave feminism among some other Jewish women has been to back away entirely from gender egalitarianism and other aspects of secular, post-modern culture. Seeking to achieve their own version of spiritual recuperation, they have drawn closer to sectarian Orthodox (haredi) communities, where, in a highly gender-separated culture, they adhere strictly to the exclusively distinct roles and identities marked out for men and women, respectively.[72]

Some attention has also been garnered by the emergence from obscurity of "closet" Jews, descended from colonial-era New Christians and Crypto-Jews who had settled in New Spain, South America, and the Caribbean. Families whose private folklore preserved special customs, of which they never spoke to their neighbors, began to reveal to their children and to researchers doing ethnographic fieldwork in the American Southwest, that these folkways were connected to their ancestors' Iberian Jewish heritage.[73]

Finally, beginning around 1967, a small but cumulatively significant stream of American Jews has migrated to Israel. As of 1980, an estimated 48,000 US-born persons, most of them Jews, had registered with the State Department as living in Israel (a conservative estimate, since not all are

of Passage," in Wertheimer, *The Uses of Tradition*, pp. 349–76; Shulamit S. Magnus, "Reinventing Miriam's Well: Feminist Jewish Ceremonials," in Wertheimer, *The Uses of Tradition*, pp. 331–47; Fishman, *Breath of Life*, pp. 130–1; Lisa D. Grant, "Finding Her Right Place in the Synagogue: The Rite of Adult Bat Mitzvah," in Prell, *Women Remaking American Judaism*, pp. 279–301; and "Restorying Jewish Lives Post Adult Bat Mitzvah," *Journal of Jewish Education* 69(2) (2003): 34–51; Keren S. Vergnon, "An Exploration of Middle-Aged and Older Women's Experiences of Bat-Mitzvah within the Framework of Erikson's Theory of Human Development" (PhD dissertation, University of South Florida, 2006).

[72] Lynn Davidman, *Tradition in a Rootless World. Women Turn to Orthodox Judaism* (Berkeley: University of California Press, 1991); Debra R. Kaufman, "Engendering Orthodoxy: Newly Orthodox Women and Hasidism," in *New World Hasidim: Ethnographic Studies of Hasidic Jews in America*, ed. Janet S. Belcove-Shalin (Albany, NY: SUNY Press, 1995), pp. 135–60.

[73] Henry J. Tobias, *A History of the Jews in New Mexico* (Albuquerque: University of New Mexico Press, 1990), pp. 194–6; Janet Liebman Jacobs, *Hidden Heritage: The Legacy of the Crypto-Jews* (Berkeley: University of California Press, 2002); Michael Caroll, "The Debate Over a Crypto-Jewish Presence in New Mexico: The Role of Ethnographic Allegory and Orientalism," *Sociology of Religion* 54 (2002): 67–78; Stanley Hordes, *To the End of the Earth: A History of the Crypto-Jews of New Mexico* (New York: Columbia University Press, 2005); Cary Herz, *New Mexico's Crypto-Jews: Image and Memory*, photographs by Cary Herz, intro. by Ori Z. Soltes (Albuquerque: University of New Mexico Press, 2007); Freedman, *Klezmer America*, pp. 216–27; Seth Kunin, *Juggling Identities: Identity and Authenticity among the Crypto-Jews* (New York: Columbia University Press, 2009); Ben-Ur, *Sephardic Jews in America*, pp. 178–82.

registered). By no means were most of them religiously inspired; indeed, many were not religiously observant at all. But, in terms of recuperative modes of Jewish identity, many of them sought in Israel a Jewish-majority culture where self and society could be conceived as cohering rather than merely co-existing. It should be noted that the annual emigration rate of United States residents to countries abroad nearly quadrupled between 1960 and 1974, which helps to place the Jewish instance in somewhat broader context. The American Jewish immigrant contingent in Israel continues to grow, and by the year 2000 was estimated at around 107,000.[74]

Let us turn, lastly, to the third aspect of religious identity and behavior, which I have dubbed the "embedded" type. Embedded religious behavior refers here to an affective identification with the extended group of fellow Jews. The "embedded" Jewish person is one for whom there is a "we" beyond the "I": a collective in which the individual asserts a stake. Such embeddedness is actualized, for instance, when parents give their children dual (American and Jewish) names. Jews called upon to perform rites in the synagogue (such as reading a portion from the Torah) are addressed by an ancestral Hebrew name, indicating their place in the community. Thus, Robert Lewis might also answer to the complete Hebrew name of Reuven ben Moshe ha-levi ve-Rivkah (i.e. Reuben, son of Moses the Levite and Rebecca).

Most American Jews, who rarely frequent the synagogue and who are still less frequently called upon to perform a Torah reading, have few occasions on which to recall or to be addressed by their ancestral names. For many, such an occasion might occur at the time of their bar- or bat-mitzvah. Another such occasion would be in the naming of the bride and the groom in the written nuptial agreement (*ketubah*) that practicing Jews incorporate in their wedding rites. Yet, even when such uses are relatively

---

[74] Halkin, *Letters*; Kevin Avruch, *American Immigrants in Israel: Social Identities and Change* (Chicago, IL and London: University of Chicago Press, 1981); Arnold Dashefsky and Bernard Lazerwitz, "The Role of Religious Identification in North American Migration to Israel," *Journal for the Scientific Study of Religion* 22(3) (1983): 263–75; Warren and Kraly, *The Elusive Exodus*; Chaim I. Waxman, *American Aliya, Portrait of an Innovative Migration Movement* (Detroit, MI: Wayne State University Press, 1989); Arnold Dashefsky, *Americans Abroad: A Comparative Study of Emigrants from the United States* (New York: Plenum Press, 1992); Edward W. Fernandez, "Estimation of the Annual Emigration of U.S. Born Persons by Using Foreign Censuses and Selected Administrative Data: Circa 1980," *Population Division Working Paper No. 10* (Washington, DC: Population Division, U.S. Bureau of the Census, 1995), Appendix, Table 2; Bernt Bratsberg and Dek Terrell, "Where Do Americans Live Abroad?," *International Migration Review* 30(3) (1996): 788–802.

few and far between, it says something that in many American Jewish families there has been a history of name-changing, but a retention of Hebrew names. Thus, "Anglicized" surnames – usually in order to facilitate easy spelling and pronunciation – are fairly common. "Lewis," for instance, might once have been Loewenstein, Lewinsky, or Lewisohn. But no one has ever sought to alter a Hebrew name: the ancestral moniker retains an aura of sanctity. At times it may be regarded as tantamount to Jewish identity as such – an inalienable boundary-setter and a "birthright."

Synagogue affiliation, ritual performance, and even belief in God may – in comparison with this quasi-"dynastic" element – be considered optional, without actually denying the underlying premise of family-based heritage. That helps to explain, in part, the more mercurial aspects of American Judaism. It accounts, for instance, for some Jews' ability to embrace certain kinds of sectarian behavior (philanthropy and other forms of social action, or an avid interest in Jewish literature) even as they neglect or reject other elements. Even in an era of institutional Judaism, complete with an ordained and articulate, professional, religious leadership, Judaism has retained or re-acquired some of its folk element.

Clearly, "embedding" Judaism within a matrix of birthright-determined modes of identification is intertwined with social forces. From without, the distance or antagonism that used to face many Jewish men and women in the social and economic marketplace, as experienced subjectively and as voiced and acted out by others, tended to reinforce group boundaries. From within, the preference for Jewish mates (endogamy), which was considered a bedrock definition of Jewish family life until well into the 1960s, ensured a "safety net" for airing and containing inter-generational frictions as well as "safe zone" in which to process the in-group/out-group tensions that most Jews accepted as a normal way of life.[75]

The extended family paradigm was always, in part, porous. Access by outsiders to the Jewish fold via conversion, though never widespread, was always available and it prevented the notion of "family" from being

---

[75] Dinnerstein, *Antisemitism in America*; Benjamin B. Ringer, *The Edge of Friendliness: A Study of Jewish-Gentile Relations*, Vol. II of the Lakeville Studies, directed by Marshall Sklare (New York: Basic Books/American Jewish Committee, 1967); Herbert J. Gans, "The Origins and Growth of a Jewish Community in the Suburbs: A Study of the Jews of Park Forest," in Marshall Sklare, *The Jews*, pp. 205–48; Fred Massarik and Alvin Chenkin, "United States National Jewish Population Study: A First Report," *American Jewish Year Book*, vol. LXXIV (New York and Philadelphia, PA: American Jewish Committee/Jewish Publication Society, 1973), p. 292; Arnold Schwartz, "Intermarriage in the United States," *American Jewish Year Book*, vol. LXXI (New York and Philadelphia, PA: American Jewish Committee/Jewish Publication Society, 1970), pp. 101–21.

wholly restricted to genealogical kinship alone. The increasing frequency of marriages between Jews and spouses, who were neither raised as Jews nor converted to Judaism, has tended to further reinforce the voluntary aspects of Jewish identification and, by the same token, to problematize the kinship-based aspects. By the end of the 1980s, one-third of Jewish adults were living in households where their partners were not Jewish.

In 1983, rabbis of the Reform movement, the most liberal Jewish denomination, decided to "distinguish between descent and identification." They altered the conditions under which interfaith couples might choose to introduce Judaism into the lives of their children – not via the formal conversion of the non-Jewish spouse or of the children to Judaism, but via "acts of identification":

> The Central Conference of American Rabbis declares that the child of one Jewish parent is under the presumption of Jewish descent. This presumption [...] is to be established through appropriate and timely public and formal acts of identification with the Jewish faith and people [which will] include entry into the covenant [i.e. circumcision of male infants], acquisition of a Hebrew name, Torah study, Bar/Bat Mitzvah, and [...] Confirmation.[76]

That declaration, popularly known as the "patrilineal descent" decision, breached rabbinical precedents dating back to late antiquity, by which *mothers* were singled out as the signal guarantors of their children's Judaism. The new policy voided this older "matrilineal" model and assigned equal weight to Jewish fathers. Shifting ground from pre-feminist notions of the maternally anchored household, it conferred decisive influence, instead, upon the formal institutions of synagogue communities. It established a new, conditional status of "potential" Judaism, contingent upon inter-faith families' interactions with a sponsoring Jewish community. It also ignored persistent findings in American social studies concerning women's greater activity in religious life.[77] Most of the other Jewish denominations, however, have not followed suit and, for them, natality has largely retained its status as an independent component of Jewish identity.

[76] *CCAR Responsa*, at http://data.ccarnet.org/cgi-bin/respdisp.pl?file=38&year=carr. The proposal to recognize children of one Jewish parent (father or mother) was already made by the CCAR in 1947, but was formalized only in 1983. The movement for Reconstructionist Judaism recognized the child of a Jewish father (and a non-Jewish mother) as Jewish in 1968: Sarna, *American Judaism*, p. 322.

[77] Cohen and Eisen, *The Jew Within*, p. 54. Jonathan Sarna observed (Sarna, *American Judaism*, p. 360) that there were from 1.5 to 2.5 million Americans today whose grandparents were Jewish, but who now practice other religions ("mostly as a result of marrying non-Jews").

Nonetheless, marriage across ethno-religious lines has produced a large sector of families with multiple or amorphous religious identities. Now into its second generation, this paradigm has a self-replicating effect, since adult children of mixed-religion households are apt, in their turn, to establish new, mixed-religion families at a substantially higher rate (74 percent).[78] In households formed by couples who had been raised in different religions, engagement with Jewish holidays and other forms of Jewish heritage perseveres, if at all, mainly informally. It is rarely formalized in terms of long-term memberships in communal or religious institutions. Thus, a growing new sector of the population is making its own way, according to its own rules, in affirming some affinity for Judaic practices (or none at all). Denomination is hardly a serious consideration, although the Reform movement has been the most accommodating. Instead, the self-guided approach is a standard feature of the burgeoning popular literature in the field. Akin to the discourse of "pride" that holds sway in much of contemporary Jewish culture, Jewish heritage is largely presented in such literature as something positive and worth acknowledging.[79]

Two Worthy Causes

In the face of religious diversification, several centralizing political causes influenced postwar American Jewish life. We have touched briefly upon the initial impact of Israeli statehood as a galvanizing force in Jewish

[78] Joel Perlmann, "Ethnic Group Strength, Intermarriage, and Group Blending," in *Ethnicity and Beyond: Theories and Dilemmas of Jewish Group Demarcation. Studies in Contemporary Jewry*, vol. XXV, ed. Eli Lederhendler (New York: Oxford University Press, 2011): 49–61; Bruce Phillips, "Children of Intermarriage: How 'Jewish'?" in *Coping with Life and Death: Jewish Families in the Twentieth Century. Studies in Contemporary Jewry*, vol. XIV, ed. Peter Y. Medding (New York: Oxford University Press, 1998), pp. 86–91; Kotler-Berkowitz, Cohen, et al., *The National Jewish Population Survey 2000–2001*, pp. 16–19.

[79] Sylvia Barack Fishman, *Double or Nothing: Jewish Families and Mixed Marriage* (Waltham, MA: Brandeis University Press and Hanover, NH: University Press of New England, 2004); Keren R. McGinity, *Still Jewish: A History of Women and Intermarriage in America* (New York: New York University Press, 2009); Paul Cowan and Rachel Cowan, *Mixed Blessings: Marriage Between Jews and Christians* (New York: Doubleday, 1987); Joan C. Hawxhurst, *The Interfaith Family Guidebook: Practical Advice for Jewish and Christian Partners* (Kalamazoo, MI: Dovetail Publishing, 1998); Lee Ferguson Gruzen, *Raising Your Jewish/Christian Child: How Interfaith Parents Can Give Children the Best of Both Their Heritages*, 2nd ed. (New York: Dodd, Mead and Co. /Newmarket Press, 2001 [1987, 1990]); Cokie and Steve Roberts, *Our Haggadah: Uniting Traditions for Interfaith Families* (New York: HarperCollins, 2011); Susan Katz Miller, *Being Both: Embracing Two Religions in One Interfaith Family* (Boston, MA: Beacon Press, 2013).

public affairs. It is tempting to view the post-1948 development of American Jewish involvement with Israel as an outgrowth of past pro-Zionist activities. It was, no doubt, a continuation from the past; however, that is also an oversimplification.

Jewish undertakings, missions, and contributions to civic and religious institutions in Palestine before 1940 had focused on social, educational, medical, and other philanthropic projects. Sometimes, economic investment in agricultural development and other enterprises was added to this agenda. Overall, most of these activities entailed few if any political connotations. Indeed, the leading American Zionist figurehead of the First World War era, Justice Louis D. Brandeis, had formulated pro-Zionist work as a liberal-progressive project in economic and social uplift.[80]

The regnant pattern of Jewish public activity on the world scene had historically entailed "donor" communities and "recipient" communities. Recipients were never the equals or the superiors of their benefactors in political status, political effectiveness, and internal hierarchical organization. With statehood, Israel became, simultaneously, both a "recipient" (of immigrants, other human resources, technical and financial resources, and political support) and a sovereign entity in its own right. It was not politically subordinate to its supporters abroad, but rather was answerable to its own citizens; donor groups abroad, in contrast, were apolitical, voluntary associations, owing comparatively little public accountability and wielding no legal authority. Thus, the establishment of the State of Israel was a game-changer that moved the political dimension to the front burner. Even a menu of philanthropic, social welfare, or cultural projects, which continued to be the staples of American Jewish engagement with Israel, now possessed an inherently political complexion.[81]

Right from the start, therefore, it became necessary to establish a new protocol for these activities. In light of American Jews' political allegiance to United States, arrangements were required to buffer the political sphere per se from that of the trans-national, pro-Israel functions of voluntary Jewish organizations. That was accomplished by a verification of US government postures on civilian, overseas philanthropic projects,[82]

[80] Halpern, *A Clash of Heroes*, pp. 197, 210, 233–4; Urofsky, *American Zionism*, pp. 294–7; and *Brandeis*, pp. 533–5, 537–8, 543.

[81] Zohar Segev, "American Zionists' Place in Israel after Statehood: From Involved Partners to Outside Supporters," *American Jewish History* 93(3) (2007): 277–302.

[82] *Foreign Relations of the United States*, 1952–1954, vol. IX, p. 1676; *ibid.*, 1956, vol. XV, pp. 163–6, 585; *Te'udot limediniyut hahuts shel medinat yisrael* (State of Israel Foreign

and by a written commitment, conveyed by the Israeli Prime Minister, David Ben-Gurion, to the leaders of the American Jewish Committee, in which Israel acknowledged that it sought no political claim upon or authority over the Jewish citizens of any other country.[83]

This separation of functions meant that world Jewry – including the American Jewish leadership – would retain only a supporting role vis-à-vis Israeli policy-makers and institutions, without formal political involvement. (This was particularly tailored to American sensibilities. A number of countries in Europe and elsewhere routinely reserve seats in their parliaments for their overseas and expatriate co-nationals; American norms, however, are far more defensive against dual citizenship and dual loyalties.)[84]

This, however, did not remove political aspects from the pro-Israel work done in the US. Indeed, Israel became an effective contender for Jewish resources precisely because of its political status. The Israeli counterparts of American Jewish philanthropic board members and executives were members of parliament, cabinet ministers, or other senior public officials who bore governmental responsibility. The joint governing boards of semi-private Israeli institutions, on which American Jewish delegates sat together with Israeli representatives, became platforms for engaging American Jewish leaders in Israeli civic life (immigration, settlement, education, health and welfare, and so forth).

Working Toward Statehood

The politicization of American Zionism did not emerge fully blown in 1948. Rather, a chain of events marked the progression of Zionist work in America from a philanthropic to a politicized project: the proposed partition of British Palestine, first broached in 1937; the British White Paper of 1939; and the Zionist Conference in New York (the Biltmore

Policy Documents), vol. IX (1954): 730–2; Bernard M. Gwertzman and Haynes Johnson, *Fulbright, the Dissenter* (New York: Hutchinson, 1969), p. 171; Randall Bennett Woods, *Fulbright: A Biography* (Cambridge: Cambridge University Press, 1995), pp. 306, 310; Confidential Report on the Fulbright Hearings, August 21, 1963, Central Zionist Archive (Jerusalem), A370/1083, p. 25. My thanks to Moshe Fox for sharing with me the fruits of his research in this field.

[83] Cohen, *Not Free to Desist*, pp. 310–15, 318–26; Zvi Ganin, *An Uneasy Relationship: American Jewish Leadership and Israel, 1948–1957* (Syracuse, NY: Syracuse University Press, 2005), pp. 3–104; Ariel L. Feldstein, *Ben-Gurion, Zionism, and American Jewry, 1948–1963* (New York: Routledge, 2006), pp. 145–6.

[84] Among the countries whose parliamentary representatives include those residing in expatriate communities are: France, Algeria, Italy, Portugal, and the Dominican Republic.

Conference) in 1942. It may be worth dwelling on this pre-1948 history briefly in order to understand its evolution.

In the wake of three years of violent Arab rioting that began in 1936, several proposals were broached to bring the British Mandate in Palestine to an end via either a two-state solution, as briefly contemplated in the 1937 Peel Partition plan, or a one-state solution (the 1939 MacDonald White Paper). This was the first occasion on which Jewish statehood had been explicitly and publicly discussed as a real option, which altered the tenor of Jewish public debate not only in Palestine and Europe, but in the United States as well.[85]

Neither plan proved tenable, as Arab opposition to either partition or to power-sharing with the Jews of Palestine remained adamant. Britain then decided in 1939 to cut off further Jewish population growth through immigration, with only minimal and finite allowances for the coming several years. This caught the Jewish world at its most vulnerable moment, just when Nazi Germany was gearing up for war and most other nations had severely restricted the entry of Jewish refugees. In the ensuing months and years, securing the freedom of Jewish immigration into Palestine became the absolute "red line" of the Zionist movement and, in later years, the raison d'être of the State of Israel.[86]

The Zionist movement leadership met in New York City in May, 1942. Gathering some 600 delegates at the Biltmore Hotel (and hence, known as the Biltmore Conference), the represented groups resolved that a Jewish "commonwealth" in Palestine be secured by international law after the end of the world war. At the time, some apparently hoped that

---

[85] Gabriel Sheffer, "British Colonial Policy-Making Towards Palestine (1929–1939)," *Middle Eastern Studies* 13(3) (1978): 307–22; Raider, *The Emergence of American Zionism*, pp. 187–90; and "Where American Zionism Differed: Abba Hillel Silver Reconsidered," in *Abba Hillel Silver and American Zionism*, ed. Mark A. Raider, Jonathan D. Sarna, and Ronald W. Zweig (London and Portland, OR: Frank Cass, 1977), pp. 99–100; Urofsky, *American Zionism*, pp. 403–7; and *Brandeis*, p. 738; Berman, *Nazism, the Jews, and American Zionism*, pp. 51–63; Bernard Wasserstein, *The British in Palestine: The Mandatory Government and Arab-Jewish Conflict, 1917–1929* (Oxford: Blackwell, 2nd ed., 1991); Martin Kolinsky, *Britain's War in the Middle East: Strategy and Diplomacy, 1936–1942* (New York: Macmillan, 1999); Michael Cohen, *Palestine: Retreat from the Mandate. The Making of British Policy 1936–45* (London: P. Elek, 1978); Lauren Elise Apter, "Disorderly Decolonization: The White Paper of 1939 and the End of British Rule in Palestine" (PhD dissertation, University of Texas at Austin, 2008), pp. 21–60; Alon Gal, "Mima'arav letsiyon: meafyenai hatsiyonut haamerikanit" (West of Zion: Characteristics of American Zionism), in *Hatsiyonut le'ezorehah* (*Zionism by its Regions*) (Jerusalem: Merkaz Zalman Shazar and Be'er Sheva: Ben-Gurion University of the Negev, 2010), vol. III, p. 135.

[86] Raider, *American Zionism*, pp. 195–6; Urofsky, *American Zionism*, pp. 413–16.

the British government could be persuaded to cancel its restrictions and afford sanctuary to some of Hitler's victims. In any case, the argument that carried the day – put forth by Cleveland's Abba Hillel Silver – was that no peaceful and democratic postwar order could be contemplated by the Allies without some historic reckoning with the human cost of Jewish statelessness.[87] Political nationhood was, thus, placed firmly on the American Jewish public agenda and it reflected a consensus that spread far beyond the narrow confines of the Zionist organizations.

In the intervening years prior to 1948, Jewish groups took the matter of Palestine to the American public square. In contrast to the dilatory response of American politicians, churchmen, and the media to the question of refugee immigration into the United States, in the matter of providing for a Jewish future in Palestine there appeared to be a happier connection between Jewish aims and American public opinion. The proposal for postwar Jewish statehood carried enough popular ballast to win a plank in the 1944 party platforms of both major parties (but not in Congress until late in 1945). It was during this prelude to Israeli statehood that American Jewish figures were able to act as partners in decision-making along with the Jewish Agency Executive (the pre-state Jewish administration in Palestine), precisely because it did not violate another state's sovereignty. Emanuel Neumann (1893–1980), a key Zionist functionary, recalled this phase as one of direct and intense involvement: "The most humble Zionist was an unofficial ambassador. In short, they were not merely fundraisers and donors, but nation builders."[88]

---

[87] Zvi Ganin, *Truman, American Jewry, and Israel, 1945–1948* (New York and London: Holmes and Meier, 1979), pp. 4, 8–11; Ilan Amitzur, *Amerikah, britaniah ve'erets yisrael – reshitah shel me'uravut artsot haberit bamedeiniut habritit be'erets yisrael, 1938–1947* (*America, Britain, and Palestine: The Beginnings of American Involvement in British Policy in Palestine, 1938–1947*) (Jerusalem: Yad Itzhak Ben-Zvi, 1979), pp. 86–104; Urofsky, *American Zionism*, pp. 424–9; Feingold, *A Time for Searching*, pp. 244–6; and *Bearing Witness*, pp. 220; Hurwitz, *Jews Without Power*, pp. 189–205; Raider, *American Zionism*, pp. 205–7; Wyman, *The Abandonment of the Jews*, pp. 157–77; American Jewish Conference, *Report of the Interim Committee* (New York: American Jewish Conference, 1944); Berman, *Nazism, the Jews, and American Zionism*, pp. 78–128; *American Jewish Year Book*, vol. XLV (1943–4), pp. 206–14; *American Jewish Year Book*, vol. XLVI (1944–5), pp. 169–77; Meyer, *Response to Modernity*, p. 331; Cohen, *Not Free to Desist*, pp. 249–60, 293–4; James L. Gelvin, *The Israel–Palestine Conflict: One Hundred Years of War* (New York and Cambridge: Cambridge University Press, 2005), pp. 116–43.

[88] Emanuel Neumann, "Towards the World Zionist Congress," *Zionist Quarterly* (June 1951): 5–15, quoted in Ganin, *Uneasy Relationship*, p. 112; see also Berman, *Nazism, the Jews, and American Zionism*, pp. 124–80; Peter Grose, *Israel in the Mind of America* (New York: Knopf, 1983), pp. 162–83; Zohar Segev, *Mipolitikaim etniim lemanhigim*

Advocating Israel

Pro-Israel activists had to argue the merits of American engagement with Israel against the considerable counter-pressure of pro-Arab interests, including the large petroleum industry. During the Truman, Eisenhower, and Kennedy Administrations, the State Department had to be convinced that stabilizing the Middle East within a precariously balanced global doctrine could somehow accommodate Israel's economic and security needs while also satisfying the strategic and petro-dollar interests America had in Arab countries.[89]

Public advocacy – turning to publicity and politicking to "bump" marginal issues farther up on the list of national priorities – provided Jewish activists a unique niche in national affairs. In later years, the infrastructure for this work was institutionalized, combining the efforts of a lobby, the America-Israel Public Affairs Committee (AIPAC, 1951); a policy coordination council called the Conference of Presidents of Major Jewish Organizations (1956); and a firmly bipartisan and non-sectarian strategy that sought allies across the whole political and religious spectrum.

A gauge of just how tentative their successes were, up to the mid-1960s, may be read in the modest levels of US loans and grants awarded to Israel in those years. Annual US aid to all foreign recipients during the 1950s and 1960s averaged around $30 billion (in 2010 dollars). Aid to Israel was just a fraction of that sum. Apart from one large loan in 1949 (worth about $965 million in today's currency), American government aid to Israel during the 1950s and early 1960s was the equivalent (in total) of some $500 million (in 2010 dollars). To put that into further perspective, the contributions (including the purchase of Israel government bonds) by voluntary campaigns among world Jewry, led by US Jewish donors, were sufficiently large to roughly match the largesse of the US government, despite the huge disparity in the volume of resources

---

le'umi'im: hahanhagah hatsiyonit-amerikanit, hashoah, vehakamat medinat yisrael (From Ethnic Politicians to National Leaders: The American Zionist Leadership, the Holocaust, and the Establishment of the State of Israel) (Be'er Sheva: Ben-Gurion University of the Negev, 2007), pp. 205–58; Henry L. Feingold, *Jewish Power in America: Myth and Reality* (New Brunswick, NJ and London: Transaction, 2008), pp. 25–42; Michael J. Cohen, *Truman and Israel* (Berkeley: University of California Press, 1990).

[89] Cohen, *Not Free to Desist*, pp. 318–26; Steven L. Spiegel, "American Jews and United States Foreign Policy (1945–90)," in *Terms of Survival: The Jewish World Since 1945*, ed. Robert S. Wistrich (London and New York: Routledge, 1995), pp. 168–76; and *The Other Arab-Israeli Conflict: Making America's Middle East Policy, from Truman to Reagan* (Chicago, IL and London: University of Chicago Press, 1985); Feingold, *Jewish Power in America*, pp. 65–83; David Paul and Rachel Anderson Paul, *Ethnic Lobbies and US Foreign Policy* (Boulder, CO: Lynne Rienner, 2009).

available. Moreover (and in contrast to US policy starting in the later 1960s), during the 1950s the United States continued to refuse to sell Israel advanced weapons systems.[90]

At the same time, Israel's cause was promoted along quite another front: in the cultural, academic, and media community. Israel in its early years was widely showcased as a model of progress, social experimentation, cooperative enterprise, and government planning – a leading "new nation" in the post-colonial world, and one that was considered safely anti-Soviet.

Even before the ink on the cease-fire agreements between Israel and the Arab belligerents (in 1949) was dry, the redoubtable journalist I. F. ("Izzy") Stone (*né* Isidor Feinstein, 1907–89), a Philadelphia-born left-wing activist, collaborated on the publication of a strongly pro-Israel photo-journalism essay. (Stone later became a stout critic of Israel, and we may take his 1949 writings as a fair sample of how far things had changed by the post-1967 decades in the Left's orientation toward Middle East affairs.) In his essays, Stone lavished praise on Israelis' mettle in defending their state against all odds, as well as their pioneering idealism and particularly their heavyweight labor movement: "[Israel's] mixed economy, its voluntary farm collectives, its network of cooperatives, already indicate how socialist devices and democratic methods could be combined, social justice achieved without sacrifice of individual freedom."[91]

---

[90] Kenneth M. Kaufman and Helena Stalson, "U.S. Assistance to Less Developed Countries, 1956–65," *Foreign Affairs* (July 1967): 715–25; Clyde R. Mark, *Israel: U.S. Foreign Assistance*, CRS Issue Brief for Congress (Washington, DC: Congressional Research Service, Library of Congress, 2005), www.fas.org/sgp/crs/mideast/IB85066.pdf; Curt Tarnoff and Marian Leonardo Lawson, *Foreign Aid: An Introduction to U.S. Programs and Policies*, CRS Report for Congress (Washington, DC: Congressional Research Service, 2011), www.fas.org/sgp/crs/row/R40213.pdf; Haim Barkai, "The Diaspora's Contribution to Israel's Economic Development," in *The Six-Day War and World Jewry*, ed. Eli Lederhendler (Bethesda: University Press of Maryland, 2000), p. 68; see also President's News Conference of February 17, 1960, Public Papers of the Presidents of the US, 1960–61; Dwight D. Eisenhower, http://heinonline.org/HOL/Page?handle=hein. presidents/pppo60000&id=237&collection=presidents&index=presidents/eisenhower#1 (my thanks to Moshe Fox for retrieving the information on foreign aid and weapons sales and bringing it to my attention). See Moshe Fox, "American Jewish Political Support for Israel, 1948–1963" (Hebrew) (PhD dissertation, Hebrew University of Jerusalem, 2015).

[91] I. F. Stone, *This is Israel*, foreword by Bartley C. Crum, photographs by Robert Capa, Jerry Cooke, and Tom Gidal (New York: Boni and Gaer, 1948), pp. 68, 127; Berman, *Nazism, the Jews, and American Zionism*, pp. 146–7. Stone was a suspected Soviet agent in the period before the Molotov-Ribbentrop Pact of 1939. He covered the emergence

Given the constellation of international forces, it was flattering – and it made political sense – to portray Israel as uniquely straddling the divisions between East and West, North and South: a parliamentary democracy with an egalitarian and collectivist ideology, poised between the free world and the emergent "people's democracies" of that era; and a developing, mixed economy set to emulate Western innovation, leapfrogging its hostile neighbors to reach out to potential friends in post-colonial Africa and Asia. Thus, the Cold War context of the 1950s and 1960s supplied an ideological platform upon which American liberals and Zionists forged a view of Israel as a pioneering liberal society.[92] Like American efforts throughout the Cold War era (and beyond) to win the hearts and minds of people in countries around the world, Israel and its friends aimed at a high moral diction. It was, perhaps, understandable that a people that had been so recently hated to death, with devastating results, should feel so compelled to be well received, at last.

American Jews' connection to Israel between 1948 and 1967 was implemented under the aegis of Jewish institutions and organizations. The important functions in this regard were carried out by metropolitan and regional Jewish philanthropic federations, in cooperation with a national office for fundraising, the United Jewish Appeal (UJA, founded 1939). Other ancillary bodies, such as an organization to promote Israeli government bonds and the Hadassah Women's Zionist Organization (which maintained its ongoing involvement with health care in Israel), undertook particular tasks and partnerships with Israeli institutions. Political advocacy functions were carried out, as noted, by newly organized groups, such as AIPAC and the Conference of Presidents of Major Jewish Organizations.

However, many American Jews remained largely unaffected in their private lives by what appeared to be so central to the public life of their community. Examples of Israel's cultural influence on grassroots Jewish

---

of Israel as a journalist and published a sympathetic book on the Zionist campaign to smuggle Holocaust survivors into British Palestine before 1948: I. F. Stone, *Underground to Palestine* (New York: Boni and Gaer, 1946).

[92] Allon Gal, "The Mission Motif in American Zionism (1898–1948)," *American Jewish History* 75(4) (1986): 363–85; and "Independence and Universal Mission in Modern Jewish Nationalism: A Comparative Analysis of European and American Zionism," in *Israel, State and Society. Studies in Contemporary Jewry*, vol. V, ed. Ezra Mendelsohn (New York: Oxford University Press, 1989), pp. 242–74; see also *Envisioning Israel: The Changing Ideals and Images of North American Jews*, ed. Allon Gal (Jerusalem: Magnes Press/Hebrew University, 1996), pp. 15–23, 31–7, 41–59.

activities abounded – such as the nearly universal adoption of Israeli-inflected Sephardic Hebrew in American Jewish schools and (eventually) synagogues, which replaced the old-style, European, Ashkenazic pronunciation. But personal visits to Israel, for example, were not widely popular: only small percentages of American Jews undertook such ethno-tourism.[93]

Russia Revisited: Отпусти народ мой! *(Let My People Go!)*

Meanwhile, an issue that signaled a quite different sort of engagement with overseas affairs began to appear with greater frequency in Jewish media in the mid-1960s: concern about the lives of Jews behind the Iron Curtain. Reports regularly surfaced about discrimination against Jews in Soviet life, restrictions on their access to synagogues and to Yiddish- and Hebrew-language print media, and the sharp tone of Soviet "anti-Zionist" propaganda that featured strongly anti-Jewish caricatures and stereotypes.

Efforts by Israel to raise such human rights violations before the UN led to an impasse. The vulnerability of the United States on the question of bias and discrimination, based on its unresolved racial segregation problems, provided the Soviet government with the diplomatic leverage it needed to effectively block any specific mention of antisemitism in international human rights conventions. By the mid-1960s, therefore, those who were actively concerned with the problem of Soviet Jewry began to shift away from diplomacy. Toward the end of that decade, a public protest movement was organized around a new rallying point: upholding the right of Soviet Jews wishing to emigrate to do so – particularly to Israel.

---

[93] Sklare, *Suburban Frontier*, pp. 214–49; and *Observing America's Jews*, pp. 89–27; Liebman, *Ambivalent American Jew*, pp. 88–108; Charles S. Liebman and Steven M. Cohen, *Two Worlds of Judaism: The Israeli and American Experiences* (New Haven, CT and London: Yale University Press, 1990), pp. 67, 83–8; Waxman, *America's Jews in Transition*, pp. 118–20; "The Limited Impact of the Six-Day War on America's Jews," in Lederhendler, *The Six-Day War and World Jewry*, pp. 99–115; "Weakening Ties: American Jewish Baby Boomers and Israel," in Gal, *Envisioning Israel*, pp. 374–96; and *Jewish Baby Boomers: A Communal Perspective* (Albany, NY: SUNY Press, 2001), pp. 81–4; Elazar, *Community and Polity*, pp. 98–9, 102–10, 170–1, 260–3; Cohen and Eisen, *The Jew Within*, pp. 135, 142–52; Arnold Eisen, "Israel at 50: An American Jewish Perspective," in *American Jewish Year Book 1998* (New York: American Jewish Committee/Philadelphia, PA: Jewish Publication Society, 1998), p. 47; Jack Wertheimer, "American Jews and Israel: A 60-Year Perspective," in *American Jewish Year Book*, vol. CVIII (New York: American Jewish Committee/Philadelphia, PA: Jewish Publication Society of America, 2008), pp. 3–79.

Thus was born the slogan that would accompany the Soviet Jewry campaigns over the next two decades: "Let My People Go!"[94]

The 1960s and 1970s were a pivotal time for the emergence of a new American political culture, which provided the context for the Soviet Jewry movement in the United States. Political activism in this period was both democratized and personalized. It drew in much wider sections of the population, particularly among students and members of racialized minorities, but also including more women, church groups, well-known figures in the arts and popular culture, and academics. Activists engaged in political action on university campuses, in the streets and parks of cities, and in mass, grassroots campaigns. While the sixties to early seventies became best known for protest activities surrounding the war in Vietnam and the Civil Rights movement, the same era was also the seedbed for conservative and neo-conservative politics and religious activism on the political Right.[95]

The growing array of protests also promoted a personalized political style. Activists aimed not just at eliciting participation in organized political rallies or mobilizing for elections, but also sought to arouse a heightened personal commitment ("consciousness") on the part of individuals. The new ethos portrayed political involvement as being personally transforming, since activism was defined as motivated by values and as subjectively liberating the individual from suppressed grievances. "Taking it

---

[94] Jonathan Frankel, "The Soviet Regime and Anti-Zionism: An Analysis," in Mendelsohn, *Essential Papers on Jews and the Left*, pp. 440–82; Ofra Friesel, *Aflayah giz'it, ma'azan haeimah, ve'antishemiut: sipur leidatah shel amanat zekhuyot adam (Racial Discrimination, the Balance of Fear, and Antisemitism: The Story of How the Human Rights Convention was Born)* (Nevo: Srigim-Leon, 2010); William W. Orbach, *The American Movement to Aid Soviet Jews* (Amherst: University of Massachusetts Press, 1979), pp. 1–51, 82–95, 96–110; Henry L. Feingold, *Silent No More: Saving the Jews of Russia. The American Effort, 1967–1989* (Syracuse, NY: Syracuse University Press, 2007), pp. 28–36, 37–63, 70–108; and *Jewish Power in America*, pp. 45–51, 55–9; Fred A. Lazin, *The Struggle for Soviet Jewry in American Politics* (Lanham, MD: Lexington Books, 2005), pp. 19–54.

[95] John Morton Blum, *Years of Discord: American Politics and Society, 1961–1974* (New York and London: W. W. Norton, 1991), pp. 252–81; David Farber, *The Age of Great Dreams: America in the 1960s* (New York: Hill and Wang, 1994), pp. 67–116, 167–211; David R. Colburn and George E. Pozzetta, "Race, Ethnicity, and the Evolution of Political Legitimacy," in *The Sixties, From Memory to History*, ed. David Farber (Chapel Hill and London: University of North Carolina Press, 1994), pp. 119–48; Richard H. King, "American Political Culture since 1945," in Agnew and Rosenzweig, *Companion to Post-1945 America*, pp. 163–8; Van Gosse, "A Movement of Movements: The Definition and Periodization of the New Left," in *ibid.*, pp. 292–4; Chafe, *Unfinished Journey*, pp. 302–36, 378–80; James T. Patterson, *Grand Expectations: The United States, 1945–1974* (New York: Oxford University Press, 1996), pp. 637–77.

personally" and "taking it to the streets" were tactics that enabled small or previously marginal sections of the population to draw attention to their particular issues. Subgroups sought in this way to mobilize their own constituencies and to concretize their presence on the social and cultural scene.[96]

This was the context in which the protest movement on behalf of Soviet Jewry developed, and it therefore shared some of these broader characteristics. Traditional organizational activity as practiced over the course of several generations, and even publicity campaigns and mass-mail techniques, did not fit the new climate. Indeed, an integral part of the new mobilizing work was an attempt to discredit older, more genteel methods, as having been both too self-effacing and ineffectual. The struggle of Soviet Jews to breach the Iron Curtain appeared to warrant an equally urgent "struggle" in America to raise Jewish consciousness against apathy and "assimilation" – a struggle that the Jewish "establishment" (a word plainly borrowed from the 1960s counterculture) was accused of having neglected. It is no accident that one of the most effective groups took the militant-sounding name, Student Struggle for Soviet Jewry.

Eminent figures like the author Elie Wiesel (1928–2016) and theologian Abraham Joshua Heschel publicly proclaimed that American Jewry was facing a historic challenge; that it was honor-bound to respond to the Soviet Jewish situation in a way that it had not succeeded in doing adequately in the previous generation, when faced with the European Jewish catastrophe. To mobilize for Russian Jews was a matter of honorable self-affirmation, as well as conscience. It was this rhetoric that altered the image of an organizational campaign, similar to other lobbying efforts, to that of a "movement," akin to the other movements across the contested American political and cultural spectrum.[97]

The new Jewish politics was not just an extension of identity politics of the post-1960 variety, however. Insofar as Jews brought their ethno-religious identification to bear on their politics, the Soviet Union and Israel were areas of foreign policy that lent the Jewish population the contours of a constituency. At the end of the 1970s, focus groups of men

---

[96] Ellen Herman, "Being and Doing: Humanistic Psychology and the Spirit of the 1960s," in *Sights on the Sixties*, ed. Barbara L. Tischler (New Brunswick, NJ: Rutgers University Press, 1992), pp. 87–101; Donald E. Phillips, *Student Protest, 1960–1970: An Analysis of the Issues and the Speeches* (Lanham, MD: University Press of America, 1985).

[97] Lederhendler, *New York Jews*, pp. 186–94; *The Jewish Sixties: An American Sourcebook*, ed. Michael E. Staub (Waltham, MA and Hanover, NH: Brandeis University Press and University Press of New England, 2004), pp. 121–35.

and women being groomed for lay-leadership positions in the communal funding apparatus readily identified "the conflict between Israel and its neighbors" and "the treatment of Jews in the Soviet Union" as the two leading problems facing the American Jewish community.[98]

As the United States and the USSR, after the Berlin and Cuban missile crises, groped their way toward what was then termed "co-existence" and, later (in Secretary of State Henry Kissinger's terms), "détente" – Jewish advocacy groups sought common ground with legislators on Capitol Hill who were involved with reframing American security and trade policies vis-à-vis the Soviet government. In 1974, Congress passed the Jackson-Vanik Amendment, which made it possible for favorable trading terms to be made contingent upon the USSR's willingness to grant emigration rights.[99]

The earlier precedent for this type of action that most readily comes to mind is the 1911 abrogation of the US-Russian commercial treaty, which similarly placed the protection of Jewish rights on the diplomatic bargaining table. Unfortunately for Jewish interests in the short run, Jackson-Vanik had little immediate impact on the status of Russian Jewry – similar, in fact, to what occurred with the 1911 treaty abrogation. Having failed to attain favorable credit and trade advantages (due to further Congressional action: the Stevenson-Byrd Amendment, which put a cap on loans to Eastern Bloc nations), the Soviets nullified the proposed bilateral trade agreement. They turned instead to Canada, Argentina, and Europe for their import requirements. Emigration was selectively permitted to some Jews during the ensuing decade and a half, and denied to others. The ultimate fall of the Soviet regime at the end of the 1980s made free migration possible.[100]

---

98 Jonathan Woocher, *Sacred Survival: The Civil Religion of American Jews* (Bloomington and Indianapolis: Indiana University Press, 1986), p. 123. See also Feingold, *A Time for Searching*, pp. 204–5; Spiegel, "American Jews and United States Foreign Policy," pp. 175–8; Connie L. McNeely and Susan J. Tolchin, "On the Hill: Jews in the United States Congress," in *Jews in American Politics*, ed. L. Sandy Maisel et al. (Lanham, MD: Rowman and Littlefield, 2001), pp. 54–63; Ira N. Forman, "The Politics of Minority Consciousness: The Historical Voting Behavior of American Jews," in *ibid.*, pp. 142–60.

99 Isaacs, *Jews and American Politics*, pp. 27–42, 181–267; Peter Y. Medding, "The New Jewish Politics in America," in Wistrich, *Terms of Survival*, pp. 86–114; Orbach, *American Movement to Aid Soviet Jews*, pp. 117–54; see also Blum, *Years of Discord*, pp. 374–83, 453–9, 465–6; Feingold, *Silent No More*, pp. 109–48.

100 Franklyn D. Holzman, "The Economics and Politics of International Trade and Financial Relations between the United States and Czarist and Soviet Russia 1800–1980," chapter XI (unpublished, available from the Association for Comparative

One more aspect of the Soviet Jewish crisis merits some discussion. A conflict of interest developed during the 1970s between Israeli officials and elements of the Jewish organizational apparatus in the United States. The issue concerned the initially small but growing proportion of Jewish émigrés who, having secured Soviet exit permits to go to Israel on the strength of family-reunion applications, then changed course. Rather than traveling to Israel, they remained in Western Europe and applied for refugee status and asylum in one of several other countries (chiefly the United States and the German Federal Republic). The American Jewish immigrant aid association, HIAS, arranged for their temporary lodging and other services in Italy, where they awaited the processing of their immigration papers.

Israeli policy-makers argued that "abuse" of Israeli immigration papers – that is, the apparently false declarations being signed by prospective émigrés concerning their motivation and destination – might result in the Soviets' cutting off further emigration. In any case, they pointed out, Jewish public money was being used to bring these émigrés to freedom; accordingly, those community resources should serve collective, national priorities (Jewish repatriation to Israel) and not be siphoned off to support re-emigration to a third country (the United States), ostensibly out of private individuals' personal or economic considerations.

American Jewish opponents of that position reasoned, instead, that Americans (Jews as well as non-Jews) had fought to obtain emigration rights for Soviet Jews on the strength of universal human freedoms; that those freedoms included the free choice of destination; and, therefore, it was improper for Jewish agencies to constrain the choices made by emigrants or to make their move to Israel appear involuntary. The Americans thought of global Jewish solidarity and co-responsibility as a moral commitment, based upon an aggregate of *individual* rights and choices. That mirrored, after all, the way that they defined their own status within American society. Public representatives of Israel, in contrast, thought of trans-national Jewish ties as an affirmation of their nationally defined right of self-determination. Their obligation was to undertake the

Economic Studies at www.acesecon.org/index.php?option=_content&task=view&id=32&Itemid=20; Feingold, *Silent No More*, pp. 109–48; and *Jewish Power*, pp. 45–57; Lazin, *Struggle for Soviet Jewry*, pp. 19–77; Marshall I. Goldman, "Soviet-American Trade and Soviet Jewish Emigration: Should a Policy Change be Made by the American Jewish Community?," in *Soviet Jewry in the 1980s*, ed. Robert O. Freedman (Durham, NC: Duke University Press, 1989), pp. 141–59.

national tasks of Jewish immigrant absorption – a central premise of Israeli statehood itself.

In the end, the intramural crisis abated for several reasons. First, the Soviet regime steeply curtailed Jewish emigration in the latter 1970s and first half of the 1980s (though not for the reasons feared by the Israelis), which tended to make the argument moot. Second, elections in Israel in 1977 brought Menachem Begin (1913–92), leader of the center-right Gahal (later Likud) Party bloc, to the premiership. Imbued with a sense that the historic moment at hand was a near analogy to pre-Holocaust rescue attempts, Begin was not inclined to make aid to Jewish émigrés contingent upon their choice of destination. For all he knew, they were all escaping certain danger, and such rescue took priority over other national concerns.[101]

When the volume of emigration finally attained mass proportions after the fall of the Communist regime, bringing over a million new immigrants to Israel and approximately 300,000 to the United States, the American administration ceased to classify ex-Soviet Jews as refugees and, accordingly, cut back on its immigration allowance for former Russian residents. This, as well as the role of Israel as the main receiver nation, placed Israel's needs in a more focal position. On a per capita basis, one new ex-Soviet immigrant was added for every five Israelis; in the United States, the corresponding figure was one Russian immigrant added for every 1,000 US citizens. That, in turn, reframed the issue for American Jews.[102]

Given the huge outlay involved in immigrant absorption expenditures, Israel sought financial assistance in the form of both private resources, through mobilizing Jewish community donations abroad, and American credit (loan guarantees), at the government-to-government level. American Jewish organizations, wielding their philanthropic potential in one executive operation, facilitated the loan guarantees and netted over $900 million in donations from 1990 to 1996 in a special campaign expressly to support ex-Soviet Jewish resettlement in Israel.[103]

---

[101] Feingold, *Silent No More*, pp. 149–86; Lazin, *Struggle for Soviet Jewry*, pp. 79–178.

[102] The population of Israel expanded from 4.4 million (3.66 million of them Jews) in 1988 to 6 million (4.9 million Jews) in 1998. Net migration accounted for over half the total growth from 1990 to 1995. Moshe Sicron, *Demografiah: ukhlusiyat yisrael – me'afyenim umegamot (Demography: Israel's Population – Characteristics and Trends)* (Jerusalem: Carmel, 2004), pp. 25, 31.

[103] Feingold, *Silent No More*, p. 288; Jack Wertheimer, "Current Trends in American Jewish Philanthropy," in *American Jewish Year Book*, vol. XCVII (New York and Philadelphia,

Beyond the Crisis Mode

American Jewish overseas engagements in the post-1945 era grew out of the crisis of European Jewry in the 1930s and World War II. After the extermination of most of Europe's Jews, the attention of organized Jewish communities and their supporters turned primarily to Israel. Beginning with the plight of the DPs in the early postwar years, continuing through the 1950s and 1960s with the need to resettle a million Jews from Arab countries, and shifting in the 1970s and 1980s to Russian Jewry and the Jews of Ethiopia – Jewish populations in distress remained a crucial consideration. Their resettlement mainly in Israel framed the issue of foreign assistance as, in substance, a continuation of older refugee-oriented philanthropic and political activity.

Politicization fostered centralized, national offices and mass fundraising campaigns. It thrived on a quasi-permanent state of high alert and it offered energetic men and women an outlet for intensive public work. Inevitably, it also had the side-effect of alienating those who were not organization-minded, whose drift toward personalism ran counter to politicized discourse, and who were left uninspired by and uninvolved in high-pressure fundraising campaigns. When the urgency of "the cause" began to slacken, domestic arrangements for Jewish communal life appeared to claim greater attention, and with that focus, a host of questions emerged regarding communal governance under conditions of normalcy.

The end of the twentieth century marked a watershed in that respect. The centralized functioning of networks formed by cooperating local communal agencies closely corresponded with the pattern of organized, nationwide, religious denominations and their hegemony over the sphere of synagogue life. But toward the 1990s and the turn of the new century, privatization occurred in both areas – philanthropy and religion alike. Individual initiatives in funding selected domestic and foreign-based projects proliferated. By the same token, nearly a third of Jews surveyed (in 2012) declined to define their religion along specific denominational lines – twice the proportion of those who answered likewise in 1990.[104]

PA: American Jewish Committee and Jewish Publication Society of America, 1997), p. 19; see also www.jewishfederations.org/page.aspx?id=222910.

[104] Wertheimer, "Current Trends," pp. 3–22, 30–40, 45–6, 77–83 (quote from p. 77); Steven M. Cohen, "Reengineering the Jewish Community," *Journal of Jewish Communal Service* 73(1) (1996): 10; and "Trends in Jewish Philanthropy," in *American Jewish Year Book*, vol. LXXX (New York and Philadelphia, PA: American Jewish Committee and Jewish Publication Society of America, 1980), pp. 29–51; Sarna, *American Judaism*, pp. 372–3.

The agitation produced by the Second World War, the Cold War, the urban crisis, racial and ethnic tensions – alongside the recapitulation of historical American Jewish engagements overseas – had produced a lively public and intellectual discourse, a constituency that was available for "mobilization," and an organized infrastructure that sometimes elicited the envy of other subgroups. Toward the new millennium, it seemed, some part of this energy was released, absorbed, and re-channeled elsewhere. That, in turn, presented questions about where Jews, as a group, might be headed. These and related questions lie beyond the scope and aims of this book. They have been recently discussed at length by a number of writers.[105] From the historical perspective, these most recent trends appear to warrant close scrutiny, though perhaps the passage of time will permit a longer-term analysis.

For the 2012 survey, see www.ajc.org/site/c.ijITI2PHKoG/b.8073029/k.B021/2012_AJC_Survey_of_American_Jewish_Opinion.htm.

[105] Wertheimer, "American Jews and Israel: A 60-Year Retrospective"; Theodore Sasson, *The New American Zionism* (New York and London: New York University Press, 2013); Jonathan Rynhold, *The Arab-Israeli Conflict in American Political Culture* (Cambridge: Cambridge University Press, 2015); Dov Waxman, *Trouble in the Tribe: The American Jewish Conflict Over Israel* (Princeton, NJ: Princeton University Press, 2016).

Epilogue

> When certain minorities create protected enclaves as preserves of memory
> to be jealously safeguarded, they reveal [...] that without commemorative
> vigilance, history would soon sweep them away. These bastions buttress
> our identities, but if what they defended were not threatened, there would
> be no need for them.
> — Pierre Nora, "Between Memory and History"[1]

Ethnic history, generally speaking, is considered a subsidiary and sup-
plementary effort, appended to the national history (the history of the
United States in this case) that defines its larger narrative setting. Indeed,
the ethnic historian usually regards the canvas of national history as the
ultimate "destination" of the ethnic narrative – the place where it "right-
fully" belongs. Jews, like members of other groups in American society,
are enthusiasts of the national heritage precisely in order to be able to lay
claim to it. Thus, many ethnic or multicultural studies tend to verify and
support the larger national narrative, simply by virtue of repeating its
major themes in a minor key.

Yet, unless ethnic history challenges the usual contours of national
history, both geographically and culturally, it loses some of its inherent
purpose. That is to say, ethnic histories would be largely unnecessary if
they were merely smaller replicas of the nation's history at large – min-
iatures with an accent, as it were. Recapitulations of accepted national
narratives, even under the guise of multicultural diversity, merely add
another level of ideological conformity, as historian and literary scholar,

---

[1] *Realms of Memory: Rethinking the French Past*, under the direction of Pierre Nora, English
edition ed. Lawrence D. Kritzman (New York: Columbia University Press, 1996), p. 7.

Sacvan Bercovitch, once pointed out: "The patchwork quilt is the reverse side of the familiar stars and stripes; multi-culturalism is the hyphenated American writ large."[2]

As conveyed in the opening quote cited from Pierre Nora's seminal work on collective memory, it is the offbeat, the transient, and the relative obscurity of minority history that lend it its characteristic blend of elegy and urgency. It is a counter-history, because its version of the past is never comfortably ensconced within the majority's point of view. The starting point for considering American Jewish history is that Jewish life in America reflects a minor voice, never attaining majority-culture status in the national setting, despite the ample opportunities that Jews have had to meld within the hegemonic majority. Much of the time, Jews in American history were (in the felicitous, oxymoronic phrase of one recent observer) "integrated outsiders."[3] The emphasis in more recent times has been more on "integration" than on "outsider" status, compared to past times, perhaps.

Nevertheless, this minor history cannot be addressed adequately unless it is set up *alongside* the national history of America, but *apart* from it, as well. National histories are defined by their territorial boundaries (the line where national history ends and international relations begin); but it is hard to delimit the story of Jews in America by making it stop at the US border. Over half the Jews in the world live outside the United States, and they are and have been an ever-present factor in American Jewish discourse. As I have argued, Jews, unlike some other sub-groups in the American population, are apt to preserve their overseas engagements well beyond the immigrant generations. Spain, Germany, and Russia were our paradigmatic examples for the nineteenth and for much of the twentieth century. After 1948, Israel acquired a similar function as an "offshore" engagement that many Jews in America have been willing to undertake. This distinctive attribute is what makes the Jews stand out in particular, among all of America's varied groups.

One might conceivably account for the distinctive dimensions of the American Jewish experience under the rubric of the *religious* bond that links Jews in different countries, across political boundaries. Indeed, it was common in the nineteenth century for American Jews to refer to fellow Jews in other lands as their "co-religionists." However, that term now has an antiquarian ring to it, and for good reason. Religious difference is

---

[2] Bercovitch, *Rites of Assent*, p. 373.
[3] Hieke, *Jewish Identity in the Reconstruction South*, p. 108.

probably the easiest way of sorting out the Jews from everyone else; but Jews, as individuals, do not all subscribe to a common or exclusive set of sacred beliefs and practices. Religion often divides them more than it unites them. Hence, religious solidarity and common faith are not necessarily the best or the only lens through which to assess American Jewry's historical experience.

It is remarkable that the notable achievements of which Jews in America regularly boast are rarely those belonging to the domain of religion. Rather, they tend to cite outstanding individual achievements by Jews in the arts, sciences, and medicine; politics and the law; enterprise and industry; the media and popular culture. They notoriously keep track of the number of Jewish Nobel Prize winners. The National Museum of American Jewish History in Philadelphia features a Hall of Fame, where notable American Jewish figures from the past are showcased. Of the eighteen names initially selected for this gallery of luminaries, only four were religious leaders (Isaac Leeser, Isaac Mayer Wise, Mordecai M. Kaplan, and Menachem Mendel Schneerson).[4]

The extent to which Jews are involved in or concerned about overseas Jewish affairs, however, depends upon a non-private form of consciousness and sense of co-responsibility that goes against the grain of domestic, American-oriented, individualistic achievement and self-reliance. Moreover, while religious behaviors are often confined to the home, the house of worship, or some other location set aside for sacred rites (including cemeteries), the actions required in order to translate the subjective sense of Jewish co-responsibility into practical work are nearly all related to the public sphere, and nearly all require collaboration with others at a much greater order of magnitude.

The tension and linkage between these two forms of socialization – one, individual-based within the American civic polity; the other, group-based within a wider construct of world Jewry, spanning both time and space – are the hallmarks of the American Jewish experience. Instead of one grand synthesis that satisfies both parts in equal measure (individual consciousness and group behavior), there is, rather, an inherent ambiguity or dialectic at the heart of American Jewry's history. These are dynamic qualities in every sense: they defy attempts to reify American Jewry's past into a single, canonical pattern. We must, as observers of that history, be able to identify the architecture of displacement, the metaphorical "reset button" positioned along the various lines of its development.

---

[4] See www.nmajh.org/CoreExhibit.aspx.

Migration has brought Jews repeatedly to settle on American shores, beginning with sixteenth-century Iberian New Christians and extending to twentieth-century survivors of Nazi concentration camps and twenty-first-century émigrés from the former Soviet Union. Each new "first" generation of migrants has discovered that America is a place where multitudes of other people are always arriving, always making a new start.

Apart from multiple origins and a long series of "new beginnings," the history of American Jews also involves some aspects of closure. We have seen this with certain patterns of occupational change, for example. Although American Jewry continues to be characterized by a wide range of income and employment statuses, there is no longer a large sector of factory hands (who once numbered in the hundreds of thousands) as part of that range. Similarly, there were once more than just a handful of individual Jewish farmers, and that, too, appears to be a closed chapter. Jewish industrial workers and farmers appeared on the American stage in tandem with the large-scale arrival of foreign immigrants, and this corresponded with the completion of the nation's westward expansion, the modernization of American farming methods, and the rapid build-up of domestic consumer goods manufacturing. Those conditions no longer apply, and most Jews today are part and parcel of the post-industrial and service branches of the occupational structure.

The native language of most of the Jewish immigrants of earlier times – Yiddish – continues to this day to resonate, albeit faintly, in the lives of some American Jews; but here, again, we appear to be witness to a phenomenon that has largely run its course. The centuries-long historical career of Yiddish as the vernacular of millions, as a global lingua franca for Jews living in dozens of countries, and as the primary aesthetic vehicle for writers, journalists, dramatists, poets, and lyricists has tapered toward a "post-vernacular," commemorative phase.[5]

Another end-passage involves those households in which, after three, four, or sometimes five generations, the basis of their attachment to other Jews has become latent or, indeed, has been relinquished. The Pew Research Center study on Jewish identity in America reported in 2013 that there are nearly 2.5 million adult Christian Americans (that is, individuals whose religious self-description is solely Christian) who, nonetheless, answer "yes" to possessing a "Jewish background" or "Jewish

---

[5] Jeffrey Shandler, *Adventures in Yiddishland: Post-vernacular Language and Culture* (Berkeley: University of California Press, 2006); see also *Choosing Yiddish: New Frontiers of Language and Culture*, ed. Lara Rabinovitch, Shiri Goren, and Hannah S. Pressman (Detroit, MI: Wayne State University Press, 2013), pp. 319–75.

affinity" (about 1.6 million and 0.8 million, respectively). In households made up of such adults, there are also about 1 million children. The great majority, seven out of ten, are being raised as "not Jewish at all" (as Christians or without any religion); two out of ten are being raised with a dual religious identity (Jewish and other); and one out of ten has no Jewish religious upbringing, but their non-religious, partly Jewish background is acknowledged in the home.[6]

On the other hand, some anticipated end-points have signally failed to arrive on schedule. Prophecies of Orthodox Judaism's demise under conditions of America's secularity and benign religious tolerance have not been vindicated. Although the proportion of the Orthodox within the American Jewish population fell from the late nineteenth century until around 1950 – declining from at least one-third to no more than one-tenth of American Jewry – in the most recent decades no further such decline has occurred. Orthodoxy has, rather, become the Judaism of choice for a stable proportion of American Jews (still around 10 percent), particularly among younger Jews raised in Orthodox households, who no longer drift automatically and enthusiastically out of Orthodoxy upon reaching adulthood. Among young Jewish adults, aged eighteen to twenty-nine, who were raised as children in Orthodox Jewish homes, fully 83 percent still claim an Orthodox affiliation. Given the higher birth rates obtaining in Orthodox communities, the proportion of Jewish young adults today who are living according to Orthodox commitments appears, indeed, to be growing.[7]

At the same time, however, at the other end of the spectrum, predictions once touted by Reform Judaism's more traditionalist opponents – namely, that its liberal, ritually "light" form of religion would never last – have not been borne out. Reform Judaism's mission to bridge the gaps between Judaism and mainstream American values was thoroughly accomplished, it would seem, several generations ago; yet, as a denomination, it has continued to recruit members and to sustain congregations, to the point that it can (again) claim to be the largest American Jewish denomination.[8]

Thus, there have been many new beginnings, several closures, and even a few surprises. There are also some new ambiguities to ponder. The religion once touted as the third of America's supposedly three religions

---

[6] www.pewforum.org/2013/10/01/chapter-1-population-estimates.
[7] www.pewforum.org/2013/10/01/chapter-3-jewish-identity.
[8] *Ibid.*

now represents less than 2 percent of the population. What, then, can be said of a religious heritage that, given the dwindling share of its adherents in the national gallery of cultures, still apparently commands a good deal of public attention?[9] This remains, as yet, uncertain.

Another ambiguity, with which we began, and to which we return as we conclude our discussion, concerns the place of the Jews in American historical research. American Jews identify strongly with the United States, its history, and its way of life. The Jews of America are part of the national history. Ironically, the intensity of that identification is such that the history of American Jews as a discrete narrative has begun to seem superfluous. Due to the multicultural turn in our culture, the question occurs as to what specific part of American history Jews may be said to inhabit: are they part of the dominant majority, and as such indistinguishable; or are they still to be reckoned among the minorities – and in what sense?

In this book I have tried to question and to stretch the terms of this contest. The evidence and perspectives required for a history of the Jews in America are not limited to the social relations taking place within the borders of the fifty states; hence, all that there is to say about the Jews is not exhausted by delving into their status situation vis-à-vis other Americans. There is something reductionist, perhaps even parochial, in limiting the discussion to one of hierarchy (majority–minority). The challenge of American Jewish history lies in doing justice to its larger issues.

If one tries to discern in American Jewish history one common denominator, it is that Jews had led a diasporic existence on three continents for many centuries before any of their relatives ever set foot in the Americas. Given that history, Jews resemble Greek, Armenian, Chinese, and South Asian people – that is, groups having some formative history of trans-continental and overseas dispersion as minorities in other host cultures – more closely than they resemble Irish, Germans, Italians, Poles, or Mexicans (most of whom spoke a single language and migrated to the United States directly from a single ancestral land). Whereas many descent groups in America have a bi-polar relation to their former homelands, the Jewish heritage looks graphically more like a far-flung network of separate strands. America is another in a series of such diasporas.

Living in America, however, has affected more than just the language and civic culture of the Jews; it has re-configured their image of that open

9 Jonathan D. Sarna, "North American Jews in the New Millennium," in Liwerant et al., *Identities in an Era of Globalization and Multiculturalism*, pp. 347–8.

network of strands, so that they have come to see it more like the spokes of a closed wheel, with America at the axial point. As a historian might see these things, that image has all the trappings of legend: a corrective, ideological, and redeeming version of the past that, with the passage of time, acquires the feel of higher truth. Although historians, faced with a myth, may demur or might hope to restore some natural proportion to the legend, it is not at all certain that historians will have the final word.

Index

abrogation of Russian-American treaty,
  see Russia: US passport question
Adath Israel
  Cincinnati congregation, 29
Adler, Cyrus, 124, 127
Adler, Samuel (rabbi), 213*t*. 4.1.
affinities and values
  cultural explanations for mobility, 80
African Americans, 11, 32, 35, 96, 102,
    105, 141, 169, 257, 261, 263,
    268, 285
  culture, 185
  Jewish representations of, 185, 186
  music industry, 183
  relations with Jews, 264
  religion, 185
agriculture
  agrarian ideal, 98, 99
  and Jews, 37, 38, 77, 81, 99–101, 187,
    251, 291, 309
  associations, 100–1
  farm colonies in US, 98–9
  philanthropic projects, 98
  post-1940, 181–2
  poultry farming, 100, 148
  Russia, 97–8
  higher education, 147
  in Soviet Union, 243
Agro-Joint, *see* American Jewish Joint
    Distribution Committee (AJDC):
    and Jewish agriculture in Russia
Agronsky (Agron), Gershon, 161, 162,
  164
Agudas harabbonim, 117, 125

Ahavath Chesed
  New York congregation, 115
aid to Jews in distress, 192, 242, 247, 256,
    257, 304
  World War I era, 130, 131, 225
  landsmanshaftn, 129
aid to non-Jews
  as form of social conscience, 268
Alabama, 70, 187
Albany, NY, 15, 25
alcohol
  consumption, 27, 33, 34, 35, 78, 123,
    141, 142
Alexander II, Russian tsar, 234
Alexander III, Russian tsar, 234
Allen, Woody, 259
Allgemeine Zeitung des Judenthums, 198
Alliance Israélite Universelle, 98
Am oylom, 98
Amalgamated Clothing Workers of
    America (ACWA), 137, 139
America Firsters, 170, 231, 232
America-Israel Public Affairs Committee
    (AIPAC), 295, 297
American aliya, *see* Israel: American Jewish
    immigration
American century idea, 188
American Civil War, 54, 55, 56, 78,
    119, 169
American Communist Party, 233
American Federation of Labor, 222, 227
American Hebrew, 76, 197, 217
American identity, 37, 38, 141, 149, 183,
    184, 222, 232, 246

American Jewish Committee, 192, 227, 229, 238, 240, 292
American Jewish Congress, 192, 229
American Jewish Historical Society, 127, 128
American Jewish Joint Distribution Committee (AJDC), 130, 192, 225, 242, 243
and Jewish agriculture in Russia, 139, 244
American Jewish tricentennial 1954, 188
American Labor Party, 168
American neutrality, 222
Neutrality Acts, 203, 207
WWI prior to 1917, 219, 221
American Red Cross, 223
American Relief Administration, 243
American Revolution, 6, 7, 16, 23, 30, 45
American Society for Cultural Relations with Russia, 139
American Southwest
crypto-Judaism, 286
American Zionist Medical Unit (AZMU), 155, 161
Amsterdam, 9
anarchism, 78, 163
Anschluss (German annexation of Austria 1938), 205
Anshe Chesed
Cleveland congregation, 49
anti-communism, 138, 148, 243, 273
anti-German sentiment
in WWI era, 221
Antin, Mary, 222
anti-Nazi activities in America, 227, 229
antisemitism, 95, 144, 148, 172, 205, 206, 209, 216, 288, 298
in Russia, 220, 237
anti-war sentiment
American Jews in WWI era, 220, 221, 222, 231
anti-Zionism
haredim and, 268
Ararat, *see* Noah, Mordecai M.
Arbeter ring, see Workmen's Circle
Arendt, Hannah, 177, 272, 274, 275
Argentina, 98, 159, 257
Arion Society, 211
Arizona, 68
Armenians, 311

army, *see* Jews: in armed services
army chaplains
Civil War, 54
arts and entertainment, 251, 308
Ashkenazim, 7, 10, 18, 23, 194
assimilation, 186, 300
Association of American Orthodox Hebrew Congregations, 116
Atlanta, GA, 67
Atlantic Charter, 231
Auschwitz, 171, 186
Auster, Paul, 259
Australia, 36, 172
Austria, 21n. 36, 28, 133, 193, 205, 209, 210
immigrants from, 61
Jews from, 71, 87, 88t. 2.2.

B'nai B'rith, 25, 29, 52, 120, 122, 129, 192, 210
B'nai Jeshurun
Lincoln, Nebraska congregation, 113
New York City congregation, 48
Baltimore, MD, 22t. 1.2., 23, 24–5, 47, 50, 62, 88, 115, 124, 176, 179, 217, 258, 259, 262, 266
banking, 34, 79, 144
Barbados, 8, 9, 16, 26
bar-mitzvah, 156, 287, 289
Barondess, Joseph, 222
Baruch, Bernard, 168
Basinski, Julius, 68
bat-mitzvah, 156, 287, 289
adult bat-mitzvah, 285
Bavaria, 212
Jews from, 7, 27, 68, 115
Bedford-Stuyvesant, Brooklyn, 261
Begin, Menachem, 303
Belarus, 97, 114, 234, 254
Bell, Daniel, 146
Bellow, Saul, 160, 259
Bene Israel
Cincinnati congregation, 26
Bene Yeshurun
Cincinnati congregation, 29
Benevolent Society, *see* cemeteries
Ben-Gurion, David, 158, 292
Benjamin, Judah P., 198, 239
Ben-Zvi, Yitzhak, 158
Bercovitch, Sacvan, 141, 307
Berkman, Alexander, 163

Berlin, Germany, 212, 215, 276
Berlin crisis, 301
Berlin, Irving (Israel Baline), 134
Bessarabia (Moldova), 90, 147
Beth Elohim, *see* Charleston, SC
Charleston congregation, 50
Beth Hamedrosh Hagodol
New York congregation, 62
Beth Israel
Milwaukee congregation, 117
Bethlehem, SD, 99
Bible, 39, 48, 49, 50, 53, 96, 110, 185, 200
swearing-in, 17
Biltmore Conference, 293
Binghamton, NY, 181
blacks, *see* African Americans
blasphemy, 15
Jacob Lumbrozo charged with, 14
Bloomingdale, Benjamin, 68
Board of Delegates of American
Israelites, 192
Board of Jewish Education
New York City, 123
Boas, Franz Uri, 218, 219
Bogen, Boris, 93
Bohemia, 28, 71
Bolsheviks, 130, 133, 158, 240, 242–3
US-British military intervention
against, 234
Bonaparte, Napoleon, 18, 23, 61
boom towns, 33, 35, 36
Borochov, Ber, 158
Boston Hebrew College, 281
Boston, MA, 6, 25, 26, 58, 59t. 2.1., 67,
104, 105, 143, 157, 206, 222, 258,
262, 266, 275
boycott
counter-boycott against German goods,
227–8, 229, 231
Nazi boycott against Jews, 227
Boyle Heights, Los Angeles, 263
Brandeis University, 144, 177
Brandeis, Louis D., 105, 217, 223, 291
Brazil, 4, 8, 9, 36
Breslau (Wrocław, Poland), 33, 115
Britain, *see* England
British White Paper of 1939, 292
Brody, Alter, 96, 131, 163
Bronx, New York, 211, 263
Brooklyn Tablet, 206
Brooklyn, NY, 105, 157, 183, 261

Budapest, Hungary, 212
Buffalo, NY, 38, 71n. 29, 160
building trades, 82
bungalow colonies, 187

Cahan, Abe (Abraham), 195, 196,
197, 244
California, 25, 33, 34, 35, 67, 68, 99, 142,
182, 214
Calvinists, 14
Camden, NJ, 100
Camp Upton, *see* Jews: in armed services:
World War I
Canada, 18, 36, 98, 164, 181
and Jewish farming, 98
Jewish trans-migrants, 159–61
Jewish war volunteers, 161
capitalism
and social values, 270
effect on Jewish settlement, 5, 8, 10, 57
effect on religious toleration, 2, 13
Caribbean, 1, 5, 7, 8, 9, 11, 20, 70,
196, 286
Catholics, 7, 8, 14, 16, 19, 20, 27, 28, 30,
35, 54, 94, 95, 119, 142, 143, 168,
169, 195, 201, 202, 207, 208, 223,
250, 270
anti-communism, 206, 207
England, 18
Catskills, 38, 100
Caucasus
Jews from, 255
cemeteries, 8, 26, 31, 32, 37, 44, 60,
113, 283
burial societies, 34
Central Conference of American Rabbis,
124, 205, 217, 289
Chabad, *see* Hasidic Jews: Chabad
Chagall, Marc, 246
chaplains, *see* army chaplains
charity
secular and sectarian, 118
Charleston, SC, 6, 7n. 7, 9, 10, 22t. 1.2.,
23, 24, 25, 27, 29, 32, 47, 50
Chicago, IL, 25, 33, 37, 38, 57, 59t. 2.1.,
62, 63, 66, 67, 70, 78, 83, 102, 107,
109, 110, 117, 141, 143, 145, 147,
154, 160, 164, 177, 179, 217, 230,
258, 259, 262, 266
politics, 103, 104, 111
Chile, 257

Chinese, 311
  in America, 35
cholera, 34
Churchill, Winston, 163
Cincinnati, OH, 12t. 1.1., 25, 26, 27, 29,
    30, 51, 66, 104, 114, 115, 120, 126,
    183, 230, 276
cities
  Jewish settlement patterns, 25, 31
  Jews' representations of in
      literature, 259
  westward expansion and, 24
civil rights, 78, 102, 268, 277, 299
  Jews in early America, 16, 19
  Jews' support for African American
      equality, 177
civil service, 145, 251
Civil War, *see* American Civil War
class and class conflict, 78, 79, 80, 111,
    122, 134, 264–5
  stereotypes, 79
Cleveland, Grover, 103, 239
Cleveland, OH, 25, 49, 50, 58, 59t. 2.1.,
    66, 67, 294
  Jewish philanthropic institutions,
      119–20, 121
clothing industry, *see* garment
      manufacturing
Cohen, Elliot, 190
Cold War, 177, 189, 250, 257, 273,
    297, 305
Columbia University, 217, 218, 222, 274
Columbus, Christopher, 128, 200, 203
  and Jewish origin myth, 200–1
Commercial Advertiser, 195
Commonweal, 207
communism, 148, 158, 163, 164, 195, 206,
    207, 232, 271, 273, 277
  after 1917, 241, 243
  volunteers in Spanish Civil War, 203–5
  WWII era, 232, 233
Communist Party, *see* communism
Confederacy, 54, 239
Conference of Presidents of Major Jewish
      Organizations, 295, 297
Connecticut, 182
conservatism
  and social values, 94
Conservative Judaism, *see* Judaism:
      Conservative
conversion, 3, 45, 285, 288, 289

conversos, *see* New Christians
cookbooks, 108
Cooper, James Fenimore, 184
Copland, Aaron, 183
Coughlin, Charles, 168, 206
Crémieux, Adolphe, 99
Crémieux, SD, 99
Crimea, *see* American Jewish Joint
      Distribution Committee (AJDC):
      and Jewish agriculture in Russia
criminality, 79
  effect on inner-city neighborhoods, 264
  Jews and, 34, 79, 104, 122, 142,
      146–7, 260
  Prohibition, 142
crypto-Jews, *see* New Christians
Cuba, 172, 179, 194, 254, 255, 274
  and Jewish trans-migrant refugees, 181
  and Spanish-American War, 196,
      197, 198
  Cuban missile crisis, 301
Cukor, George (Zukor), 134
Curaçao, 5, 8, 9
Czechoslovakia, *see* Bohemia,
      Moravia, 133

Dallas, TX, 69
Darwin, Charles, 53
Davenport, IA, 66
Day of Atonement, *see* Yom Kippur
de Lancey, Oliver, *see* Franks, Phila
Debs, Eugene V., 197
Delaware, 17
democracy, *see* democratization: in
      communal governance
Democratic Party, 102, 104, 105, 120, 271
  Jewish support, 143, 167
democratization
  in communal governance, 121
Denver, CO, 69
deportation, 92, 163
Der Tog, 222
Des Moines, IA, 29, 30, 231
desegregation, 263
Detroit, MI, 25, 29, 58, 59t. 2.1., 230, 258,
      262, 264
Dewey, John, 139
diamond trade, 266
Die Deborah, 27, 53
Director, Aaron, 167
discrimination, 271

effect on employment, 80, 87, 88,
    94, 143–4
higher education, 159
issue in foreign affairs
    Russia and US passport
        question, 240
    psychological effects, 145–6
disease and hygiene, 85
Displaced Persons, 173n. b, 178, 181, 304
Disraeli, Benjamin, 199
Doctorow, E. L., 259
Drachman, Bernard (rabbi), 115, 124,
    213t. 4.1.
Dreyfus affair, 216
Dropsie College, 124
Du Bois, W. E. B., 215
dual loyalties, 292
Dubinsky, David, 227, 243
Dubuque, IA, 30
Duluth, MN, 66
DuPont Corporation, *see* Shapiro, Irving S.

Easton, PA, 29
economists, 167
Edlin, William, 222
egalitarianism
    gender in the synagogue, 281, 285, 286
Eichmann in Jerusalem, see
        Arendt, Hannah
Eichmann, Adolph, 273
Einhorn, David (rabbi), 212, 213t. 4.1.
Eisenhower, Dwight, 295
Eisenstein, Ira (rabbi), 280
elderly, 260, 261
elections, 16, 103, 104, 105, 106, 167, 231,
    259, 270, 271
Electoral College, 259
Ellis Island, 69, 92, 133, 175
Emerson, Ralph Waldo, 178
endogamy, 86–8, 90
Engel, David, 181n. 101
England, 4, 7, 10, 11, 23, 44, 70, 71, 172,
    205, 215, 256
    in Palestine, *see* Palestine: British
        Mandate
    in WWI, 148, 155, 161, 220, 221, 223
        Zionist support for, 223, 224
    Jewish community, 65
    Jewish immigrants from, 26
    Jewish refugees in, 174, 175
    Jews expelled from, 3

New World colonies, 1
WWII ally, 231
English language
    and Jewish prayer, 47, 57, 124
entrepreneurship, *see* self-employment
Ethiopian Jews, 304
ethnic and national history, 306–7
Etz Chayim Yeshiva, 114, 115
Europe
    Jewish disabilities in, 13–14, 18
    Jews in 1600s, 2
exile, *see* Judaism: religion: concepts: exile

family
    kinship networking as economic
        asset, 87
farmers, *see* agriculture: and Jews
Fascism, 178, 195, 203, 205, 207
Federation for the Support of Jewish
        Philanthropic Societies of New York
        City, 123
Federation of Jewish Charities, Cleveland,
        OH, 121
Federation of Oriental Jews, 202
federations, 121, *see also* philanthropy:
        and Jewish community: governance
Feingold, Henry, 140, 181n. 101
fellowship communities (*havurot*), 281
Felsenthal, Bernard (rabbi), 53, 111,
    213t. 4.1.
Female Hebrew Benevolent Society
    Philadelphia, 52
feminism
    and Judaism, 285, 286
Ferber, Edna, 95, 210
fertility and family planning, 95
film and film industry, 90, 134, 152, 228,
    245, 259
Finkelstein, Louis (rabbi), 269–70, 271
Finns, 83
    and radical politics, 106
first settler myth, 29, 31
Fischer, Louis, 164
Fitzgerald, F. Scott, 147
Florida, 38, 166, 187, 255, 257
folk Judaism, 278, 288
folk religion, 40, 52
Forverts (Forward), 103, 221
France, 4, 11, 18, 205, 216, 223, 256, 274
    Jews expelled from, 3
    New World colonies, 1, 7, 31

Franco, Francisco, 164, 203, 205,
    206, 207
Frankel, Zacharias (rabbi), 115
Frankfurter, Felix, 168, 170, 217, 223
Franks, Abigaill, 10n. 12, 44, 45, 52
Franks, David, 45
Franks, Naphtali, 44
Franks, Phila, 45
Fredman, J. George, 228
free-loan associations, 92, 260
Freemasonry, 46, 47, 49
Friedenwald, Harry, 217
Friedlaender, Israel, 224, 242
Friedman, Milton, 167
Fromm, Erich, 177, 178

G. I. Bill, 249
Gadol, Moise, 202
Galicia, 28, 115
Galveston, TX, 69
garment manufacturing, 26, 82, 89, 137,
    140, 153
Gay, Peter, 181n. 101
Gedalecia, Joseph, 202
Geist, Raymond, 229
gender ratio among immigrants, 90
    effect on endogamous marriage, 87
    Jews from Eastern Europe, 84
    relation to permanent settlement and
        economic integration, 84
General Electric Corporation, 243
geography
    regional distribution of US Jews, 85,
        90, 259
    urban, 36, 97, 267
    urban vs rural, 37, 95
        and Prohibition, 142
George, Henry, 105
German language, 27, 28, 210, 211,
    212, 215
    and education, 49
    literature, 214, 215, 224
    press, 53
German philosophies, 48, 274
German social science, 215, 218
German-American Bund, 230
German-American Business League
    (DAWA), 230
German-Americans
    and Nazism, 229, 230
    WWI era, 220

Germanization
    Jews and, 209
Germany, 4, 21n. 36, 23, 127, 138, 159,
    193, 205, 274
    American Jewish attitudes in 19th
        century, 209–16
    and antisemitism, 215
    and Soviet Jewish emigrants, 302
    culture, 28, 221, 224
    immigrants from, 27, 28, 31, 32, 61, 69,
        88t. 2.2., 103, 106, 208, 210, 311
    in WWI, 223
    Jewish expulsions, 3
    Jewish leadership in 1930s, 226
    Jews from, 8, 10, 23, 26, 27, 30, 49, 61,
        71, 87, 88t. 2.2., 114
    and agriculture, 181
    and employment of east European
        Jewish immigrants, 91
    and Jewish communal leadership, 91
    in Palestine, 174
    Nazi era, 175–8, 181, 182
    Jews migrating to, 70
    Nazi regime, 174, 203, 209, 225,
        232, 274, 275, 276, 293,
        see also Nazism
    trans-migration through Europe, 63, 65
Gershwin, George and Ira, 185
ghetto, 78, 92, 133, 141, 258, 264
Gilded Age, 214
Glatzer, Nahum N., 177, 181n. 101
Gold Rush, 33, 214
Goldberg, Harvey E., 284
Goldfogle, Henry M., 102, 105
Goldman, Emma, 163–4
Gomez family, 8
Gompers, Samuel, 222
Gordin, Jacob, 245
Gottheil, Gustav (rabbi), 199, 213t. 4.1
Gottheil, Richard, 217, 223, 224
Graetz, Heinrich, 214
Grant, Ulysses S., 103, 120, 236
Gratz, Benjamin, 12t. 1.1
Gratz, Michael, 12t. 1.1
Gratz, Rebecca, 48, 49n. 91, 51, 52
Great Awakening, 41
Great Depression, 134, 140, 165, 175, 188,
    203, 207, 225, 253, 265
Greece
    Jews from, 62
Green, Arthur (rabbi), 281

Ha'avarah agreement, 228
Habsburg Empire, 2, 3, 62, 64, 70, 133
Hadassah, 155, 156, 161, 297
Halivni, David Weiss, 181*n*. 101
Halkin, Abraham S., 284
Halkin, Hillel, 284
Harby, Isaac, 47, 51
Harding, Warren G., 149
haredim, 180, 255, 266, 267, 268, 286
Harlem, New York City, 221
Harris, Maurice (rabbi), 221
Harrison, Benjamin, 235, 236
Harvard University, 217, 273
Hasidic Jews, 180, 185, 194, 261, 276
    Chabad, 268
Havurat Shalom, 281
havurot, see Havurat Shalom; fellowship
    communities (havurot)
Haymarket Riot, 78, 111, 164
hazan (cantor), 50
Hebrew Emigrant Aid Society
    (HEAS), 74
Hebrew language, 39, 298
    and Jewish liturgy, 49, 57, 124
Hebrew literature in America, 185, 199
Hebrew Theological College, 154
Hebrew Union College, 276
Hebrew Union College (HUC), 114
Hebrew University of Jerusalem, 162
Hebrews
    category tabulated by US immigration
        authorities, 133
Hebron, 162*n*. 64
Heifetz, Jascha, 246
Heine, Heinrich, 199, 211, 214
Heller, Max (rabbi), 217
Henry Street Settlement, 220,
    see also Wald, Lillian, 139
Henry, Jacob, 17
Herzl, Theodor, 77, 216, 217
Heschel, Abraham Joshua, 181*n*. 101,
    300
Heschel, Abraham Joshua (rabbi),
    272, 276–7
Heschel, Susannah, 181*n*. 101
HIAS (Hebrew Sheltering and Immigrant
    Aid Society), 239, 302,
    see also HIAS (United HIAS
        Service), 226
HIAS (United HIAS Service), 179
High Holidays, 34, 150

higher education, 80, 145, 250
    discrimination, 143, 144
Highland Park, IL, 252
Hilberg, Raul, 181*n*. 101, 272, 274–5
Hilfsverein der Deutschen Juden, 98
Hillman, Sidney, 139
Hillquit, Morris, 221
Hirsch, Emil G. (rabbi), 213*t*. 4.1.
Hirsch, Maurice de, 98
Hirsch, Samuel (rabbi), 213*t*. 4.1.
Hispanics, *see* Latinos
Hitler, Adolf, 172, 204, 225, 226, 229, 294
Holland, 4, 10, 11, 70
    Jewish immigrants from, 7, 23
    New World colonies, 1, 4, 5, 14
Holocaust, 131, 181, 181*n*. 101, 188, 248,
    268, 274, 277, 300, 303, 304
Holocaust survivors, 173, 174*n*. a, 178–80,
    181, 182, 309
Holtzman, Jack, 183
Holy Land, *see* Palestine; Zionism
hometown associations, *see*
    landsmanshaftn
Hook, Sidney, 272–3
Hoover, Herbert, 143, 165, 243
Horowitz, Horowitz, 246
hospitals and health care, 92, 94, 122, 144,
    155, 251, 258
Howells, William Dean, 244
Huebsch, Adolph (rabbi), 220
Huebsch, Ben W., 220
Huguenots, 20
human capital, 81, 82
Hungary, 70, 133, 138, 180, 195, 210,
    216, 267
    Holocaust era, 172
    immigrants from, 28, 106
    Jews from, 62n. 11, 71, 102, 114,
        115, 134
    post-WWII, 179

IBM, 252
identity politics, 299–300
illegal immigration to America, 134*n*. 6
Illinois, 68, 86
Illowy, Bernard (rabbi), 212, 213*t*. 4.1.
immigration
    quotas and restrictions, 133–4, 136, 141,
        143, 174
    US immigration policy after 1960, 254
Indiana, 67

Indians, 30, *see also* Native Americans
Industrial Removal Office (IRO), 69
Inquisition, 3, 205
    New World, 3, 200
inter-faith couples, 289, 290
inter-faith dialogue, 208, 277
Intergovernmental Committee on
    Refugees, 228
intermarriage, 7, 21, 45, 52, 86, 175, 249,
    289, 290
    depiction of in Zangwill's "The Melting
        Pot", 236
    Gentile Americans from different ethnic
        stocks, 87
International Brigade, *see* Spanish
    Civil War
International Ladies Garment Workers
    Union (ILGWU), 137, 138,
    140, 243
International Refugee Organization
    (IRO), 179
Iowa, 67, 95, 99
Iran
    Islamic Republic, 268
    Jews from, 255
Irish
    in America, 31, 32, 70, 79, 83, 88t. 2.2.,
        94, 168, 202, 311
    attitudes on WWI, 220
    opinion on Spanish Fascism, 206
Islam and Moslems, 2, 3, 193
isolationism, 149, 207
Israel, 77, 174, 181, 188, 248, 254, 256,
        257, 277, 287, 291, 292, 294, 296,
        297, 299, 300, 303, 304, 307
    American Jewish immigration, 286, 287
    American Jewish support, 291, 292–8
    criticism of, 296, 298
    disagreements with US Jewish
        groups over Soviet Jewish
        emigration, 302–3
    effect on American Jewish organizational
        life, 290
    effect on Jewish culture, 297–8
    Jews from, 255
    Likud Party, 303
    representation of in liberal
        discourse, 296–7
Israel, House of (as synonym for Jewish
    people), 43
Italy, 3, 4, 11, 70, 302

    immigrants from, 64, 84, 85, 88t. 2.2.,
        89, 103, 148, 186, 202, 208, 311
    and socialism, 106
    political opinions on Spanish
        Fascism, 206
    volunteers in Spanish Civil War, 206
    Jews from, 115

J. Seligman & Co., 34
Jackson-Vanik Amendment, 301
Jamaica, 8, 16
Japan, 237, 237n. 88
Jastrow, Marcus (rabbi), 213t. 4.1.
Jefferson, Thomas, 17, 18
Jerusalem, 41, 49, 77, 125, 161, 162, 162n.
    64, 221
Jewish Agency, 294
Jewish Agricultural Society, 182
Jewish Chautauqua Society, 127
Jewish Colonization Association, 98
Jewish commonwealth in Palestine, *see*
    Biltmore Conference
Jewish Defense Association, 238
Jewish Encyclopedia, 127
Jewish Immigrants' Information Bureau
    (JIIB), 69
Jewish Institute of Religion (JIR), 154
Jewish Labor Committee, 227, 229
Jewish law, *see* Judaism: religion: concepts:
    halakhah
Jewish leadership
    US Administration and
        refugee question, 170
Jewish Legion, 148, 161, 164
Jewish migration
    19th century, 61
    after 1945, 254
    as response to human rights crisis,
        235
    Europe
        late 19th century, 61–3
    from Russia, 234
    mass migration era, 64, 65–6, 238
    median age, 81
    post-Soviet migration to US, 255
    return-migration, 64
Jewish nationalism, 216, 218
Jewish organizations
    expansion in 1920s, 149
Jewish Orphan Asylum, Cleveland, OH,
    119, 120

Jewish Publication Society of America, 124, 127, 236
Jewish Renewal, 280
Jewish Social Service Association (New York), 166
Jewish Social Service Bureau (Los Angeles), 166
Jewish Spectator, 177
Jewish Studies
  in the American academy, 181, 195
Jewish Theological Seminary (JTS) Association, 115
Jewish Theological Seminary of America, 115, 117, 154, 224, 269, 276, 281, 284
Jewish War Veterans, 228
Jewish Welfare Board (JWB), 123
Jews
  and anti-Catholicism in US, 201–2, 247
  and Germans in America, 27, 28, 210–11, 218
    identities, 28
  and rural America, 95–101, 185–7
  civil status of, 71
  Diaspora history, 126, 311
  ethnocentrism, 112
  foreign interests
    compared with other Americans, 190–5, 246–7
    impact on centralization of Jewish organizations, 191–2
  foreign-born as percent of US Jews, year 2000, 255
  German vs Russian stereotypes, 73–4, 79, 117–18
  in armed services, 126, 148, 251
    Civil War, 54
    Spanish-American War, 197
    WWI, 123, 125, 161, 223
    WWII, 247, 249, 274
  middle-class social profile after WWII, 252
  occupational patterns after 1945, 250–1
  occupations
    after 1880, 78–9
    early 1900s, 81
    in early America, 16, 20–1, 24, 26, 32
    mobility, 80–2
    work force participation, 81
  population

birth rates, 267
distribution in US, 1820, 21
distribution in US, 1900, 68
distribution in US, 1970 (cities), 258
organized redistribution, 69
post-1950, 248
prejudice against, 18
Russian influences in culture and the arts, 245
upper class, 135
upward class mobility after WWI, 135
Jim Crow, 145
Johnson, Albert, 133
Johnson, Lyndon B., 253
Joint, *see* American Jewish Joint Distribution Committee (AJDC)
Joint Boycott Council, 230
Joseph, Jacob (rabbi), 116
  funeral riot, 116
Judaism, 39, 271
  and Americanization, 46, 54, 125, 189
  as America's third religion, 310
  biblical, 41
  Conservative, 113, 115, 116, 151, 154, 156, 253, 269, 278, 280, 281, 285
    and women's rabbinical ordination, 281
  denominations in, 107, 151, 278–82, 304
  in civic affairs, 54
  Orthodox, 113, 114, 116, 122, 125, 151, 154, 155, 193, 218, 278, 279, 280, 284, 310
    and religious education for girls, 157
    growth of haredi (ultra-Orthodox) Jewry, 266–9
    in Palestine, 223
    separation of gendered roles, 286
  post-biblical, 41
  Reconstructionist, 149, 280
  Reform, 48, 51, 53, 107, 108–9, 112, 113, 114, 117, 125, 151, 194, 205, 217, 218, 278, 279n. 60, 290, 310
    and religious education for girls, 156
    Charleston, 47, 214n. 44
    patrilineal descent policy, 289
  religion, 19, 39, 41, 212, 282
    concepts
      charity, 111
      creed, 43, 48, 109
      ethics, 43

Judaism (*cont.*)
  exile, 43
  God, 271, 272, 276, 277, 280, 288
  halakhah, 155, 275
  messiah, 11–13
  repentance and forgiveness, 109, 110
  salvation, 43
  shame, 41, 43, 44, 51, 54
  sin, 41, 42, 43, 109, 110, 267, 272
  universalism, 271
  divisive character, 308
  heresies, 11
  liturgy, 48
  orientalism, 39, 107
  practices, 41, 279, 282
    circumcision, 39, 40, 42, 283, 289
    death and burial, 44, 47
    domestic, 43, 52, 282, 285
    food, 42, 44, 108, 267
    Hebrew names, 287, 288, 289
    marriage and divorce, 40, 41, 287
    mezuzah, 283
    pietism, 267
    sexuality, 41, 42, 267
    calendar, 39
  spiritual life in Europe vs
    America, 128
  World War I, 123–5
 spiritual life in colonial times, 11–13
 theology, 11

K. A. M.
 Chicago congregation, 109, 110
kabbala and kabbalism, 194
Kafka, Franz, 177
Kahan, Arcadius, 181*n.* 101
Kallen, Deborah, 162
Kallen, Horace M., 162, 217, 223
Kansas, 33, 68, 99
Kansas City, MO, 69
Kaplan, Marion, 181*n.* 101
Kaplan, Mordecai M. (rabbi), 149,
  280, 308
Kassow, Samuel, 181*n.* 101
Kennedy, John F., 295
Kennedy, Joseph P., 168
Kentucky, 96, 97, 132, 187
King, Martin Luther, Jr., 277
Kishinev, 90, 148, 236
Koenig, Samuel, 102
Koenigsberg (Kaliningrad), 274

kohen (cohen), 41, 108, 114
Kohler, Kaufmann (rabbi), 107, 108,
  213*t.* 4.1.
Kohut, Alexander (rabbi), 115, 213*t.* 4.1.
kosher food, 39, 40, 42, 49, 108, 123, *see also*
  Judaism: religion: practices: food
Krauskopf, Joseph (rabbi), 108, 198
Kuhn, Fritz, 230
Kuznets, Simon, 89

La America, see Ladino language: press
La Convivencia, see Spanish
    Golden Age
labor unions, 79, 90, 91, 101, 136, 142,
  168, 169, 222, 262, 265
 industrial unions, 90
 response to Nazism, 227
Labor Zionism, 161, 222
Ladino language
 press, 202
LaFollette, Robert M., Sr., 105
LaGuardia, Fiorello, 207
Lancaster, PA, 23
landsmanshaftn, 129, 180
Latin America, *see* South America
Latinos, 257
 and Spanish-speaking Jewish
  immigrants, 194
Lauterbach, Edward, 102
law, *see* legal profession
law enforcement, 142, 145
lay leadership
 in synagogues, 40, 47, 50, 72, 279
Lazarus family, 57, 59–60
Lazarus, Emma, 56, 59, 60, 61, 76, 77, 78,
  134, 199, 214, 217, 235
League of Nations, 171
Leeser, Isaac, 48, 49, 51, 52, 109, 308
legal profession, 33, 212, 251, 308
Lehman, Herbert, 138, 227
Lehman, Irving, 227
Leopold and Loeb murder case, 147
Lester, Julius, 285
Levi Strauss Company, 147
Levinson, Barry, 259
Levites, 114
Levy, Asser, 9
Levy, Leonard, 221
Levy, Moses, 38
Lewisohn, Ludwig, 224
Lexington, KY, 12*t.* 1.1., 97

Leyeles, Aharon (Glanz), 132, 189
liberalism, 121, 197, 208, 210, 230, 262,
        269, 270, 271, 273, 277, 291, 297
    "tikkun olam", 268
Liebman, Joshua Loth (rabbi), 272
Lilienthal, Max (rabbi), 48, 51, 212,
        213t. 4.1.
Lincoln, Abraham, 102
Lincoln, NE, 113, 114
Lindbergh, Charles, 231, 232
liquor, *see* alcohol: consumption
Lisitzky, Ephraim E., 185
Lithuania, 2, 9, 29, 97, 117, 180, 234, 252
Livorno (Leghorn), 4, 8
Łódź, Poland, 245
London, 4, 7, 7n. 7, 8, 9, 18, 23, 60, 276
    Jews and entrepreneurship in, 89
London, Meyer, 106
Longfellow, Henry Wadsworth, 56, 59,
        60, 184
Lorelei Fountain, *see* Heine, Heinrich
Los Angeles, CA, 68, 69, 147, 166, 175,
        179, 187, 188, 203, 255, 258,
        262, 266
Los Angeles, LA, 264
Louisiana, 7, 86
    Louisiana Purchase, 7
Louisville, KY, 12t. 1.1., 25, 105, 120
Lower East Side, 105, 195, 196, 197
Lutherans, 28, 209, 222
lynchings, 35, 186

Mack, Julian, 170, 217, 223
Madison Square Garden, 229, 230
Madison, IN, 53
Magnes, Judah L. (rabbi), 122, 123, 162,
        220, 238
Maimonides (Rabbi Moshe ben Maimon)
    as cultural icon, 194
Maimonides School, 157, 275
Manhattan, *see* New York City
manual trades, 81
Marcuse, Herbert, 177
Mark Twain (Samuel Clemens), 237
Marshall, Louis, 238, 243
Marxism, 78, 177, 215, 241, 272
Maryland, 14, 15, 17
Masonic rites, *see* Freemasonry
Massachusetts, 86, 187, 281, 285
Mayer, Louis B., 228
McDonald, James G., 171

McKinley, William, 196
medicine, 33, 144, 145, 159, 212, 215, 308
Mediterranean, 9, 11, 193
    Sephardim from eastern
        Mediterranean, 70
memorialization, *see* memory
memory
    collective
        history, nostalgia, grief, 126–31, 191
Memphis, TN, 25, 31, 32, 120, 261
    Federation (Jewish Service
        Agency), 261
Mendes, Henry Pereira (rabbi), 115,
        116, 197
Menuhin, Yehudi, 148
meritocratic standards, 145
Merzbacher, Leo (rabbi), 213t. 4.1.
Messersmith, George S., 229
Mexican-American War, 33, 54
Mexicans
    in United States, 35, 169, 263, 311
Mexico, 3, 194, 286, *see also* Spain: New
        World colonies
    Inquisition in, 3
Meyer, Michael A., 181n. 101
Miami, FL, 188, 258, 262
Michigan, 30, 99, 168
Middle East
    emerging nations, 256
    in geopolitics, WWI era, 223
middle-class
    lifestyle, 28, 48
Midwest, 25, 57, 69, 86, 101, 143, 187
migration
    early 19th century, 23
    effect on family ties, 126
    re-emigration, 157–60, 287
    temporary migrants, 64
    trans-migration, 71
    United States domestic migration, 66,
        67, 68, 69
        planned population redistribution, 70
migration regime, 174
    Trans-Atlantic migrants, 63
Mikveh Israel, 6, *see also* Philadelphia, PA
    Philadelphia congregation, 48
Milgram, Stanley, 272, 275, 276
    and Milgram experiment, 273
Mill Street synagogue, 14
Milwaukee, WI, 25, 58, 99, 117, 210, 230
Minneapolis, MN, 58, 222, 252

minyan, 31
missionaries, 41, 119
Mississippi (State), 187
Mississippi Valley, 214
Mobile, AL, 30, 90
Molotov-Ribbentrop agreement, 232
Montana, 68
Montgomery, AL, 29, 30, 179
Montreal, Canada, 160
Moore, Deborah Dash, 188
Moorish-style synagogues, 72, 212
Morais, Sabato (rabbi), 115
Mordecai, Abram, 30, *see also*
     Montgomery, AL
Mordecai, Rosa, 49*n*. 91
Morgen frayhayt, 233
Morgen zhurnal, 103
Morgenthau, Henry, Jr., 168, 170
Morgenthau, Henry, Sr., 223
Mormons, 20, 33
Morocco, 172
Mortara affair, 192*n*. 1
Moscow, Russia, 216, 245
Moses, I. S. (rabbi), 109, 110, 117
Moskowitz, Belle, 140
Mosse, George, 181*n*. 101
mother tongue
    census data, 62*n*. 11
mothers and motherhood, 53, 212, 289
movies (motion pictures), *see* film and film
    industry
Mugwumps, 105
Muncie, IN, 66
Museum of Modern Art
    (New York), 246
music
    composers and performance artists,
      183, 246
    in German culture, 215
    in the synagogue, 39, 50, 281
    popular music, Jews and, 183–4
Mussolini, Benito, 204

Napoleonic Wars, *see* Bonaparte, Napoleon
Nathan, Isaac Mendes Seixas, 57
National Conference on Jewish
    Employment, 148
National Council of Jewish Women, 129,
    155*n*. 49
National Federation of Temple Sisterhoods,
    155*n*. 49

National Museum of American Jewish
    History, 308
National Socialist Teutonia Society, 230
Native Americans, 30, 35, 186
    Jewish representations of, 184–6
nativism, 141, 142, 240
Naturalization Act, 15
Navigation Acts, 15
Nazism, 170, 171, 172, 175, 177, 205,
    226, 227, 276, 277, 309
Nazi-Soviet pact, *see* Molotov-Ribbentrop
    agreement
Nebraska, 67
Netherlands, *see* Holland
Neumann, Emanuel, 294
New Age, 281
New Amsterdam, *see* New York City
New Christians, 3, 4, 10, 209, 286, 309
New Deal, 139, 140, 165, 167, 168, 169,
    172, 265, 271
    "Jew Deal" epithet, 168
New England, 13, 57, 150
New Haven, CT, 6, 9
New Jersey, 9, 86, 142, 147
    Jewish farms in, 100, 182
New Left, 178
New Odessa, OR, 99
New Orleans, LA, 7, 23, 24n. 40, 25, 30,
    50, 66, 185, 217
New Spain, *see* Mexico
New York Association for New Americans
    (NYANA), 179
New York City, 6, 8, 9, 10, 15, 21, 22t.
    1.2., 23, 24, 25, 29, 38, 45, 46,
    48, 57, 59t. 2.1., 67, 86, 88, 99,
    102, 114, 115, 141, 150, 179, 207,
    211, 230
    foreign-born population, 58
    freeman status in colonial era, 15
    growth of Jewish population
      1860s, 56
    Holocaust survivors, 183
    immigrants from Soviet Union, 254
    incomes compared
      Jews and non-Jews after 1945, 252
    Jewish immigrants, 66, 68, 70, 103
    Jewish population after 1945, 188
    Jewish population in 1960, 248
    Jewish poverty, post-1950, 261
    Jews in manual trades after 1945,
      251, 260

Orthodox Jews, 266
politics, 104, 143, 232
public schools, 62
teachers' strike of 1968, 263
urban decay, 263
New York Kehillah, 122–3, 220
New York metropolitan area, 258
New York State, 23, 67, 68, 86, 103, 142, 182
Newark, NJ, 58, 59t. 2.1., 62, 151, 259, 264, 281
Newburyport, MA, 150
Newport, RI, 6, 8, 9, 37, 56, 57, 59, 60, 61, 70
Nicholas II, Russian tsar, 73
Nidche Israel
    Baltimore congregation, 47
Niebuhr, Reinhold, 270
Nietzsche, Friedrich, 276
Niger, Shmuel (pen-name of Shmuel Charney), 97
Niles, David, 168
Noah, Mordecai M., 38, 46, 51, 71n. 29, 198
Nobel Prize, 308
non-Aryans
    Christians of Jewish ancestry in Nazi Germany, 226
Nora, Pierre, 307
Norich, Anita, 181n. 101
North Africa, 4, 11
North Carolina, 17, 68, 86
North Dakota, 99
Novick, Paul, 233

Odessa, Ukraine, 239, 245
Ohio, 67, 68, 224
Old Testament, *see* Bible
Omaha, NE, 69
Opatoshu, Joseph, 186
Opatów, Poland, 276
Oregon, 33
Orthodox, *see* Judaism: Orthodox
Ottoman Empire, 70, 71, 77, *see also* Turkey
    Jews in, 2, 4
Ottumwa, IA, 95
Ozick, Cynthia, 259

Pacific Coast, 33, 57, 101, 187
pacifism, *see* anti-war sentiment

Palestine, 73, 76, 77, 98, 108, 123, 155, 156, 159, 161, 163, 172, 177, 181, 205, 216, 217, 223, 228, 242, 291, 293, 294
    and Jewish statehood, 294
    Arabs, 156, 162, 293
    bi-nationalism, 162, 221
    British Mandate, 161, 162, 162n. 64, 174, 293
    partition plans, 292, 293
    in WWI, 223
Palestine farm colony, Michigan, 99
Paley, Grace, 259
Passover, 40, 51, 218
passport question, *see* Russia: US passport question
pastoral imagination, 37, 38, 97, 183
patrilineal descent, *see* Judaism: Reform: patrilineal descent policy
Peace of Mind, 272
peddlers, 20, 24, 26, 32, 33, 50, 57, 67, 78, 88, 96, 97, 212, 265, 285
Peixotto, Benjamin Franklin, 120
    Romania mission, 120, 192
Pennsylvania, 16, 23, 30, 67, 68, 86, 142
Per capita income
    United States according to occupation, 153
    United States according to region, 86
Perkins, Frances, 138, 140, 170
Petaluma, CA, 147, 148, 182
Petuchowski, Jakob, 181n. 101
Pew Research Center, 309
Philadelphia, PA, 6, 9, 10, 17, 21, 22t. 1.2., 23, 24, 25, 27, 29, 31, 45, 48, 49, 52, 57, 59t. 2.1., 60, 89, 100, 108, 109, 115, 124, 161, 164, 198, 214, 258, 262, 264, 280, 296, 308
    public schools, 62
philanthropy, 166
    and civic recognition, 119
    and Jewish community, 29, 37, 40, 93, 118–23, 223, 288, 304
        alternate field of leadership, 118
        governance, 120, 121, 122–3, 149, 153, 191, 297, 304
        projects in Palestine pre-1948, 291
    and self-esteem, 119
    donor-recipient model, 291
    secular and non-sectarian, 261
Philip II, Spanish king, 3

Pinski, Dovid (David), 184
Pittsburgh Platform, 108, 109, 112
Pittsburgh, PA, 12t. 1.1., 59t. 2.1.,
    215, 221
Poale Zion, 161
pogroms, 65, 73, 98, 203, 234, 236, 238
    Western responses to, 73
Poland, 2, 3, 11, 21n. 36, 127, 133, 180,
    205, 212, 225, 226, 232, 234,
    267, 274
    immigration from, 88t. 2.2., 106, 133,
        202, 311
    Jews from, 10, 26, 29, 31, 34, 61, 71,
        133, 147, 181
    in Palestine, 174
    partition of, 209
    Russo-Polish War, 241, 242
politics
    Jews and
        US political parties, 101–7
Portland, OR, 68
Portugal, 1, 3, 10, 194
Poznanski, Gustav, 50, 51
prayer books, 57, 124
preaching, *see* sermons
Presbyterians, 14
press, 38, 51, 52, 71, 76, 103, 139, 197,
    205, 215, 224, 236, 259, 267
    German-language, 27
Prinz, Joachim (rabbi), 176
professionals, 78, 123, 153, 162, 175,
    180, 251
Progressive Era, 79, 102, 103, 111, 149
Prohibition, 136, 142
    Jews' attitudes, 141
promised land motif in literature, 185
Proskauer, Joseph M., 227
prostitution, 79
Protestants, 19, 20, 41, 110, 142, 187, 247,
    270, 285
    Non-Anglicans in England, 18
Providence, RI, 25, 83
Prussia, 209, *see also* Germany
public image of American Jews, 208
public schools, 27, 61, 82, 90, 122, 129,
    144, 145, 263
    education and mobility among
        Jews, 82–4
Puerto Rico, 197
Puritans, 13, 14
Pyke, Rachel Peixotto, 48

Quakers, 14, 20
quotas
    in higher education, *see* higher
        education: discrimination

Rabbi Isaac Elchanan Theological
    Seminary (RIETS), 115, 116, 154,
        155, 275
rabbinical schools
    in America, 72, 114, 115, 153–4, 195,
        270, 279
rabbis, 39, 40, 44, 47, 51, 52, 72, 107,
    109, 115, 116, 117, 124, 125, 126,
    128, 142, 176, 191, 199, 268, 282,
    283, 289
    attitude toward women in religious
        life, 53
    from Germany, 212
Rabin family (Nehemiah and Yitzhak), 161
racial hierarchies, 35, 184, 187, 257, 264
    and anthropology, 218
    Jews and, 79–80
racial science, 219
racism, 169, 216, 219, 268, 298
radio industry, 90
railroads, 32, 63, 66, 68
Raphall, Morris, 213t. 4.1
Reconstructionism, *see* Judaism:
    Reconstructionist; Kaplan,
    Mordecai M.
Reconstructionist Rabbinical College,
    280, 281
Red Army, 241, 242
Red Scare, 136, 240
Reform, *see* Judaism: Reform
refugees, 71, 73, 74, 76, 77, 92, 130, 145,
    260, 261, 294, 302, 303
    after WWII, 256
    from Arab lands, 179, 248, 254, 304
    Nazi era, 170, 171, 172, 173t. 3.1., 174,
        175, 178, 180, 226, 229, 293
Reinharz, Jehuda, 181n. 101
Reiss, Abraham, *see* Rice, Abraham
    (rabbi)
relief, *see* welfare
religion
    in schools, 48
religiosity, forms of
    in contemporary American Judaism, 283
religious toleration
    United States, 46

Republican Party, 102, 103, 104, 105, 143
 Jewish support, 167
 political positions, 102
republicanism, 269
restoration to Palestine, *see* Zionism
Revel, Bernard Dov, 155
Rhode Island, 16
Rice, Abraham (rabbi), 47, 50, 212, 213t. 4.1.
Richmond, VA, 12t. 1.1., 22t. 1.2., 23, 25, 33
riots, 264
Rochester, NY, 103, 105, 107
Rock Island, IL, 66
Rodeph Shalom
 Pittsburgh congregation, 221
Romania, 195, 205, 209
 Jews from, 61, 62, 64, 77, 114, 115
 Peixotto diplomatic mission, 120
 Romanian "Iron Guard", 203
 violence against Jews, 122
Ronch, Itzhok (Isaac), 186
Roosevelt, Eleanor, 138
Roosevelt, Franklin D., 140, 165, 168, 170, 171, 172, 207, 231, 243
 critics of, 169
Roosevelt, Theodore, 103, 105, 128, 165, 239
Root, Elihu, 158
Rosenau, William (rabbi), 124
Rosenfeld, Isaac, 259
Rosenwald, Julius, 244
Rosenzweig, Franz, 177
Rosh Hashanah, 122
Roskies, David G., 181*n.* 101
Rosmarin, Trude-Weiss, 177
Roth, Henry, 259
Roth, Philip, 259
Rothschild, Edmund de, 98
Rothstein, Arnold, 147
Rozenblit, Marsha, 181*n.* 101
Rubinow, Isaac M., 140
Ruef, Abel, 104
Russia, 18, 36, 70, 98, 102, 133, 139, 158, 163, 193, 209
 1905 revolution, 237
 antisemitism
  American Jews' opinions of, 236–7
  American public opinion, 236, 239, 240

atrocities
 1905–1906, 238
 WWI through Russian civil war, 130, 148, 220, 241, 243
culture and the arts, 244, 245
history of Imperial policy toward Jews, 234, 239
history of relations with United States, 233
in WWI, 220, 241
Jewish living conditions, 65, 72–3, 76, 81, 91
Jews from, 61, 63, 64, 88t. 2.2., 89, 90, 147
post-1881 civil restrictions on Jews, 234–5
radicalism, 98, 106, 126
Soviet government, 139, 188, 206, 243, 254, 273
 American Jewish relations pre-1940, 240–4
 and Jewish migrants, 164, 195, 298
 Jewish postwar population, 248
 Middle East policy, 257, 298
 posture toward Jews, 242, 298, 302, 303
 postwar Jewish emigration, 254
 suppression of Hungary rebellion 1956, 179
 WWII, 232
US passport question and abrogation of 1832 treaty, 239–40, 301
violence against Jews, *see* pogroms
Russian Information Bureau, 243
Russian revolution, 130, 133, 138, 158, 163, 164, 240, 241, 242
Russian-American commercial treaty of 1832, 233
Russo-Japanese War, 237, 239

Sabath, Adolph Joachim, 102
Sabbath, 7, 19, 39, 50, 107, 128, 129, 267
Sabbetai Zevi, 11
Sacco and Vanzetti affair, 170
Sacramento, CA, 34
Salt Lake City, UT, 33
Salvador, Francis, 16
Sampter, Jesse, 162
San Diego, CA, 68

San Francisco, CA, 25, 33, 34, 36, 58, 68, 103, 104, 108, 120, 147, 148, 227, 246, 262
Savannah, GA, 7, 22t. 1.2., 46
Schaechter, Mordkhe, 181n. 101
Schechter, Solomon (rabbi), 115
Scheinfeld, Solomon Isaac (rabbi), 117
Schiff, Jacob H., 74, 117, 139, 223, 224, 237, 238, 239, 240, 243
Schneerson, Menahem Mendl (rabbi), 268, 308
Schneiderman, Rose, 138, 140, 160
schools, 26, 29, 48, 49, 95, 282
    parochial religious, 27, 253
    parochial religious schools, 94
Schorsch, Ismar, 181n. 101
Schurz, Carl, 197
scientists, 175, 180, 252, 308
Sears, Roebuck Company, *see* Rosenwald, Julius
Seattle, WA, 108
second day observance of festivals, 50
Second Vatican Council, 209
sectionalism, 36
Secular Humanistic Judaism, 281
secularization, 95, 194
Seixas family, 56
self-employment, 80, 88, 89, 90
Seligsberg, Alice, 161
seminaries, *see* rabbinical schools
Sephardim, 3, 4, 5, 6, 7, 9, 13, 115, 126, 197, 202, 218
    France, 18
    from Balkans and Turkey, 62
    from eastern Mediterranean, 114, 194, 202
sermons, 40, 47, 51, 52, 109, 128, 129, 185
Shapiro, Irving S., 252
Shavelson, Clara Lemlich, 140
Shearith Israel, 23, *see also* New York City
    Cincinnati congregation, 29
    New York congregation, 57, 115, 197
Sheinin, John Jacobi, 145
shohet (kosher slaughterer), 23, 44, 51
Sholem Aleichem (Sholem Rabinovich pen-name), 203
Shomrim, 251n. 7
Shuster, George N., 207
Shvarts, Israel Jacob, 96, 97, 132, 189
Sicily Island, LA, 99

Siegel, Benjamin ("Bugsy"), 146
Silkiner, Benjamin, 199
Silver, Abba Hillel (rabbi), 294
Silver, Joan Micklin, 259
Simon, Neil, 259
Singer, Isaac Bashevis, 160, 259, 268
slaves and slaveholding, 32, 36, 184, 269
    colonial era, 1, 7, 8
    employment of hired slaves, 32
    small business, 78, 81, 87, 89, 145, 263, 265
Smith, Alfred E., 140, 143, 209
Social Darwinism, 76
Social Democrats, *see* socialism and the Left
social feminism, 155
social gospel, 92
social justice, 270, 277, 288
    and government, 269, 271
Social Security, 260
social services, *see* welfare
social work, 123, 161, 251
    Jewish clients in US cities post-1945, 260
socialism and the Left, 105–7, 136, 138, 139–40, 148, 168, 188, 194, 196, 197, 207, 221, 222, 232, 238, 241, 270
    German influence, 215
Socialist Party, 105, 106, 139, 143n. 24, 221, 232
Society for the Advancement of Judaism, *see* Judaism: Reconstructionist; Kaplan, Mordecai M. (rabbi)
Solis-Cohen, Solomon, 198
Soloveitchik, Joseph Ber (Dov) (rabbi), 157, 272, 275–6, 277
Soloveitchik, Tonya Lewit, 157, 275
South America, 5, 171, 194, 205, 254, 286
South Carolina, 6, 16, 17
Soviet Jewry, 257, *see also* Russia: Soviet government: posture on Jews
    migration to the US, 302, 303, 309
    US Jewish support for, 257, 277, 298–303
    Soviet Jewry movement, 299, 300
Spain, 3, 10, 13, 127, 193, 198, 208
    initiative to attract Sephardic immigrants, 202
    Jews expelled from, 3, 4, 198, 200, 209
    New World colonies, 1, 3, 7, 31, 199

Spain, Germany, and Russia construct, 246
  axial cultures and historical icons for
    American Jews, 193–5
Spanish Civil War, 164, 203, 206, 207,
    231, 232
  American Jewish volunteers, 203–5
  clash between Jews and Catholics in
    America, 205–7
Spanish Golden Age, 208, 214
Spanish Hebrew poets, 199
Spanish-American War, 221, 247
  Jews' opinions of, 195–8, 201–2
Spanish-Portuguese synagogue, *see*
    Shearith Israel
St. Louis, MO, 12t. 1.1., 25, 31, 120, 230
St. Petersburg, Russia, 239
  Music Conservatory, 246
Stalin (Joseph Stalin) and Stalinism, 139,
    164, 233, 244, 272
Stanislawski, Michael, 181*n*. 101
Statue of Liberty, 61
Stevenson, Adlai, 271
Stiles, Ezra, 16, *see also* New Haven, CT
Stoecker, Adolph, 215
Stone, I. F., 296
Stowe, Harriet Beecher, 184
Straus, Nathan, 168
Straus, Oscar, 103, 127, 197, 202, 239, 243
strikes, 140, 148
Student Struggle for Soviet Jewry, 300
students, 281
suburbs, 135, 252, 253, 263, 278
suffrage movement, *see* women: suffrage
Sullivan, Timothy (Big Tim), 104
summer camps, 187, 278, 281
Sunday business closings, 50
Sunday prayer services, 107
Sunday School, 48, 49
sweatshops, 79, 265
Switzerland, 77, 159
synagogues, 10, 14, 15, 19, 23, 26, 29, 31,
    32, 34, 36, 40, 46–7, 48, 50, 52, 53,
    56, 68, 72, 110, 113, 122, 253, 262,
    266, 267, 287, 289, 298, 304
  and children, 282
  architecture and design, 151–2, 194,
    212, 253
  as multi-purpose facilities, 151
  as venue for fostering community, 282
  building and attendance in 1920s,
    150–1

expansion in number
    1860s, 57
  German influence, 212
  membership, 278, 288
  mixed seating in, 53
  of Polish Jews, 62
  postwar growth, 278
Syracuse, NY, 103, 105
Syria
  Jews from, 254
Syrkin, Nachman, 222
Szold, Benjamin (rabbi), 115, 213t. 4.1
Szold, Henrietta, 155, 156, 161, 162,
    217, 218
Szold, Robert, 217

Tacoma, WA, 68
Taft, William Howard, 240
Talmud, 154, 157, 276
Tammany Hall, 102, 104
teachers, 263
Temple de Hirsch
  Seattle congregation, 108
Temple Emanu-El
  New York congregation, 199, 217
Temple Sinai
  Chicago congregation, 107, 111
tenements, 69, 78, 85, 89, 92, 135,
    258, 264
Tenenbaum, Joseph, 230
Texas, 33, 69, 70, 99
Thanksgiving, 126
The Melting Pot, see Zangwill, Israel
The Nation, 164
The New Colossus, Emma Lazarus sonnet,
    see Statue of Liberty
The Promised Land Mary Antin memoir, 222
The Rise of David Levinsky, 244
the South, 25, 67, 85, 86, 96
the West, 69
theology, 271, 276, 280, 282
third parties, 105, 106, 271
Third Reich, *see* Nazism
Thirty Years' War, 3
Thomas, Norman, 143*n*. 24, 232
Thoreau, Henry David, 178
Tifereth Israel
  Lincoln, Nebraska congregation, 113
tikkun 'olam (repairing the world), 268
Torah, 9, 34, 40, 47, 114, 283, 287, 289
Toronto, Canada, 160

330 *Index*

Touro Synagogue, 37, 61
trade networks, 5, 8, 9, 13, 20, *see also* capitalism: effect on Jewish settlement
trade union, *see* labor unions
Treue Schwestern, 52, 210
Trotsky, Leon (Lev), 139, 158
Truman, Harry S., 178, 271, 295
Trunk, Isaiah, 181*n*. 101
tuberculosis, 85
Turkey, 4, 11, 128, 172, 197, 202, 223
    in WWI, 155, 223
    Jews from, 62, 126
Turner, Frederick Jackson, 36

US financial assistance to Israel, 295
US Congress, 103, 106, 170, 203, 207, 235, 236, 239, 240, 294, 301
US Constitution, 17
US foreign policy, 256
    Middle East, 295, 296
    plight of Russian Jews, early 20th century, 239
    Soviet Union, 301
    trade with Soviet Union, 243
US House of Representatives, 102, 103, 123, 133, 143
US Justice Department, 252
US Senate, 103, 133
US State Department, 133, 139, 170, 172, 207, 229, 239, 286, 295
US Supreme Court, 105, 170, 217
US Treasury Department, 172
Ukraine, 11, 97, 98, 130, 131, 139, 163, 234, 241, 244, 254, 267
    Jews from, 69, 140, 147
    partisans in civil war, 242
    violence against Jews, 17th century, 11
Ulster County, NY, 100
ultra-Orthodox, *see* haredim
Union for Traditional Judaism, 281
Union of American Hebrew Congregations, 151
Union of Orthodox Jewish Congregations, 116, 124, 151
Union Prayer Book, 125
Union Theological Seminary, 270
United Federation of Teachers, 263
United Hebrew Relief Association, 111
United Hebrew Trades, 139
United Jewish Appeal (UJA), 297

United Jewish Organizations, Cleveland, OH, 122
United Nations, 256, 298
United Nations Relief and Rehabilitation Administration (UNRRA), 179
United Service for New Americans (USNA), 179
United States Immigration Commission, 82, 240
United Synagogue, 124, 151
Untermyer, Samuel, 228
urbanism
    Jews and, 13, 33, 36, 38, 57, 58, 95, 183, 244, 258, 264
    urban crisis and poverty, 258–66
Utah, 33
Utica, NY, 12t. 1.1., 32

Vatican, 192, 209, 277
Venice, Italy, 4, 7, 9, 21n. 36
Vermont, 17
Vienna, Austria, 216
Vietnam War, 277, 299
Vilna (Vilnius, Lithuania), 116, 245
Vineland, NJ, 182
Virginia, 17, 67
    Act for Religious Freedom, 17
Vladeck, Baruch (Charney), 97*n*. 65, 227
Volstead Act, *see* Prohibition

Wage Earners League for Woman Suffrage, 140
Wagner, Robert F., Sr., 229
Wald, Lillian, 139, 220, 237n. 88
Wall Street, 223
Wallace, Henry, 271
Waltham, MA, 144
War Refugee Board (WRB), 172
Warburg, Felix, 223, 224, 243
Ward's Island, New York City immigrants' shelter, 74, 76
Warsaw, Poland, 245
Washington Heights, New York City, 176
Washington State, 33
Washington, D.C., 67, 162n. 64, 170, 187, 223, 244, 258
    Jews in, 25
Washington, George, 190
Weinreich, Max and Uriel, 181*n*. 101
Weizmann, Chaim, 223
welfare, 169, 260, 261

government social benefits, 87, 165, 166, 265, 266

Jewish institutions, 92, 93, 153, 166, 191, 249, 250, 258, 260

settlement houses, 92

voluntary service agencies, 165

Wertheimer, Jack, 181*n.* 101

West Coast, *see* California

West Point, 126

Wexler, Jerry, 184

whiteness, 169

Wiesel, Elie, 300

Wilkes-Barre, PA, 69

Williamsburg, Brooklyn, 261

Wilson, Woodrow, 103, 105, 136, 165, 217

Wine, Sherwin T. (rabbi), 281

Wisconsin, 30, 67, 99

Wise, Isaac Mayer, 51, 52, 53, 120, 212, 213t. 4.1., 308

Wise, Stephen S., 217

Wise, Stephen S. (rabbi), 154, 217, 218, 223, 224, 230, 231, 243

Wisse, Ruth R., 181*n.* 101

Witte, Sergei, 239

Wolff, Milton ("El Lobo"), 204

women, 27

  and charity, 26, 53

    philanthropic leadership, 118, 120

  domestic crafts, 126

  femininity, 126

  first-wave feminism, 140–1

  in higher education, 250

  in immigrant households and quality of life, 84–5

  in public life, 156, 169

  in religious life, 39, 40, 42, 43, 44, 51, 52, 53, 54, 140–1, 155, 282, 285, 289

  burial societies, 32

  national organizations, 101, 129, 155, 278, 297

  refugee assistance, 176

  suffrage, 101, 136, 140

  synagogue clubs, 279

  volunteer activism, 153

  volunteers in Spanish Civil War, 204

  work and employment, 78, 85, 135

  domestic service, 28

  haredi sector, 266

Women's League of the United Synagogue of America, 155*n.* 49

Women's Trade Union League, 138

women's movement in contemporary Judaism, *see* feminism: and Judaism

Woodbine, NJ, 100

Workmen's Circle, 107, 222

World Jewish Congress, 176

World War I, 70, 102, 122, 123, 130, 132, 148, 155, 158, 161, 163, 164, 169, 218, 232, 234, 238, 240, 241, 245

  American Jews and, 123–5, 219–25

World War II, 171, 172, 175, 181, 187, 224, 225, 247, 293, 304, 305

  German occupation in Russia, 244

writers, 259

Wyschogrod, Michael, 181*n.* 101

Yale University, 273

Yemen

  Jews from, 77

Yeshiva University, 115, 275

yeshivas, 157, 180

Yiddish language, 80, 107, 113, 180, 194, 196, 217, 222, 267, 298, 309

  as mother tongue, 62*n.* 11

  literature, 96, 97, 184, 186, 189

  press, 103, 221, 222, 228, 233

  theater, 244, 245

Yiddishes tageblatt, 103

Yom Kippur (Day of Atonement), 43, 50, 109, 283

youth culture, 281, 283

Zangwill, Israel, 236

Zion

  prayers for, 125

Zionism, 77, 161, 162, 163, 176, 177, 194, 216, 223, 268, 293

  in America, 77, 216–18, 291, 294, 297

  migration to Palestine, 161–3

  politicization of, 292

  leadership of in America, 294

Zionist Organization of America (ZOA), 161, 217